THE MUSLIMS ARE

THE MUSLIMS ARE COMING!

Islamophobia, Extremism, and the Domestic War on Terror

Arun Kundnani

VERSO
London • New York

This paperback edition published by Verso 2015
First published by Verso 2014

3 5 7 9 10 8 6 4 2

Verso
UK: 6 Meard Street, London W1F 0EG
US: 20 Jay Street, Suite 1010, Brooklyn, NY 11201
www.versobooks.com

Verso is the imprint of New Left Books

ISBN-13: 978-1-78168-558-7 (PB)
eISBN-13: 978-1-78168-521-1 (UK)
eISBN-13: 978-1-78168-212-8 (US)

British Library Cataloguing in Publication Data
A catalogue record for this book is available from the British Library

The Library of Congress Has Cataloged the Hardback Edition as Follows:

Kundnani, Arun.
The Muslims are coming! : Islamophobia, extremism, and the domestic war on terror / Arun Kundnani.
pages cm
Includes bibliographical references and index.
ISBN 978-1-78168-159-6 (hardback)
1. Terrorism—United States—Prevention. 2. Terrorism—Great Britain—Prevention. 3. Domestic terrorism—United States. 4. Domestic terrorism—Great Britain. I. Title.
HV6432.K856 2014
363.325'160973—dc23
2013041108

Typeset in Minion Pro by Hewer Text UK Ltd, Edinburgh
Printed and bound by
CPI Group (UK) Ltd, Croydon, CR0 4YY

Contents

Introduction

> The tradition of the oppressed teaches us that the "emergency situation" in which we live is the rule.
>
> —Walter Benjamin, *On the Concept of History*

Death came instantly to Imam Luqman, as four FBI agents fired semiautomatic rifles from a few feet away. Sixty law enforcement officers—including a special operations team the FBI had flown in from Quantico, Virginia, a SWAT team from the FBI's Detroit field office, and officers of the Royal Canadian Mounted Police—had surrounded the warehouse in Dearborn, Michigan, where the imam and his four colleagues were loading television sets into a trailer on the morning of October 28, 2009. Luqman Abdullah had been the leader of the Al-Haqq Mosque on Detroit's impoverished West Side for thirty years. Every Sunday he and his followers had run a soup kitchen, providing some of the basic needs of the local community. The majority of the people in the neighborhood were either unemployed or in low-paying jobs, and they depended on such initiatives for their survival. The landscape of mostly empty and burned-out buildings was testimony to the exodus of huge swathes of the city's population and the practice of families sharing houses when they could no longer afford the rent on their own homes. Imam Luqman was a familiar face, always available to help out Muslim and non-Muslim alike. His favorite word was "grassroots," says his son Omar Regan.

> He had a strong desire to change the neighborhood. He believed that Islam would help people get off drugs, alcohol, and depression. But he wouldn't even really preach for them to be Muslim more than he

> would push for them to at least act like they were Muslim. He'd just give it to you real. Everybody always talked to him, because they appreciated his direct approach. He believed we got to change the condition of our people, because the government ain't going to do it. And he would say we need to stand up and fight for our rights, because the government's pushing us around, trying to make us feel like we got something to do with 9/11 when we ain't got nothing to do with that kind of stuff. That's how my dad would talk—he's from back in the sixties.[1]

Luqman Abdullah had converted to Islam in the early 1980s, after serving in the military and then falling into depression. The inspiration for his conversion was Jamil al-Amin, who in the 1960s, under the name of H. Rap Brown, had been a leading activist with the Student Nonviolent Coordinating Committee (SNCC). Over the course of a decade, in the face of racist violence and the Democratic Party's sluggish response to the organization's attempts to break southern segregation, SNCC had radicalized; it came to advocate black power and opposition to the Vietnam war, and eventually merged with the Black Panther Party. Rap Brown rose to the top of the FBI's target list of black revolutionaries, and soon enough, the bureau found its opportunity to imprison him—on incitement to riot charges. Brown converted to orthodox Islam while in prison in New York in 1971 for reasons no doubt similar to those which led Luqman Abdullah to do the same a decade later. For both, Islam preached active struggle for racial justice alongside individual spiritual development; it offered a way to live and a vision of a better life. This interpretation of Islam offered a framework for continuing the black radical tradition of the Black Panther Party and Malcolm X after a period of defeat for black political struggle.The FBI's Counterintelligence Program (known as COINTELPRO) had secretly destabilized the movement and entrapped its activists. Brown, now calling himself Jamil al-Amin, was released from prison in 1976 and settled in Atlanta, Georgia. He opened a community grocery store and helped rid the neighborhood of drugs. But he continued to face regular law enforcement harassment and arbitrary arrests. Eventually, in 2000, al-Amin was arrested on murder charges after a shootout with two Fulton County Sheriff's deputies occurred. Al-Amin was identified by the surviving officer as the shooter who had been wounded in the exchange of gunfire—even though he had no injuries and another person had confessed to the crime. He is now caged in the "domestic Guantánamo," the supermax prison in Florence, Colorado, where the US government incarcerates those it accuses of being among the most dangerous al-Qaeda terrorists.

By the time the war on terror was launched in 2001 much of the sixties generation of black radical activists had been exhausted, co-opted, imprisoned, or killed, to a large degree victims of the FBI's efforts to destroy the movement. But Luqman Abdullah, who was leading the campaign to free Jamil al-Amin, was still preaching radicalism to his small congregation in Detroit. As Omar Regan puts it, he was "unfinished business" from the days of COINTELPRO. And now the war on terror provided a new lens through which to view his activities. Soon the FBI was categorizing Abdullah as a "highly placed leader of a nationwide radical fundamentalist Sunni group consisting primarily of African-Americans" who had called his followers to "an offensive *jihad*, rather than a defensive *jihad* [in order] to establish a separate, sovereign Islamic state . . . within the borders of the United States, governed by Shariah law."[2] The implication was that he shared an ideology with al-Qaeda. In the sixties, figures such as Malcolm X and Muhammad Ali had been portrayed by the media as "Muslim extremists"; now a new set of images of Islamic extremism had come to the fore, images that could be used to manufacture an ideological connection between a radical black preacher on Detroit's West Side and the events of September 11, 2001.

In 2007, the FBI found its opportunity to begin targeting Imam Luqman's mosque. A member of the congregation had recently been arrested on murder charges, and in a deal with law enforcement, he agreed to work with the counterterrorism squad of the FBI's Detroit field office as part of a sting operation. Two other informants were also recruited, and a two-year undercover operation to infiltrate the mosque began. Many of the congregants had criminal records; all were struggling with poverty. The offer of an FBI payout was bound to be tempting. And when the FBI implemented its plan to lure those around Imam Luqman into helping fence stolen goods, it is easy to see how some of them were drawn in. The FBI's informants pretended they had a contact who needed help moving merchandise stolen from trucking companies. Just for turning up to discuss the plan, the contact, played by an FBI agent, gave everyone one hundred dollars. The second time they met, the FBI undercover agent paid one thousand dollars to the group before anything had even happened, and promised another fifteen hundred dollar payment the following night. All they had to do was turn up at a warehouse in Dearborn and help move what they thought were stolen television sets and laptops from one semitrailer to another. This was repeated a number of times over the coming months, gradually drawing Imam Luqman himself into the operation so that he would also be present at the FBI's warehouse when the time came to carry out the raid.

An indictment was issued against Imam Luqman the day before the raid in October 2009 that charged him with conspiracy to sell stolen goods transported in interstate commerce, firearms possession violations, and alterations to a vehicle identification number. No terrorism-related charges were included, despite the involvement of the FBI's counterterrorism squad and the multiagency Joint Terrorism Task Force. But the indictment included claims, based on reports by the FBI-paid infiltrators, of conversations in which Imam Luqman had advocated "the spread of Islam through violent *jihad*, and violence against the United States government and against law enforcement."[3] These claims were never tested in court, since Iman Luqman was dead, and none of these conversations were taped. In one of the few conversations that was recorded by an informant, Imam Luqman was asked to donate money for someone to "do something" during the Super Bowl in Detroit. But he replied that he would not be involved in injuring innocent people. There seems little doubt that Imam Luqman viewed the US government as an oppressor and called on his followers to organize against it. Like the Black Panther Party, members of the mosque also carried guns. But there was no evidence of any plot to carry out a terrorist attack, just small-time hustlers in an impoverished neighborhood struggling to pay the bills while denouncing America. As Abdullah Bey el-Amin, another African-American imam from the same neighborhood and a friend of Imam Luqman, put it, the radical talk was no more than "selling wolf tickets"—street corner bragging. "You don't need all these crack-shot FBI and helicopters for somebody stealing a laptop."[4] Andrew Arena, the special agent in charge of the FBI's Detroit field office, maintains that Imam Luqman was "the leader of a domestic terrorist group." When asked why no terrorism charges were brought, he replied: "There's a lot of cases where we don't charge a person with terrorism. We charge them with whatever we can, to get them off the streets."[5] With no evidence of terrorism strong enough to hold up in a court, some other charge had to be concocted. But at the same time, in order to justify a sting operation on this scale, journalists were told that the mosque was a hotbed of violent fundamentalists. It proved easier to convict the imam of terrorism in the court of public opinion than in a court of law.

When the time came to finally spring their trap, the FBI's informants once again lured Imam Luqman to the Dearborn warehouse. At a prearranged time, the three informants exited the warehouse and explosives were let off inside as a distraction. A dozen federal agents approached Imam Luqman and his colleagues and commanded them to get down and show their hands. His four associates complied, but Imam Luqman delayed for a moment. Accounts of what happened next differ. Most likely suspecting that Imam Luqman was hiding a gun, the agents released a dog trained to grab an arm and, as the dog bit at his face, Imam Luqman fired at its chest, prompting return fire from four of the agents, who were positioned nearby, killing him instantly. While an agent handcuffed his body as it lay motionless on the warehouse floor, the police dog was evacuated by helicopter to a hospital for possible life-saving treatment. The federal agents commented later that in the seconds before they opened fire, Imam Luqman was looking directly at them and did not appear to be afraid.[6]

A thousand people attended the four-mile procession to Imam Luqman's funeral. The Department of Justice exonerated the FBI's handling of the arrest and declared his killing lawful. But there is little doubt that had the government chosen not to infiltrate his mosque and entrap him in a criminal conspiracy of its own invention, he would still be alive.

* * *

The killing of Imam Luqman barely registered in the news media. From one point of view, the manner of his death was hardly different from dozens of other killings of African Americans each year at the hands of militarized law enforcement agencies.[7] From another perspective, he resembled the thousands of unnamed militants killed by drones in Pakistan, Somalia, and Yemen. Whether as an "Islamic extremist" or as an African American, his death was a perfectly normal occurrence. If the war on terror was the stuff of high-profile debates about war, torture, and surveillance in the Bush years, under President Obama it became a matter of bureaucratic routine, undramatic and unopposed. Although Obama was elected on a wave of opposition to Bush's war on terror, he then failed to take the US in a fundamentally different direction; the administration thereby effectively neutered any remaining opposition and made permanent what had been a "state of emergency." The minor shifts that did occur were largely already in train in the closing years of the Bush administration. Obama continued along the same track with the same aim in mind: to find ways to continue projecting force in the Middle East and to maintain a national security state at home—but without the noisy and divisive political conflicts that had plagued Bush from 2003 onward. Thus, the US military occupation of Iraq was wound down while the war in Afghanistan, where the number of US troops was trebled, was presented as the "good war." The number of prisoners at Guantánamo was decreased by around a third, but the 171 who remained were slated for indefinite detention in what was now a permanent internment camp. Speaking in Cairo in 2009, Obama attempted to draw a line through the clash of civilizations imagery of the post-9/11 period and offered instead a picture of respectful dialogue between cultures. But he did so without offering any of the changes in US foreign policy that would give such rhetoric substance. The PATRIOT Act was renewed and the state secrets doctrine was invoked to protect Bush-era officials from prosecution for their torture policy. Extraordinary rendition was wound down, while extrajudicial killings were stepped up.[8] The American Civil Liberties Union (ACLU) called it the "new normal."[9] The very banality of counterterrorism discourse secured its ideological power much more effectively than the confrontational rewriting-the-rules strategy of the Bush years. Neoconservatives invented the terror war, but Obama liberalism normalized it, at which point, mainstream journalists stopped asking questions.

What should, by any objective measure, have been the moment the war on terror finally ended actually marked its entry into banality. The killing of Osama bin Laden on May 2, 2011, just a few months before the ten-year anniversary of the 9/11 attacks, came as uprisings in Tunisia and Egypt were providing a practical refutation of al-Qaeda's argument that violence against Western civilians was the only way to defeat the near enemy of autocratic regimes in the Middle East. Yet the terror war did not end. The chants of "U-S-A" on the streets of New York and Washington, led by Democrats happy that their president now had his own narrative of conquest, captured the mood. What was being celebrated was a victory in a continuing war rather than the outbreak of peace. There was little chance that this would be a moment to remember the hundreds of thousands killed around the world as a result of the conflict between al-Qaeda and Western governments. On that Sunday night, hours after bin Laden's death, CNN's resident terrorism expert, Peter Bergen, announced that it would mean the end of the war on terror. By Monday morning, after Hillary Clinton had said "the fight continues," he was back on to correct his earlier assessment, echoing the official line: there could be no end to the war.[10] A war that from the beginning had no clear limits or objectives could not now be concluded with the death of one man. The Authorization for Use of Military Force Against Terrorists, passed by Congress three days after 9/11, established the war on terror paradigm of an open-ended, perpetual, global war. Today the Obama administration continues to rely on that authorization for the claim that it has a legal basis to carry out extrajudicial killings without geographical limit.[11] The enemy had come to be understood as more than a single individual or organization; it was a set of ideas—radical Islam—that was defined vaguely enough that even the death of bin Laden would not halt the hundreds of billions of dollars in spending the war involved. Thus, the national security pundits warned, even greater dangers lurked at this very moment of apparent victory. The same terrorism experts who with the death of bin Laden pronounced the near elimination of what they called "core al-Qaeda" in Pakistan and Afghanistan also heralded new threats of Muslim radicalization in other parts of the world: Yemen, Somalia, Nigeria, Europe, and in the US itself. If the wars in Afghanistan and Iraq had been justified on the grounds that fighting them "over there" was the best way to prevent attacks "over here," a new phase of the war on terror under President Obama intensified the fear that Western Muslim citizens were also a threat.

In August 2011, the White House published its new strategy to prevent violent extremism within the US, which for the first time referred to the need to combat the circulation of extremist ideology among American Muslims.[12] The following month the US government used Predator drones to kill two American citizens in Yemen—Anwar al-Awlaki and Samir Khan. Security officials described the two as "radicalizers" who had pioneered the use of the Internet to influence Western Muslims.[13] It was the first time the US government had openly ordered the extrajudicial killing of its own citizens. In another drone attack three weeks later, al-Awlaki's sixteen-year-old son, Abdulrahman, was killed, along with his teenage cousin and at least five other civilians.[14] Former White House press secretary Robert Gibbs, then a senior adviser to Obama's reelection campaign, was asked by journalists about the killing; he said Abdulrahman should have had "a far more responsible father."[15] Congress began to consider the National Defense Authorization Act at the same time, which would not only lead to Guantánamo being kept open indefinitely but also codify the indefinite military detention without trial of American citizens arrested on US soil. President Obama declined to veto the act. The common theme in these developments was the focus of the war on terror on the domestic front: the enemy now existed as much among our fellow citizens as in foreign lands. The government was no longer imagining the threat as foreign terrorist sleepers living among ordinary American Muslims; now it was the radicalization of ordinary American Muslims themselves that it feared. Polling carried out after bin Laden's killing suggested that Americans were more anxious about Muslim Americans being terrorists than they had been before.[16]

Whereas 9/11 was the defining event of the early war on terror, its later phase was shaped at least as much around acts of violence in

Europe: the train station bombing in Madrid; the murder of filmmaker Theo van Gogh in Amsterdam in 2004; and the 7/7 attacks on the London transportation system in July 2005. The Obama administration's domestic war on terror borrowed heavily from the counterradicalization practices Britain introduced after 7/7, which aimed to embed surveillance, engagement, and propaganda in Muslim communities. The linkages between the US and the UK approaches were multiple: ideas, analyses, and policies traveled back and forth between Washington and London. A flurry of public intellectuals, journalists, and think-tank activists from Britain—such as Peter Bergen, Timothy Garton Ash, Christopher Hitchens, Ed Husain, Bernard Lewis, Melanie Phillips, and Salman Rushdie—played prominent roles in forming American perceptions of Islam and extremism. Quintan Wiktorowicz, the architect of the Obama White House's approach to counterradicalization, developed his ideas while working for the US embassy in Britain after 7/7. US terrorism experts gave evidence in British courts, and the State Department conducted its own outreach with Muslims in the UK. Meanwhile, a highly distorted picture of Britain's Muslim "ghettos"—summed up by the specious term "Londonistan"—was circulated by journalists and bloggers in America as an apparent warning from across the Atlantic of what happens when Islam is accorded too much tolerance.[17] There are significant demographic differences between the Muslim populations in the UK and in the US. In Britain, Muslims make up a larger percentage of the national population, are more often working class, and are less diverse in their ethnic origins. There are also important differences in the two countries' political histories of multiculturalism and antiracism, attitudes toward religion and civil rights, and official cultures of counterterrorism. But especially since 2005, these differences have not been the barriers to the convergence of counterterrorism policies and the shared project of counterradicalization between the two countries that might be expected.

This book explores the domestic fronts of the war on terror in the US and the UK. It argues that radicalization became the lens through which Western societies viewed Muslim populations by the end of the first decade of the twenty-first century. Theories of radicalization that purport to describe why young Muslims become terrorists are central to counterterrorism policies on both sides of the Atlantic. But these models make an unfounded assumption that "Islamist" ideology is the root cause of terrorism. To do so enables a displacement of the war on terror's political antagonisms onto the plane of Muslim culture. Muslims became what Samuel Huntington described as the "ideal enemy," a group that is racially and culturally distinct and ideologically hostile.[18] The political scientist Mahmood Mamdani had earlier identified such "culture talk" as the default explanation for violence when proper political analysis is neglected.[19]

Two main modes of thinking pervade the war on terror, one predominantly among conservatives, the other among liberals. The first mode locates the origins of terrorism in what is regarded as Islamic culture's failure to adapt to modernity. The second identifies the roots of terrorism not in Islam itself but in a series of twentieth-century ideologues who distorted the religion to produce a totalitarian ideology—Islamism—on the models of communism and fascism. The problem with both of these approaches is that they eschew the role of social and political circumstances in shaping how people make sense of the world and then act upon it. Moreover, these modes of thinking are not free-floating. They are institutionalized in the war on terror's practices, actively promoted by well-resourced groups, and ultimately reflect an imperialist political culture. Together they give rise to the belief that the root cause of terrorism is Islamic culture or Islamist ideology; they thus constitute an Islamophobic idea of a Muslim problem that is shared across the political spectrum. As a result, a key aspect of national security policy has been the desire to engineer a broad cultural shift among Western Muslims while ignoring the ways in which Western states themselves have radicalized—have become more willing to use violence in a wider range of contexts.

Islamophobia is sometimes seen as a virus of hatred recurring in Western culture since the Crusades. Others view it as a spontaneous reaction to terrorism that will pass away as the effects of 9/11 recede into history. Many believe it does not exist. My emphasis is on Islamophobia as a form of structural racism directed at Muslims and the ways in which it is sustained through a symbiotic relationship with the official thinking and practices of the war on terror. Its significance does not lie primarily in the individual prejudices it generates but in its wider political consequences—its enabling of systematic violations of the rights of Muslims and its demonization of actions taken to remedy those violations. The war on terror—with its vast death tolls in Afghanistan, Iraq, Pakistan, Somalia, Yemen, and elsewhere—could not be sustained without the racialized dehumanization of its Muslim victims. A social body dependent on imperialist violence to sustain its way of life must discover an ideology that can disavow that dependency if it is to maintain legitimacy. Various kinds of racism have performed that role in the modern era; Islamophobia is currently the preferred form. The usual objection to defining it in this way is that Muslims are not a race. But since all racisms are socially and politically constructed rather than reliant on the reality of any biological race, it is perfectly possible for cultural markers associated with Muslimness (forms of dress, rituals, languages, etc.) to be turned into racial signifiers.[20] This racialization of Muslimness is analogous in important ways to anti-Semitism and inseparable from the longer history of racisms in the US and the UK. To recognize this obviously does not imply that critiques of Islamic belief are automatically to be condemned as racially motivated; it does mean opposing the social and political processes by which antipathy to Islam is acted out in violent attacks on the street or institutionalized in state structures such as profiling, violations of civil rights, and so on.[21]

The academic and official models of radicalization that have been central to the domestic war on terror have emerged within what the US and UK governments call a preventive approach to counterterrorism, in which an attempt is made to identify individuals who are not terrorists now but might be at some later date. But how do you identify tomorrow's terrorists today? That was also the implied question posed by Steven Spielberg's 2002 film, *Minority Report*, in which a specialist PreCrime Unit uses three psychics called PreCogs to predict who will be murderers in the future. The unit is then able to arrest precriminals before they have committed the crimes for which they are convicted. Likewise, a preventive approach to the war on terror would need its own PreCogs' capability to identify the terrorists of the future. To meet this need, security officials turned to academic models that claim scientific knowledge of a process by which ordinary Muslims become terrorists; they then inferred the behavioral, cultural, and ideological signals that they think can reveal who is at risk of turning into a terrorist at some point in the future. In the FBI's model, what they call "jihadist" ideology is taken to be the driver that turns young men and women into terrorists. They pass through four stages: preradicalization, identification, indoctrination, and action. In the second stage, growing a beard, starting to wear traditional Islamic clothing, and becoming alienated from one's former life are listed as indicators; "increased activity in a pro-Muslim social group or political cause" is a sign of stage three, one level away from becoming an active terrorist.[22] Only the last stage in this model involves criminal conduct but, as a New York Police Department (NYPD) paper on radicalization put it, the challenge is "how to identify, pre-empt and thus prevent homegrown terrorist attacks given the non-criminal element of its indicators."[23] What this implies is that terrorism can only be prevented by systematically monitoring Muslim religious and political life and trying to detect the radicalization indicators predicted by the model. Sharing an ideology with terrorists is thus considered a PreCrime, a stage in the radicalization process. "The threat isn't really from al-Qaeda central," explained former FBI assistant director John Miller, "as much as it's from al-Qaeda-ism."[24] Deciding that al-Qaeda-ism—an ideological construct devised by the FBI—is a threat means that radicals who do not espouse violence but whose ideas can be superficially associated with al-Qaeda, such as Imam Luqman, come to be seen as would-be terrorists. In *Minority Report*, the PreCrime Unit is eventually shut down when the fallibility of the PreCogs is exposed. The FBI and other law enforcement agencies continue to rely upon radicalization models with no predictive power in order to shape policies of surveillance, infiltration, and entrapment.

The consequences of making the notion of radicalization central to the domestic war on terror are far-reaching. When the government widened the perceived threat of terrorism from individuals actively inciting, financing, or preparing terrorist attacks to those having an ideology, they brought constitutionally protected activities of large numbers of people under surveillance. Most discussion of state surveillance attends to wiretapping, collection of Internet communications data, closed-circuit television cameras, and other forms of electronic surveillance of our online and offline lives. Edward Snowden's whistle-blowing has made clear the extent to which the US National Security Agency conducts warrantless surveillance of Internet and phone communication globally and domestically.[25] But central to counterradicalization practice is another form of surveillance that is addressed less often: using personal relationships within targeted communities themselves for intelligence gathering. When community organizations and service providers such as teachers, doctors, and youth workers develop surveillance relationships with law enforcement agencies, when government community engagement exercises mask intelligence gathering, and when informants are recruited from communities, surveillance becomes intertwined with the fabric of human relationships and the threads of trust upon which they are built. The power and danger of these forms of surveillance derive from their entanglement in everyday human interactions at the community level rather than from the external monitoring capabilities of hidden technologies. Moreover, having established such structures of surveillance in relation to Islamist extremism, it becomes easy to widen them to other forms of radicalism—occasionally to cover the far Right, but more often to left-wing protesters and dissidents. Following from the widening of surveillance is the criminalization of ideological activities previously understood to be constitutionally protected. This can happen through the entrapment of individuals by law enforcement agencies or through measures criminalizing the material support of terrorism, the definition of which has been widened to include a broad range of ideological activities. Then, because ideologies circulating among Muslim populations have been identified as precursors to terrorism, the perception grows that Muslims have a special problem with radicalization. In this context, leaders of targeted Muslim communities have become intimidated by the general mood and aligned themselves with the government, offering themselves as allies willing to oppose and expose dissent within the community.

Everyone who rejects the game of fake patriotism falls under suspicion, as opposition to extremism becomes the only legitimate discourse. Finally, the spectacle of the Muslim extremist renders invisible the violence of the US empire. Opposition to such violence from within the imperium has fallen silent, as the universal duty of countering extremism precludes any wider discussion of foreign policy.[26]

The planting of informants and agents provocateurs among networks of political radicals is a practice dating back at least 125 years, to the Russian tsar's secret police, the Okhrana, and the early special branch at Scotland Yard. Lightly regulated intelligence services have long used techniques of provocation to disrupt political opposition, spread misinformation, and engineer violent crimes that would otherwise not have happened, thereby securing the conviction of dissidents. This was the countersubversion model the FBI's COINTELPRO initiative drew on in its sustained and coordinated campaign to thwart constitutionally protected activism and counteract political dissent during the 1960s. Targets included the civil rights, black liberation, Puerto Rican independence, antiwar, and student movements. In an attempt to neutralize Martin Luther King Jr., who, the FBI worried, might abandon his "obedience to white liberal doctrines," he was placed under intense surveillance, and attempts were made to destroy his marriage and induce his suicide. The Black Panther Party was disrupted in various cities by using fake letters and informants to stir up violence between rival factions and gangs.[27] The congressional hearings initiated by Senator Frank Church in 1975 to examine the intelligence agencies concluded that the FBI's activities

> would be intolerable in a democratic society even if all of the targets had been involved in violent activity, but COINTELPRO went far beyond that. The unexpressed major premise of the program was that a law enforcement agency has the duty to do whatever is necessary to combat perceived threats to the existing social and political order.[28]

Those at the agency behind the initiative were never brought to justice for their activities, and similar techniques continued to be used in the 1980s against, for example, the American Indian

Movement and the Committee in Solidarity with the People of El Salvador.[29]

In recent years, the US domestic national security apparatus has effectively revived the countersubversion practices of COINTELPRO. Campaign groups such as the Bill of Rights Defense Committee have dubbed "COINTELPRO 2.0" tactics that amount to a twenty-first-century countersubversion strategy: the extensive surveillance of Muslim-American populations; the deployment of informants; the use of agents provocateurs; the widening use of material support legislation to criminalize charitable or expressive activities; and the use of community engagement to gather intelligence and effect ideological self-policing of communities. Significantly, such practices have been encouraged, organized, and legitimized by the radicalization models that law enforcement agencies adopted in the first decade of the twenty-first century. Yet radicalization—in the true sense of the word—is the solution, not the problem. Al-Qaeda's violent vanguardism thrives in contexts where politics has been brutally suppressed or blandly gentrified. Opening up genuinely radical political alternatives and reviving the political freedoms that have been lost in recent years is the best approach to reducing so-called jihadist terrorism.

In 1966, after the phantasmagoric anticommunism of the early cold war had been discredited and before its revival by Reagan, Hollywood released a characteristically liberal take on it. *The Russians Are Coming! The Russians Are Coming!* is in many ways a film that reflects our own moment in the war on terror. When a Soviet submarine accidentally runs aground near a small island off the coast of Massachusetts, a section of the crew goes ashore, leading the conservative townsfolk to think a Russian invasion has commenced. A ragtag citizens' army is formed to hunt down the Russians. Only Walt Whittaker, a liberal writer visiting from New York, grasps the more mundane reality of the situation. As the sailors and the townsfolk confront each other, the hysteria is eventually broken when a young boy who has climbed up a church steeple to watch the showdown loses his grip and hangs precariously. Russians and Americans unite in forming a human pyramid to rescue the boy, and international harmony ensues. Film historian Tony Shaw notes that *The Russians Are Coming!* "depicted America not as a united, peace-loving nation, but divided between paranoid warmongers . . . and level-headed liberals willing to talk with the Russians, like Walt Whittaker."[30] The film positions itself on this liberal center ground, directing its humor at the excesses of early cold war paranoia while presenting the Russians not as dangerous communist ideologues but as human beings who—displaying a mixture of incompetence, heroism, and romance—behave just like Americans. This portrayal is an improvement on the "machine-like automatons bent on the enslavement of the Free World" who peopled the cold war films of the 1950s.[31] However, the price the Russians pay for this advance is their depoliticization. "They do not make any explicitly political statements or hold any political conversations among themselves. Neither they nor the islanders make any reference to the long-standing ideological differences between East and West."[32] The film's implicit message is that conservatives are wrong to fear Russians en masse; instead, Russians should be admitted to the circle of humanity, so long as they leave behind their political ideology. This liberal version of the cold war thinks of ideology as what the other side has; America itself is essentially neutral.

Similarly, today liberal America finds it easy to condemn the early war on terror of the Bush years as a moment when hysteria took over, leading to blanket fears of Muslims and misguided warmongering. But now, liberals say, we have moved beyond that, and we understand that Muslims in America are just like the rest of us. However, just as in *The Russians Are Coming!*, the liberal caveat is that Muslims are acceptable when depoliticized: they should be silent about politics, particularly US foreign policy and the domestic national security system, and not embrace an alien ideology that removes them from the liberal norm. Two of the aims of this book are to ask what reasons there are for thinking Islamic ideology is the root cause of terrorism, and why the acceptance of Muslims as fellow citizens should be conditioned on their distancing themselves from any particular set of ideological beliefs.

Which is not to say we do not still need our level-headed liberals to expose hysteria and warmongering. Indeed, the Muslims are not "coming," in the sense of presenting a distinct threat of violence.[33] While the possibility of another 9/11-style attack taking place in the US or UK cannot be ruled out, official and popular understandings of terrorism are more a matter of ideological projection and fantasy than of objective assessment. At first glance, the bombing of the Boston Marathon in April 2013—resulting in the deaths of three spectators and injuring dozens of others—and the stabbing a month later of British soldier Lee Rigby on the streets of Woolwich, South London, appear to suggest an ongoing domestic threat from jihadists. Both incidents seem to fit the current war on terror paradigm of young Muslim men becoming radicalized through their exposure to Islamist ideology. The events were quickly inserted into the preexisting script of the terror war on both sides of the Atlantic. Peter King, chair of the House Subcommittee on Counterterrorism and Intelligence, for example, claimed the Boston attack showed "the war from terrorism is far from over." Claiming "the new threat is definitely from within," he argued that "political correctness" should not get in the way of even wider surveillance of Muslim communities.[34] Texas congressman Louie Gohmert added that the government should deport "Chechens coming here . . . if there's violence in their background."[35] The homemade pressure-cooker bombs used in Boston, assembled with explosive material from commercially available fireworks, were described by prosecutors and establishment commentators as "weapons of mass destruction"—a dramatic widening of the term's use from its original reference to nuclear, chemical, and biological devices (as if the nondiscovery of weapons of mass destruction in Iraq could be redeemed by their imaginary discovery in Boston!).[36] In the UK, Prime Minister David Cameron spoke of "a conveyor belt to radicalization that has poisoned [young Muslims'] minds with sick and perverted ideas."[37] "We have to drain the swamp which they inhabit," he added.[38] A government task force on tackling "extremism and radicalization" was established, which would renew efforts to stem the circulation of radical ideologies in universities and prisons and on the Internet. New powers to stop broadcast interviews with extremists were floated.[39] London mayor Boris Johnson wrote that thousands of young Muslims were suffering from the "infection" of "the Islamist virus." Universities needed to be "much,

much tougher in their monitoring of Islamic societies" in order to "to stamp out the virus."[40] The formula in London and Washington was the same: the cause of these recent acts of violence was taken to be the same dangerous ideology as that behind 9/11, which was continuing to capture the minds of young Muslims. By presenting Boston and Woolwich as traumatic repetitions of 9/11 and 7/7, fear and anxiety could once again be harnessed to perpetuate the war on terror with a renewed focus on domestic threats and used to legitimize further surveillance, criminalization, and demonization. There was nothing new in the metaphors of "swamps," "conveyor belts," and "viruses," all of which had been repeatedly deployed since 9/11 to sustain a particular way of thinking about radicalization and camouflage the limits of official analysis.

What was most significant about the Boston and Woolwich attacks was left unmentioned. Unlike the image of terrorists in popular culture, the perpetrators were not members of any terrorist organization, had received no training, and barely had a proper plan for what they were doing. This amateurism was rarely commented on because it conflicted with an interpretative frame in which every act of terrorism was, at some level, a repeat of 9/11—with all of its associated emotional energies. Moreover, in both cases, the connections between acts of violence in the US and the UK and the normalized violence of the US and UK militaries went unexamined. In Boston, the pressure-cooker bombs represented an importing of the improvised explosive devices used in the Afghan war to a US civilian context. That the Boston attack might be linked to the wider violence of US foreign policy was what terms like "weapons of mass destruction" and "radicalization" sought to disavow. As he was hiding from police in a dry-docked boat in Watertown, Massachusetts, Dzhokhar Tsarnaev, one of the alleged perpetrators of the Boston bombings, made this connection explicit. On the inside wall of the boat, he wrote:

> The US government is killing our innocent civilians . . . I can't stand to see such evil go unpunished . . . We Muslims are one body, you hurt one, you hurt us all . . . Now I don't like killing innocent people it is forbidden in Islam but due to said [unintelligible] it is allowed . . . Stop killing our innocent people and we will stop.[41]

It was this message, horribly flawed yet clearly stated, that official and media reflections on the causes of the bombings gave little attention to. In Janet Reitman's investigation for *Rolling Stone*, for example—the most detailed media account of the two brothers—the relationship between acts of mass violence on the streets of Boston and that of US foreign policy was not explored at all. While the magazine attracted controversy for its "rock star" cover image of Dzhokar Tsarnaev, the real problem with the article was its attempt to present the brothers' alleged actions as solely the product of a psychological "disintegration" brought about by a series of individual misfortunes. Triggers for the brothers' acts of violence, according to Reitman, include the separation of their parents; their failure to build a successful life in the US; the stress of struggling to pay college fees and rapidly rising rents; and cuts to the family's welfare payments. The article suggested that rather than admit they were struggling emotionally, ideology gave them a defense mechanism and a way to project blame onto America. This deployment of a psychological radicalization model—supported, of course, with quotes from the terrorism-expert industry—enabled the writer to avoid a political analysis of such violence that placed it within the context of the global war on terror and its vast civilian death toll.[42]

Likewise, in Britain after the Woolwich murder, it remained taboo to suggest any connection between the killing of a British soldier on the streets of London and the killings by British soldiers in the villages of Helmand. The coverage of the event in the age of twenty-four-hour news channels and social media, with their supposed demand for diverse content, was actually strikingly one-dimensional: it was restricted to the official narrative of radicalization by a dangerous ideology. Yet again, the perpetrators offered a clear statement of what they thought they were doing, choosing to speak to the cell-phone video cameras of gathered bystanders rather than flee the scene. Bloodied knife in hand, and with the body of a murdered solider by his feet, one of the attackers announced:

> The only reason we have killed this man today is because Muslims are dying daily by British soldiers. And this British soldier is one. It is an eye for an eye and a tooth for a tooth. By Allah, we swear by the

> almighty Allah we will never stop fighting you until you leave us alone . . . So leave our lands and we can all live in peace. That's all I have to say.

Interestingly, the only religious quotation in these words was from the Bible. In the ten minutes or so before the police intervened, an even more striking illustration of the politics of this violence emerged, as women who happened to be passing by approached the attackers to protect the body of the victim and challenge the attackers about their actions. One of the women, Ingrid Loyau-Kennett, asked the knife-wielding perpetrator why he had done it and was told that the victim was a British soldier who had "killed Muslim people" in other countries. They drop their bombs on women and children and no one cares, he told her. Loyau-Kennett responded by telling him that if he wanted to join a war, he should have gone to an actual battlefield and joined an army rather than acting as if the streets of London were such a setting. This simple, spontaneous riposte, barely mentioned in the media, was perhaps the most important comment made during the entire episode and subsequent public discussions, because it pointed to the dangers of the idea of a global battlefield. To the perpetrators there is a war taking place between Western governments and an Islamic resistance, a war that is essentially global in its reach. To them the streets of London are as much of a battlefield as the streets of Mogadishu or Baghdad, and if almost every other Muslim in London did not look at it that way, that was because they were intoxicated by the riches and comforts of a Western consumer society. But the attackers likely thought that a dramatic action like the one in Woolwich might shake the Muslims of London out of their slumber. "I want a war in London," the attacker told Loyau-Kennett, by which he probably meant he wanted Londoners to stop acting as if they were not already at war, to choose sides, and take action.[43] In the event, it was only the far Right which took the Woolwich murder as a rallying cry and began a rampage of violent assaults on Muslims and bombings of mosques around England.[44] But, more significantly, in thinking of the war on terror as having a global reach, the Woolwich attackers were taking at its word the US government, which had itself defined the whole world as a battlefield in its interpretation of the September 2001 Authorization for Use of Military Force—the basis for its use of drone strikes outside of recognizable areas of combat. If the US government believes itself to be involved in a war with no geographical limits, it is hardly surprising that its enemies might themselves adopt that view.

As scholars such as Eqbal Ahmad pointed out even before the war on terror, to designate an act of violence as terrorism is to arbitrarily isolate it from other acts of violence considered normal, rational, or necessary. The term "terrorism" is never used to refer to the military violence of Western states, or to the daily reality of gender-based violence, for example, both of which ought also to be labeled terrorism according to the term's usual definition: violence against innocent civilians designed to advance a political cause (the maintenance of patriarchy is eminently political). As such, each use of the term "terrorism" is an inherently political act. The definition of terrorism is never applied consistently, because to do so would mean the condemnatory power of the term would have to be applied to our violence as much as theirs, thereby defeating the word's usefulness.[45] Ahmad's point finds no better illustration than Congressman Peter King, who today rails against the radicalization of Muslim Americans but in the 1980s gave what would now be called material support to the Irish Republican Army by encouraging fund-raising among Irish Americans and telling a 1982 rally in Nassau County, New York: "We must pledge ourselves to support those brave men and women who this very moment are carrying forth the struggle against British imperialism in the streets of Belfast and Derry."[46] If the British army's presence in Northern Ireland in the 1980s was imperialism, then presumably its more recent presence in Afghanistan must also be so described.

If terrorism is defined as violence against innocent civilians designed to advance a political cause, the Woolwich attack in London is properly described as an act of terrorism. The victim was a combatant, but he was not present on a battlefield, so it is appropriate to describe him at that time as a civilian. However, by the same definition, all the racist murders that occur in Britain and the US are also acts of terrorism, because the perpetrators are trying to send a political message to minority communities (i.e., intimidate them into a subordinate status). Like the violent acts we normally think of as terrorism, racist violence not only takes the lives of its immediate victims, but also sends a larger message of fear to the wider population.[47] Yet terrorism and racist violence are not considered to be equally significant threats by governments and the establishment media echo chamber. While the murder of Lee Rigby was a major national event, prompting a flurry of government actions, policy responses, and public discussion, racist murders are rarely reported beyond the local newspaper. This difference cannot be explained as a matter of the scale of harm each form of violence inflicts. In Europe, the violence carried out by far Right groups, which have racism as a central part of their ideology, is of a similar magnitude to that of jihadist violence: at least 249 people died in incidents of far Right violence between 1990 and 2012; 263 were killed by jihadists over the same period.[48] In the US, between 1990 and 2010, there were 145 acts of political violence committed by the American far Right, resulting in 348 deaths.[49] In comparison, 20 people were killed over the same period in acts of political violence carried out by Muslim-American citizens or long-term residents of the US.[50] Both categories of violence represent threats to democratic values from fellow citizens. Whereas the former uses violence to foment a change in the ethnic makeup of Western countries or to defend racial supremacy, the latter uses violence to try to intimidate Western governments into changing their foreign policies. Ultimately, to be more concerned about one domestic threat of violence rather than the other implies governments and mainstream journalists consider foreign policies more sacrosanct than the security of minority citizens.

The political act of labeling certain forms of violence as terrorism is also usually a racialized act. This was revealed clearly in the hours after the attacks in Boston and Woolwich, before the identities of the perpetrators were known. Speculation in the US media as to whether the attacks were domestic or international terrorism used those terms as codes to talk about whether the perpetrators were white (and therefore assumed to be either crazed "lone wolves" or far Right "patriots") or Muslim (and therefore to be understood as driven by the same alien ideology that produced 9/11). When CNN's John

King commented that the person arrested for the Boston attack had been identified as a "dark-skinned man," it was not just an individual gaffe but the making explicit of the racial subtext to the entire discourse of counterterrorism.[51] On MSNBC, Chris Matthews asked his terrorism expert guests whether government analysts would be able to tell from the surveillance images of the suspects if they were "from Yemen or other parts like that."[52] The suspect's face was being asked to reveal a racial identity that would, in turn, tell us whether he was one of "them" or one of "us," and therefore what kind of emotional response to the bombing would be appropriate. As it turned out, the suspects were in every sense Caucasian.

In reporting the Woolwich murder, the BBC's political editor, Nick Robinson, made a strikingly similar slip, describing one of the assailants as being of "Muslim appearance."[53] The black man he was referring to was wearing jeans, a hoodie, and a wooly hat; nevertheless his "Muslimness" had somehow become visible, thereby justifying the use of the term "terrorist". A month earlier, another UK murder had taken place that was barely noticed, let alone named as a terrorist act. Mohammed Saleem, a seventy-five-year-old Muslim man from Birmingham, had been stabbed three times in the back as he left his local mosque. Only later in July, when the perpetrator was arrested and found to have also bombed two mosques in the weeks after the Woolwich attack, did pressure from community activists force the police to also describe his crimes as terrorism.[54] The default assumption remains that the term "terrorist" is reserved for acts of political violence carried out by Muslims.

The events of 9/11, of course, stand out as the worst single day of nonstate terrorism in the modern era. But the stream of similarly devastating attacks that security officials predicted in the years after 2001 has not materialized while the basic mind-set of counterterrorism has not adjusted: its reflexes are much the same as they were on September 12, 2001. Certainly there have been a handful of plots, such as that of Najibullah Zazi in 2009, in which a terrorist act would likely have occurred in the US were it not for the government's investigative efforts (although the argument that successful investigations depended on warrantless surveillance did not stand up to scrutiny).[55] And a series of potentially devastating jihadist plots have been detected in Britain. Of course, governments claim the absence of a greater number of successful attacks is a result of their policy choices. But a closer look at the actual arrests made by governments suggests a somewhat different account. Those arrested for terrorist crimes bear scant resemblance to the popular image of Muslim fanatics out to destroy Western civilization through spectacular acts of violence. Of the 176 Muslims indicted or arrested for involvement in terrorism in the US between 2001 and 2010, a significant number were prosecuted not for violence but for "expressive" and charitable activities that the government considers "material support" for terrorism—but which would likely have been considered lawful before 9/11.[56] Others are accused not of threatening violence in the US but of traveling to other parts of the world to join local insurgencies. Most of the remainder are individuals who have been convicted because agents provocateurs spent months pressuring them to agree to participate in imaginary plots they would never have been able to organize by themselves—in these cases, the only radicalization taking place was that carried out by the FBI. To a large degree the US government is fantasizing into existence the very threat of domestic jihadism it claims it is fighting.

In dedicating tens of billions of dollars a year to fighting a domestic threat of terrorist violence that is largely imagined, the US government has neglected the challenge of creating a genuinely peaceful society.[57] An ideologically driven focus on Muslim Americans as the prime threat of violence goes hand in hand with a normalization of the fact that in the US fifteen thousand people are murdered each year.[58] Indeed, the political scientist John Mueller has illustrated how our conception of the terrorist threat is shaped more by ideology than objectivity. He has calculated as follows: "In almost all years the total number of people worldwide who die at the hands of international terrorists is not much more than the number who drown in bathtubs in the United States."[59] In the United Kingdom, despite the focus on al-Qaeda, the number of deaths caused by sectarianism in Northern Ireland over the last decade is similar to the number of lives lost in jihadist attacks. According to the University of Ulster, there were sixty-two deaths related to the conflict in Northern Ireland between 2002 and 2011. There were fifty-three deaths as a result of jihadist violence in the UK over the same period.[60]

Contrast those numbers with the loss of life in Afghanistan, Iraq, and Pakistan as a result of the wars the US has fought since 9/11. Scholars at the Eisenhower Research Project at Brown University's Watson Institute for International Studies calculated in 2013 that those wars had led to the deaths of 270,000 people, the most conservative of such estimates.[61] A study by the Johns Hopkins Bloomberg School of Public Health estimated that the Iraq war had led to 655,000 deaths as of July 2006, before the worst period of violence.[62] One of the key arguments of this book is that to comprehend the causes of so-called jihadist terrorism we need to pay as much attention to Western state violence, and the identity politics that sustains it, as we do to Islamist ideology. What governments call extremism is to a large degree a product of their own wars.

A Note on Sources

The Muslims Are Coming! is based on three years of research in both the US and the UK that was supported by the Institute of Race Relations in London and the Open Society Foundations in New York. Research for the book was carried out in a number of locations in the US (Dallas, Dearborn, Detroit, Houston, Minneapolis–St. Paul, New York City, and Washington, DC) and the UK (Birmingham, Bolton, Bradford, London, Luton, and Manchester). In all, 160 interviews were carried out with activists, campaigners, religious leaders, law enforcement officials, policy makers, government advisers, and young people. In partnership with the civil liberties organization Liberty, the Freedom of Information Act was used to obtain previously classified data on the demographics of individuals profiled as extremists by the UK's Prevent policy.

CHAPTER 1

An Ideal Enemy

> The ideal enemy for America would be ideologically hostile, racially and culturally different, and militarily strong enough to pose a credible threat to American security.
>
> —Samuel P. Huntington, *Who Are We?*

As a teenager in the 1980s, Farasat Latif was a Marxist. Politicized by his experience of racism while growing up in England, he thought that abolishing capitalism was the only way to create a just world. He began to travel at the age of fourteen, from Stevenage, the small town north of London where his family had settled, to the capital, where he hung around with anarchists and leftists. When he wasn't fighting fascists on the streets of east London he was in demonstrations fighting the police. He read books by Marx and Lenin and became a student at the London School of Economics. When, in 1990, the Thatcher government introduced the new poll tax that shifted the local government's tax burden from the rich to the poor, he joined the hundreds of thousands of other protesters who had gathered in Trafalgar Square. Panicking at the unexpected turnout, Scotland Yard ordered mounted police into the crowds, and the square descended into violence. Demonstrators, Farasat among them, grabbed bricks from a building site to use as missiles. He was caught red-handed and arrested. While he was detained in a police cell officers asked him to sign a form for his personal property on which they had written "a brick" as one of his possessions. He declined to sign the incriminating form until it was corrected. After his release on bail he was advised that he faced a prison sentence. The trial was scheduled for nine months' time.

Around the same time, Farasat's 107-year-old grandfather fell ill in Pakistan, and he decided to visit him for the last time. While there he happened to browse a bookshop and came across a text entitled *Marxism and Islam* published by the International Islamic University, Islamabad. Before, when people had asked if he was a Muslim, he had answered that although he grew up in a Muslim family, he was not really sure anymore. He did not drink alcohol or eat pork, and occasionally he would visit a mosque, but more for social than religious reasons. His lack of deeper religious conviction had never troubled him. But now, his reading of this book forced him to decide between his Marxist and Muslim identities. The book, written as propaganda material to support the mujahideen fighting the communist regime in neighboring Afghanistan, gave a systematic critique of Marxism from an Islamic perspective. Farasat returned to England with his Marxist beliefs shattered and realized he no longer knew what he believed in. And he thought he was about to go to prison. As it turned out, a character reference from Farasat's professor impressed the judge, and he only received a £400 fine. By then he also had found that Islam was able to address the same needs that had earlier been met by Marxism.

I met Farasat twenty years later at a Salafi mosque in Luton, a town thirty miles north of London that had attracted immigrants, mainly from Pakistan, to work in its auto industry. Looking back, he explained how Islam had supplanted his commitment to Marxism. "It answered the same questions, which were about injustice. And it also put a perspective on this life, that it is a small part of your overall existence. At that time I was very angry and frustrated. There was the total massacre in Iraq in 1991. There was so much injustice, and they were getting away with it. Thatcher had smashed the unions, and the Left was too busy arguing over silly little things. And then Islam took me back to fundamental questions: What's the purpose of life? What's the purpose of creation? and, How does one achieve justice? It didn't happen overnight, but that's what started dawning on me." He began spending time with the different Islamic sects in England—Barelvis, Deobandis, and the Tablighi Jamaat—asking the questions that had been thrown up by his crisis of meaning. In the end it was the clarity of the Salafis, a tiny trend within Islam with less than 5 percent of British Muslims as followers, that attracted him most. "Salafism is very literalist: This is what

Allah says, this is what the messenger said, this is what the companions said, this is what you do—end of story. I prefer that. The idea that the message is infallible appealed to me." His attraction to the Salafis solidified further a few years later, when they proved the most willing to volunteer to defend Muslims against the atrocities being carried out by Serb forces in Bosnia. While others had talked about "jihad" to defend Muslims from oppression, the Salafis actually went and did it.[1]

Farasat joined the Salafi mosque in Luton and soon found he had a knack for winning over young people on the fringes of society to his puritan worldview. The mosque reached out to those in prisons or involved in crime, most with Pakistani backgrounds, and tried to transform their lifestyles. So successful was the group's approach that Luton's most prominent drug dealer was won over and gave up his old life of casual sex, violence, and fast cars for the austerity of praying five times a day and lawful work on the minimum wage. Soon other young people from working-class African-Caribbean and white backgrounds were converting to Islam and following the same Salafi lifestyle.

The Salafis preached "self-rectification," a process of individual purification aimed at modeling one's life as closely as possible on the Prophet's example. "When it comes to religious things, dress sense, character, morals, manners, behavior, it should be exactly as it was in the time of Prophet Muhammad," says Farasat. The political oppression of Muslims was central to this Salafi discourse but interpreted as a punishment from God for failing to adopt the correct lifestyle. Unlike other groups, such as the Muslim Brotherhood, Jamaat-i-Islami, Hizb ut-Tahrir, or their offshoots, which focused on using political power to create an Islamic society, the Saudi-aligned Salafis thought there was no point in engaging in such political struggles until individual Muslims first corrected their own beliefs and practices. For the time being, they believed, the struggle involved self-transformation: doing away with South Asian cultural practices seen as diluting the original Islamic message and rejecting innovations introduced by Islamic scholars after the early generations of Muslims. "We don't say that the solution is a political one," notes Farasat.

> We don't blame [King] Fahd [of Saudi Arabia] or Mubarak or Saddam Hussein for the ills of the Muslim *ummah* [global community]. Even

> though every Muslim country is ruled by a tyrannical leader, we do not call the people to rise up against them. We warn people against revolution. We say that the reason you have these dictators is because we are sinful, and so we need to change ourselves and better ourselves, and Allah will give us a leader who loves us. So in that sense, we are antirevolutionary. We need to pray five times a day, respect our parents, and do all the things that Allah has ordered us to do. When we do that Allah will give us victory. That is why we talk about the political situation as the illness that has befallen Muslims, but the cure lies in self-rectification.[2]

While the Salafis of Luton hope their comrades in Chechnya, Kashmir, and Palestine will be victorious in fighting what they consider to be foreign occupiers, they reject violence against civilians and against the British state. "In England we would strongly oppose any armed conflict," states Farasat, "because it is not a situation where Muslims are being massacred and raped in large numbers. If that happened, our call would not be jihad, but emigration."[3] Nevertheless, they believe individuals should participate where they consider legitimate armed struggles to be taking place in other parts of the world if they have undergone a successful process of rectification and "got things right in other aspects of their life." Thus, in the 1990s, a small number of young Salafis from Luton volunteered to fight in Bosnia and Kashmir.

Britain's security services had tacitly approved of Muslim volunteers fighting Serb militia in Bosnia and Kosovo. But after 9/11, the Salafi networks came under greater suspicion. The national media, too, descended on Luton in the weeks after 9/11, when it emerged that the city's branch of a rival group, al-Muhajiroun (local membership: six), had sent two men to Afghanistan to join the Taliban; they had been killed in a US bombing raid on Kabul. Unlike the Salafis, al-Muhajiroun's rhetoric included calls for political struggle in Britain to establish an Islamic state. The media attention soon gave Luton a reputation as a hive of extremist activity. At football matches, Luton Town supporters were mocked by opposing fans for having Muslim extremists in their city. Racial animosity mounted among elements of Luton's white majority. In an effort at appeasement, the Salafis found al-Muhajiroun's local leader, beat him up, and warned him not to continue his activities in the town. Then they called a press conference and publicly denounced the group. "Their activities will no longer be tolerated here," read their statement. "If we see al-Muhajiroun on the streets spreading their poison, we will drive them off the streets."[4] The Salafis wanted to send a message to the city and to the security services that there was a difference between themselves and al-Muhajiroun, that their agenda within the UK was purely religious, and that they were willing to police their own community and drive out "violent extremists." For a while, the threats of racial violence against Luton's mosques declined, although a few years later some Luton Town Football Club supporters would be central to forming the English Defence League, a new far Right political group with a violent anti-Muslim agenda.

Farasat Latif was not alone in his struggle to make sense of a world that seemed plagued by vast injustices yet was without any prospect of radical change on the horizon. The children and grandchildren of the African-Caribbean and South Asian settlers who had come to the UK in the decades after World War II had grown up in a society that usually saw them as a problem to be solved rather than as fellow citizens with an equal right to shape British life. They were disproportionately stopped and searched by the police on the streets, subjected to racist violence and harassment on their way to and from school or college, and pilloried and mocked in newspapers and television programs, so a sense of racial injustice—often understood as a continuation of the colonialism their parents and grandparents had fought—was an enduring feature of their lives. Their very presence in Britain was only explicable within the broad sweep of a colonial history that most British people preferred to forget. When Britain had needed cheap labor to rebuild after the war, British subjects from South Asian and Caribbean colonies were recruited. Since colonialism had already made them subjects of the British Crown, they were technically not immigrants but subjects moving from one part of Britain's multiracial empire to another. As Britain's imperial project finally collapsed in the 1950s, the people of color who had begun to settle in the "mother country" were left as a kind of historical anomaly, and their settlement was construed as an external intrusion into the body politic. Both liberals and conservatives among the governing elite in the 1960s looked anxiously across the Atlantic at the urban uprisings occurring in the US and hoped they could avoid similar problems by passing immigration laws to close the colonial "open door" to those who were not white at the same time that they implemented antidiscrimination measures to integrate the new communities of color. In the event, official efforts to end racial discrimination proved largely symbolic, while the new immigration laws worsened matters by reinforcing the perception that people of color were not really part of Britain, conveniently erasing the colonial history that had brought them there. A. Sivanandan, a Sri Lankan writer who had settled in London in 1958, refused this false separation of immigration from imperialism by inventing the slogan: "We are here because you were there."

Community movements against racism, influenced by Black Power movements in the US and anticolonial struggles in the Caribbean, Africa, and Asia, emerged in the 1960s and 1970s. Their starting point was that Britain's color line was also the cord that held British capitalism together—fighting racism was therefore necessarily connected to a radical anticapitalism. For instance, the Asian Youth Movements, youth-led organizations which had sprung up in various South Asian neighborhoods in England in the 1970s to coordinate community self-defense against racist violence, were modeled on the US Black Panther Party. Like the Panthers, they understood racism as inherent to Western capitalism. Local government leaders responded to such radicalism with a formula of soft multiculturalism, looking to conservative identity politics as a useful counter. Giving "ethnic minorities" a cultural stake in the existing system would, it was hoped, prevent their search for a socialist alternative. In the city of Bradford, the heart of Britain's Pakistani community, the city council encouraged a council of mosques to be constituted in 1981, as an alternative community voice to the secular Asian Youth Movement. The city council legitimized the mosque leaders as a new class of community leadership through funding and consultation exercises, hoping they would become conservative allies in a process of undermining the younger radicals.[5] Bradford's approach was replicated elsewhere, and by the end of the decade, religious identity politics was on the rise among young South Asians as secular leftist radicalism was declining.

The official language of multiculturalism was more about managing ethnic identity than dealing with institutional discrimination. Government ministers hoped institutionalizing ethnic identity would sever it from political radicalism. The introduction of multicultural television programming, for instance, was described by William Whitelaw, then the home secretary, in the following terms:

> If you are Home Secretary in any government, you are going to take the view that there are a lot of minority interests in this country, [for example] different races. If they don't get some outlet for their activities you are going to run yourself into much more trouble.[6]

Political trouble was to be avoided with the sop of cultural identity. Yet culture itself could be a field of political contest: the question of what it meant to be British was itself becoming politicized.

Between 1991 and 1993 there were nine racist murders in London.[7] The murder of African-Caribbean teenager Stephen Lawrence by a racist gang in the southeast of the capital attracted as little attention as the others when it first occurred in 1993. The police refused to take action, despite a number of people coming forward to identify the perpetrators. But Stephen's family spent years campaigning for justice, making legal history by launching a private prosecution. The case collapsed, but the momentum of the campaign—helped especially by the support of Nelson Mandela during his first visit to London—pushed the government to announce a public inquiry into the murder in 1997. Two years later, Sir William Macpherson released the inquiry's report, identifying a pervasive problem of institutional racism in the police.

Outside London, where communities of color included significant numbers from South Asian Muslim backgrounds, the picture was, if anything, bleaker. In the northern textile-mill towns of Yorkshire and Lancashire, for example, Pakistanis and Bangladeshis had been recruited from the 1950s onward to work night shifts, which were unpopular with the existing white work force. But as new machinery was developed, the need for labor diminished, and such labor as was needed could be obtained for less elsewhere. The work once done cheaply by Asian workers in the north of England could by the 1980s be done even more cheaply by Asian workers in Asia. The decline of the mills left entire towns on the scrap heap. With the end of the textile-mill industry, the largest employers were the public services, but discrimination kept most of those jobs for whites. The future for South Asians lay in the local service economy. A few brothers would pool their savings and set up a convenience store or a takeout restaurant. Otherwise, there was taxi driving, with long hours and the risk of violence and racist abuse. In one of the former mill towns, Oldham, a quarter of Pakistanis in their thirties were unemployed by 1992; for those age eighteen to twenty-four, the unemployment rate was 37 percent.[8] Industrial collapse led ethnic groups to turn inward on themselves in different ways. The depressed inner-city areas, lined with old terraced houses built for millworker families, were abandoned by those whites who could afford to move out to the suburbs. Others took advantage of discriminatory public housing policies which allocated whites to new housing estates cut off from South Asian areas.[9] Those South Asians who did get public housing on predominantly white estates soon found their homes targeted: bricks were thrown through windows; sometimes gasoline and a lighted match were tossed through the door. The fear of racial harassment and violence meant most South Asians sought the safety of their own areas, in spite of the overcrowding, the damp and dingy houses, the claustrophobia of a community penned in. The geography of the balkanized northern towns became a chessboard of mutually exclusive areas.[10] It was no surprise that, in this ghettoized context, dirty linen was washed neither in public nor in private: problems of drug abuse and forced marriage in South Asian communities went unaddressed.[11]

The violence that accompanied de facto segregation was vividly illustrated in January 2000. Sarfraz and Shahzad Najeib, two South Asian brothers attending university in Leeds, went to a nightclub in the city center, crossing the implicit lines of ethnic separation that marked the social life of the city. A group of white men got into an argument with them and struck Sarfraz, who, as a court would later hear, "had the temerity to punch back"—the South Asian stereotype was to not retaliate. In response to this so-called provocation, the group chased Sarfraz out of the club and into an alleyway, beat him to the ground, and kicked his head to within an inch of his life. The next day the brothers discovered that two of those accused of the attack were celebrities: Jonathan Woodgate and Lee Bowyer, stars of the Leeds United football club and the English national team. Woodgate was eventually convicted of being part of the chase but was not jailed, and he continued his successful football career; Bowyer was acquitted. Because of poorly designed laws on prosecuting racial violence, Sarfraz was unable to testify in court on the racial epithets he had heard. The brothers' father, who in a racist attack thirty years before had also been beaten unconscious, said: "If I had had even a small inkling that something like this might happen, perhaps I would not be in this country. I would have gone back to Pakistan."[12] The following year, a string of towns in the north of England erupted in riots, as young South Asians battled with police forces that had both criminalized them and failed to protect them from racist violence.

Earlier generations of South Asian youth had made sense of these kinds of experiences through a secular and leftist political framework. But this was less true of the 1990s. Farasat Latif's disillusion with a declining Left was not unusual. Nor was the influence on him of Islamic movements that had flourished in Pakistan as a side effect of the US sponsorship of the mujahideen in Afghanistan in the 1980s. The fatwa against Salman Rushdie issued by the Iranian regime in 1989 further illustrated that Islamic movements were ascendant. In South Asia itself, the Indian army's attack on the Sikh Golden Temple in Amritsar in 1984 and the Hindu nationalist mobilization that ended in the destruction of the mosque at Ayodhya in 1991 had undermined the credibility of Indian-style secularism. British Muslims arriving at university in the 1990s, with experiences of personal racist violence as teenagers, institutional racism in the police, and a growing awareness of global injustices such as the Bosnian genocide, were more likely to encounter Islamic politics than South Asian forms of leftism. Groups like Hizb ut-Tahrir (HT) offered a way of making sense of these experiences and were able to recruit thousands of young supporters to what would come to be known as "Islamism."

Islamic movements like HT, founded in Jordan in the 1950s, the Muslim Brotherhood (MB) in Egypt, and the Jamaat-i-Islami (JI) in South Asia, which had emerged in the context of decolonization in the mid–twentieth century, were essentially attempts to respond to the legacy of colonialism at the cultural level. Frantz Fanon, the psychiatrist from Martinique who joined the Algerian anticolonial struggle, had noted: "Colonial domination, because it is total and tends to oversimplify, very soon manages to disrupt in spectacular fashion the cultural life of a conquered people."[13] Like all colonized peoples, Muslims in the Middle East and South Asia recognized that formal political independence did not by itself resolve the issue of how to reconstruct identity. Leaving the nation-state structures established by colonialism in place and simply replacing Europeans with native leaders was insufficient: it ignored the more complex question of what kinds of political subjectivity they would need to create to sustain newly decolonized states, what Fanon described as the demand for "not only the disappearance of colonialism but also the disappearance of the colonized man."[14] For the Muslim Brotherhood in Egypt and the JI in Pakistan, the answer was to be found in turning Islam into a form of identity politics. It was as Muslims, rather than as nationals of a colonially defined territory, that a sense of shared belonging was to be established and a more fundamental breach with European cultural domination enacted. In this respect, these Islamic movements were similar to groups mobilizing other religious identities in decolonizing settings—such as the Hindu nationalist Rashtriya Swayamsevak Sangh in India. In practice, as these movements began to increase their influence in the 1970s, they tended toward stabilizing the social inequalities left behind by colonialism. They campaigned for conservative positions on gender relations and mobilized support through agitation against minorities, whether it was the Ahmadiyya minority in Pakistan or the Copt minority in Egypt. They bore little resemblance to Fanon's hopes of setting "afoot a new man" in the aftermath of colonialism that would offer new models for humanity.[15]

The appeal of these movements to some young Muslims who were living as minorities in Britain in the 1990s therefore seems hard to explain at first. The political program of HT, for instance, had little to say about Britain itself. Before the Rushdie affair, HT's UK-based leadership did not even target British-born Muslims for recruitment, preferring to focus on visiting Arab students and professionals who might participate in an HT-led coup d'état on their return home. Such a program was of little practical relevance to minority Islam in a secular Western state such as Britain.[16] HT's success in this period rested not on its political program as such but on its ability to act as a vehicle for a new kind of globalized Islamic identity. As the French scholar Olivier Roy has argued, this notion of a globalized Islam is not the product of any specific "Islamist" organization but a broad sociological trend that has developed across Europe as a result of racism, migration, and globalization.[17] Young Muslims felt alienated not only from the racism of the wider society, but also from the inward-looking mosque life of their parents, which was centered upon specific ethnic identities (for example, Sylheti, Gujarati, or Mirpuri) and mingled Islam with South Asian folk traditions. The idea of identifying with the global *ummah* proved an attractive third alternative to either assimilating into a racist society or following the inherited religio-cultural traditions of their parents. The version of Islam that suited this approach was one that was delinked from the ethnic folk practices drawn from South Asia (such as reverence for holy men, or *pirs*); these were to be stripped away on the grounds of their being impure accretions that had contaminated the original universal message of Islam. While their parents had imbibed their religion through an oral tradition bound up with South Asian languages and poetry, the new, globalized Islam was at home in English and on the printed page (and later, the Internet). It was this concept of a globalized Islam rather than a Pakistani Islam or a Bangladeshi Islam that appealed to some young British Asian Muslims in the 1990s, whether it led to the ranks of HT or, as for Farasat, to Salafism. Through these new Islamic movements, young Muslims thus carried out their own globalization, transcending inherited ethnic and national belongings in favor of an allegiance to the global Islamic community. As new immigrant communities from Somalia, Afghanistan, Algeria, and Iraq began to form in the UK during the 1990s, the idea of a global Islam, as opposed to a mosaic of ethnicities, made all the more sense. The world was now pictured differently.

The South Asian neighborhoods of Britain and the original towns and villages of South Asia from which communities had migrated remained the central axes of young Muslims' mental geography. But alongside them came a growing knowledge of other parts of the world where the *ummah* was oppressed: Palestine, Chechnya, Kashmir, Bosnia, Kosovo, and Iraq. In principle, all the struggles for justice of Muslims around the world were to be regarded as equally important. Ultimately, there was no homeland and no diaspora but a global Islamic consciousness unbounded by geography. This new sense of identity was fundamentally political: It provided a new language for describing injustice and offered a way of filling the void opened up by the decline of the Left. It countered the globalization of capitalism not with a return to local tradition but with a transnationalism of its own.

There was a range of ways in which this trend manifested. For some, having stripped Islam of South Asian cultural accretions, it was easier to establish a sense of belonging as a Muslim in Western society. This was the model offered by reformists such as the Swiss philosopher Tariq Ramadan, who emphasized the need to apply Islam's universal principles to the specific context of when and where one lived. By going back to the original sources, Ramadan argued, universal Islamic values, after being separated from the particular immigrant cultures with which they had become bound up, are found to be broadly compatible with liberalism. This then provided an Islamic basis for active citizenship and engagement for social justice rather than isolation or a one-sided adaptation to British cultural norms.[18] The unities between Muslims and others in the movement against the 2003 Iraq war rested on this assumption, that Islamic and liberal values could be aligned on specific political struggles. For others, like Farasat Latif, the path led to literalism and the attempt to model one's life as closely as possible on the Prophet's. While both of these approaches involved issues of identity, they could only be fully understood in the context of a political history of racism, the decline of leftist politics, and Western neocolonialism.

Three of the four men who carried out the 7/7 terrorist attacks on the London transport system in 2005, resulting in the deaths of fifty-two passengers, had also been shaped by the generational gap between a parental folkloric Islam and a new global Islam. In the aftermath of the attacks, the pundits, think tanks, academics, and intelligence analysts who were called on to explain this new threat of "homegrown" terrorism tended to assume because those perpetrating the violence had made a break with their parent's Islam in favor of something called Salafism or Islamism, that these isms must be the cause of their violence, the drivers of their radicalization. In the most influential study of the causes of 7/7, the journalist Shiv Malik argued that the bombers were the product of a much wider trend in Britain's Muslim communities, of a younger generation using Islamism to reject the traditional practices of their parents.[19] The claim that the cultural origins of homegrown terrorism could be found in the general trend of young Muslims rethinking their identities was a convenient alternative to recognizing more political factors, such as Britain's foreign policies. And such a claim had the implication that a whole range of behaviors associated with this generational conflict could be used by security officials as "indicators" of the risk of radicalization—for example, choosing to leave the congregation of one's parents' mosque in favor of an attachment to one with a more globalized idea of Islam. It also meant that government projects to intervene in the cultural dynamics of Muslim life to try to shore up alternatives to Islamism could be legitimized as part of a counterterrorism strategy. Finally, it implied that multicultural tolerance of these new forms of identity, in which Muslims identify with their coreligionists around the world, was in itself a national security risk.

Such analyses became the main lens through which Muslim identity in the West was viewed. In Prime Minister David Cameron's much-discussed speech to the Munich Security Conference in 2011, he made the same argument: behind Muslim terrorism lay "a question of identity"; "the passive tolerance of recent years" had to be abandoned in favor of a much more assertive defense of British values against "Islamist extremism"; Muslims had to privilege their Britishness over their global allegiance to Muslims.[20] On the same day, the far Right English Defence League marched through Farasat Latif's hometown of Luton making roughly similar demands in less genteel language. By remaining within an exclusively cultural analysis, and ignoring the political histories of racism and the foreign policy practices of the war on terror, Cameron's speech was unable to come to grips with the real roots of political violence. Ironically, demanding that Muslims be more British simply reminded them that as things stood they did not have an equal say in what Britishness meant.

In later chapters I argue that analyses of terrorism that locate its root cause in Islamist ideology and underlying cultural conflicts are conceptually flawed and inconsistent with the available evidence. In short, there is no demonstrable cause and effect between holding an Islamist ideology and committing acts of terrorist violence. The notion that "extremist ideas," perhaps enabled by identity conflicts or group dynamics, by themselves turn people into violent radicals does not stand up to scrutiny, and it detaches the question of terrorist violence from the wider context of Western governments' foreign policies. It is noteworthy that in the July 7, 2005, bombings the usual theories of radicalization, such as Shiv Malik's, have to ignore the story of Germaine Lindsay, the suicide bomber who killed 26 people and injured over 340 on a Piccadilly line underground train between King's Cross and Russell Square stations. He was born in Jamaica in 1985 and immigrated to Britain with his mother as a young child. His mother converted to Islam when he was fifteen, and he followed immediately afterward, before she left to live in the US. Thereafter, Lindsay seemed to live a life of petty crime but engaged in some political activities. He was reported to have been a drug dealer for a time, who was "always going on about racism" and "thought all white people were trash."[21] He attended a national demonstration in October 2002 against the impending war on Iraq and for the rights of Palestinians; there he met a woman with whom he would have a long-term relationship and two children. He was only nineteen years old when he carried out his act of mass murder. There was nothing in this story to correspond to the generally accepted radicalization models, which is why pundits normally neglect to discuss him.

At the Door of Whiteness

In July 2011, Arizonans complained that local television news stations were referring to the massive dust storms that sweep through the state as "*haboobs*," an Arabic term long used by meterologists in the Southwest. One resident wrote to a local newspaper asking: "How do they think our soldiers feel coming back to Arizona and hearing some Middle Eastern term?"[22] One wonders if soldiers would also object to their children learning algebra. That "some Middle Eastern term" could provoke this reaction points to the way in which signifiers of perceived alien cultures can designate racialized enemies. Just as the story of Muslim identity in Britain is inseparable from questions of race, so too is race a necessary part of understanding what it means to be Muslim in the US. In both settings, the social history of Muslim life attests to the shifting construction and reconstruction of racial meanings.

Compared to the UK, the American Muslim population is less concentrated on South Asia as a region of origin. In the last fifty years, Muslims have settled in the US from various Arab countries, other countries in Asia and Africa, Turkey, Iran, and southeastern Europe—and different parts of this mixed Muslim population have experienced distinct patterns of racialization. It is estimated that 20 to 30 percent of Muslims in the US are African American.[23] Indeed, one in four of those brought to the Americas with the Atlantic slave trade originated from Muslim-majority parts of West Africa. The 1977 television miniseries *Roots*, based on Alex Haley's novel, reflected historical realities when it portrayed Kunta Kinte, the African captured as an adolescent and sold into slavery in the US, as a Muslim.[24] By the late nineteenth century the African-American connection to Islam had been largely erased, but as blacks moved north from southern segregation, they began to forge new and syncretic religious movements, often oriented toward Islam. Meetings of Marcus Garvey's Universal Negro Improvement Association in Harlem often featured South Asian missionaries of the Ahmadiyya sect, who claimed kinship with African Americans because of their own hardships under British colonialism. The Moorish Science

Temple, formed in Newark in 1913 by an African American named Timothy Drew (who renamed himself Noble Drew Ali), was the first significant organization in the US to identify itself as Islamic, though its knowledge of Muslim life in other parts of the world was sketchy. In 1926, the Egyptian Dusé Mohamed Ali formed the Universal Islamic Society in Detroit, a precursor to Wallace Fard Muhammad's Nation of Islam, which was founded in the city four years later. These heterodox forms of religious practice were attractive as a basis for both spiritual salvation and reconceptualizing what it meant to be a black American. By proclaiming themselves "Moorish Americans" or "Asiatics" rather than "Negros," followers imaginatively left behind their racial subordination within the US and aligned themselves with a transnational Islamic community, within which racial classifications were transcended.[25] Islam became known as a religion that freed its followers from America's racial definitions; the impact in the black community went beyond the number of actual followers.[26] When Malcolm X claimed conscientious objector status during the Korean War draft, he identified his country of citizenship as Asia. By the early 1960s, when he was the Nation of Islam's most dynamic leader, the organization had attracted a membership of tens of thousands and the admiration of millions.[27]

As well as a base for new forms of African-American religion, Detroit, and the neighboring factory city of Dearborn, built by Henry Ford, were also major centers of Arab immigration in the twentieth century. The majority of Arab immigrants to the US have been Christians, but in later decades Muslims made up an increasing proportion. Arab Americans are reckoned to make up around a quarter of Muslims in the US today.[28] Ford began recruiting Palestinians, Yemenis, and Lebanese to work in his auto factories in 1913. Arab communities sprung up around the auto plants, the largest in the Southend area of Dearborn, in the shadow of Ford's mammoth River Rouge complex. By the early 1970s, two thousand Arab Americans were working at Chrysler's Dodge Main auto plant in Detroit. Like black workers, they were singled out for worse conditions in an attempt to divide the workforce along ethnic lines and undermine industrial labor organizing, following a tradition of racial division first systematized by Henry Ford. In 1973, three thousand Arab workers staged a militant parade through the streets of Dearborn to protest the leadership of the United Auto Workers; the union was accused of aligning itself with management and white workers, marginalizing blacks and Arabs, and purchasing $300,000 in Israeli bonds, in effect supporting the military occupation of Palestinian territories.[29] (Arabs, mainly from Yemen, were also a significant segment of the agricultural work force in California in the 1960s and 1970s, and were active in César Chávez's United Farm Workers union.)[30] As a result of the auto industry, Dearborn became a national center of Arab-American life, even as, with the decline of US manufacturing, its communities were forced to seek new kinds of work. "Ask any family in Dearborn where their father used to work," notes Rachid Elabed, a local youth worker,

> and they will say Chrysler, Ford, or GM. My dad worked at Ford. My uncle worked at GM. A lot of those jobs have gone now. Most Arab Americans went into small businesses: running gas stations, groceries, you name it.[31]

Today, despite the working-class black and Arab origins of American Islam, the mean family income of Muslims in the US is roughly similar to that of the population as a whole. For every cab driver, cleaner, or unemployed refugee there is a doctor or engineer living in the suburbs.[32] Following reforms of immigration policy in 1965, the US government began to carefully admit selected immigrants from Africa, Asia, and the Middle East. Who was allowed to settle was fine-tuned to the needs of US capitalism, and the geopolitical imperatives of the cold war. High-flying students from the Third World were recruited to American campuses as part of a brain drain rivalry with the Soviet Union. Many, including significant numbers of Muslims, stayed on. The proportion of South Asians in America's Muslim population increased. These settlers were destined for professional employment—the immigration selection process had already filtered out those without technical or professional skills of use to the US economy. But it was easy for Asians themselves and others to believe there was something inherent to "Asian culture" that made them a model minority in the US against which blacks and Latinos could be unfavorably compared.[33]

For the new Arab-American middle class there was the possibility of making what the law scholar John Tehranian has called a "Faustian pact with whiteness": choosing to pass as white in order to avoid racial discrimination.[34] The US government's Office of Management and Budget, which is responsible for identifying official racial and ethnic categories, formally defines people from "Europe, the Middle East, or North Africa" as white.[35] Assimilation to a suburban American whiteness was an option for many Arab Americans, especially Christians and nonpracticing Muslims, but it came at a price: collective invisibility and loss of identity. In its own way, this invisibility amounted to a form of second-class citizenship within the emerging parameters of post–Civil Rights Act multiculturalism: hiding in the mainstream was a racial performance that threatened to fall flat if the actors raised political issues on behalf of their group. When Arab organizations turned to the question of Palestine, they quickly lost their whiteness and came to be seen as dangerous aliens.

In the late 1960s, Arab Americans formed organizations such as the Association of Arab-American University Graduates and the Organization of Arab Students to contest US support of Israeli aggression in the Middle East. These were immediately the target of the pro-Israel lobby, which portrayed Arab activists as spies and foreign radicals.[36] In 1972, the Nixon administration issued a set of directives known as Operation Boulder that enabled the FBI and CIA to coordinate with the pro-Israel lobby, subjecting nonviolent Arab-American political activists to surveillance and harassment.[37] Such surveillance continued into the 1980s, as media coverage of the Iranian revolution and conflict in the Middle East gave rise to new stereotypes of Arabs as dangerous fanatics. In 1985, Alex Odeh, a leader of the American-Arab Anti-Discrimination Committee in California, was murdered in a bomb attack, likely carried out by the Jewish Defense League.[38] Two years later, the FBI and the Immigration and Naturalization Service (INS) arrested seven Palestinians and the Kenyan wife of one of them in Los Angeles, accusing them of distributing subversive literature. The investigation turned up no criminal activity but, as foreign nationals, the "LA8" were nevertheless vulnerable to deportation proceedings due to their political allegiance, under the McCarthy-era McCarran-Walter Act. Government documents made it clear the aim was to disrupt constitutionally protected political activity.[39] The government continued its efforts to deport them until it finally gave up twenty years after the initial arrests. Around the time of the arrests, a secret INS document was leaked to the *Los Angeles Times*. It outlined plans for the roundup of up to five thousand foreign nationals suspected of links to "terrorism"—i.e., support for the Palestinian cause—and their incarceration in camps in Louisiana. The May 1986 document, entitled "Alien Terrorists and Undesirables: A Contingency Plan," detailed how "selected aliens" from eight Middle Eastern countries who were suspected of being "engaged in support of terrorism" could be arrested on nebulous charges and deported on the basis of secret evidence.[40]

It was in the 1980s that the template of the war on terror was first hammered out: a fight against terrorism as ideological cover for state violence directed at those resisting US and Israeli power, whether they happened to be terrorists or not; a selective use of the term "terrorism" to exclude all those state and nonstate actors using violence to achieve our political ends (such as the Contras in Nicaragua); and a suturing of Israel and the US as defenders of "Western values" against "Islamic fanaticism." The message worked perfectly for the US television news audiences. The idea that Israel might be involved in suppressing a legitimate movement for national liberation became unthinkable. Much of the groundwork for this approach was laid by Benjamin Netanyahu, then the Israeli permanent representative to the United Nations, through a conference organized in Washington, DC, in 1984. In a subsequent collection of articles edited by Netanyahu—entitled *Terrorism: How the West Can Win*—a number of contributors argued that terrorist violence was endemic to Islam. For instance, the political scientist P. J. Vatikiotis claimed that terrorism is rooted in the "dichotomy, in fact, between the Islamic and all other systems of government and authority," an ideological clash that is "clear, sharp, and permanent" and "marked by hostility." While he accepted their "nothing in Islamic doctrine links it specifically to terrorism," there is nevertheless "a general Islamic injunction that power belongs to the believers for use against unbelievers, and that the latter should be fought until the earthly order is established under Allah."[41] President Reagan reportedly decided to launch his attack on Libya in 1986 after reading excerpts from the conference in *Time* magazine.[42] The Reagan administration was further encouraged by Claire Sterling's book *The Terror Network*, which claimed the Soviet Union was conducting a secret campaign of terrorism against the West.[43] When Reagan's newly appointed CIA director, William Casey, told his analysts to investigate the book's claims, he was unaware that its findings were in part based on earlier CIA disinformation campaigns in Italy, the aim of which had been to deliberately confuse terrorism with communism.[44] Terrorism became the number-one foreign policy issue for the US. The link in the popular mind between Islam and terrorism was sealed. Cultural theorist Edward Said described how, by the late 1980s, Islam called up "images of bearded clerics and mad suicidal bombers, of unrelenting Iranian mullahs, fanatical fundamentalists, and kidnappers, remorseless turbaned crowds who chant hatred of the US, 'the great devil,' and all its ways."[45]

By the end of the cold war the model minority, or passing-for-white, approaches were becoming less workable for American Muslims. US multiculturalism had tended to function as a selective openness to ethnic identity, requiring that groups entering the mainstream abandon any desire to reshape the basic contours of American political life. Cultural diversity was tolerated up to the point that it challenged the continuity of the existing system. In the early twentieth century, Jews and southern Europeans were welcomed into the American mainstream if they distanced themselves from communism and anarchism; to those who did not, the state responded with the Palmer raids and deportation. But for American Muslims, the perceived association with radicalism and terrorism was getting harder to avoid. The experience of Rehan Ansari, a Pakistani living in New York in the 1990s, was typical of the Muslim professional class:

> I had a job on Wall Street with a brokerage house in 1993 and one of the brokers used to think it was funny asking me how the Hizbollah was doing at least once every morning. He used to like rolling the word around in his mouth. My response to him was model minority. When the World Trade Center bombing happened that year, I was no longer with the firm and wondered what he would say if we were to meet again.[46]

For reasons similar to those in the UK, Muslim identity became an increasingly common basis for community organization in the US of the 1990s. These organizations had grown from the root of the Muslim Student Association (MSA), which had been created at a meeting at the University of Illinois, Champaign-Urbana, in 1963. The MSA's early activists were students from the Middle East and South Asia who had been influenced by the Muslim Brotherhood and Jamaat-i-Islami movements in their home countries. After their studies, they settled in the US and took up professional jobs, and were conservative in religion and politics; the local and national organizations they founded, such as the Islamic Society of North America (ISNA), reflected this. Some, having been active in Islamic politics in the dangerous context of Arab autocracies, now wanted to leave political activism behind; for them, the chief objective of Muslims in America should be to preserve cultural and religious identity within the framework of official multiculturalism while assimilating socioeconomically, as they had seen Jews do successfully. For others there was a desire to build social movements that could engage the wider society, either with an Islamic message or to lobby on foreign policy issues. In neither case was there a strong connection with the African-American Muslim experience.

Insofar as they had a political agenda, the national Islamic organizations that came to prominence in the 1990s were concerned with campaigning in support of Palestine—an activity that was increasingly in danger of being criminalized. The 1996 Antiterrorism and Effective Death Penalty Act gave birth to the "material support statute," which became the basis for prosecution of Muslim Americans for expressing an "ideology" and allowed government evidence to be heard in secret in detention hearings and trials, effectively removing the right of defendants to challenge the prosecution. It was a power used mainly against Arabs and Muslim Americans. In the LA8 case, the judge had refused to allow the government to present evidence in secret; the 1996 act was designed to remedy that. Meanwhile, the Democratic Party had deepened its ties with the pro-Israel lobby during the 1990s. In what is now a largely forgotten piece of pre-9/11 history, the major Islamic organizations decided to respond to these trends by allying with the Republicans in the 2000 elections, hoping that in return for American Muslim votes, the GOP would be a vehicle for a more balanced Middle East foreign policy. In 1999, George W. Bush hosted meetings between Muslim and Republican leaders and visited an Islamic center in Michigan. On the campaign trail he celebrated Americans who regularly attend a "church, synagogue, or mosque." And in one of his presidential debates with Vice President Al Gore, Bush criticized the 1996 secret evidence legislation, which President Clinton had signed into law. Conservative activist Grover Norquist proclaimed in the *American Spectator* that "Bush was elected President of the United States of America because of the Muslim vote."[47]

After the heyday of the cold war, the pattern of immigration had shifted again: Muslims coming to live in the US were now more likely to be seeking asylum, fleeing conflict, joining family, or entering on H1B temporary work permits linked to employment in information technology (IT) or engineering. A significant Muslim population developed in northern Virginia based on the local tech industry. In the western suburbs of Houston, Texas, Muslim immigrants came to take up jobs in the energy sector. Somali refugees settled in Minneapolis and St. Paul, Minnesota, and Columbus, Ohio, beginning in the late 1980s, often facing severe unemployment in their new homes. In Bay Ridge, Brooklyn, refugees from Egypt and Lebanon who arrived in the 1990s likewise struggled to live anything like the American Dream. They were often at risk of raids by the immigration authorities and disproportionately stopped and frisked on the subways.[48]

It was the more precariously situated refugee populations that bore the brunt of the post-9/11 government crackdowns on Muslims in the US: the roundups of foreign nationals, intensifying surveillance, and racial profiling. The majority of American Muslims—perhaps as many as 80 percent—do not attend mosques and have a secular outlook. But irrespective of their own lack of belief in, affiliation with, or practice of Islam, since 9/11 they have become "Muslim," because others perceive them as such.[49] In his analysis of French anti-Semitism, Jean-Paul Sartre wrote of a similar process in which being Jewish was ultimately not based on a biological race or a religious belief but on a social relationship: "The Jew is one whom other men consider a Jew."[50] Similarly, after 9/11, the experience of being Muslim was rooted more in a social than a theological identity. Many suburban Muslims hoped that the negative atmosphere after 9/11 would be temporary, and that, after it had passed, they could return to their status as Asian model minorities or go back to passing for white. In the meantime, the best strategy was thought to be excessive displays of patriotism and declarations of loyalty to the American way. A 2011 Pew survey of Muslim Americans found that 44 percent display the United States flag at home, at the office, or on their car.[51] To these more affluent Muslims, more recently arrived working-class immigrants who had not assimilated were something of an embarrassment, bringing what a Muslim businessman in Houston, Texas, refers to as "a lot of baggage from back home" such as "anti-American sentiment."[52]

For the national organizations, the basic question raised by the new after-9/11 climate was whether to follow a strategy of declaring one's loyalty to America and presenting Muslims as model citizens, or to instead move in the direction of protests against the war on terror foreign policy and attacks on Muslims' human rights in the US, particularly those of foreign nationals. Overwhelmingly, the leadership chose the former path: they were ill equipped to do anything else, given their own conservative outlooks. The traditions of civil rights organizing that existed among African-American Muslims were an obvious resource, which by and large was not drawn upon by the major Islamic organizations. Having generally discounted the African-American experience from their idea of what it means to be an American Muslim, it was hard for the national organizations to embrace it; and while the activities of African-American Muslims might on occasion be seen by wider society as un-American, their social being was not considered alien as such, and their experience was therefore significantly different from that of Arabs and South Asian Muslims after 9/11. Beginning in the 1990s, there had been some attempts to unify African-American and immigrant Muslim experiences, as the former drew closer to orthodox Sunni Islam and the latter grew accustomed to seeing themselves within the framework of US multiculturalism The Muslim American Society, for example, tried to bring the movement-building tradition of black civil rights to

US Muslims, arguing that organizing against the government on foreign policy and civil rights issues was not disloyalty but a truer form of patriotism. It launched a civic education program and voter registration drives and sought to build coalitions with other minorities. But fear in the community was a major barrier.[53]

Race proved at least as strong a factor as religion in shaping the experiences of US Muslins in the period after 9/11. As Dawud Walid, an African-American Muslim activist in Detroit, notes:

> Arab Americans were right at the door of what's called "whiteness" in America. Whiteness in America doesn't mean skin color. It's a level of assimilation and social fluidity. Even on the census, Arabs are considered white. But now socially they're not white any more—9/11 took away their social white card. So some of these people want to do whatever they can do to be accepted as white. To be accepted in the mainstream. Now, I'm black, and we have a different history in this country. I've never desired to be white, and it's impossible for me to be white. Hence, from us black Americans who are Muslims, you will hear a different type of talk. And sometimes they think that we're more like the angry black people. It's not that. It's just that I want a dignified space for us in America. It's not my goal to be accepted by certain people. And I don't have any fear of being deported. I'm coming from a totally different psychological disposition.

While some were still hoping that the door to whiteness might in time open again, for the moment, after 9/11 their treatment by the federal government reflected their reracialization. Dawud added:

> Even those people who have made it—successfully, financially, and educationally—their money won't stop them from getting handcuffed at the Canadian border or being questioned by the FBI. I know people who are millionaires who this has happened to. Even a political relationship with the Bush administration didn't help them. One of the wealthiest Muslims in this area, an Arab American, who is a big donor to the Republican Party and has given a million dollars to the GOP—it didn't stop him from getting handcuffed when he flew back into the country.[54]

The Arab-American comedian Dean Obeidallah joked:

> It's so weird. Before 9/11, I am just a white guy, living a typical white guy's life. All my friends had names like Monica, Chandler, Joey, and Ross . . . I go to bed September tenth white, wake up September eleventh, I am an Arab.

Despite the losses of civil liberties, the hate crimes, and the launching of wars causing the deaths of hundreds of thousands in the Middle East and South Asia, there was no mass-movement building among American-Muslim communities to protest against the war on terror, as there had been to some extent in the UK. Instead, most American Muslim organizations favored attempts at behind-the-scenes political lobbying and judicial activism. Even public statements by Muslim organizations against the 2003 Iraq war were wrapped in declarations of loyalty. The Muslim American Society on its Web site on March 27, 2003, stated:

> Our opposition to some government policies does not diminish our love for our country and our commitment to its security and prosperity. We strive to serve its best interests by standing out firmly for justice at home and abroad, and calling for meaningful reforms.

For young American Muslims growing up in the period after 9/11, the contradictions were glaring. The excessive loyalty declarations inadvertently revealed how insecure Muslims actually were in America. Youth worker Rachid Elabed explained that before 9/11, young Muslim Americans in Dearborn were reaching the point where they "felt like they're American." But that ended with the war on terror.

> And they see all this stuff on TV, like the Peter King congressional hearing on Muslim radicalization and the guy who wants to burn the Qur'an. They feel like: What's up with this? Just because one Muslim does something bad, doesn't mean all Muslims are bad. They love to be American, they love the freedom, but things like this pull down their self-esteem. Deep down it hurts them, but they don't show it.

> They don't feel like anything's going to happen if they speak out, so they keep it to themselves.[55]

Young Muslims outside the largely Arab neighborhood of Dearborn feel such sentiments even more intensely. The dissonance between public patriotism and private anger at what was happening in Iraq, Afghanistan, and Palestine was striking. Many middle-class Muslim professionals continued to genuinely believe in the American Dream; others just felt they had to be careful what they said in public. To many young Muslims, America's rhetoric of freedom began to ring hollow. At school, those who seemed, from their color, dress, or name, to be Muslim—including Sikhs, Hindus, and Christian Arabs—were often victimized. A 2009 survey revealed that the majority of Sikh school students in the San Francisco Bay Area suffered racial bullying or harassment.[56] (The Muslim terrorist is stereotypically depicted in US popular culture with a turban, which is traditionally worn by Sikh men.)

For many young Muslims, the war on terror forced a rethinking of their identities as Americans. Suhail Muzzafar, a Pakistani American who chairs a mosque on Staten Island, New York, remembers:

> On 9/11, all the schools in New York were locked down. Afterwards, I went to pick up my eight-year-old daughter. She said: "Dad, our teachers told us someone bombed the World Trade Center. We should go and bomb whoever did this." She was thinking like a pure American. Like many other American Muslims of her generation, she didn't know anything about Palestine or Pakistan. However, when American-Muslim children returned to school after 9/11, they suddenly discovered they were being called "terrorists" and "extremists." Muslims came under suspicion, and their loyalty to America was questioned. In the post-9/11 climate our kids were made to think of themselves only in terms of their Muslim identity. Prior to 9/11 we identified ourselves to each other based on ethnic and national identity—as Italian Americans or Pakistani Americans, for example. After 9/11 we were identified more by our religion, as American Muslims, and this was new to us. The older generations of American Muslims generally did not react to this, but we noticed our children often

> responded by highlighting their Muslim identity. Young women began to wear hijab and young men wore Muslim caps in public. By their dress code, they were saying, "You think I'm an extremist. OK, I'll give you extremism." On the other hand, others went the other way and called themselves "Mo" instead of Mohammed.

As in the UK, one way that young Muslims have tried to reconcile these tensions is by distancing themselves from the specific ethnic heritage of their immigrant parents and identifying with the *ummah*. But such an identity is not easily expressed publicly—in some quarters, it makes you a potential enemy of the state—so many find online venues to explore who they are. Many, too, search for answers to the question of what being an American Muslim might mean. Tariq Ramadan's model is, for many, an attractive way of rethinking Islam for life as a Muslim in the West, with its emphasis on individual interpretation, reconciling basic values, and engaging the wider society in struggles for justice.[57] In various ways, a new narrative is beginning to emerge among the younger generation, which starts from the premise, I want my parents' religion but not their culture.[58] Figures like Suhaib Webb, imam of the Islamic Society of Boston Cultural Center, and Hamza Yusuf, cofounder of Zaytuna College in Berkeley, California, are at the forefront of this movement to create an American-style Islam that combines Islamic principles with US culture. At the 2007 ISNA annual convention, Yusuf argued not only that Muslim and American values are aligned, but also that American Muslims are the true inheritors of "old-fashioned American values" which have otherwise been lost.[59]

Looking back in 2011 on ten years of Muslim activism that was mainly focused on reassuring the mainstream, Khalilah Sabra of the Muslim American Society asked:

> Did we affect those who have the power to act against the injustices that still seem to have significant traction? I wonder if we did more than just fortify a comfort zone . . . I cannot help but believe that many Muslims were more apologetic than honest, hoping to avoid the appearance of being more antagonistic than moderate. It's pretty common to disguise indignation with moderation, because it offers

an individual self-protection. Is there no escape from this circular reasoning in which Muslims are urged to prove their loyalty to the nation, and after presenting themselves as loyal, are then accused of concealing their disloyalty?[60]

CHAPTER 2

The Politics of Anti-Extremism

> The central conservative truth is that it is culture, not politics, that determines the success of a society. The central liberal truth is that politics can change a culture and save it from itself.
>
> —Daniel Patrick Moynihan, *Family and Nation*

The terror war's policy makers, scholars, ideologists, and political activists have developed two broad approaches to making sense of "Islamic extremism." In the first one, Muslim communities are seen as failing to adapt to modernity as a result of their Islamic culture. Islam, they say, fails to separate religion from the state, and to render unto Caesar the things which are Caesar's. Because its founder was a statesman as well as a prophet, they hold, Islamic culture is inherently antithetical to a modern, secular containment of its aspiration to impose itself on society. Further, because the teachings of Islam fail to separate it from the political sphere, the atavisms of religious fanaticism are dangerously introduced into the public realm. This approach to analyzing extremism, which emphasizes what adherents regard as inherent features of Islamic culture, I refer to as "culturalism."

In the second approach, extremism is viewed as a perversion of Islam's message. Rather than the legacy of a premodern, Oriental religion, extremism is the result of twentieth-century ideologues who transformed Islam's essentially benign teachings into an anti-modern, totalitarian, political ideology. In this view, the classical religious texts themselves are not the basis for terrorism. Instead, ideologues who reinterpreted Islam based on the models of communism and fascism lie at the root of al-Qaeda's violence. The war on terror is not, then, a clash of civilizations between the West's modern values and Islam's fanaticism; the clash is instead between a traditional, apolitical Islam that is compatible with Western values and a totalitarian appropriation of Islam's meaning that has transformed it into a violent political ideology. I refer to this view as "reformism," both because it seeks to reform what it regards as the counterproductive stereotyping of the early war on terror and because its project is to, in effect, reform Islamic culture itself.

The concept of ideology is central to both the culturalist and reformist accounts. They both find terrorism's origins in the content of an ideology that is rooted in an alien culture, whether that ideology is thought of as Islam itself or as Islamist extremism. This concept of ideology is ultimately derived from cold war views of totalitarianism, in which theorists assume a direct causal connection between holding a certain ideology and committing acts of political violence. The role of Western states in coproducing the terror war is thereby obscured. Rather than seeing terrorism as the product of an interaction between state and nonstate actors, who together constitute themselves in a relationship of conflict between the West and radical Islam, both culturalists and reformists take the content of an alien ideology as sufficient explanation for the conflict's existence; they eschew the role of social and political circumstances in shaping how people make sense of the world and then act upon it. In the following chapter I explore the cold war origins of this account of ideology in more detail. But I first consider the different antiextremist strategies that flow from culturalist and reformist ways of thinking.

The Culturalists

The culturalists' argument can best be illustrated by considering Bernard Lewis's much-circulated 1990 *Atlantic Monthly* article, "The Roots of Muslim Rage," a major source for their analysis.[1] Muslims and the West, Lewis says, are in a deeply rooted conflict that is not linked to a set of political issues such as racism, the Israel-Palestine conflict, or Western backing for Middle Eastern autocrats but must be understood as a product of Islamic culture itself and its unique structural problem with modernity. For Lewis it is this fixed content of Islamic culture rather than various political contexts that lies at the root of what he calls "Muslim rage." "It should by now be clear," writes Lewis,

> that we are facing a mood and a movement far transcending the level of issues and policies and the governments that pursue them. This is no less than a clash of civilizations—the perhaps irrational but surely historical reaction of an ancient rival against our Judeo-Christian heritage, our secular present, and the worldwide expansion of both.[2]

While Lewis referred to Islamic fundamentalism as the current expression of this deeper problem in Islamic culture—keeping open the possibility of nonfundamentalist Muslims finding their way to a reconciliation with Western modernity—Samuel Huntington went further, popularizing the clash of civilizations notion as a general formula for understanding post–cold war international relations and seeing Islam itself, rather than Islamic fundamentalism, as an underlying problem for the West. "The great divisions among humankind and the dominating source of conflict will be cultural," wrote Huntington. "Islam has bloody borders [and a] centuries-old military interaction" with the West that is unlikely to disappear and "could become more virulent."[3] In either form, the clash of civilizations thesis assumes that Muslim politics can be explained simply as the mechanical and repetitive expression of an underlying cultural abstraction called Islam that is preprogrammed for fanaticism, has remained the same over centuries, and whose content can be known through a reading of its religious texts. The more literally one reads those texts, the more forcefully their inherent violence captures the reader: terrorism is simply the product of a literalist reading of classical Islam. This view has been taken up with enthusiasm by the Christian Right and by right-wing Zionists; together they have driven the culturalist agenda to a significant if not dominant position in American political life. For them it conveniently posits Islam as inherently alien to the Western values that they say underlie the alliance between Israel and the US.

As a method of understanding the "Islamic world," this approach has the advantage of offering a simple, endlessly recyclable formula that does not require attending to what individual Muslims actually say or do. And, much like the Salafis, it takes Islam to have only one possible meaning. This kind of view of Islam reduces a complex social, economic, and political history to an underlying cultural essence that is taken to be the root cause of a wide range of phenomena spread across vastly different historical and geographic contexts.[4] In a July 2011 comment, Republican presidential candidate Mitt Romney offered a variation on this theme: The Israelis have outpaced the Palestinians economically because "culture makes all the difference," ignoring the decades of military occupation and ethnic cleansing suffered by the Palestinians.[5] Culture here plays the same role as race: a hidden force that underlies a whole people's behavior; a single rule that can be applied everywhere to explain anything that Muslims do. According to the culturalists, Muslims live hermetically sealed within their homogenous culture, their lives entirely determined by it, whereas Westerners exist outside any specific culture in the universal space of modernity. In the West, people make culture; in Islam, culture makes people.

Using the language of culture in this way to define a "Muslim problem" produces the same outcomes that more obviously racial languages had achieved.[6] Cultural tropes such as wearing a hijab have come to serve as twenty-first-century racial signifiers, functioning in ways analogous to the more familiar racial markers of "color, hair and bone" that W. E. B. Du Bois identified.[7] In the same way that some claim racial inequities are natural, a product of blacks having a lower innate intelligence, the political origins of violence in the Middle East are masked when culturalists invoke the idea of Muslims as culturally prone to violence and rage. As the philosopher Étienne Balibar writes, with these new forms of racism "culture can also function like a nature, and it can in particular function as a way of locking individuals and groups a priori into a genealogy, into a determination that is immutable and intangible in origin."[8] Culturalists introduce an ontological chasm between us and them—their violence is the natural product of their inner culture while ours is the necessary response to their fanaticism. Thus, the imperial violence of the US state and its allies is disavowed and projected onto the enemy other. In doing so, culturalists displace what are essentially political conflicts onto a more comfortable cultural plane.

The problem is their culture not our politics. Islam becomes, as Huntington puts it, the "ideal enemy" against which an America fractured by multiple antagonisms can be bound together, a phantomlike image of external danger to mask the cracks within the social body.[9] This culturalist view of Islam remains the default position among conservatives, even though it has long been discredited intellectually. In his *Orientalism* Edward Said demonstrated that the West's homogenized and reified culturalist view of Islam has its roots in European colonialism.[10] In his *Covering Islam* he showed how these colonial notions continued to influence US news coverage of the Middle East in the 1990s.[11] Against the culturalist view that Islam has a special problem distinguishing religion and politics, the writer Eqbal Ahmad pointed out in his 1984 essay, "Islam and Politics," that religious and political power in Muslim-majority countries have been separate for at least ten centuries. In 945, the Abbasid caliph's dual role as Islam's temporal and spiritual leader came to an end. Since then the exercise of state power by temporal governments generally has been accepted. Where insurrections in the name of Islam have occurred against such power, the causes are to be found more in the secular political context than in some eternal Muslim propensity to apply religion to politics.[12] Anticolonial uprisings that coalesced around a religious ideology, or the politicization of the Shi'ite clergy in Iran from the late 1960s in opposition to the shah's regime, demonstrate not an Islamic failure to separate mosque and state but the possibility that Islam, like any religion, can be mobilized for political purposes.[13] Like other religions, Islam provides at most a language and a broad moral outlook with which to make sense of political crises. What matters are the specific ways in which people apply an Islamic discursive tradition, one open to wide-ranging interpretation, in particular political settings.

Whatever its intellectual flaws, culturalism has proved useful as ideological ballast for US foreign policies. President George W. Bush's official statements tended to reject a straightforwardly culturalist analysis in the days after the 9/11 attacks. He told a joint session of Congress that "a fringe form of Islamic extremism that has been rejected by Muslim scholars and the vast majority of Muslim clerics" was responsible, and that these extremists constituted a movement "that perverts the peaceful teachings of Islam"—the problem was not Islam itself but a small number of individuals who had hijacked the religion.[14] But the neoconservatives who shaped his foreign policy in the early years of the terror war did have a culturalist analysis of the Muslim problem. It was their analysis that was reflected in Bush's characterization of the war on terror as a "crusade."[15] Bernard Lewis himself was a key adviser to the administration. And among members of the Christian Right, a key base of Bush's support, the idea of an apocalyptic crusade against Islam was prevalent. Such views sometimes emerged among military leaders. In 2003, William Boykin, Bush's deputy undersecretary of defense for intelligence and an evangelical Christian, told a meeting in Oregon that the war on terror is a battle against Satan fought by "the army of God."[16]

To the culturalists, the Islamic world was inherently prone to fanaticism and violence. Revolution there could only mean Islamic revolution along the lines of Iran in 1979. Pro-Western democracy could not emerge except by force from outside—the script for the disastrous Iraq war begun in 2003. Neoconservatives presented their Middle East policy as a call for democratic transformation, appearing to break radically with the conventional wisdom of maintaining alliances with autocratic regimes in the name of stability. But behind the apparent differences, neoconservatives and those favoring more conventional policies shared the same culturalist logic: Muslims could not produce an acceptable form of democracy by themselves. Within this logic the only foreign policy options were autocracy or war. The US backing of autocratic regimes—for example, in Egypt, Saudi Arabia, Jordan, and Pakistan—was the traditional method of restraining Islamic fanaticism. The neoconservatives proposed a new alternative: war as a way of erasing the substrate of Muslim culture to such an extent that a new value system no longer prone to fanaticism could be erected upon the resulting tabula rasa. For Bernard Lewis, the key intellectual influence on neoconservative thinking about the Middle East, the model for this revolution from above was Atatürk's violent "modernization" of Turkey in the 1920s and 1930s—an attempt to impose a total cultural transformation on a majority-Muslim country.[17] This more radical solution to the Muslim problem defined the early war on terror, and especially the invasion and occupation of Iraq. Neoconservatives fantasized about rebuilding Iraq from scratch in the image of US neoliberalism—a project that in practice implied the destruction of the country's entire social fabric. The wars of the time were, as British prime minister Tony Blair noted, "not just about changing regimes but changing the values systems governing the nations concerned. The banner was not actually 'regime change'; it was 'values change.' "[18]

But the ways of thinking advanced by Lewis and Huntington did not restrict themselves to questions of international relations, their original topic. Precisely because they relied on an essentialist notion of Islamic culture, it was easy for their methodology to be used in the analysis of Muslims living in the West. The application of the culturalist thesis to a substantially different context was made possible by the underlying assumption that Muslims are everywhere the same. Protests against Danish cartoons in European cities, urban unrest in French *banlieues*, or young Muslims volunteering to leave the West to fight foreign occupations in the Middle East, Africa, or Asia—all these different actions are not made sense of by culturalists in terms of the specific social and political histories involved but explained away as symptoms of an inevitable, underlying conflict between Islam's regressive cultural identity and Western values.[19] Thus, a culturalist writer like *Weekly Standard* senior editor Christopher Caldwell can dismiss the social and political factors that motivated the rioters in France in 2005 and instead declare Islam the cause: "Even if they did not believe in Islam, they believed in Team Islam."[20]

In both Britain and the US, anti-Muslim culturalists were able to appropriate and rework culturalist arguments that had long been central to popular forms of racism. In the US, the 1965 Moynihan report had claimed that higher rates of unemployment among African Americans ultimately derived from a culture of weak families rather than from structural racism. Conservatives would resuscitate this theme in the ensuing decades, as they sought to roll back the gains of the civil rights movement, culminating in today's racially coded attacks on welfare dependency.[21] In Britain, beginning in the late 1960s, African Caribbeans and South Asians were regarded by conservatives as bearers of alien cultures that disrupted the homogeneity supposedly essential to the national political order.[22] As

Margaret Thatcher put it in 1978, a year before she was elected prime minister, there was a worry that unless nonwhite immigration was halted, Britain "might be rather swamped by people with a different culture."[23] Such themes continued into the 1990s and beyond, but their force was gradually diminished by pressure from antiracist movements. In response, conservatives shifted their attention to Muslims, against whom their culturalist arguments enjoyed greater success.

For example, the British journalist Anthony Browne had, in 2002 and 2003, written a series of articles on Third World immigration that recycled the same language of cultural fear that Thatcher had earlier mobilized. In *The Times* (London), he wrote:

> Britain is losing Britain [as] an unprecedented and sustained wave of immigration [is] utterly transforming the society in which we live against the wishes of the majority of the population, damaging quality of life and social cohesion . . . In the past five years, while the white population grew by 1 per cent, the Bangladeshi community grew by 30 per cent, the black African population by 37 per cent and the Pakistani community by 13 per cent.

What he called "little Third World colonies" had appeared in Britain.[24] (Contrary to the impression given by these numbers, Britain's population remains 88 percent white.)[25] In the same year, Browne wrote in *The Spectator* magazine that immigration "especially from the Third World [is] letting in too many germs."[26] Following the July 2005 terrorist attacks on London's transport system, Browne abandoned Third World immigration as his target and directed his aim at Islam. Excessive multicultural tolerance, he claimed, had led to the creation of "Muslim ghettoes." That tolerance now needed to be abandoned so that arranged marriages could be banned, imams who support the Muslim Brotherhood deported, and a French-style ban on wearing head scarves in schools considered. The Pakistani and Bangladeshi women whom he earlier saw as helping form "Third World colonies" now needed to be rescued from the ghetto extremism of their male coreligionists.[27] With the war on terror, racisms directed generally at people of color in Britain honed in on the figure of the Muslim as a convenient symbol of threatening cultural difference.

Similarly, New York–based lawyer David Yerushalmi, whose group, the Society of Americans for National Existence, received about $1.1 million in donations from 2007 to 2009, spearheads a campaign to identify shari'a as the greatest threat to US security.[28] But his targeting of American Muslims is the thin end of a larger racial wedge. In a 2006 essay published in a little-read bulletin of the far Right, he wrote that most "of the fundamental differences between the races are genetic." He asked why "people find it so difficult to confront the facts that some races perform better in sports, some better in mathematical problem-solving, some better in language, some better in Western societies and some better in tribal ones?" And he called on the US to reject the political correctness that prevents asking why "the founding fathers did not give women or black slaves the right to vote."[29] His campaign to focus popular anxieties on Muslim culture—symbolized by shari'a—is an attempt to rework racial ideology in an age when more obviously racist rhetoric had become publicly unacceptable but white America's fears of its diminishing demographic weight remained. In both the UK and the US, existing forms of racism did not disappear after 9/11, but the racial terrain underwent a transformation, as new alliances and new enemies were constituted.[30]

Domestically, culturalism is strongly bound up with discriminatory immigration and policing practices that construct Muslims as a "suspect community."[31] For culturalists, Muslim extremists are a threat to Western civilization, and the state can legitimately use wide-ranging emergency powers to counter them. But other Muslims, who do not adopt a literalist interpretation of Islam, must also be regarded with suspicion. Douglas Murray, the associate director of the Henry Jackson Society, a UK-based neoconservative think tank, has said: "Conditions for Muslims in Europe must be made harder across the board: Europe must look like a less attractive proposition."[32]

In the months after 9/11, the US Justice Department detained thousands of Muslim, South Asian, and Middle Eastern men, through various initiatives. Many were deported, others held for months without charge; all had their lives turned upside down and their reputations destroyed.[33] The only basis for such a policy was a general suspicion directed at those thought to be Muslim; only one or two convictions on terrorism charges resulted from the roundup.[34] One of those detained, Mohammed Rafiq Butt, died of a heart attack after being taken to a New Jersey jail. He had come to New York from Pakistan to work as a waiter in Jackson Heights, Queens, but after 9/11 some of his neighbors had called the police, saying they thought he looked suspicious. As a result, he joined other foreign nationals who were held without charge. The FBI passed him on to the Immigration and Naturalization Service, which detained him for overstaying his visa.[35]

Similarly, the National Security Entry-Exit Registration System, introduced in 2002, required men aged sixteen to sixty-four who were present in the US or planning to enter on nonimmigrant visas, and who were from twenty-three majority-Muslim countries, or from Eritrea or North Korea, to be interviewed under oath, fingerprinted, and photographed by a federal official. The Department of Homeland Security stated that these nationalities were singled out because they were a "risk to national security." More than 200,000 Arab and Muslim men underwent this "special registration," all of whom were cleared of terrorism. Nevertheless, 13,424 of them who were present in the US were placed in removal proceedings, and faced deportation.[36] According to one estimate, as of 2004, at least 100,000 Arabs and Muslims living in the United States had personally experienced one of the various post-9/11 state security measures, including, arbitrary arrests, secret and indefinite detentions, prolonged detention as "material witnesses," closed hearings, the production of secret evidence, government eavesdropping on attorney-client conversations; FBI home and work visits; wiretapping; seizures of property, removals for technical visa violations, and mandatory special registration.[37] All of these measures embodied the notion that Islam was, by its very nature, a threat. They thus, as scholar Moustafa Bayoumi put it, "created a race out of a religion" by assuming that, by virtue of an inner, fixed cultural essence, Muslims were potentially violent.[38]

Women wearing head scarves were especially at risk of harassment and discrimination. After 9/11, the hijab was taken to signify that its wearer was "sympathetic to the enemy, presumptively disloyal, and forever foreign."[39] Women faced discrimination in employment and violence on the streets, often involving attempts to pull off their head scarves.[40] A post-9/11 study of young, college-educated Arab-American Muslim women in Chicago, some of whom wore hijabs, found that all of those interviewed had been the victims of physical or verbal abuse, or knew someone close to them who had been.[41]

For culturalists there is only one political act that Muslim fellow citizens can perform without suspicion: rejection of their own Muslim identity. On this view, liberation for Muslims consists in leaving their culture behind rather than autonomously changing it from within. Ayaan Hirsi Ali, the Somali-born former Dutch parliamentarian recruited by the neoconservative American Enterprise Institute, serves as an icon for this form of politics. She describes herself as a "combatant in the clash of civilizations."[42] "Violence is inherent in Islam," she says. "It's a destructive, nihilistic cult of death . . . The battle against terrorism will ultimately be lost unless we realise that it's not just with extremist elements within Islam, but the ideology of Islam itself."[43] After the Boston bombings and Woolwich murder in 2013, she reiterated once more the basic culturalist argument: the violence simply reflected "the problem with Islam" that Muslim leaders had repeatedly refused to address.[44]

The Reformists

By 2006, the war on terror was in crisis. Despite Secretary of State Condoleezza Rice's comment that the violence in Iraq was merely the "birth pangs" of the new Middle East, the war on terror had clearly failed to establish the hoped-for transformation of values.[45] With France and Germany's opposition to the Iraq war, the Atlantic alliance had fractured. Images of human rights abuses in Abu Ghraib and Guantánamo discredited the talk after 9/11 of spreading democracy around the world. In Madrid, Amsterdam, and London, for the first time, "homegrown" Muslim terrorists were carrying out acts of violence against fellow citizens.

Waiting in the wings to respond to this crisis were a number of reformists who, since the inception of the terror war, had been arguing for a rethinking of its basic assumptions. In the first four years of the war, their influence had been modest. But as failures mounted, they took center stage, and a second view of Muslim extremism became prominent. The reformists made three main points. First, they rejected the view that Islamic culture was inherently oppositional to Western interests. What mattered, they said, was not Islamic culture itself, but the politicization of Islamic culture among an extremist minority. Whereas culturalists saw Islam as having an inherent tendency to generate extremism, the reformists argued that extremism was a product not of Islam but of its perversion. In this view, what distinguished extremist Muslims from moderate Muslims was their misinterpretation of Islam as bearing a political message. Against the culturalists, who argued that Islam is inherently reluctant to separate itself from the political sphere, the reformists viewed the majority of Muslims as practicing their religion apolitically in ways that presented no threat to the West. But, they said, a minority remained who distorted Islam's essentially benign message and turned it into an anti-Western political ideology. The reformists usually used the word "Islamism" to label this political distortion of Islam; sometimes the term "Salafism" was preferred.

Culturalists had sought to illustrate Islam's dangers by borrowing the imagery of totalitarianism. Bernard Lewis regarded Islam and communism as having affinities: both were totalitarian doctrines with "complete and final answers to all questions on heaven and earth" in contrast to "the eternal questioning of Western man."[46] For Lewis, Islam's totalitarian tendency was an outgrowth of its core religious beliefs. The reformists countered that Islam only became totalitarian when its core beliefs were distorted into a political ideology. They argued that such Islamist extremism was best understood as a Muslim version of the totalitarianisms—communism and fascism—that had taken hold in twentieth-century Europe. Both culturalists and reformists made use of the term "Islamo-fascism" to refer to the totalitarian content of the ideology they saw as the cause of terrorism. To culturalists "Islamo-fascism" referred to Islam's inherent tendency to fanaticism; to reformists it named a political misreading of Islam not to be confused with Islam as a mainstream religion. The term's ability to straddle both modes of analysis made it useful in political campaigning. President Bush used the ambiguous term in his 2005 speech to the National Endowment for Democracy, and in 2007, the Islamophobic activist David Horowitz launched a series of protests on college campuses under the banner of Islamofascism Awareness Week.[47]

Liberal writer Paul Berman has produced the most sophisticated statement of the reformist position. His best-selling *Terror and Liberalism* contends that there is a single template underlying all totalitarian ideologies: the myth of "a people of God, whose peaceful and wholesome life had been undermined . . . [by] the subversive dwellers in Babylon." Restoration of the reign of God, of "a society cleansed of its pollutants and abominations" that would be governed by a great Leader, would only be achieved by "the war of Armageddon—the all-exterminating bloodbath."[48] In the European "counter-Enlightenment" the elements of this originally religious "ur-myth" were given secular form. For the communists the proletariat were the people of God; for the Nazis it was the Aryan race. Detecting the same template in the texts of the influential Egyptian radical Sayyid Qutb, Berman concluded that Islamist totalitarianism is "the Muslim variation on the European idea."[49] Similarly, the journalist Peter Beinart, in his book *The Good Fight*, argued for fighting the war on terror in the tradition of cold war liberalism. The enemy, in this view, was "a new totalitarian movement that lacks state power but harnesses the power of globalization instead."[50] Inspired by Qutb, Salafism, though a social movement rather than a state, has a "totalitarian character."[51] In Britain, the *Observer* columnist Nick Cohen and former Hizb ut-Tahrir activist Ed Husain made essentially the same argument in best-selling books.[52] For the reformists the clash was not between civilizations but between extremists and moderates within Islamic civilization itself—an internal struggle over Islamic identity. Rather than a battle between the Judeo-Christian West and Islam, there was an extremist version of Islam on one side and a pro-Western, moderate Islam on the other.

The second part of the reformists' argument was the claim that ideology—which they took to mean any set of ideas radically rejecting the existing system—was bound to lead to violence as a direct result of its illiberal ideological content. For Berman, if we pay close enough attention to the content of Islamist texts, we can see that the ideology they embody is, like Nazism, "bound to end in a cult of death."[53] The third point the reformists made flowed from the first two. Because the battle was between competing definitions of Islamic identity, the war on terror was as much a cultural war as a military one. Berman called for a new "mental war" against "Islamism" that is "partly military but ultimately intellectual, a war of ideas, fought around the world."[54] Rather than a singular enemy, the Islamic world was a cultural terrain within which Western states needed to intervene to reshape identities in an antiextremist mold. They believed the right kind of antitotalitarian politics could change Islamic culture and save it from itself. In this global campaign "shock and awe" had to be complemented by attempts to win over the hearts and minds of Muslims around the world.

If the key reference point for the reformists was the cold war concept of totalitarianism, they found that the word itself, with its connotation of state repression, was unsuited for general use in the war on terror—after all, the new enemy was clearly characterized by its lack of attachment to any state. The term "extremism" came instead to serve as the anchor for the war on terror. Extremism is a term peculiarly amenable to naturalizing the status quo. Since at least the French Revolution, politicians have used the accusation of extremism to denounce enemies on their flanks, and to present themselves as occupying a moderate center. But used in this way, the concept is somewhat arbitrary. The German liberal Heinrich Bernhard Oppenheim asked in 1850, "Would the middle not lie elsewhere if only the extremes were moved?" On the principle that truth is always to be found in the middle ground, political movements would be "right to increase their 'demands' to the utmost extreme in order to gain a bit more of the centre for themselves."[55] In British political discourse, the term "extremism" was first used at the beginning of the twentieth century. Police reports produced by the colonial administration in India categorized anticolonial militants who favored full independence as "extremists," while those, such as the Indian National Congress, whose demands were limited to administrative reform, were dubbed "moderates." English-language newspapers in India used the terminology before it spread to the British press.[56]

During the cold war, the old formula of the moderate center was revived. Historian Arthur M. Schlesinger Jr. wrote in his 1949 book, *The Vital Center*, that American liberalism was the defender of a down-to-earth process of gradual reform, which was endangered by communism on the left and antidemocratic reactionaries on the right—both of which captured minds by exploiting the "darker passions."[57] Just as war on terror intellectuals would later look for the causes of terrorism in sexual frustration, so too did Schlesinger describe communism's appeal apolitically, highlighting what he thought was a reliance upon "lonely and frustrated people" who were "craving sexual fulfillment they cannot obtain in existing society."[58] After the 1960s, when social movements came to be regarded as presenting threats to Western governments as great as communist states, the term "extremism" began to be used to designate the same ideological dangers in them that totalitarianism had pointed to in states. The war on terror continued this approach. "Extremism" referred to either the religious fanaticism of Islam itself (culturalists) or to the political ideology of Islamism (reformists). Since the term widened the focus from specific acts of violence to the ideas, values, or mind-sets assumed to cause the violence, a much wider set of trends, ideologies, and peoples could be subsumed under a single category of threat. Instead of analyzing political Islam in such a way that located its emergence within specific material circumstances, the only public discussion was of how its ideological content produced anti-Western violence.

The Cultural War

Just as the reformists turned to cold war theories of totalitarianism to make sense of terrorism, so too did they turn to cold war history for ideas on how to combat it. One approach was to oppose extremist ideology using the same cultural techniques that had been favored in the early cold war, in which the CIA had sought to recruit the noncommunist Left in an ideological battle against Moscow. Updated for the war on terror, this meant recruiting moderate Muslim leaders to speak out against extremism and funding those within Muslim communities willing to propagate a pro-Western argument. By 2006, some erstwhile neoconservatives, such as Francis Fukuyama, had joined liberals like Berman in favoring this approach. The talk in Washington and London was of the importance of "soft power." Interventions by the State Department, the US Agency for International Development, and the National Endowment for Democracy were as important as those by the Pentagon, they argued.[59] A year later, military planners at the RAND Corporation released a study that argued for an ideological campaign in which the West's "good Muslims" would be counterposed against al-Qaeda's "bad Muslims." They recommended deriving "lessons from the experience of the Cold War" in order to "develop a 'road map' for the construction of moderate and liberal Muslim networks."[60] One of the most influential of the war on terror experts, Marc Sageman, a former CIA operations officer who had been based in Islamabad in the late 1980s, argued around the same time that governments should quietly partner with pro-Western Muslim leaders, advising them on the techniques of "political and cultural influence" in order to "battle for the soul of the community" and win the "hearts and minds of the Muslim community."[61]

In Britain, the newly installed prime minister, Gordon Brown, spoke of the need for a "cultural effort" against "Islamic extremism," to be fought with the techniques used

> during the cold war in the nineteen-forties, fifties and sixties, when we had to mount a propaganda effort, if you like, to explain to people that our values represented the best of commitments to individual dignity, to liberty, and to human life.[62]

Senior civil servants had been studying Frances Stonor Saunders's book *The Cultural Cold War*, which examined the covert battle of ideas waged by the CIA and British Foreign Office to discredit communism in the postwar literary world.[63] Rather than read her study as the critical account she intended, they adopted it as a manual.[64] This methodology was presented on both sides of the Atlantic as the progressive and smart alternative to fighting an overly militarized war on terror. The war of ideas could not substitute for actual military force, but it was necessary and complementary.

Another strand of reformist thinking drew on the cold war tradition of counterinsurgency theory, which is where the phrase "hearts and minds" had its origins. It had reportedly first been used by the British general Sir Gerald Templer to describe the counterinsurgency strategy he deployed during the so-called Malaya Emergency of 1948 to 1960. Counterinsurgency theorists' founding principle was the need to isolate insurgents from the wider base of potential support among the population. The methods they recommended to achieve this included soft power (political measures, such as propaganda) as well as hard power (military force and coercive policing). What they considered essential for success was a coordinated government machinery that could act strategically across the military, political, judicial, and social spheres; emergency legal powers; an effective, integrated nationwide intelligence organization able to build up detailed information on the insurgents as well as the population the insurgents were trying to win over; and a communications strategy to address grievances and win popular support. In seeking to defeat communist guerrillas fighting against colonial rule in Malaya, the British army recognized that the insurgency's strength was the political support it was able to attract among the population. Various techniques were deployed in response to try to isolate the population from the guerrillas: the forced resettlement of half a million people; mass arrests; the death penalty for carrying arms; detention without trial; censorship; arson attacks against the homes of communist sympathizers; collective punishment; and massacres of unarmed civilians. This bloody record was hardly likely to win over the population. Nevertheless, conquering hearts and minds came to signify an approach in which military force was subsumed within a wider political strategy. In the end, British colonialism was defeated in Malaya, but not before the communist insurgency had been sufficiently weakened for other political forces to assume power upon independence. Following the US defeat in its war against the Vietnamese communists, many military planners considered the Malaya model a superior alternative.[65]

The counterinsurgency techniques that had been tested in other British colonial territories were further refined during the conflict in

Northern Ireland, in a context where democratic institutions had to be accorded greater respect. Less emphasis was placed on the use of the British army than in Malaya and more on emergency policing and a rigged judicial process, which involved no-jury courts and confessions extracted under duress. But the key objective remained the isolation of insurgents from their base of potential support through a coordinated military, political, judicial, and communications strategy.

By 2005, a number of influential military thinkers in the US and the UK, such as David J. Kilcullen (who worked for the US Department of Defense beginning in 2004 and helped the Pentagon rethink the war on terror after Donald Rumsfeld's departure as defense secretary) and John Mackinlay (a fellow of the Royal United Services Institute and the Department of War Studies of King's College, London, both of which are closely linked to the Ministry of Defence), were arguing that the war on terror was failing because it did not include the lessons of counterinsurgency theory. They claimed that winning the ideological allegiance of Muslims around the world—the prize in a battle of ideas, or an information war—was as important as killing or capturing terrorists. Success, Mackinlay said, as with the anticommunist counterinsurgencies fought during the cold war, "lies in having a genuine political counter strategy and being able to co-ordinate a campaign that embraces all the organs of the state."[66] In his influential 2005 article for the *Journal of Strategic Studies*, Kilcullen redefined the war on terror as a global counterinsurgency in which the emphasis should be on the disaggregation of "local players" from "global sponsors" by discrediting the latter's ideological authority, winning the hearts and minds of target populations, "countering Islamist propaganda" with a counterextremist political narrative, creating alternative institutions, engaging influential community leaders as allies, amassing information on Muslim populations to an anthropological level of detail, and seeking to effectively manage grievances and other drivers of popular support for the insurgents.[67] Given the global nature of the insurgency, such a strategy was thought to be needed as much in Bradford as in Basra.

The US rediscovery of counterinsurgency theory came at a moment of crisis in its war on terror. In Iraq and Afghanistan it became clear that the US was fighting colonial wars in all but name. The US military found counterinsurgency theory a way of connecting with a longer European tradition of colonial warfare that promised victory through the smarter application of power. These ideas were reflected in the influential US Army and Marine Corps's *Counterinsurgency Field Manual*, published in 2006, which was key to restoring the war on terror's legitimacy, particularly among a section of liberal critics. The cult of General David Petraeus rested largely on his associating himself with such ideas and presenting them as an alternative "intellectual" strategy for the occupations of Iraq and Afghanistan: the "graduate level of war," as the army's counterinsurgency manual described it.[68] Winning, he argued, meant fighting a political battle of ideas as well as a military battle of physical force. US forces would need officers who were as good at mounting a political defense of "the virtues of market-based economics" as they were at directing military campaigns.[69]

To a compliant US media, Petraeus appeared as the savior of the war on terror who would channel the lessons learned not only from twentieth-century European counterinsurgency campaigns, but also from US colonial wars in Indo-China, the Caribbean, and Latin America. (As a graduate student at Princeton he had written a paper entitled, "The Invasion of Grenada: Illegal, Immoral, and the Right Thing to Do.")[70] A series of articles in *Time* magazine by Joe Klein, with titles such as "The Return of the Good Soldier" and "David Petraeus' Brilliant Career," described the general as the "exemplar of the creative new thinking" that would transform the US military "from a blunt instrument, designed to fight tank battles on the plains of Europe, into a 'learning institution' that trains its troops for the flexibility and creativity necessary to fight guerrilla wars in the information age."[71] Klein's account presented the US military in Iraq and Afghanistan as engaged in a kind of benign educational exercise whose main aim was to understand local cultures. The reality of the 2007 troop surge in Iraq, masterminded by Petraeus, was that it achieved a form of pacification through entrenching sectarian divisions, sponsoring local militias, and disempowering populations. Later, as director of the CIA, Petraeus became "one of the most experienced operators of and thinkers on lethal drones for targeted killing."[72] The proponents of US counterinsurgency strategy, like British colonial planners who, with a strategy of "define and rule," constructed their subject populations as a multitude of "tribes," started from the assumption that tribes were the basic unit of Iraqi society.[73] The political component of counterinsurgency meant in practice reducing local political structures to a mosaic of tribes whose leaders could be bought off to suit military and political exigencies. Ethnographic knowledge of these tribal structures was therefore essential. For Kilcullen, counterinsurgency is "armed social science." Clever manipulation of local culture was thought essential to defeating insurgencies.[74] In 2007, a US military program known as Human Terrain Systems was introduced; it sought to embed anthropologists and social scientists with combat units, using them to develop knowledge of local cultures in order to engineer the "trust of the indigenous population."[75] As in Malaya, the application of counterinsurgency techniques in Iraq and Afghanistan brought with it large-scale programs of torture and targeted killings (often carried out by private military contractors) of those thought to be members of oppositional tribes. Meanwhile, US journalists reporting on the war on terror increasingly referenced the tribal codes prevalent among Arabs and in the region US military planners dubbed "AfPak," recalling Orientalist fantasies of the past. *New York Times* columnist Thomas Friedman, for example, regularly bemoaned the "oft-warring Arab tribes" who could only be disciplined by an "iron-fisted leader" or the presence of "150,000 US soldiers to referee"—as if the US occupation of Iraq was the solution to Iraqi violence rather than its cause.[76] As we shall see in later chapters, these tropes also found their way back to the domestic national security apparatus and shaped the FBI's approach to countering homegrown Muslim radicalization.

With President Obama, the emphasis on winning hearts and minds came fully to the fore. His speech in Cairo in 2009, addressed to "Muslims around the world," rested on the assumption that multicultural recognition of mainstream Islam could win over moderate Muslims and help isolate and defeat extremism. At the same time, Obama sought to rebuild partnerships with governments in the Middle East that had been undermined by neoconservative unilateralism, and which would be needed in a global antiextremist campaign of soft power. Unilateralist talk of exporting democracy had already reverted to a more conventional, pragmatic approach in the last two years of the Bush administration, following Hamas's election to the Palestinian Authority in 2006 and Hezbollah's success in elections in Lebanon around the same time. Obama continued this trend by shoring up international alliances with autocratic regimes and outsourcing security to regional clients. As he pointed out: "The truth is that my foreign policy is actually a return to the traditional bipartisan realistic policy of George Bush's father, of John F. Kennedy, of, in some ways, Ronald Reagan."[77] What was new was a belief that, alongside the hard power of US military violence, cultural recognition of Islam could play a soft power role in reducing Muslim opposition to American foreign policy.

The Home Front

The reformists' emphasis on opening a cultural front went hand in hand with a turning inward of the terror war to the domestic sphere. Commentators and policy makers on both sides of the Atlantic had begun to focus heavily on the perceived threat from Europe's Muslim communities; in contrast, American Muslims were counterposed as embodying a story of successful assimilation. In late 2005, Francis Fukuyama warned that European Muslims were as serious a threat to the US as Muslims in the Middle East. Europe's multiculturalist policies had failed to assimilate the Muslim population, he argued.[78] He went on to comment: "Europe's failure to better integrate its Muslims is a ticking time bomb that has already contributed to terrorism."[79] Robert Leiken of the Nixon Center and the Brookings Institution wrote in *Foreign Affairs* of Europe's "angry Muslims, [who were] distinct, cohesive, and bitter [and] eligible to travel visa-free to the United States."[80] Marc Sageman wrote in 2008 that the "individuals we should fear most" are "homegrown wannabes—self-recruited, without leadership, and globally connected through the Internet," mostly living in Europe, whose "lack of structure and organizing principles makes them even more terrifying and volatile than their terrorist forebears."[81] In what has become a familiar ideological maneuver in the war on terror, attributes that would normally be considered reasons to downplay a threat (the absence of competent training by a terrorist organization or direct access to an experienced leadership) were themselves taken as evidence of an even greater threat. The question of how Muslims in Europe could be brought to identify more closely with European nation-states became a hot topic in Washington national security circles.

The answer from policy-minded reformists on both sides of the Atlantic had three parts. First, unlike the culturalists, whose outlook led to an alienation of Muslims from national life, the reformists wanted a mainstream Islam to be recognized in Europe as a valid identity within an official discourse of cultural tolerance. This would, it was thought, facilitate political assimilation. They argued that European governments needed to foster moderate Muslim leadership within their own nations that, in partnership with the state, could promote acceptable ways to be Muslim and publicly speak out against extremism. The liberal commentator Timothy Garton Ash, whose reputation had been established through his reporting on Eastern European dissidents in the 1980s, became a major advocate for a reformist agenda that involved searching for what he called the "dissidents within Islam."[82] Europe's Muslims were presented as balanced on a knife edge between good citizenship and terrorism:

> An invisible front line runs through the quiet streets of many a European city. Like it or not, whether you live in London or Oxford, Berlin or Neu-Ulm, Madrid or Rotterdam, you are on that front line—much more than you ever were during the cold war . . . The larger part of this struggle . . . is the battle for the hearts and minds of young European Muslims—usually men—who are not yet fanatical violent jihadists, but could become so. All over our continent, and around its edges, there are hundreds of thousands of young Muslim men who could go either way. They could become tomorrow's bombers; or they could become good citizens, funders of our faltering state pension schemes, tomorrow's Europeans.[83]

Clever use of the West's soft power could tilt the balance.

> This struggle for Muslim hearts and minds should be decided by Muslims arguing among themselves, but we non-Muslims undoubtedly shape the context—and control many of the media—in which it is conducted.[84]

Speaking at the launch of a new antiextremist think tank in London in 2008, Garton Ash said he hoped Islamism could be undermined in the same way that communism was with the publication of *The God That Failed* in the 1950s.[85] As we shall see in later chapters, the belief that huge swathes of Muslim populations were "not yet fanatical"—supposedly on the verge of becoming extremists—fed programs of mass surveillance reminiscent of the operations of the East German Stasi that Garton Ash had famously documented.

In France, Belgium, the Netherlands, Britain, and Germany the search was on for suitably moderate Muslim leaders who were both credible within Muslim communities and reliably loyal to Western states. If, as the reformists argued, the problem of extremism lay in a misreading of Islam's core teachings, then a state-sponsored Islamic leadership could play an important role in promoting the correct way to interpret theological terms like "jihad" and "shari'a." To enable such a leadership to emerge, a form of multicultural recognition was granted to new religious identities rather than just the ethnic identities that had been central to earlier multicultural policies. The development of this "multi-faith-ism" had already begun in a piecemeal fashion in some contexts, but now its creation was embarked upon more systematically. Paradoxically, this led liberal states, which otherwise proclaimed a secular separation of religion and politics, to, in effect, endorse an official version of Islam. Government officials became de facto theologians who implicitly approved particular interpretations of the religion over others.[86]

The second part of the reformist argument claimed that while offering recognition to a mainstream Islam, European governments also needed to curtail the circulation of Islamist ideology, which was for them the key driver of Muslim violence. Clear limits needed to be set on the expression of extremist forms of Islam. In Britain, the new crime of glorifying terrorism, introduced in the Terrorism Act 2006, was not about preventing incitement to violence, which was already covered under legislation dating from the nineteenth century, but about criminalizing a wider set of Islamist ideological messages. Britain's Prime Minister Tony Blair tabled a call for such legislation to be introduced globally and made clear at the UN Security Council meeting on September 14, 2005, that what was to be criminalized was "a movement with an ideology and a strategy," which would only be defeated when

> the [Security] Council united . . . in fighting the poisonous propaganda that the root cause of terrorism lay with [us] and not them. [That] root cause . . . was not a decision on foreign policy, however contentious, but was a doctrine of fanaticism.[87]

A similar law was proposed by the European Union the following year, to prevent "public provocation to commit a terrorist offence," which was defined as the expression of messages that could "cause a danger" of terrorism, whether or not terrorism was directly advocated.[88] For non–European Union citizens residing in Britain, or for those with dual nationality, the grounds on which residence rights or citizenship could be removed were widened to include such vague violations as "distributing material, speaking publicly or running a website which fosters hatred which might lead to inter-community violence."[89] This opened the possibility of Home Office ministers stripping British citizens of their citizenship for no other reason than the opinions they expressed.

As the British civil rights lawyer Gareth Peirce noted, more and more young men and occasionally women were imprisoned in the UK based on their possession of pamphlets or videos or on the records of their Internet use, any of which could be cited as evidence of encouraging or glorifying terrorism. "Previously accepted boundaries of freedom of expression and thought have been redefined and are now in effect being prosecuted retrospectively."[90] In March 2012, for example, Azhar Ahmed, a nineteen-year-old from Dewsbury, Yorkshire, posted a comment on his Facebook page bemoaning the level of media attention British soldiers killed in Afghanistan received in comparison to civilian victims of the conflict. In concluding his posting, he expressed himself without restraint: "All soldiers should die and go to hell! The lowlife fokkin scum!" He was labeled an "Islamist extremist," charged with sending a grossly offensive communication, and ordered to do 240 hours of community service. A police spokesperson said: "He didn't make his point very well and that is why he has landed himself in bother."[91] Meanwhile, safeguards on not removing foreign nationals if they would be at risk of cruel and inhuman treatment in the receiving country were eroded. Reformist writers who saw the war on terror as an ideological battle to defend liberal values against a new totalitarian enemy were often less than liberal in applying those values to the treatment of extremists. Nick Cohen, for example, argued that extremists should be deported from Britain even if it led to their being tortured.[92] Ed Husain called for membership in the group Hizb ut-Tahrir to be a criminal offense, despite there being no evidence of the group's involvement in terrorism.[93] This points to the second contradiction within the reformists' agenda: in the name of defending liberal values, the liberal freedom to express an Islamist ideology or identity is curtailed. If Islamist ideology is a totalitarian threat to liberal society, then placing limits on the freedom to express that ideology is seen as the lesser evil.[94]

The third aspect of the reformists' program was a call for a public campaign to celebrate and promote the liberal values upon which they saw Western society resting. A positive defense of such values was regarded as a necessary part of the battle of ideas against extremism in Europe. Governments could play a role in this campaign. For example, they could introduce a requirement that new citizens declare an oath of allegiance to those values or require that immigrants pass tests of their values before being admitted. But more generally, this was an appeal to commentators, journalists, academics, and the general public to become more forceful in defending Western liberal democracy and in criticizing the new Muslim totalitarianism the reformists thought they had identified. National security demanded a change in public attitudes, argued the reformists. The chief barrier to such a change was the European doctrine of multiculturalism, which they claimed discouraged forceful criticism of aspects of other cultures. Such attitudes of tolerance had to be swept aside. This was an argument that had been made repeatedly in

Britain since the mid-1990s, but the war on terror boosted its appeal, particularly after the 7/7 terrorist attacks in London. A widely publicized essay pleading for national leadership in the face of multicultural weakness—penned in 2008 by a group of British former generals, senior diplomats, and intelligence services officers—was typical of a genre of hardened multiculturalism-bashing.

> The United Kingdom presents itself as a target, as a fragmenting, post-Christian society, increasingly divided about interpretations of its history, about its national aims, its values and in its political identity. That fragmentation is worsened by the firm self-image of those elements within it who refuse to integrate. This is a problem worsened by the lack of leadership from the majority which in misplaced deference to "multiculturalism" failed to lay down the line to immigrant communities, thus undercutting those within them trying to fight extremism. The country's lack of self-confidence is in stark contrast to the implacability of its Islamist terrorist enemy, within and without.[95]

Throughout the first decade of the war on terror, Britain's politicians repeatedly announced to the public that multiculturalism had gone too far and now needed limits set on it. What Timothy Garton Ash called "a more demanding civic-national identity" was needed.[96] That identity was increasingly defined less through conservative notions of England's ancient inheritance and more in terms of post-1960s liberal values of gender equality, freedom of expression, sexual equality, and secularism. Presumed lack of allegiance to these values became one of the ways in which liberals identified who was to be considered a Muslim extremist. Hence the third tension within the reformists' project: they need some form of multiculturalism to recognize and incorporate mainstream Islam, but they also denounce multiculturalism as an enabler of extremist ideas and identities, and as a danger to liberal values. While liberals try various formulae to reconcile these two imperatives, it is no wonder that across Europe, multiculturalism is said to be in crisis.

Through these techniques, the reformist approach to tackling homegrown Muslim extremism aims at a cultural transformation in which the identity of European Muslims is reshaped in a pro-Western mold. For policy makers, the reformists' distinction between Islam as a religious identity, to be granted multicultural recognition, and Islamism, a totalitarian ideology to be fought, provides a more productive grid for thinking about Muslims domestically and internationally than that offered by the anti-Muslim generalizations of culturalism. It allows governments to avoid confrontational language that overtly demonizes huge numbers of people and to engage instead in a process of identifying allies in Muslim communities who can assist with programs designed to tackle extremism. The language of diversity, reform, and partnership can plausibly be deployed to win support for this approach from across the political spectrum. Those defined as moderate Muslims can have their religious traditions valued within the parameters of Western tolerance, while the state focuses its powers of surveillance, coercion, and violence on those categorized as extremist. Yet the reformists' progressive rhetoric masks a vast, ambitious program of intervention. They seek to use both hard and soft power to "battle for the soul" of Muslim communities, domestically and internationally, and to redraw the contours of Muslim identity in Europe.[97] The state wants to create a new kind of more palatable Muslim to be integrated through cultural respect and tolerance while those who mount a political refusal see their civil rights disintegrate.

Until 2009, most reformists thought the US largely immune from domestic Muslim radicalization. Analysts like Marc Sageman believed America's free-market society had been better at integrating Muslim immigrants than the European welfare-state model, which he thought fostered dependency and indolence.[98] Similarly, the US government's 2007 *National Strategy for Homeland Security* claimed:

> The fact that our country has not experienced the level of homegrown violent Islamic extremism that has begun to plague other Western democracies is, in large measure, a tribute to American society, which values free expression and encourages all to engage politically and economically.[99]

The picture was one in which Muslims in the US were smoothly assimilated by a successful melting pot, while in Europe they were left angry and violent. In fact, comparing the number of terrorist offenses in the US and Europe is difficult, due to differing definitions, legal and policing practices, and time periods in the published data. Moreover, the numbers on both sides of the Atlantic are too small and too distorted by law enforcement biases (as we shall see in Chapter 6) to allow for comparative conclusions about Muslim behavior, let alone to ascribe any differences to European welfarism.[100]

In any case, a number of events in 2009 undermined the perception that the attractions of the American Dream made the US immune. In June, Abdulhakim Mujahid Muhammad, an African American from Memphis who had converted to Islam, shot at US soldiers outside an army recruiting center in Little Rock, Arkansas, killing one and wounding another. In September, Najibullah Zazi, a Pakistani-born permanent US resident, was arrested and later pleaded guilty to planning to bomb the New York City subway system. It emerged that he had acquired the ingredients to make an explosive device.[101] Colleen R. LaRose, known in the media as "Jihad Jane" and described as having an "all-American appearance," was arrested the following month and accused of supporting terrorism online from her home in suburban Pennsylvania and plotting to murder a Swedish artist.[102] On November 5, 2009, Palestinian-American army major Nidal Hasan entered the military base at Fort Hood, Texas, shot thirteen people dead, and wounded another thirty-two. Hasan was a US citizen and an army psychiatrist. The following May, Faisal Shahzad's attempt to detonate a car bomb in New York's Times Square was intercepted at the last minute by a vigilant street vendor who happened to be a Muslim from Senegal.[103] The Pakistan-born Shahzad had become a US citizen a year earlier.[104]

In September 2010, the influential Bipartisan Policy Center published a report by two leading US-based terrorism experts, Peter Bergen and Bruce Hoffman, which claimed:

> Al-Qaeda and its allies arguably have been able to establish at least an embryonic terrorist recruitment, radicalization, and operational infrastructure in the United States.

The report went on to warn:

> The American "melting pot" has not provided a firewall against the radicalization and recruitment of American citizens and residents . . . By stubbornly wrapping itself in [a] . . . false security blanket, the U.S. lost five years to learn from the British experience.

Finally, the report concluded:

> It is fundamentally troubling . . . that there remains no federal government agency or department specifically charged with identifying radicalization and interdicting the recruitment of U.S. citizens or residents for terrorism.[105]

Calls for such a policy of counterradicalization were forcefully advanced by the Washington Institute for Near East Policy (WINEP), an influential part of the pro-Israel lobby and, according to an Israeli newspaper report, an organization with a secure phone line linking it to Obama's White House.[106] WINEP argued that "Islamism—a radical political ideology separate from Islam as a religion—[be] recognized internally within the US government as the key ideological driver of the violent extremist threat posed by al-Qaeda and other radical Islamist groups." Domestically, the US government should "identify, connect, and empower local Muslim opinion leaders to compete with the message of radical extremists within the United States."[107] Then-senator Joseph Lieberman, as chair of the Senate Homeland Security and Governmental Affairs Committee, repeatedly called for a comprehensive plan to combat homegrown Islamist radicalization, and Congressman Peter King's hearings on Muslim radicalization in 2011 further raised the issue's prominence.

Homeland Security Secretary Janet Napolitano agreed that radicalization in the US needed addressing, stating: "Home-based terrorism is here. And like violent extremism abroad, it is now part of the threat picture that we must confront."[108] Her department organized meetings with some of the large private philanthropic foundations to suggest they fund community-based initiatives to counter radicalization in American Muslim communities.[109] A Countering Violent Extremism Working Group was established at the department to coordinate efforts by local, state, and federal agencies to confront this emerging domestic theat. US policy makers began to import modes of thinking from the UK on how to tackle homegrown Muslim terrorism. Much of the agenda that had emerged in Britain—official recognition of a moderate Islam and curtailing the civil rights of those who dissented—took hold in the US, albeit in different forms. There was growing attention paid to developing partnerships between government agencies and moderate Muslim community leaders, in an effort to prevent extremism. Officials of the Department of Homeland Security toured America's Muslim communities, holding meetings with community representatives. Farah Pandith, the State Department's special representative to Muslim communities, engaged not only internationally but with those in the US as well. And FBI special agents working on counter-terrorism investigations made appearances at specially organized outreach events in Muslim communities. A White House paper published in August 2011 held up such initiatives as central to the US strategy: "Mainstream Islam" was to be officially recognized by the government, the better to counter "extremism."[110] Speaking about this new strategy in an interview with NPR radio, Denis McDonough, then deputy national security adviser to the White House, highlighted the extent to which a range of public authorities were to play a role—even schools, which were to monitor communities for signs of radicalization: "Well, I think it's not just local law enforcement, although local law enforcement is addressing this issue and is ready. It's also local community leaders. It's teachers. It's principals. It's coaches."[111] The strategy thus envisaged a web of surveillance and engagement by a range of professions that might interact with young Muslims and spot signs of radicalization.

Government representatives came close to speaking of a "true" meaning of Islam that should be officially recognized as the acceptable way to be a Muslim in America. Rashad Hussain, President Obama's most senior Muslim adviser and a special envoy to the Organization of Islamic Cooperation, spoke about the meaning of Islam as a bulwark against violence: "I am of the opinion that one of the strongest tools that you can use to counter radicalization and violent extremism is Islam itself, because Islam rejects violent extremism."[112] A year before his first appointment to the Obama

White House, Hussain had coauthored a paper for the well-connected Brookings Institution, arguing that "in order to win the 'battle of ideas,' the United States government must carefully reformulate its strategy and work with the Muslim world to promote mainstream Islam over terrorist ideology."[113] What is striking about those taking such a position of multicultural recognition is that they were often the very same officials involved in the most repressive counterterrorism measures. Take, for example, the current CIA director, John Brennan. In February 2010, as a top adviser to President Obama on counterterrorism, he gave a speech to Muslim students at New York University in which he offered the audience an official position on what jihad does and does not mean—"Jihad is a holy struggle, an effort to purify for a legitimate purpose"—and offered his "respect for a faith that has helped to shape my own worldview."[114] At the time he said these words he was at the helm of the government's drone program that was carrying out extrajudicial killings of Muslims in at least three different countries. He had earlier been a senior counterterrorism official at the CIA when it was involved in torturing terrorist suspects. Such contradictions run through Obama's war on terror: hunger-striking Guantánamo prisoners are brutally force-fed, but at night, to comply with fasting during Ramadan; bin Laden was buried at sea—but according to what officials called "traditional procedures for Islamic burial."[115] The point here is not one of hypocrisy but of the way in which a paternalist multicultural respect for Islam is central to a counterextremism strategy that seeks to reshape Muslim politics by both hard and soft power.

Domestically, part of the hard power aspect of this strategy took the form of federal law enforcement agencies increasingly seeking to prosecute individuals for expressing Islamist ideology. Expressive activities, such as distributing radical documents and videos online, were criminalized more and more frequently as material support for terrorism, punishable with up to fifteen years in prison. The number of terrorism-related indictments brought in the US nearly doubled in 2009 and 2010 compared to previous years. Of these indictments, the proportion involving material support charges rose from less than 12 percent in 2007 to nearly 70 percent in 2010.[116] For instance, in 2009, Tarek Mehanna, a US citizen from Boston, was charged with conspiring to provide material support to a terrorist organization for translating a widely available online text and distributing videos online—activities historically understood as free expression protected by the First Amendment to the Constitution. In April 2012, he was sentenced to seventeen and a half years in prison.[117] He had earlier twice refused to work as an informant for the FBI.

In theory, the First Amendment to the US Constitution should have acted as a barrier to these developments. Its establishment clause requires the government to refrain from adopting an official position on any point of religious doctrine or holding up particular interpretations of theological terms as correct or incorrect. Unlike in Europe, where religion is regulated by the state through a variety of institutional arrangements, the US system claims to construct religious identity as a privileged space of near-absolute freedom from the state. The official regulation of Islam recommended by the reformists' antiextremist agenda ought therefore to have been impossible to achieve in the US.[118] Furthermore, the First Amendment's freedom of speech clause was interpreted in the three decades before 9/11 as constitutionally protecting the expression of any political or religious view that was not "intended and likely to incite imminent lawless action"—the formulation that the US Supreme Court adopted in the 1969 *Brandenburg v. Ohio* case. Based on this definition the government could not criminalize expressions of extremist ideology except in those rare circumstances where it could be shown to directly incite terrorist activity.

In practice, however, the First Amendment proved less of a barrier than might have been expected. The US Supreme Court's 2010 decision in *Holder v. Humanitarian Law Project* found that expressive activity coordinated with, or under the direction of, a foreign group which the speaker knows to be a terrorist organization may constitutionally be prohibited as material support for terrorism. The government's argument was that a person who is not a member of a terrorist organization but advocates on behalf of it is indirectly supporting terrorism, because as a result of such advocacy, the organization needs to invest less of its own resources in communicating its message and can focus more on increasing its capacity for violence. The Mehanna case implicitly widened still further what might qualify as material support. There was no evidence that he was acting in coordination with or under the control of a terrorist group, yet he was still convicted on the basis that his expressive activities amounted to material support for terrorism. There was certainly no plausibility to the claim that his expressive activities were likely to "incite imminent lawless action" as that phrase had normally been understood. But under the influence of radicalization models in which ideology is seen as the root cause of terrorism, the legal interpretation of free speech shifted.

Since around 2007, the reformist approach has constituted the official narrative of the global war on terror among state bureaucracies and mainstream policy think tanks in the US and UK, and has represented the default position of liberal writers and analysts. Beginning in 2009, US officials began to believe they needed to apply this approach domestically, too. But culturalism remains a trend among elements of the national security apparatus, and its narrative continues to be propagated by right-wing agitators and propagandists. Together, reformism and culturalism set the terms of a narrow debate on the Muslim problem. Reformists criticize the crude generalizations of the culturalists—their assumption that Islam can only be interpreted as a doctrine of fanaticism and their counterproductive alienating of Islam from the West. Culturalists respond by charging reformists with naiveté for thinking governments can bring about cultural change in Muslim communities, with wishful thinking in attempting to find a moderate Islam, and with overlooking the danger that partnering with Muslims facilitates infiltration. Culturalists argue that the war on terror is a battle between Judeo-Christian civilization and Islam's premodern values; reformists reply that it is better conceived as a battle between liberal values and an antimodern political ideology called Islamism. The reformists are optimistic that their assimilatory strategy can transform Islamic culture and draw Muslims into a pro-Western stance, while the culturalists, believing Islamic culture unreformable, pessimistically peddle fear, suspicion, and distancing. Both reify Muslim culture, the former to manipulate it, the latter to vilify it.

To the culturalists, Western Muslims can never be equal citizens. To the reformists, the equal citizenship of Muslims is, in practice, precariously dependent on their being able to prove their allegiance to ill-defined Western values. But placing Muslims under constant suspicion for fear they are about to break the rules of the liberal political game is a poor basis for true equality.[119] The only question becomes how to integrate Muslims into a preexisting liberal society that remains basically the same. But what if citizens do not want just to be accepted in the existing system but seek to change it, for example, by challenging fundamental assumptions of its foreign policy? The solution for liberals is to allow difference so long as it does not make a difference. Culture is held to be a private matter of quaint lifestyle choices that present no real challenge to the system. But that only works if a set of universal values can be presumed, at some deep level, to be shared by everyone.[120] In times of political conflict, when that assumption looks less plausible, liberals tend to abandon their principles and reach for coercive methods to defend the status quo. Conservatives are more consistent in asserting that the basis for political order is a single cultural tradition organically rooted in a particular people, but such a notion also offers no answer to the question of multicultural coexistence, except to declare it impossible. What both neglect is the basic political question thrown up by multiculturalism: how can a common way of life, together with full participation from all parts of society, be created?

The debate between culturalists and reformists raises real and significant issues. But the real ideological message contained in this debate is not any of the particular positions taken within it but the very fact that such a debate is taking place at all and the unspoken assumptions that underlie it. At a more basic level, the positions in this debate form a joint paradigm in which extremist ideology, whether literal Islam itself or a political perversion of it, is seen as the root cause of terrorism. For both, Muslim culture is reified and singled out as an object of wide-ranging state intervention—whether through hard or soft power. Through their dominance of the mainstream discussion of terrorism in the US's and UK's political cultures, these two modes of thinking, in effect, collude to sustain a shared discourse that defines Muslims as a problem.

CHAPTER 3

The Roots of Liberal Rage

> The link between belief and behavior raises the stakes considerably. Some propositions are so dangerous that it may even be ethical to kill people for believing them . . . If they cannot be captured, and they often cannot, otherwise tolerant people may be justified in killing them in self-defense. This is what the United States attempted in Afghanistan, and it is what we and other Western powers are bound to attempt, at an even greater cost to ourselves and to innocents abroad, elsewhere in the Muslim world. We will continue to spill blood in what is, at bottom, a war of ideas.
>
> —Sam Harris, *The End of Faith*

Jesse Curtis Morton did not have cable television when he was growing up in the US in the 1980s. "When I was a child, the new wave was cable TV and MTV, and I didn't have access to it," he said. "And I think it's a major reason why I had some level of human consciousness as I grew up. And I could see through the lies and the hypocrisies of my own society, from the beginning." Jesse hated the consumerism he thought had brainwashed his fellow students at his working-class high school. "They watch their favorite TV show, and they eat their favorite cereal, and they buy their favorite shoes. And that's what life's about. I think they're sick. I was never part of it." Jesse left home at an early age to escape his abusive family. For a while he traveled with the Grateful Dead, attracted to the countercultural band's rejection of materialist values. By 2002 he was struggling with drug addiction and, while in Virginia, was charged with petty larceny and possession of crack cocaine.

But within a few years he had converted to Islam, graduated from college, and earned a master's degree from Columbia University. He described his first reading of the Qur'an as an "overwhelming epiphany," and his subsequent conversion seemed to have given him a sense of focus and discipline. He changed his name to Younes Abdullah Muhammad and found work as a substance abuse counselor in New York. He also sought to understand the history, politics, and economics of the Middle East, and spent time in Saudi Arabia. To his dismay he encountered the same materialism that had alienated him from US society. He came to believe that through the "straitjacket of globalization" the commercialism rampant in America was being imposed around the world. The sickness he thought he had seen around him as a teenager was infecting the whole world, and nobody seemed to care. But he also started to think that Islam, the religion that had saved him from drug addiction, would, if properly followed, save Muslim societies from Western materialism. "Under the religion we have to control our resources, we have to control our own society, and we have to rule by a very basic principle-based system that Allah has given to us," he said.

Islam, in this view, demanded freedom from US-led globalization. Abdullah Muhammad thought the US government was aware that the survival of its economic system depended on eradicating any application of Islamic principles. He concluded that to defend its empire America had declared war on Islam, calling it a war on terror. "On the periphery the people are plundered, while at the heart of the empire the people benefit," he said. "And as long as they can carry back the spoils of war, keep the price of oil down, keep consumption up, only a few people will speak out." The anger at American hedonism Abdullah Muhammad felt as a teenager was now channeled into a struggle to defend Islam from the destruction wrought by US-led capitalism:

> Their religion is the religion of wealth, the religion of consumption, the religion of globalization, which is a satanic system. It exploits women, it exploits the family, and it exploits all of what is moral and good. It says there are no values: do what you want, no matter who it hurts or what it affects.

While he did not "want anybody to blow up any civilians in America" as part of this struggle, he nevertheless was able to see "some strategic benefit" to the 9/11 attacks. He was clear that US forces in majority-Muslim countries "who are invading other people's houses and homes . . . should be annihilated."[1]

In December 2007, Abdullah Muhammad and a fellow radical, Yousef al-Khattab, created an organization called Revolution Muslim. It functioned primarily online, through a Web site, blogs, Facebook page, and YouTube channel. Videos, such as "Knowledge is for Acting upon—the Manhattan raid," which celebrated the 9/11 attacks, were circulated online. So too were speeches by radical preachers such as Abdullah Faisal, who had been convicted in Britain in 2003 for inciting violence and later deported to Jamaica. The group also attempted to preach its message on the streets of New York. On the sidewalk outside the Islamic Cultural Center on New York's Upper East Side, Abdullah Muhammad would denounce the silence of Muslims in the face of US foreign policy abuses; the congregants leaving the mosque after their prayers largely ignored his speeches. By 2009 the Revolution Muslim Web site was attracting a number of angry young American men and was under the close surveillance of government agencies. Samir Khan—a twenty-three-year-old online radical, who had grown up on Long Island—was in touch with Abdullah Muhammad at this point and contributing to the Web site. He would later travel to Yemen, produce propaganda material for al-Qaeda in the Arabian Peninsula, and eventually be killed in a US drone strike, in 2011. In January 2010, Zachary Adam Chesser, a twenty-year-old from northern Virginia who had converted to Islam two years previously and, like Samir Khan, made a name for himself within the community of online radicals, began to administer the Web site jointly with Abdullah Muhammad.[2]

Abdullah Muhammad saw Revolution Muslim as having a double ideological purpose. On the one hand, its role was "countering the bullcrap propaganda coming out of the American empire, and saying, 'Look, that's not true.' " On the other hand, he wanted it to develop social and economic policies that could be put into practice were an Islamic state to emerge somewhere in the world.

> We're starting to show how you can issue your own money into the economy, and you don't need to borrow from a central bank. Or how you would be able to create livable wages for workers, and how that creates a distribution of wealth across society. We talk about environmentalism from an Islamic perspective. And, at the same time, we're not afraid or ashamed to say that we support those fighting the imperialists across the globe. We don't want to see the Muslim population annihilated in the way of the Native Americans.[3]

In his manifesto, *By All Means Necessary*, he imagined what would happen if an Islamic state were to be consolidated in, say, Somalia. The new state would be isolated and in need of assistance. Abdullah Muhammad fantasized that Revolution Muslim would be "the right crew with the right connections [who] could come in with some serious policy recommendations," a kind of World Bank for emerging Islamist states.[4]

In April 2010, Zachary Adam Chesser heard about a forthcoming episode of the Comedy Central television series *South Park*, in which the Prophet Muhammad was to be depicted wearing a bear suit. To alert Revolution Muslim followers, Chesser posted a graphic picture of the murdered Dutch filmmaker Theo van Gogh online and predicted that the program's writers, Trey Parker and Matt Stone, would probably suffer a similar fate. Details of the neighborhood where Parker and Stone lived in Colorado were added, with the suggestion that readers "pay a visit." The posting was soon picked up by the mainstream news media. The television news channels had a field day. Comedian Bill Maher told the audience of his *Real Time* show:

> Though America likes to think it's number one, we have to admit that we're behind the developing world in at least one thing: their religious wackos are a lot more wacko than ours . . . Our culture isn't just different from one that makes death threats to cartoonists—it's better.[5]

"Revolution Muslim" entered Google's list of the hundred most-searched-for phrases. Then hackers took down the site. Abdullah Muhammad got calls from journalists asking about the organization's position, so he decided to work on a "clarification statement" with Chesser. But it hardly clarified. It began by saying that Revolution Muslim was "not against a rational dialogue" before (incorrectly) claiming that Islamic scholars are unanimous in supporting the death penalty for those who mock Muhammad. "Thus our position remains that it is likely the creators of *South Park* will indeed end up like Theo Van Gogh. This is a reality." Still, they claimed, "We are not trying to directly incite violence." Finally, they quoted Osama bin Laden's remarks on the Muhammad cartoons published by the Danish *Jyllands-Posten* newspaper: "If there is no check in the freedom of your words, then let your hearts be open to the freedom of our actions."[6]

Three months later Chesser was arrested while attempting to travel to Somalia, accused of seeking to join al-Shabaab, and later sentenced to twenty-five years in federal prison.[7] Around the same time, Abdullah Muhammad quit his job and left the US for Morocco. While he was there I was able to conduct a telephone interview with him. He told me he had "made some mistakes" with the Revolution Muslim Web site. "I had some buffoons work alongside of me, and you learn as you go." But his new project, Islampolicy.com, would, he said, focus more on developing policy solutions for a future Islamic state. Nevertheless, he said, "I have no doubt that I'll probably end up in prison some day."[8]

For a while his new Web site published discussions of how to create financial systems without interest, so as to be shariʿa-compliant. But when Osama bin Laden was killed in Pakistan in May 2011, Abdullah Muhammad posted an admiring tribute that called for an "army of Osama."[9] Later that month, he was arrested in Morocco, then extradited to the US and charged with conspiracy to solicit the murder of his fellow citizens, primarily for his role in coauthoring the *South Park* clarification statement with Chesser. Back in the US he was held in solitary confinement for months until he agreed to take a plea the government offered rather than risk a trial. He was sentenced to eleven and a half years in prison.

Abdullah Muhammad embodies the radicalization threat that many in the US national security apparatus most fear: a white American who rejects the society in which he was raised and becomes an admirer of its most feared enemy, Osama bin Laden. It is easy to devise psychological theories to explain his journey to extremism. Could his abusive upbringing have produced a rage that was then projected onto American society as a whole? Was his only way of escaping drug addiction to structure his life according to absolute moral precepts, a Manichean mind-set vulnerable to a fanatical belief in violent struggle between forces of good and evil? Did his childhood experiences give rise to a failure to adjust to reality, a relentless longing for a utopia where his life's struggles could be redeemed? Maybe those were parts of the explanation. But remaining on a psychological level leaves out the bigger question of why his ideological journey took the particular form it did. In recent years, this question has been explored in theories of radicalization that attempt to explain the relationship between ideology and violence; those are examined in detail in the following chapter. In fact, the radicalization literature fails to offer a convincing demonstration of a causal relationship between holding an ideology and choosing to use violence. Nevertheless, within the logics of culturalism and reformism there is a shared mechanical view of the effectivity of ideologies. Extremist ideas—whether expressed in the classical Islamic texts or in Islamist discourse—are regarded as, in themselves, the ultimate cause of violence. The metaphors used to describe the impact of extremist ideology are illustrative: ideology is a "conveyor belt" that propels its adherents toward violent action, a "funnel" down which they slide toward terrorism, or a "virus" that infects those with whom it comes into contact.

Abdullah Muhammad was not directly involved in violence himself. He published online material that could be interpreted as a threat of violence against fellow citizens. The case raised the issue of whether Abdullah Muhammad's online statement about the creators of *South Park* amounted to a threat that had the effect of undermining their right to free expression. There was certainly a case to answer. On the other hand, it is not hard to find other US Web sites that praise murderous violence without facing criminal sanction: the "Army of God," for example, a Christian antiabortion group based in Virginia, openly praises the murder of abortionists as "justifiable homicide."[10] Yet in the prosecution's submission, there was a different argument running alongside this legal question: what was at stake was not just an individual making a threat against someone perceived to have insulted his religion but an attempt to prevent a truth about Islamic ideology from being spoken. In his sentencing statement, federal prosecutor Neil H. MacBride centered his argument upon the following point:

> The role of Muslims in the United States, the relationship between the United States and the Muslim world, and the existence of links between Islam and terrorism are issues of major public importance. Yet anyone choosing to address them publicly must carefully weigh the risk of being marked for death by the likes of Morton for saying or writing something perceived as insulting while doing so. Left unchecked, that risk will hamper public policy decision making by dampening public discourse over some of the most consequential issues of our age.[11]

Abdullah Muhammad's actions, in this view, presented the danger that America would stop speaking of the possibility of links between Islam and violence. He was not just threatening violence against those perceived to have insulted Islam but seeking to intimidate those who wanted to publicize Islam's violent nature. This was his real crime, the basis for his long sentence, and why his online activity was considered completely differently from non-Muslim terrorist organizations that promote violence on the Internet without facing prosecution.

Macbride must have been aware that the episode of *South Park* was hardly an attempt to explore questions of Islamic theology and political violence. And there was no other evidence to ascribe to Abdullah Muhammad the wider motive of seeking to hide Islam's alleged violent nature. But MacBride was following a generic war on terror paradigm in which ideology and violence are seen as functionally interdependent. In this view, Islamic ideology was the force that radicalized Abdullah Muhammad to make threats of violence, and the purpose of those threats was to prevent discussion of precisely this radicalizing force. Having presented the case as involving basic questions of Islam, it naturally followed that for Macbride the trial was a part of the ongoing clash of civilizations. He continued:

> Determined enemies are striving through all means to destroy the West and snuff out our traditions of free thought, free speech, and freedom of religion. If they succeed, we will be enslaved . . . Failing to punish Morton in a manner that recognizes the true magnitude of his crimes will be—in the words of Mark Steyn—just another shuffling step into a psychological bondage of our own making.

The reference to the neoconservative Mark Steyn—who has written that Europe is being subjected to an Islamic "recolonization" due to its falling fertility rate[12]—indicated that a far Right decline of the West mythology was being drawn on.

But the larger problem with a paradigm that sees political violence as the mechanical product of an alien ideology is that it fails to comprehend the part played by Western states themselves in constituting the global conflict between the West and radical Islam. The only way to explain any one party's behavior in the conflict is by analyzing its interaction with the other, and how each interprets the other's actions. Abdullah Muhammad accepted at face value the official narrative that radical Islam was an existential threat to an American society he had come to despise, and he acted on that basis. He did not need an Islamist ideology to radicalize him into thinking the West was at war with Islam; the war on terror's own militarized identity politics was enough. His definition of Islam as a violent rejection of Western values was ultimately derived from the very culturalist ideologues who were cited in his prosecution. He merely wrenched the labels of good and evil from the official war on terror discourse and inverted their positions. The technocratic, gentrified politics of post–cold war liberal societies, which no longer offered ideological alternatives promising to remedy the world's injustices, had nothing to offer Abdullah Muhammad, but in his fringe version of Islam he could find a total opposition to global capitalism and a community of fully committed radical believers.

Antitotalitarianism

The war on terror paradigm that makes ideology the root cause of political violence derives from the cold war theory of totalitarianism, which presumed a similar direct causal connection between ideology and the repressive practices of political control. To understand the modes of thinking that have been central to war on terror analyses of extremism and radicalization, it is instructive to begin by tracing the contours of cold war antitotalitarianism. Like today's liberal analysts of extremism, liberal theorists of totalitarianism constructed political threats as external ideological intrusions into an essentially benign Western cultural space, failing to acknowledge their own positioning as participants in violent political conflicts. Ideologies were thought of as sets of alien ideas that by their very nature gripped followers and produced a fanatical mind-set that led mechanically to violent modes of politics.

During the cold war, the violence of ideology was seen as the aspiration to control every aspect of life, down to the very thoughts of citizens—a total approach to government that communism was meant to share with fascism. In both cases, the origins of state political repression were seen as lying in unrestrained ideological thinking and contrasted with Western societies, in which Lockean liberalism was held to have inspired postideological forms of government that protected basic freedoms. The American proposition of liberal democratic capitalism positioned itself between twin extremes of right and left, which shared a commitment to ideologically driven totalitarian government. The slogan *Les extremes se touchent* (The extremes meet)—originally a middle-class polemic against the moral corruption of both upper and lower classes in prerevolutionary France—became a staple formula of cold war discourse. The political spectrum was not a single line but one that looped round, so that communism was paradoxically closer to nazism than liberalism. In *The Vital Center* Arthur Schlesinger wrote that the

> integrity of the individual [was] the unique experience and fundamental faith of contemporary liberalism [and] will continue to be

> under attack from the far right and the far left . . . The totalitarian left and the totalitarian right meet at last on the murky grounds of tyranny and terror.[13]

On this basis, the energies unleashed in World War II against Nazism could thereafter be redirected to the cold war fight against communism, as former ally the Soviet Union was rebranded an enemy as monstrous as Nazi Germany.

The formula of antitotalitarianism did designate real differences between systems where social and political freedoms were more or less available. But the straight lines it tried to draw between ideology and practices of political control were too neat and convenient. It was mistaken to think of even the most politically tolerant of societies as somehow free of their own ideological drives. There is perhaps nothing more ideological than claiming to be postideological. As the theorist Terry Eagleton has noted, the cold war use of the concept of ideology was inconsistent: it stood for both a passionate, rhetorical, fanatical, pseudoreligious way of seeing the world as well as for a schematic, coldly rational conceptual system which seeks "to reconstruct society from the ground up in accordance with some bloodless blueprint."[14] Certainly the West's slogans of political tolerance bestowed an aura of innocence on liberal states, shielding their own ideological practices from scrutiny in the name of defeating the greater evil of Soviet totalitarianism. At least as much evidence could be gathered to suggest that what led societies to fall under systems of total political repression was not the ideas of the party in power but the material circumstances that prevailed there. Was not totalitarianism in Europe inseparable from the new forms of mass warfare that unfolded on the continent during the twentieth century?[15]

The most elaborate attempt to develop a liberal analysis of totalitarianism for the cold war was produced by the philosopher Hannah Arendt in her three-volume *The Origins of Totalitarianism*. The books contain within them two countervailing arguments. Written between 1943 and 1946, volumes one and two held that the "conditions of possibility" of the Nazi "total" state lay in European colonialism, anti-Semitism, and the plantocracy racism of the US South. Volume three was written in the years just before the entire series publication in

1951, by which time the cold war had begun and Arendt had shifted her attention from Nazism to the Soviet Union. At this point, the analysis changed course. Political theorist Corey Robin writes that by 1949, in Arendt's writing "racism merged with Marxism, Auschwitz with the Gulag, and Fascism morphed into Communism."[16] Totalitarianism was now taken to be a radically novel form of government that made terror its organizing principle and sought to remake reality in accordance with the logic of a ruling ideology. It aimed at accelerating history's natural laws, such that human beings became raw material for the forces that ideology revealed. The total state was made possible by modern "mass society" in which the space for a meaningful and thoughtful public life collapsed, leaving the individual unusually vulnerable to being swept up in great ideological causes that rendered him subsumed to the party. These causes had seized power in Nazi Germany and Soviet Russia, but they were a general threat in all modern societies. Rather than locating totalitarian rule within the West's history of racism and imperialism, as volumes one and two had implied, the third volume referred to its linkage to "Oriental despotism," which had, Arendt said, always rested on "the mass man's typical feeling of superfluousness," a feeling long-standing in India and China but only appearing in modern Europe with the industrial era's atomization, breakdown of social stratification, and masses of lonely individuals.[17] In this way, the concentration camps were, on some deep level, externalized from the history of the West and viewed as resulting from the corruption of European politics by an alien form—thus warding off the dreadful thought that the Holocaust was due not to the breakdown of Western modernity but to the culmination of its inner logic.[18] Her model for this process of alien corruption was Joseph Conrad's *Heart of Darkness*. European colonizers, confronted by the "savagery" of the colonized population, degenerated into "savages" themselves, setting a precedent for the would-be totalitarian leaders of the European "mob."[19] Thus, the origin of "our" savagery lies in "their" culture; Western civilization can be corrupted by the barbarism of others but does not give rise to any distinctive barbarism of its own. The experience of World War II had led Arendt to write one of the century's greatest analyses of racism; the experience of the cold war had taken her in the opposite direction.

Arendt was keenly aware of the ways in which democracies themselves could take on some of the characteristics of mid-twentieth century totalitarianism. And her analysis of European colonial expansion remains a forceful demonstration of the ways in which imperialist mass violence had a tendency to boomerang back to the metropole. But the more widely read third volume of *The Origins of Totalitarianism* offered her contemporary readers—and a good many war on terror propagandists—a way to avoid these issues by falling back on the more comforting formula that political violence was always the natural product of alien ideologies. In a 2004 *New York Review of Books* essay by Samantha Power, later a special assistant to President Obama and a member of his National Security Council, *The Origins of Totalitarianism* is offered as a model for explaining "Militant Islam." Arendt's "wisdom for today's dark times" consists in recognizing that if "one could pierce the veil of mystery that shrouds al-Qaeda, Hamas, or Islamic Jihad, one might well find some of the qualities Arendt associated with totalitarian movements." Of course, the lessons contained in Arendt's account of imperialism in Volume two are ignored. Power mentions in passing Arendt's argument that overseas empires generate racism at home but does not apply this insight to today's America.[20]

The general trend among cold war theorists of totalitarianism was to neglect material circumstances and specific political contexts, preferring to deduce the existence of total political repression a priori from an "ideological original sin."[21] In Karl Popper's two-volume treatise *The Open Society and Its Enemies*, written during World War II but going on to become another key text of cold war antitotalitarianism, he applied this approach on a grand scale. Totalitarianism was rooted in a purely intellectual error: the doctrine that a chosen people would inherit power according to an inevitable process laid down by the laws of history. In Marxism, the proletariat is the chosen people destined to inherit the earth; in fascism, it is race that plays the same role. "Both theories base their historical forecasts on an interpretation of history which leads to the discovery of a law of its development."[22] What matters is the underlying template that is essentially the same in each case and which always leads to violence and intolerance when allowed to influence society.

Such thinking ultimately derives from Plato and takes its modern form with Hegel, who is not "to be taken seriously" and has "helped to produce two world wars so far."[23] By implication, German Idealism took a wrong turn after Kant, and all continental philosophy derived from it is suspect. An open society needs to protect itself against the threat of such "historicist" ideologies that view history as following inexorable laws of development. Paradoxically, it needs to proclaim its pluralism and tolerance of different worldviews yet prevent a historicist worldview from taking hold of society. Popper turned to an odd metaphor in his attempt to resolve this paradox: we should let the "searchlight" of normal historical interpretation "play upon our past" and "illuminate the present by its reflection," but historicism, which is an ideology "of a peculiar kind," "may be compared to a searchlight which we direct upon ourselves," and which therefore "makes it difficult if not impossible to see anything of our surroundings."[24]

In a frequently quoted footnote, he argued: "We should therefore claim, in the name of tolerance, the right not to tolerate the intolerant. We should claim that any movement preaching intolerance places itself outside the law."[25] No doubt Popper was thinking of the failure of Germany's interwar Weimar Republic to prevent the rise of Nazism, and wanted liberal societies not to repeat the mistake of indulging ideological enemies. But he ignored the ways in which the coming to power of fascism in Europe was also enabled by the desire for strong opposition to communism. Fascism acquired respectability as a counterweight to Bolshevism for many liberals among the Italian and German governing elites.

In Popper's work on scientific discovery, the exceptions to laws were at the center of his model. If an empirical exception to a claimed universal law could be found, that was enough to claim it as false. It was the possibility of such falsification that distinguished genuine science from mere metaphysics. In his political work, the exception to the laws—the moment when the usual rules of pluralism are suspended in the name of defense against an ideological enemy—is accorded a mere footnote rather than being taken as the starting point for a theoretical elaboration. Like other cold war theorists, Popper held that liberal societies had to know when to break their own rules of tolerance if they were to defend themselves against the intolerance of totalitarian ideologies. But the possibility that such a moment of emergency could itself become permanent and be normalized as a paradigm of government—what the Italian philosopher Giorgio Agamben called the "state of exception"—was not explored.[26] The possibility that his antitotalitarianism could itself foster unexpected forms of totalitarian rule was alien to Popper's thought. Cited whenever cold war and war on terror liberals seek to justify the adoption of illiberal measures, his tolerance footnote was thus the backdoor by which political repression could slip unnoticed into an open society.

In ways that would later be repeated with the war on terror, cold war liberalism masked the fact that the most promising opportunities for emancipatory politics emerged in spaces outside the war's own terms of reference—in movements that sought to transcend the Moscow-Washington axis rather than take a position along it. Throughout the cold war, radical political movements found themselves on the wrong side of antitotalitarianism's vaunted liberal tolerance. The McCarthyite blacklists are well known, but the anticommunism of the early cold war was also hugely destructive to the early US civil rights movement, pressuring its leaders to detach the issues of desegregation and voting rights from the wider context of struggles for social equality in the US and the fight against colonialism internationally. Those who were unwilling to make this accommodation were marginalized. In 1948, W. E. B. Du Bois was sacked from the National Association for the Advancement of Colored People when his attempt to petition the United Nations for the human rights of African Americans clashed with the anti-Soviet propaganda of the US government (the strategy would have to wait until the early 1960s, when Malcolm X advocated the same approach).[27] The same anticommunist lens refracted Third World nationalist movements, making them appear communist pawns on the cold war chessboard rather than struggles for national self-determination.[28] A measure of liberal tolerance at home went hand in hand with brutal repression of Third World movements for national independence, whether in the form of CIA-orchestrated bloody coups in, for example, Iran (1953), Iraq (1963), and Indonesia (1965), or as full-scale military violence—as in Vietnam. The antitotalitarian discourse obscured the ways in which the domestic successes of liberal America were dependent on an illiberal foreign policy of using state terror to secure the international arteries of US-led capitalism.

Governments which joined the US-led fight against communism—such as the military regime in South Korea, General Pinochet in Chile, or the fascist governments of Spain and Portugal—were supported, irrespective of whether their own governing practices resembled the totalitarianism of Moscow. In these cases, the label "totalitarian" was not applied—they were merely "authoritarian", and therefore not to be thought of as cold war enemies. In Italy, where a strong working-class movement was by the late 1960s transcending the Communist Party as its chosen form of organization, the state, with NATO backing, manipulated emergency antiterrorism powers to undermine the Left, while secretly fostering its own right-wing terror cells to destabilize democracy. Presenting itself as a neutral mediator between *opposti estremismi* (opposing extremisms) of Left and Right, the state was able to camouflage its own hand in the violent suppression of working-class radicalism. In the name of a "sacrosanct defence against the terrorist monster," wrote left-wing radical Gianfranco Sanguinetti, the state "can exact from all its subjects a further portion of their tiny freedom, which will reinforce police control over the entire population." In this "strategy of tension," all other political questions were forgotten in the face of the "holy mission" of securing public order against totalitarian extremists.[29]

Ideology and Violence

Like the cold war theorists of totalitarianism, who ignored the specifics of political context and assumed violence to be the direct product of unrestrained ideology, both culturalists and reformists in the war on terror ignore the fact that terrorism is a mode of political action. Whether a movement makes the leap into using a particular form of violence or not cannot be reduced to the question of its ideological content. It is necessary instead to examine how states and social movements have mutually constituted themselves as combatants in a global conflict between the West and radical Islam. A key part of such an analysis is to ask under what conditions each has chosen to adopt tactics of violence and in response to what political circumstances they find themselves in, paying close attention to the relationship between their legitimizing frameworks. It is the interaction between these state and nonstate actors that produces a context in which violence becomes seen as a valid tactic.[30] This relational aspect requires us to investigate the ways in which Western states themselves became radicalized—as much as Islamist political movements—both becoming more willing to use violence in a wider range of contexts. Only by analyzing the interactions between the parties in the conflict, and how each interprets the other's actions, is it possible to explain why, for example, the number of incidents of terrorist violence increased in Britain following the launch of the Iraq war.[31] Similarly, while it is convenient for Israel's army of publicists to claim that Hamas is immutably violent because of its Islamist ideology, and therefore needs to be met by force rather than dialogue, the truth is that Hamas's political violence can only be explained in the context of the decades-long Israeli military occupation, to which it is a flawed response. That religious arguments are used by Hamas to legitimize its ceasefires as much as they are used to legitimize its violence suggests that religious ideology does not provide an adequate explanation of its behavior.[32]

Related to the question of ideology is the issue of how culturalists and reformists relate to the texts they think provide the source of ideological violence. For culturalists, the classical Islamic texts themselves are the problem: the Qur'an, and the *sunna*—descriptions of the Prophet Muhammad's life given by his companions. Culturalists compile lists of verses from these texts, which are taken to indicate an Islamic prescription to terrorism. Of course, it is possible to quote an equal number of verses that contradict or contextualize what might seem at first to be injunctions to violence. But whether the use of violence is legitimate in Islamic terms in any particular context is not something that can be straightforwardly deduced from the classical sources. The standard Islamophobic argument is that, as Melanie Phillips put it after the Woolwich murder in 2013, terrorism "arises from an interpretation of Islam which takes the words of the Koran literally as a command to kill unbelievers in a jihad, or holy war, in order to impose strict Islamic tenets on the rest of the world."[33] But there is no Islamic doctrine of "kill the unbelievers," as anti-Islam propagandists often maintain. Islam, like other religions, provides a broad moral framework for thinking about questions of violence; the real question is how Muslims apply this framework to particular situations. Disagreements over these questions reflect different analyses of particular political contexts rather than disagreements over theology. The classical Islamic precepts are themselves too broad and too open to different interpretations to be a cause of violence in themselves. Nor is there a centralized authority, like the Vatican, that can lay down an official interpretation of Islam. Culturalists have to abandon all scholarly rules of exegesis in order to present Islamic doctrine as causing violence, exclude all contextual factors, and embark on a crude reification of the texts. As the anthropologist Talal Asad has argued, religions are not reducible to a single essence which can be read from founding texts. Islamic doctrine has always interacted in complex ways with social practices rather than laid down a total blueprint for every aspect of life.[34]

At first it might appear that the reformists avoid these problems, because they at least admit Islam is usually interpreted in moderate forms. Yet their thinking about the practical effects of texts also tends to be reductive. In order to make their argument that extremist ideology directly inspires violence, they are also forced to simplify the relationship between ideas and actions. The question of how different actors find different meanings in Islamist texts in different contexts, and mobilize them for different purposes, gets lost. The problem can be illustrated by thinking of earlier debates on the political meanings of Islam. During the cold war, scholars debated whether Islam would tend to support communism or capitalism. Many, such as Bernard Lewis, believed that Islam had an inherent affinity with communism, due to their shared totalitarian tendencies—a precursor to the similarly unconvincing arguments made today. But others found equal evidence suggesting compatibility between Islam and capitalism. After all, the religion had emerged in a merchant culture.

Some went further still and thought they could detect a process of reform taking place in which innovators within Islam were pushing the religion toward a modern form of private belief based on individual conscience. For US development scholars focused on the Middle East, such as the political scientist Leonard Binder, this was thought a necessary step in the emergence of a procapitalist middle class in Muslim countries. Ironically, the innovator who was given as an example of such a trend was Sayyid Qutb, who, Binder thought, introduced an "element of individualism" that could be the basis for an Islamic liberalism.[35] Binder was picking up on the idea in Qutb's book *Milestones* that Islamic political identity is based on the individual actively choosing to join the community of believers rather than on accepting inherited tribal, ethnic, or national filiations. For Qutb, the Islamic society is based "on the association of belief alone, instead of the low associations based on race and color, language and country, regional and national interests."[36] Emphasizing the individual freed by conscience from the authority of the nation-state makes possible a model of Islamic society that is libertarian, "an anarchy of true believers" in which there is no need of earthly laws.[37] Qutb wrote:

> Islam is a declaration of the freedom of man from servitude to other men . . . Thus it strives from the beginning to abolish all those systems and governments which are based on the rule of man over men and the servitude of one human being to another. When Islam releases people from this political pressure and presents to them its spiritual message, appealing to their reason, it gives them complete freedom to accept or not to accept its beliefs . . . Whatever system is to be established in the world ought to be on the authority of God, deriving its laws from Him alone. Then every individual is free, under the protection of this universal system, to adopt any belief he wishes to adopt.[38]

In the context of the cold war, when socialist rather than religious radicalism was the greater fear, such passages were, for Binder, enough to present Qutb as embracing modern ideas of individual emancipation from traditional authority, and of religious subjectivity as an individual and intuitive experience that does not require the methods of the traditional clerics. Writing in 1988, Binder went so far as to suggest that "the political significance of Qutb's work may not be as violently revolutionary as it now appears," and its idea of individual freedom could even provide the "social preconditions for the emergence of a liberal bourgeois state."[39] Yet twenty years later the very same passages were cited in the war on terror as evidence of Islamism's totalitarianism, and the authors of the 9/11 Commission report regarded *Milestones* as the inspiration for al-Qaeda.[40] What this points to is that the practical effects of even hard-line Islamist texts are shaped by the political context within which they are read rather than just the unfolding of a violent dynamic inherent to the texts themselves. Qutb himself stated that his advocacy of violence against the Egyptian state was not an ideological principle but a product of political circumstances. On the eve of his execution, he wrote: "If we had known that arrest is merely an arrest, which ends up with a fair trial and legal penalties . . . nobody would have thought of retaliation by force against aggression."[41]

Because of the influence of the idea of a direct causal connection between ideology and terrorism, possession of books such as Qutb's *Milestones* is in danger of being criminalized in Britain. In December 2011, Ahmed Faraz was convicted in Birmingham of possessing and distributing "extremist" books, including *Milestones*, and sentenced to three years in prison (his conviction was quashed by the Court of Appeal after a year of imprisonment).[42] Much of the trial discussion consisted of attempts to interpret the meaning of *Milestones*. In his sentencing, the judge described the book as Manichean, separatist, and excessively violent, and claimed it misinterpreted the teachings of the Qur'an in order to justify a skewed position on Islam.[43] Not only was the state arrogating to itself the right to decide that certain books were too dangerous for its citizens, but in order to do so, the judge had to become a de facto theologian who could distinguish between Qutb's false interpretation of Islam and an officially endorsed moderate Islam. This reformist war on terror had become one in which governments tell believers what their religion really means, and back that up with the power to criminalize alternatives. This ultimately involves a restriction on the freedom of believers to explore their own textual tradition and interpret its meaning for themselves—ironically mirroring the approach of fundamentalists whom such policies ostensibly aim to marginalize. Government attempts to establish an official interpretation of Islam as a benign monolith are as flawed as campaigns to present Islam as a monolithic threat.

Desperately Seeking Moderate Muslims

In practice, the classifying of Muslims into extremist and moderate is highly unstable. The boundary between the two is constantly shifting, putting moderate Muslims in the precarious position of continually being scrutinized for evidence that they really have distanced themselves from Islamist ideology. The act of distinguishing a moderate from an extremist is not a matter of applying objective criteria (such as whether or not one has advocated political violence against fellow citizens) but a complex hermeneutic of suspicion, in which cultural, religious, and political signifiers are parsed for signs of allegiance. Ed Husain, in his *The Islamist*, for instance, used an array of adjectives to distinguish between "true Islam" (which is "spiritual," "moderate," "Sufi," and "traditional") and a distorted form of Islam as "ideology" (which is "extremist," "activist," "Salafi," "literalist," "anti-Western," and "political").[44] But these two sets of terms do not fall neatly into line: spiritual Islam need not be traditional; political Islam need not be literalist; one can be a Sufi who is anti-Western. Cultural attitudes, religious beliefs, and political allegiances are independent of each other. But reformists tended to assume that Muslims' cultural and religious attitudes could serve as indicators of their political allegiances and potential for violence.

In 2007, Paul Berman wrote a twenty-eight-thousand-word essay for the *New Republic* dedicated to establishing whether the Swiss philosopher Tariq Ramadan was a moderate or extremist. Ramadan had been denied entry to the US on national security grounds but was also a fellow of St. Antony's College, Oxford, a professor at Erasmus University Rotterdam, and had served on a British government task force on combating extremism. In his writings, he opposes literalism in the interpretation of Islam and argues for the use of "reason in the treatment of the Texts in order to deal with the new challenges of their age and the social, economic, and political evolution of societies." He says that through such a process Islam could be found to share the core values of Western societies. But he also opposes Western foreign policies and locates himself within the tradition of political Islam and its organizational networks.[45] Berman worked his way through what he regarded as Ramadan's "double discourse" to see if behind the mask of moderation lurked a closet extremist, and concluded that he was indeed an extremist, not really because of anything he said or did, but because he failed to completely distance himself from an Islamist intellectual tradition, which "can only serve to confer legitimacy on the revolutionary Islamist idea, which is willy-nilly bound, in turn, to elevate ever so slightly terrorism's prestige."[46]

David Goodhart, then editor of the liberal British magazine *Prospect* and another significant war on terror reformist, also scrutinized Ramadan. For a while Goodhart held him to be a positive example of a Muslim leader who appropriately called for Muslims to adopt Western values. But the admiration came to an end when Ramadan tried to talk publicly about the root causes of terrorism, writing in the *Guardian* that "a link exists between terrorism and foreign policy."[47] With this betrayal, Goodhart denounced Ramadan as "grievance-seeking" and "responsibility-avoiding." In an "open letter" to Ramadan, Goodhart announced the parting of ways like a lover betrayed: "You, I thought, were different. You were modern, confident, educated, in favour of Muslim integration against religious and ethnic balkanisation . . . I was wrong about you."[48] Ramadan, it seemed, was just like all the rest of them: he talked a nice talk, but deep down, he was not really one of us. Expressing a different view of the origins of terrorism turned him from a moderate Muslim into an extremist Muslim. For *Observer* columnist Nick Cohen, the anti-Iraq war movement in Britain had been purged of moderate Muslims by an extremist leadership.[49] What was it that made someone like Salma Yaqoob, the most high-profile Muslim leader of the antiwar movement, an Islamist, which for Cohen implies being "sexist, homophobic, racist"?[50] Was it that she wears a hijab? Or just that she is a Muslim who disagrees with US-UK foreign policy?

What is most disconcerting to the reformists is Western Muslims who identify with the victims of Western state violence in other parts of the world. To be classed as moderate, Muslims must forget what they know about Palestine, Iraq, and Afghanistan and instead align themselves with the fantasies of the war on terror; they are expected to constrain their religion to the private sphere but also to speak out publicly against extremists' misinterpretations of Islam; they are supposed to see themselves as liberal individuals but also declare an allegiance to the national collective; they are meant to put their capacity for reason above blind faith but not let it lead to criticisms of the West; and they have to publicly condemn using violence to achieve political ends—except when their own governments do so. No wonder moderate Muslims are said to be hard to find.

Identity Liberalism

Like their cold war forebears, war on terror liberals have been haunted by the thought that the individual freedom they celebrate hampers their ability to generate the collective identities necessary to mobilize their cause. Compared to culturalists, with their rousing rhetoric of defending Western civilization against Islamic fanaticism, reformists were left with apparently mediocre slogans of liberal values, pluralism, and tolerance. Would this be enough to wage a cultural war against a full-blooded ideology such as political Islam, which claimed to march in the name of God? On the one hand, reformists aspired to a politics drained of such popular enthusiasms; on the other, they felt compelled to mimic the grand ideological claims of their extremist enemies, finding their own language of life-and-death struggle. To do so they were forced to borrow from a culturalist ideological basket and adopt the idea that the West faced a fundamental cultural threat. But they also redefined what Western identity meant: whereas the culturalist version of the war on terror was presented as ultimately a campaign to defend a Judeo-Christian identity, the reformist version held it to be a battle to defend the liberal values they thought defined the post-1960s West.

In his 2007 book *The Fallout*, for example, *Observer* journalist Andrew Anthony writes in such a vein.[51] In his liberal version of the clash of civilizations, the battle lines are clear: on the one side, the Western Enlightenment and, on the other, what he calls the

"Endarkenment" of the Islamic world. The Arab world, says Anthony, suffers from a "lack of intellectual curiosity [and] self-willed ignorance."[52] Its cultural failure to produce rational, independent thinking implies Western liberals must not shy away from imposing their universal values. British culture has, he says, "over the centuries," tended toward valuing "certain rights, liberties, responsibilities, protections and opportunities," while "many traditional cultures in the Third World" value "petty corruption, sexism, homophobia, tribalism and patriarchal authoritarianism." He only finds it necessary to cite two examples: a case of voting fraud among some South Asians living in Birmingham, England, and rigged exams in an Indian university.[53] But mounting an empirical argument is not the point. Nor is he concerned to explore how, for example, homophobia in traditional cultures might be fought against. What matters is the performance of an identity, the desire for a liberal army to raise the flag of the West so that conservatives no longer monopolize the war on terror's political energies.

A similar picture emerges in Martin Amis's *The Second Plane*, a collection of writings on 9/11 and the war on terror. In a section on "the dependent mind" of "the Muslim male," Amis writes: "No doubt the impulse towards rational inquiry is by now very weak in the rank and file of the Muslim male."[54] And he sees the "Muslim problem" as ultimately rooted in a cultural frustration of sexuality. Thus, he speculates that the anti-Western anger in the Islamist writings of Sayyid Qutb stems from his lack of success in attracting women during his stay in the US in the 1950s. He imagines that suicide bombings and the practice of torture in Arab police cells are the product of sexual frustration or male impotence. The pathological hatred and violence of the enemy in the war on terror is thus presented as the product of a culture that unhealthily represses or misdirects male sexual desire, a culture that is implicitly contrasted to a post-1960s Western culture of sexual freedom. The covering of women's bodies through various kinds of head scarves is, then, the ultimate rejection of Western sexual "openness."

Amis also worries about the potency of Muslim reproduction. He endorses Mark Steyn's book *America Alone*, which argues that within a few decades, Europe will succumb to a demographic takeover by

Muslims with higher rates of reproduction. Noting, "not a single West European country is procreating at the 'replacement rate' of 2.1 births per woman," Amis adds:

> A depopulated and simplified Europe might be tenable in a world without enmity and predation. And that is not our world. The birth rate is 6.76 in Somalia, 6.69 in Afghanistan and 6.58 in Yemen.

For Amis, Europe's valuing of women's autonomy in sexual reproduction hampers the continent in its "demographic war" against immigrants from Muslim countries, because women choose to have fewer children.[55] Behind the anxiety about Muslim sexual repression and the fear of Muslim fecundity lies the question of cultural differences: what makes Muslims a threat is, for Amis, ultimately their rejection of European gender and sexual relations. Amis says: "Geopolitics may not be my natural subject but masculinity is," implying that in explaining Muslim political violence, geopolitics is of less relevance than a culture that perverts masculinity.[56] Thus, Amis stitches together a number of liberal and conservative themes, all of which lead to conventional anxieties about the infiltration of alien cultures. But precisely because this framework differs from familiar patterns of racialization associated with skin color, it can associate itself with the defense of a liberal way of life and appear postracial. In 2006, Amis told an interviewer:

> There's a definite urge—don't you have it?—to say, "The Muslim community will have to suffer until it gets its house in order." What sort of suffering? Not letting them travel. Deportation—further down the road. Curtailing of freedoms. Strip-searching people who look like they're from the Middle East or from Pakistan . . . Discriminatory stuff, until it hurts the whole community and they start getting tough with their children.[57]

What is striking here is the way that some reformists—liberals and former leftists of the 1968 generation who were shaped by their earlier experiences of campaigning on issues of gender, sexuality, religious authority, and censorship—turned the values they once fought for into icons of Western identity. What was once a call to fight for freedom in Western societies degenerated into a call to defend a liberal way of life from foreign enemies.[58] Though the slogan of Enlightenment values was repeatedly invoked, the (universal) Enlightenment principle of rejecting all authority that stands in the way of freely reasoning equal individuals was, strictly speaking, incompatible with the reformist war on terror: its aim was not to encourage autonomous thought but to reshape identity according to a state agenda. On the other hand, the (particular) Western historical experience of enlightened individuals freeing themselves from the religious authority of the church was more amenable to being presented by reformists as a model for Muslims to follow. In seeking to resolve this tension between the universal and the particular, reformists collapsed the distinction between liberalism as a set of universal principles associated with the Enlightenment (that could be the basis for critiques of social institutions) and liberalism as what Edmund Burke called an "inheritance"—the shared customs and habits thought necessary to sustain a specific way of life. Liberalism became a form of identity politics.[59]

In *Democracy in America*, Alexis de Tocqueville wrote that the citizens of the liberal US, "each of them, living apart, is as a stranger to the fate of all the rest."[60] It was this void in liberal social philosophy—its inability to generate common bonds—that historically led to liberalism borrowing from the Left and adopting ideas of social equality and welfare rights in order to embed itself in a collective culture. But the war on terror offered a different glue to hold society together: liberal values—held up as the cultural basis for Western identity and the universal standard of civilization—were taken to imply an identitarian politics of national security rather than an egalitarian politics of social security. Nowhere was this more powerfully manifested than in the image of the liberal intellectual who claimed to stand above identity politics on the hallowed ground of conscience, from where, in the name of universal values, he raged against the West's enemies. A liberal ideological positioning beyond identity made possible the knitting together of Western identity itself.

In its campaign to transform Islamic identity, liberalism itself underwent a transformation: it became an ideology of total war that led its advocates into what Italian theorist Domenico Losurdo calls "a tragic performative contradiction."[61] War on terror liberals reproduced the weaknesses of the conceptual scaffolding they inherited from the cold war. They located the problem of radical political challenges to Western society in alien ideologies that by their very nature were bound to produce violence. In so doing, they disavowed the structural violence on which liberal society itself depended: the ways in which racialized "others" live in a "state of exception" in which liberal norms are permanently suspended—paradoxically, in the name of defending the liberal way of life.[62] Fighting an extremist enemy constructed as Huntington's "ideal enemy"—both "ideologically hostile" and "racially and culturally different"—required that liberalism become an identity politics, a call to recharge the batteries of belonging, to take a stand defending a way of life—militarily, intellectually, and culturally—while still claiming the mantle of a universal civilization.[63]

CHAPTER 4

The Myth of Radicalization

Religion had nothing to do with this. We watched films. We were shown videos with images of the war in Iraq. We were told we must do something big. That's why we met.

—Hussein Omar, interviewed after participating in a plot to bomb the London Underground on July 21, 2005

How a government makes sense of political violence directed against it usually tells us at least as much about the nature of that government as it does about the nature of its violent opponents. After Ulrike Meinhof, of West Germany's Red Army Faction, was found hanged in her prison cell in 1976, officials secretly removed her brain in the hope that neuropathologists might discover why she gave up her successful career as a journalist to cofound the far Left armed group. To state officials it seemed more natural that the source of her violence was located in brain deformities than in the political conflicts of postwar Germany. Likewise, Mau Mau rebels captured in the 1950s by the British army in colonial Kenya were examined by the psychiatrist J. C. Carothers, who claimed to find "hard scientific evidence" demonstrating that the uprising was "not political but psycho-pathological," a conclusion which conveniently validated the need for continuing colonial government.[1]

In the aftermath of 9/11, public discussion of the causes of terrorism was largely curtailed, on the assumption that there could be no explanatory account of terrorism beyond the evil mind-set of the perpetrators. Culturalists, whose analysis tended to prevail, saw terrorists as motivated by a fanaticism that was inherent to Islam and did not require much in the way of further analysis. Those wanting to cover such simple formulae in the veneer of scholarship turned to the founding father of terrorism studies, Walter Laqueur, whose "new terrorism" thesis distinguished between older, political forms of terrorism inspired by nationalism, communism, or fascism and the new "Islamic fundamentalist violence" that he saw as "rooted in fanaticism."[2] By 2004, however, this account of terrorism was showing its limitations. No longer believing that killing and capturing could by themselves bring success, governments began looking for a new discourse that could better guide their counterterrorism efforts. The taboo on discussing the causes of terrorism now had to be broken. The concept of radicalization emerged as a vehicle for policy makers to explore the process by which a terrorist is made and to provide an analytical grounding for preventive strategies that went beyond the use of state violence.

Peter Neumann, director of the International Centre for the Study of Radicalisation at Kings College, London, is one of the founders of the new radicalization discourse; he is also a scholar with access to policy makers in Westminster and Washington. In 2008 he wrote about the value of the concept of radicalization:

> Following the attacks against the United States on 11 September 2001 . . . it suddenly became very difficult to talk about the "roots of terrorism," which some commentators claimed was an effort to excuse and justify the killing of innocent civilians. Even so, it seemed obvious [then] that some discussion about the underlying factors that had given rise to this seemingly new phenomenon was urgent and necessary, and so experts and officials started referring to the idea of "radicalisation" whenever they wanted to talk about "what goes on before the bomb goes off." In the highly charged atmosphere following the September 11 attacks, it was through the notion of radicalisation that a discussion about the political, economic, social and psychological forces that underpin terrorism and political violence became possible again.[3]

In the context of the evolving war on terror, this new discussion of radicalization could present itself as the wiser, more liberal alternative to the simple accounts of terrorism offered immediately after

9/11. It acknowledged that terrorism was a problem that could be investigated, analyzed, and subjected to policy solutions beyond the use of physical force. In actuality, however, the radicalization discourse was, from the beginning, circumscribed to the demands of counterterrorism policy makers rather than an attempt to objectively study how terrorism comes into being. Rather than provide a location for the scholarly understanding of the causes of terrorism—what Kant called the "public use of reason," aimed at the general enlightenment of society—the radicalization discourse limited itself to the "private use of reason" (serving the needs of a "particular civil post or office"), constraining the intellectual process to the needs of government security establishments.[4]

As such, the concept of radicalization inherited at birth a number of built-in, limiting assumptions. Those perpetrating terrorist violence are drawn from a larger pool of extremists who share an ideology that inspires their actions; entry into this wider pool of extremists can be predicted by individual or group psychological or theological factors; and knowledge of these factors could enable governments to develop policies that reduce the risk of terrorism. The study of radicalization, ostensibly a reflection on the causes of terrorism, is thus in practice limited to a much narrower question: why do some individual Muslims support an extremist interpretation of Islam that leads to violence? This question, of course, takes terrorist violence to be a product of how Islam is interpreted and so renders irrelevant consideration of terrorism not carried out by Muslims. An a priori distinction is drawn between the new terrorism, seen as originating in Islamist theology, and the old terrorism of nationalist or Leftist political violence, for which the question of radicalization is rarely posed. Answers to the question of what drives this process are to exclude ascribing any causative role to the actions of Western governments or their allies in other parts of the world; instead, individual psychological or theological journeys, largely removed from social and political circumstances, are claimed to be the root cause of the radicalization process. While some accounts acknowledge politics as a component—using euphemistic phrases such as "grievances against real or perceived injustices"—this is only done in the face of overwhelming empirical evidence, before they quickly move on to the more comfortable ground of psychology or theology. While terrorist violence is not seen as having political causes, nonviolent political activity by Muslim groups that are thought to share an ideology with terrorists is seen as another manifestation of the same radicalization process, with roots in individual theological and/or psychological journeys; it is thereby depoliticized and seen as complicit with religiously inspired terrorism. As historian Mark Sedgwick argues in one of the few critical reflections on the radicalization discourse:

> The concept of radicalisation emphasizes the individual and, to some extent, the ideology and the group, and significantly de-emphasizes the wider circumstances—the "root causes" that it became so difficult to talk about after 9/11, and that are still often not brought into analyses. So long as the circumstances that produce Islamist radicals' declared grievances are not taken into account, it is inevitable that the Islamist radical will often appear as a "rebel without a cause."[5]

In pursuing this path, radicalization analysts supply what policy makers demand. Following the murder of Dutch filmmaker Theo van Gogh in Amsterdam in 2004 and the 7/7 attacks on the London transport system in 2005, the issue of homegrown terrorism, involving citizens of European countries carrying out violence domestically, came to prominence. Government officials, first in the Netherlands and later elsewhere, began to devise counterradicalization policies they hoped would preempt such violence. Their assumption was that knowledge of the indicators of individual or group radicalization would allow for the construction of an early warning system to detect theological violence. Authorities came to believe they could monitor and profile Muslim citizens for these signs of radicalization and then intervene to prevent the drift to extremism. Rather than providing governments with a full analysis of the causes of homegrown terrorism, think tanks and terrorism studies departments—which had been established in universities after 9/11 to attract new government funding for national security research—began to model the process by which an individual was thought to become a supporter of the extremist ideologies assumed to lie behind terrorist violence. After all, addressing the wider political context of terrorism was a nonstarter with government officials, for whom the basic parameters of foreign policy in the Middle East and South Asia were written in stone.

For those establishing themselves as purveyors of this knowledge, the period from 2004 onward was a time of new opportunities, new funding, and new audiences, first in Europe and then in the US, especially following the election in 2008 of a president who wanted a new way of talking about counterterrorism and who was confronted, a year and a half into his term, with the attempted car bombing of Times Square by an American Muslim. Disraeli once remarked, at the high point of British colonial expansion, "The East is a career." Edward Said used the phrase as the epigraph to his *Orientalism*. Today counterradicalization is a career, as young scholars enter the mini-industry of national security think tanks, terrorism studies departments, law enforcement counterterrorism units, and intelligence services to work on modeling radicalization. Of course, scholars of political violence should want societies to make use of their work in order to reduce such violence. But true scholarship also involves a duty to question the underlying assumptions that define the discipline, particularly when those assumptions reflect the priorities of governments that are themselves parties to the conflict under investigation.

Whereas before 2001 the term "radicalization" had occasionally been used informally in academic literature to refer to a shift toward more radical politics (usually not referring to Muslims), by 2004 the term had acquired its new meaning of a psychological or theological process by which Muslims move toward extremist views. By 2010, over one hundred articles on radicalization were being published in peer-reviewed academic journals each year. In this chapter, I examine the work of some of the leading scholars of radicalization and show how their analyses owe more to the aims and objectives of the states that are the primary consumers of their literature than to an objective study of the subject. This is not solely a matter of biases introduced by funding, by the revolving doors between government agencies and think tanks, or by other institutional pressures, but rather a matter of ideological assumptions that determine what counts as legitimate and illegitimate within the terms of this discourse. The result is that radicalization scholars systematically fail to address the reality of the political conflicts they claim they want to understand. Instead a concept has been contrived that introduces biases and prejudices into officials' thinking; in turn, this thinking shapes government practices and structures introduced to combat radicalization, resulting in discrimination and unwarranted restrictions on civil liberties. My method is not to challenge the conclusions of radicalization scholars with alternative sets of empirical data but rather to explore the conceptual frameworks used to make sense of the data where they exist, and to show that even the limited data that are available ought to lead to different conclusions.

A Cultural-Psychological Predisposition

A 2004 article by Walter Laqueur provides a bridge between the older terrorism studies and the then–emerging radicalization literature and a useful starting point. Lacqueur, a seasoned Washington insider who first came to prominence in the 1950s as Israel's representative to the CIA-funded Congress for Cultural Freedom,[6] begins by asserting that "al Qaeda was founded and September 11 occurred not because of a territorial dispute or the feeling of national oppression but because of a religious commandment—jihad and the establishment of *shari'ah*." His argument for rejecting any linkage between terrorism and either poverty or causes such as Palestine is that there are many groups who suffer poverty or oppression but not all resort to violence. With this he moves away from a macro focus on economics or politics and descends to the level of the individual: "How to explain that out of 100 militants believing with equal intensity in the justice of their cause, only a very few will actually engage in terrorist actions?" Here we confront the founding question of the radicalization discourse, which, Laqueur states, has been hitherto neglected. Answering it will provide a root cause that no longer references the wider political context but instead focuses on what he calls "a cultural-psychological predisposition." Framing the root cause question in this way, and providing a model of this "predisposition," also, of course, offers intelligence and law enforcement agencies the possibility of an analytical framework that can be used for surveillance purposes. Scholarship that associates a particular kind of predisposition, be it cultural, psychological, or some combination, with terrorist violence enables intelligence gatherers to use that predisposition as a proxy for terrorist risk, and to structure their surveillance efforts accordingly.

To illustrate the argument, Laqueur turns his attention to Europe, which he describes as "probably the most vulnerable battlefield" and "the main base of terrorist support groups." He claims that this is the result of a process "facilitated by the growth of Muslim communities, the growing tensions with the native population, and the relative freedom with which radicals could organize in certain mosques and cultural organizations." The failure of "Muslim newcomers" to integrate into Europe—"cultural and social integration was certainly not what the newcomers wanted"—reflected a desire to maintain a separate religious and ethnic identity. This, in turn, led to "the radicalization of the second generation of immigrants" that featured acute feelings of "resentment and hostility" toward the authorities and non-Muslim neighbors, nourished by underachievement and "sexual repression." Hence a "free-floating aggression" underlies the "milieu in which Islamist terrorism and terrorist support groups in Western Europe developed."[7]

In this early account, the main components and confusions of the radicalization discourse are already present: the focus on the religious beliefs and psychology of individuals and the downplaying of political factors; the view that terrorism is rooted in a wider youth culture of anger and aggression; and the listing of factors likely to drive individuals toward support for terrorism, such as anti-Western attitudes, religious fundamentalism, and self-segregation. Already the term "radicalization" tends to merge a number of meanings—disaffection, youth alienation, radical dissent, religious fundamentalism, propensity to violence—which ought to be kept analytically distinct. Already unfounded and biased assumptions about the social and political history of Muslims in Europe are being introduced, and a causal process from a "cultural-psychological predisposition" to violence is being asserted without any substantial evidence. Finally, it is worth noting that there is no mention of US and UK government rhetoric on the need to fight a war against radical Islam, of the war on Iraq, of the uniting of millions of European Muslims and non-Muslims to actively oppose it, and of the failure of these mobilizations to prevent the war by democratic means.

Later writers of works in the radicalization discourse can be seen as attempts to systematize the basic framework laid out by Laqueur in 2004; they travel in a number of directions from this starting point. For some the question of religious belief—the cultural part of Laqueur's predisposition—is most significant. If a set of religious beliefs, an ideology, can be identified that terrorists share with a wider group of radicals but which moderate Muslims reject, then a model can be developed in which such beliefs are seen as indicators of radicalization, a point along a pathway to becoming a terrorist. This can be called the theological approach to radicalization. It offers a scientific basis for security officials to target surveillance and investigative resources at a group of people who happen to have specific religious beliefs—say, for example, Salafi Muslims. The problem is that if there is no real reason to think that these radical religious beliefs are associated with terrorist violence, then the theological radicalization model is merely legitimizing unwarranted state intrusion into the private religious lives of large numbers of citizens.

The other direction of travel from Laqueur's 2004 paper is to attend to individual and group psychology. What is the process by which some individuals' mental states of alienation or resentment escalate to extremist beliefs whereas others' do not? This psychological approach to radicalization offers the same predictive possibilities, and a more complex account is developed. A psychological process, such as a group dynamic or a struggle with identity, is seen as interacting with a process of acquiring an extremist ideology. A particular combination of psychological factors and religious beliefs becomes the best guide to identifying radicalization. Implicit in both the theological and psychological approaches is the notion that the circulation of extremist ideas, seen as a kind of virus, is able to turn people into violent radicals. This then leads law enforcement agencies to try to prevent exposure to this virus, whether it is found in the contents of books or Web sites, or in the words of preachers or radical activists.

One further point worth noting: because security officials are interested in patterns of belief and behavior that *correlate* with terrorist risk, irrespective of whether they *cause* terrorism, questions of causality are usually left unaddressed in this discourse, despite theorists' claims to be interested in root causes. Instead of answering the question of what causes terrorism—the key question demanded by Kant's "public use of reason"—radicalization discourse claims predictive powers but lacks explanatory powers. Scholars generally talk of factors or indicators that are statistically associated with radicalization, and which intelligence agencies can put to use in their efforts to detect future threats, while tending to refrain from reflecting on the larger question of causality.

Radicalization as a Theological Process

A 2009 study by Daveed Gartenstein-Ross and Laura Grossman, entitled "Homegrown Terrorists in the US and UK: An Empirical Examination of the Radicalization Process," published by the Foundation for Defense of Democracies (FDD), provides a case study of scholarship that attempts to demonstrate the central role of theology in radicalization. While the study is typical of many in its approach and conclusions, it stands out for the authors' claims to rigor—"an empirical examination of behavioral manifestations of the radicalization process in 117 homegrown 'jihadist' terrorists"—and in the interest it has attracted among policy makers in Washington.

The key question the study sets out to answer: "What clues might there be that an individual is self-identifying with, or being indoctrinated into, jihadist ideology?" The data for the study is statements by terrorists themselves, trial transcripts, and newspaper reports that provide biographical information on "every known Islamic homegrown terrorist in the US and UK who perpetrated an attack, attempted to do so, or illegally supported Islamic terrorism through the end of October 2008." Based on this data, the authors claim to discover clusters of indicators that recur sufficiently to suggest a shared trajectory of radicalization. The indicators are not regarded as sufficient conditions to produce a terrorist but as useful markers of risk.

> This study primarily focuses on specific behavioral changes that homegrown terrorists went through as they radicalized. It examines six manifestations of the radicalization process: the adoption of a legalistic interpretation of Islam, coming to trust only a select and ideologically rigid group of religious authorities, viewing the West and Islam as irreconcilably opposed, manifesting a low tolerance for perceived religious deviance, attempting to impose religious beliefs on others, and the expression of radical political views.

The study concludes that the first five factors—all associated with religious ideology—are sufficiently present in enough cases to demonstrate that

> the individuals' theological understanding was a relatively strong factor in their radicalization.

There are a number of rather obvious problems with the study that can be noted initially. The study does not include a control group of persons who are not terrorists, and so it has no basis on which to associate terrorism with the religious manifestations it is considering. There seems to be no basis on which these six manifestations of the radicalization process were chosen as opposed to other possibilities. One might also ask how much insight into ideology can be gleaned from breaking down a person's beliefs into six discrete religious and political manifestations. Even if these problems are set aside, there remains the difficulty that selecting to study the category of so-called jihadist terrorism assumes that this form of terrorism has specific causes that differ from other forms of violence. In fact, this assumption runs up against even the limited data gathered by Gartenstein-Ross and Grossman. The study's sixth ideological manifestation, what it refers to as the expression of "radical political views," is summarized:

> Western powers have conspired against Islam to subjugate it, both physically and morally. At the same time, Muslims worldwide have lost their faith, and lack the strength that they possessed during Muhammad's time. The only proper response to the present situation is military action.

It turns out that belief in this political narrative scores highest among the manifestations examined; indeed, there are no cases in which this political dimension was found to be absent. But the study seeks to evade the implications of its own data. Having noted that the political component of radicalization appears more consistently than the theological, the authors immediately caution that to conclude politics is more significant than religion would be "crude" because "when individuals are committed to a physical fight against the West, it is natural that they will try to justify this on multiple levels"—which rather defeats the purpose of looking to a person's own account of their beliefs, as the study sets out to do. The authors go on to ask whether

> individuals' religious awakening *preceded* or followed their political awakening. For the homegrown terrorists who exhibited signs of political radicalization, the religious awakening preceded the political awakening 40.7 percent of the time. In contrast, we found that political radicalization preceded any kind of religious radicalization 11.6 percent of the time. (In the other 47.7 percent of cases, it is unclear whether political or religious ideology came first.) Thus, in our view, a nuanced look at the role of religious ideology in homegrown terrorists' radicalization should find that religion likely plays an important role.[8]

But whether religious awakening or political radicalization comes first in the process of becoming a terrorist is only relevant if we assume that one must be a gateway to the other; only then does it make sense to ask the order in which these manifestations occurred. No empirical evidence is offered for this assumption. Within the study's own framework, a more natural interpretation of the data would be that religious awakening is neither a precursor to political radicalization nor vice versa, and that political radicalization is the key factor in becoming a terrorist. In any case, without including a comparison with cases of radicalization that did not result in terrorism, it is impossible to draw any positive conclusions that associate a particular set of beliefs with jihadist terrorism.

Why this eagerness to downplay political factors, even when the data suggests otherwise? Part of the answer might lie in the politics of the study's publishers and funders. The FDD is one of several neoconservative pressure groups set up in the wake of 9/11 that helped build support for the US war on Iraq. The study was funded by three private foundations, one of which was the Lynde and Harry Bradley Foundation that donated more than $1.2 million to the neoconservative Project for the New American Century and has provided millions of dollars to Islamophobic propaganda groups in the US, such as the Center for Security Policy and the David Horowitz Freedom Center.[9] For such groups it is convenient to root terrorism in religious ideology rather than in the political interaction of Western foreign policy and Muslim terrorist groups. But perhaps the main reason is a bias in favor of knowledge claims that can be put to use by national security practitioners without institutional discomfort. Breaking down religious extremism into different manifestations that can be scientifically associated with terrorism is knowledge that law enforcement and intelligence agencies can easily utilize; on the other hand, painting a more reflexive picture, in which state agencies and terrorists are caught in a dynamic political conflict, is much harder to sell. In an introductory section to the FDD study, Brian Jenkins Mead, a prominent analyst of terrorism at the RAND Corporation, makes clear its potential use by law enforcement and intelligence agencies: "The indicators identified by Gartenstein-Ross and Grossman . . . have value . . . in deciding whether to initiate a closer look or to not waste limited resources where it is not warranted."[10] And the FDD study's lead author has, according to his Web site, provided

> instruction to members of the US military preparing for deployments to the Horn of Africa, Afghanistan, and the Persian Gulf. He also designs training courses and specific modules for use by US government agencies, including the State Department's Office of Anti-Terrorism Assistance.[11]

Radicalization as a Theological-Psychological Process

Counterradicalization policy in the US and Europe is pluralist and involves making compromises among multiple approaches within the limits of the basic assumptions outlined above. Radicalization scholarship reflects this range of approaches. While accounts that focus purely on religious ideology have had a certain influence, at least as significant have been more complex models that involve processes and interactions among theological and social psychological journeys. Religious beliefs by themselves do not drive individuals to violence; rather, the picture is one in which ideology becomes more extreme in response to what is called a "cognitive opening," an identity crisis, or a group-bonding process. This implies a more sophisticated counter-radicalization practice that addresses the interdependence of theology and emotions, identity, and group dynamics.

Among the most prominent exponents of this perspective is Marc Sageman, whose *Understanding Terror Networks* and *Leaderless Jihad: Terror Networks in the Twenty-First Century* together constitute perhaps the most ambitious attempt to develop a comprehensive theory of radicalization.[12] His model has come to be known as the "bunch of guys" theory because of its emphasis on friendship and kinship as central to the radicalization process. Sageman, a psychiatrist, was, as noted earlier, formerly a CIA operations officer specializing in Afghanistan, and he was based in Islamabad from 1987 to 1989, where he ran "unilateral programs with the Afghan Mujahedin."[13] (Who better to carry out research on the causes of "jihad" than someone who used to be an official organizing the US government's funding of the Afghan jihad against the Soviets? Unsurprisingly, that particular history plays no role in his analysis.) Sageman has also been an adviser to the New York City Police Department (NYPD) for a number of years, and in 2008 was named its scholar-in-residence.[14]

In line with the basic assumptions of the radicalization literature, Sageman rejects accounts that consider economic or political circumstances as significant, on the grounds that these factors affect millions of people whereas only a small number become terrorists. And he breaks with those who think religious ideology can by itself create a terrorist: "These perspectives imply an overly passive view of terrorists, who are the recipients of social forces or slaves to appealing ideas." Instead, he argues convincingly that we need to ask how terrorists interpret the structural conditions that they are confronted with and how they attempt to forge a common struggle in response.

In addressing these questions, Sageman makes strong claims to academic rigor, claiming to bring the methods of social science (statistics, sampling theory, survey techniques, measurement, data analysis) to the study of radicalization. Yet the object of his study lacks any objective definition. The closest we get is his statement that he is interested in analyzing

> the men responsible for the September 11, 2001, attacks and all those who, like them, threaten the United States and the West on behalf of a larger community, the vanguard trying to establish a certain version of an Islamist utopia.

This, he says, gives him a database of around five hundred persons "linked" to the 9/11 attackers. Based on this sample, he claims, the most striking feature of the jihadist profile is that

> joining the global Islamist terrorism social movement was based to a great degree on friendship and kinship . . . About two-thirds of the people in the sample were friends with other people who joined together or already had some connection to terrorism.

He concludes that there are two major pathways into terrorism: the bunch of guys deciding collectively to join a terrorist organization; and joining a childhood friend who is already a terrorist. Social bonds, therefore, "come before any ideological commitment."

Sageman delves into the process by which a bunch of guys radicalizes, trying to establish what it is about the dynamics of the group that brings them to the point of supporting terrorism. He identifies four prongs to this process: first, a sense of moral outrage about a perceived injustice in the world; second, "an enabling interpretation," such as that there is a war on Islam, which places this outrage in the wider context of a moral conflict; third, personal experiences, such as of discrimination, which become "another manifestation of the war on Islam"; and fourth, mobilizing networks.

> Only other people who share their outrage, beliefs, and experiences, but who are further along the path to violence or who are willing to

> explore it with them, can help them cross the line from venting their anger to becoming terrorists.

Thus, a "natural and intense loyalty to the group, inspired by a violent Salafi script, transformed alienated young Muslims into fanatic terrorists." For Sageman it is the embedding of theological radicalism within a group dynamic that is the root cause of radicalization.

He argues that the response should be a reformist approach to the war on terror: policy makers should understand that the "war against the al Qaeda social movement is basically a battle for the hearts and minds of the Muslim community." He summarizes as follows: community policing can preempt the radicalization process by reducing alienation; the American Dream of equal opportunity and individualism is the best way of integrating Muslims; and the Iraq war was counterproductive, because it fostered moral outrage. Above all, governments should work with pro-Western Muslim leaders, and assist them to convince young Muslims that the US is not engaged in a "war on Islam."[15] Sageman's work provides an analytical basis for those who favor a managerial approach to Muslim grievances, using soft power methods to contain radical dissent and promote shared values without asking too many questions about where that radicalism comes from.

Sageman's stress on social networks has been a major influence on how law enforcement and intelligence agencies understand radicalization, and has obvious implications for investigators. If tomorrow's terrorists are likely to be today's associates of terrorists, then that gives agencies a simple formula for identifying suspects: Suspicion by association has long been a staple of counterterrorism policing anyway. But claiming social bonds to be the root cause of terrorism is inadequate. Even if we accept the implication that terrorism spreads like a virus from a person already infected to his associates, all we have done is explain the process of infection; we have said nothing of why the virus exists in the first place. More importantly, Sageman's work shares with the rest of the radicalization discourse a failure to distinguish between radical beliefs and violent methods. Despite his stated aim to explore how terrorists interpret their situation and how they decide to respond, we get no discussion of the conditions under which violence is chosen over other means. Even if his model offered a plausible explanation of how radical ideas circulate, it has nothing to say on what causes supporters of such ideas to favor violence over other means of advancing their cause. By default, then, the question of violence can only be answered by assuming certain ideologies are inherently violent. The picture is one in which the Salafi script is already a predisposition to violence that only needs a friendship dynamic to activate it. Sageman argues, with regard to al-Qaeda and the "many other terrorist groups that collaborate in their operations [that] Salafi ideology determines its mission, sets its goals, and guides its tactics."[16] In other words, as this bunching of guys intensifies their beliefs in a radical theological worldview, violence is likely to follow. For that violence to pose a terrorist threat, the only other necessary condition is that the social network is able to successfully find the "global Salafi jihad," in order to access skills and resources.[17] Thus, for Sageman, jihadi terrorism is the product of a socialization process of friendship and kinship, progressive intensification of beliefs leading to acceptance of the Salafi ideology, and a link to know-how and support.[18] At the heart of his model remains an unexamined assumption that violence has its origins in dangerous theological ideas.

A similar approach is favored by Quintan Wiktorowicz, another of the leading advocates of a combined theological and social psychological model of radicalization. Wiktorowicz spent a number of months in London in 2002 conducting ethnographic fieldwork with al-Muhajiroun, the radical Islamist group founded by Omar Bakri Muhammad. This research was published in 2005 as *Radical Islam Rising: Muslim Extremism in the West.*[19] He subsequently worked at the US embassy in London at a time, after the 7/7 terrorist attacks, when the US government became keenly interested in the potential radicalization of Britain's Muslim population. Diplomatic cables subsequently published by WikiLeaks reveal that the US embassy in London made available grants of $50,000 to support antiextremist projects among UK Muslims, including the possibility of fostering an "anti-extremist genre" of Bollywood films.[20] Wiktorowicz built up a network of links in Britain and observed the impact of the UK government's Preventing Violent Extremism policy. In early 2011, given the White House's interest in developing similar policies, Wiktorowicz was appointed to the National Security Council and credited with developing the Obama administration's counterradicalization policy.[21]

In his *Radical Islam Rising*, Wiktorowicz seeks to answer the question of why "thousands of young Britons are attracted to the panoply of radical Islamic movements with bases or branches in the United Kingdom, including Hizb ut-Tahrir, Supporters of Shariah, al-Muhajiroun, and al-Qaeda." Al-Muhajiroun is taken as a case study. Like Sageman, he emphasizes the way that groups place grievances within an interpretative "frame" and on the importance of socialization into the group's construction of reality to create a "network of shared meaning." But his account of radicalization adds still more levels of complexity while maintaining the same underlying assumptions. He introduces the concept of cognitive opening, which refers to a psychological crisis in which previously accepted beliefs are shaken and an individual becomes receptive to other views and perspectives. This might be caused by emotional distress (such as a death in the family), experiences of discrimination, political repression, confusion over identity, or as a result of "consciousness raising" or persuasion by activists. Those who experience a cognitive opening may then attempt to find religious answers to the discontent that has prompted it, through initiating a process of "religious seeking." Finally, exposure to networks of radicals socializes individuals into participation in the movement, as would-be activists are "cultured" into accepting the religious authority of the movement's leaders and adopting their ideology.[22]

Wiktorowicz begins his study with an account of two erstwhile members of al-Muhajiroun—Asif Mohammed Hanif and Omar Khan Sherif—who in 2003 attempted to carry out a suicide attack on behalf of Hamas at the Mike's Place bar in Tel Aviv. The rest of the text effectively becomes an attempt to explain how these two British citizens could possibly be willing to carry out such an act of violence. Yet the people studied by Wiktorowicz, through his interviews and participant observations, are radical activists, not terrorists, a distinction that gets lost in the attempt to construct a model of radicalization. Most of al-Muhajiroun's activities were ideological, but the group supported violence in certain contexts, and individual activists and former activists have been involved in violent actions. But Wiktorowicz offers little reflection on what factors legitimized or delegitimized the use of violence within the group. In fact, during the 1990s, Omar Bakri Muhammad made use of the Islamic concept of *'aqd al-aman*, or covenant of security, to legitimize an arrangement with the British security services in which his followers in Britain were not permitted to break the law, and he was likely a source of intelligence, in return for allowing his movement to propagate its ideology freely.[23] But in January 2005, he cited the intensifying war on terror and the pressures it was putting Muslims under in Britain as reasons for saying the covenant no longer held, and for the first time he encouraged his followers to join al-Qaeda.[24] What is significant is that this shift occurred not because of any theological reinterpretation or because of changes in group psychology, but because of the changed political context.

In Wiktorowicz's study, as with Sageman's work, the question of what causes radical religious beliefs becomes a proxy for the question of what causes violence. As Wiktorowicz himself acknowledges at the end of his study, the social psychological process by which individuals become active in radical Islamist groups is "not all that different" from moderate, nonviolent Muslim groups, or from non-Islamic social movements, even if the content of the ideology differs; it therefore becomes impossible to use his account of that process to credibly explain why violence occurs.[25] Like other radicalization scholars, Wiktorowicz argues correctly that by themselves political and economic circumstances are insufficient to account for radical activism. For support, he quotes Trotsky from *The History of the Russian Revolution*: "The mere existence of privations is not enough to cause an insurrection; if it were, the masses would be always in revolt." It follows, he states, that the real question is "why some aggrieved individuals choose to join Islamic groups while others do not"—a question which is answered by considering psychological and theological journeys.[26] This is a different inference from that made by Trotsky, who follows the above quote with these sentences, which Wiktorowicz's text does not include:

> It is necessary that the bankruptcy of the social régime, being conclusively revealed, should make these privations intolerable, and that new conditions and new ideas should open the prospect of a revolutionary way out. Then in the cause of the great aims conceived by them, those same masses will prove capable of enduring doubled and tripled privations.[27]

Wiktorowicz's rejection of a mechanical model of grievances directly causing revolutionary action is convincing. But whereas this leads him to turn to the individual religious and cognitive trajectory, he ignores the other possibilities suggested by Trotsky's text, which emphasize the perceived legitimacy of the present state of affairs and the plausibility of alternatives—in other words, politics. From this perspective the question would be, What kinds of political circumstances, combined with what kinds of political narratives (even if expressed in religious terms), are necessary for particular kinds of violence to be seen as legitimate within a given movement? This is a question Sageman and Wiktorowicz are unable to address with their models.

Radicalization Models as Policing Tools

The view shared by Sageman and Wiktorowicz—that radicalization is essentially a theological-psychological process in which dangerous religious beliefs and identities, activated by group dynamics or cognitive openings, transform individuals into terrorists—has been influential among law enforcement agencies. In 2007, the Intelligence Division and Counter-Terrorism Bureau of the NYPD published a study, entitled "Radicalization in the West: The Homegrown Threat," that outlined a simplified version of this kind of radicalization model. It was the first time the NYPD had chosen to publish a document that claimed any kind of scholarly credentials; it did so, it stated, in order "to contribute to the debate among intelligence and law enforcement agencies on how best to counter this emerging threat." The report is backed by outside experts, such as Brian Jenkins Mead of the RAND Corporation, and strongly influenced by the work of Sageman and Wiktorowicz; it identifies "jihadist ideology" as the key driver of radicalization and suggests four phases an individual passes through in going from being "unremarkable" to a person "quite likely to be involved in the planning or implementation of a terrorist act": preradicalization (before they are exposed to "jihadi-Salafi Islam"); self-identification (they begin to explore Salafi Islam as a result of a cognitive opening, which leads to the breakdown of an existing identity and to associations with like-minded others); indoctrination (the progressive intensification of their beliefs which, as a result of group socialization, leads to the complete adoption of the ideology); and jihadization (their acceptance of their individual duty to participate in jihad). These four stages are described as a "funnel" through which ordinary persons become terrorists, as their religious beliefs become progressively more radical. The NYPD study argues that each of these four stages of radicalization has a distinct set of indicators that allow predictions to be made about future terrorist risks. For example, stage two of the radicalization process has "typical signatures" that include:

- becoming alienated from one's former life; affiliating with like-minded individuals;
- joining or forming a group of like-minded individuals in a quest to strengthen one's dedication to Salafi Islam;
- giving up cigarettes, drinking, gambling and urban hip-hop gangster clothes;
- wearing traditional Islamic clothing, growing a beard;
- becoming involved in social activism and community issues.

The study acknowledges that these behaviors are "subtle and non-criminal," but nevertheless, the need "to identify those entering this process at the earliest possible stage" means that intelligence gathering based on these indicators is "the critical tool in helping to thwart an attack."[28]

The NYPD's study bases its analysis on eleven actual and alleged plots that took place in the US, the UK, Spain, the Netherlands, Canada, and Australia, each involving a handful of perpetrators. Not only is this too small a sample upon which to base positive knowledge claims about the relationship between religious behaviors and terrorism, it also lumps together individuals in widely varying social and political contexts. Additionally, there is no control group of individuals who fit the pattern of religious behaviors associated with radicalization but do not become terrorists. In order to show a correlation between a set of religious behaviors and terrorism, it would be necessary not only to show that terrorists are statistically likely to have passed through a process in which those behaviors were manifest, but also that nonterrorists are statistically unlikely to show the same behaviors. In fact, the behaviors the NYPD study associates with radicalization are common to large numbers of people who never become terrorists. Likewise, the study does not consider cases of terrorism that are not carried out by Muslims, for example, terrorist activity carried out by individuals in far Right movements. By failing to compare across cases of terrorism with different ideological motivations, the study ignores the possibility of indicators of risk that are not specific to Muslims but have a general applicability to terrorism in general. The claim that terrorism carried out by Muslims is driven by a radicalization process different from other forms of terrorism should, if made, be derived from whatever case-based evidence is available to support it rather than assumed as a given in the design of the study. Finally, even constraining ourselves to the small number of cases the NYPD study actually describes—and ignoring the absence of a control group and the absence of comparisons with other forms of terrorism—the study offers weak evidence for any correlation between religious behaviors and terrorist activity, because its assertions linking religious behaviors and terrorist acts are generally impressionistic, arbitrary, and lacking in any analytic rigor.

Following Sageman and Wiktorowicz's emphasis on the group dynamic in radicalization, the NYPD considers it crucial to identify the venues where socialization into radical ideology is occurring, what it refers to as "radicalization incubators." These the study describes as "places where like-minded individuals will congregate as they move through the radicalization process." They can be mosques but are more likely to be "cafes, cab driver hangouts, flophouses, prisons, student associations, non-governmental organizations, hookah (water pipe) bars, butcher shops and book stores [or] extremist websites and chatrooms."[29] Thus, in the hands of the NYPD, Sageman's and Wiktorowicz's radicalization scholarship becomes a prospectus for mass surveillance of Muslim populations.

An investigation by the Associated Press, published in a series of articles beginning in August 2011, revealed that the NYPD's Intelligence Division, headed by thirty-year veteran of the CIA David Cohen, has considered every aspect of Muslim life in and around New York worthy of observation and infiltration. More than 250 mosques in New York and New Jersey and hundreds more "hot spots," such as restaurants, cafés, bookshops, community organizations, and student associations, have been listed as potential security risks for reasons that included endorsing conservative religious views or having devout customers. A secret team known as the Demographics Unit has dispatched undercover officers (known as "rakers") and recruited informants ("mosque crawlers") to eavesdrop at these "locations of interest" to listen for "hostility to the United States."[30] The unit invested resources in mapping "residential concentrations" of different ethnic groups within the tristate area, seeking to "gauge sentiment" and identify locations "where community members socialize." The communities to be monitored were identified on the basis of their origins in twenty-eight majority-Muslim countries, as well as those described as "American Black Muslim." Staff of the NYPD's Moroccan Initiative have watched Moroccan restaurants, gyms, barbershops, meat markets, and taxi companies—and compiled a list of every known Moroccan taxi driver.[31] Muslims who changed their names to sound more traditionally American or who adopted Arabic names were investigated and catalogued in secret NYPD intelligence files.[32] One of the architects of this surveillance program was CIA analyst Larry Sanchez, who worked within the Intelligence Division from 2002 to 2010 while remaining on active duty with the CIA. He reportedly told associates that its methods were modeled on Israeli techniques used in the military occupation of the West Bank.[33] It is clear that none of this activity was based on investigating reasonable suspicions of criminal activity. According to a deposition by Assistant Chief Thomas Galati of the Intelligence Division, the work of the Demographics Unit produced no criminal leads between 2006 and 2012, and probably did not before then either.[34]

Another part of the NYPD's Intelligence Division is the Analytic Unit, headed until recently by Mitchell Silber, who coauthored the NYPD's radicalization study. It consists of a team of two dozen civilian analysts who are responsible for the cultural analysis of Muslim communities in the US and abroad.[35] The NYPD Intelligence Division also has a program for international efforts, the International Liaison Program, with offices in eleven foreign capitals. The NYPD's 2010 budget for counterterrorism and intelligence was over $100 million, with a thousand officers reportedly employed.[36]

Central to the NYPD's counterradicalization strategy has been the use of informants. In 2012, a Muslim-American student decided to end his relationship with the department and speak publicly. He told the Associated Press that he had been instructed to take photographs inside mosques, collect the names of innocent people attending study groups on Islam, and to "bait" Muslims into making inflammatory statements. Shamiur Rahman, aged nineteen, said he had followed a police strategy called "create and capture," which involved initiating conversations about jihad or terrorism, then capturing the response and sending it to the NYPD's Intelligence Unit. He had earned as much as one thousand dollars a month for his work. He had begun working for the police after a string of minor marijuana arrests; an NYPD plainclothes officer approached him in a Queens jail and asked whether he wanted to turn his life around. Among his assignments was spying on the Muslim Student Association at John Jay College in Manhattan, where he was asked to note down "radical rhetoric." Rahman said he never witnessed any criminal activity or saw anybody do anything wrong. He eventually felt his work for the NYPD was "detrimental to the constitution."[37] According to the Associated Press investigation, by 2006 the police had identified thirty-one Muslim student associations and labeled seven of them "of concern," including branches at Brooklyn College, Baruch College, City College, Hunter College, La Guardia Community College, and Queens College.[38] Many of the colleges had informants or undercover agents operating among the student population. In another case, the NYPD sent an undercover officer to student rallies protesting against Israel's Operation Cast Lead attack on Gaza in 2009. The officer pretended to be a fervent sympathizer with the

Palestinian cause and sought to ingratiate himself with activists. He constantly used violent and provocative rhetoric, in an attempt to incriminate those around him, but ended up producing no tangible cases. Then the agent came across Algerian-born Ahmed Ferhani, a twenty-seven-year-old with a history of mental health problems: he had been involuntarily committed to psychiatric wards thirty times during the previous ten years. Over a six-month period Ferhani was pressured by the undercover agent to buy weapons. Eventually he agreed and was prosecuted for a supposed plot to blow up Manhattan's largest synagogue.[39] Ferhani was sentenced to ten years in prison and faces deportation to Algeria upon his release. His conviction was the first under a New York State antiterrorism law that was passed in response to 9/11.[40]

Once these tactics have become commonplace in relation to Muslims, they can easily be extended to others. The NYPD monitors nonviolent political groups, such as African-American community groups protesting against police racism and pro-Palestinian groups.[41] The *New York Review of Books* has reported strong evidence that the Intelligence Division infiltrated, spied on, and aggressively harassed organizers of Occupy Wall Street. In doing so, the NYPD is renewing its long history of spying on nonviolent political activists. During the cold war, its Red Squads targeted communists, trade unionists, civil rights organizations, and black radicals. By 1970 it had collected dossiers on over 1.2 million New Yorkers, which it shared with private investigators, academic officials, and prospective employers.[42] Activists filed a class-action lawsuit the following year, which became known as *Handschu v. Special Services Division*, challenging the NYPD's harassment of political groups. The *Handschu* guidelines, agreed to in a settlement fourteen years later, required the NYPD to restrict its investigations of political activity to cases in which there was specific information that criminal conduct was afoot.

A year after 9/11, the new head of NYPD Intelligence, David Cohen, told a federal court:

> The counterproductive restrictions imposed on the NYPD by the Handschu Guidelines in this changed world hamper our efforts every day, [making it] virtually impossible to detect plans for attack

> [and placing] this City, our nation and its people at heightened and unjustifiable risk.[43]

The guidelines were rewritten, watering down the requirement that investigations be linked to specific criminal activity. The tactics of the old Red Squads were then revived, this time directed primarily at New York's Muslim populations. Moreover, there was no body with significant oversight powers to check whether the NYPD's counterterrorism and intelligence activities were violating civil rights (although New York City Council voted in August 2013 to appoint an inspector general as a potential remedy). An e-mail from a senior FBI official to the private intelligence firm Stratfor that was released by WikiLeaks in 2012 reveals an awareness that the NYPD's counterterrorism activities are unlawful and continue earlier histories of political policing:

> I keep telling you, you and I are going to laugh and raise a beer one day, when everything Intel [NYPD's Intelligence Division] has been involved in during the last 10 years comes out—it always eventually comes out. They are going to make [former FBI Director J. Edgar] Hoover, COINTEL, Red Squads, etc look like rank amatures [*sic*] compared to some of the damn right felonious activity, and violations of US citizen's rights they have been engaged in.[44]

Ironically, the FBI, which follows a model of radicalization similar to that outlined in the NYPD's report, uses the same "felonious" activities itself.[45]

The Primacy of Politics

Radicalization models, whether based solely on theology or including a social psychological component, have encouraged national security establishments to believe they can preempt future terrorist attacks through intensive surveillance of the spiritual and mental lives of Muslims. As noted earlier, radical religious ideology has been defined as a kind of virus infecting those with whom it comes into contact, either by itself or in combination with psychological processes. But we have seen that the radicalization literature fails to offer a convincing demonstration of any causal relationship between theology and violence, and there is no evidence of any significant statistical correlation between the supposed indicators of radicalization and terrorist violence. Moreover, the concept of radicalization tends to confuse a propensity for violence with an interest in radical ideas, leading the question of what causes violence to be insufficiently isolated from the question of how belief systems and ideologies come to be adopted.

In a paper that is less widely read than his better known books on Islam, the French sociologist Olivier Roy, a widely respected authority on European Muslims, argues that it makes more sense to separate theology from violence: "The process of violent radicalisation has little to do with religious practice, while radical theology, as salafism, does not necessarily lead to violence."[46] The "leap into terrorism" is not religiously inspired but better seen as sharing "many factors with other forms of dissent, either political (the ultra-left), or behavioural: the fascination for sudden suicidal violence as illustrated by the paradigm of random shootings in schools (the 'Columbine syndrome')."[47] While a Salafi vocabulary is used by certain groups to articulate their narratives, this by itself is not evidence that religious ideology is causing violence, merely that, within this milieu, theological references provide a veneer of legitimacy. Religious ideology seems to play at most an enabling role in cohering a group rather than being the underlying driver of terrorism.

In spite of its analytical problems, the radicalization concept continues to be popular among policy makers in Europe and the US. And the alternative possibilities of conceiving of terrorism, particularly of viewing it as a mode of political action, are neglected. While policing agencies search for scholarship that can give them a magical formula to predict who will be a future terrorist, the microlevel question of what causes one person rather than another in the same political context to engage in violence is probably beyond analysis and best seen as unpredictable.[48] Sizable resources have been allocated to finding a general formula of radicalization, yet no plausible one has been offered. At best, the path to becoming a terrorist can be reconstructed on an individual basis after the event. For law enforcement agencies, the best approach is therefore to investigate the active incitement, financing, or preparation of terrorist violence rather than wider belief systems which are wrongly assumed to be its precursors. On the other hand, the mesolevel question of what conditions are likely to increase or decrease its legitimacy for a particular political actor (either a social movement or a state) is amenable to productive analysis. So too is the macrolevel question of how particular social movements and states are constituted to be in conflict with each other, and how the interaction between these different political actors produces a context in which violence becomes seen as a legitimate tactic.[49] An objective study would examine how state and nonstate actors mutually constitute themselves as combatants in a global conflict between the West and radical Islam and address under what conditions each chooses to adopt tactics of violence, paying close attention to the relationships between their legitimizing frameworks.

Such an approach has the advantage of being consistent with what is known about the biographies, actions, and self-descriptions of terrorists themselves and those who publicly support terrorist violence. Consider, for example, Anwar al-Awlaki. From 2009 until his extrajudicial killing in a US drone strike in September 2011, he was regarded by the US and UK governments as constituting one of the foremost terrorist threats to their countries, and accused of radicalizing American and British Muslims via his use of YouTube, Facebook, and e-mail correspondence. Al-Awlaki was a US citizen who was born in New Mexico, attended school in Yemen, and then returned to the US in 1991, where he lived for twelve years before spending two years in the UK and then returning to Yemen. According to security officials, his familiarity with both Western and Arab cultures made him particularly influential among Western Muslims. Beginning in 2008, he was seen as a figure who could, while based in southern Yemen, drive Western Muslims on a path toward terrorism, using his Internet communications to provide the theological and psychological underpinnings thought necessary for radicalization—a new bin Laden, all the more dangerous for his ability to appeal to disaffected Western Muslims. During this time, FBI agents closely monitored his Internet traffic, including an average of seventy e-mails a day.[50] The Obama administration seems to have placed al-Awlaki on its extrajudicial kill list in January 2010.[51] When al-Awlaki's father challenged the US government's targeted killings policy in the courts in September 2010, government officials stopped describing al-Awlaki as a propagandist and began referring to him as an active terrorist. As evidence for this, the administration cited an interrogation with Umar Farouk Abdulmutallab, following his failed attempt to blow up a plane traveling from Amsterdam to Detroit on Christmas Day 2009. During the questioning, Abdulmutallab was said to have revealed al-Awlaki's involvement in the plot at an operational level. This claim was never tested in court but Homeland Security Secretary Janet Napolitano said al-Awlaki was actively involved in planning attacks.[52] And Director of National Intelligence James Clapper said al-Awlaki had joined al-Qaeda in the Arabian Peninsula and was playing a "key role in setting the strategic direction" of the group. In Britain, al-Awlaki was accused of operational involvement in a plot to exploit weaknesses in airport security via e-mail correspondence with Rajib Karim, an employee of British Airways.[53] Both Nidal Hasan, who carried out the Fort Hood attack in Texas in November 2009, and Faisal Shahzad, who attempted a car bombing in New York's Times Square in May 2010, were among the thousands of people to have reached out to al-Awlaki by e-mail, but there was no evidence that he directly instructed either of them to engage in violent acts. What is beyond doubt is that by this time al-Awlaki was publishing online material that advocated violence against the West. He praised Nidal Hasan as a "hero" for the attack at Fort Hood that left thirteen people dead, and his document "44 Ways of Supporting Jihad," published in January 2009, suggested various ways of aiding the "mujahideen," such as financial support, advocacy, and training. The text was vague about who the mujahideen are and whom they are fighting, but it was clear that their struggle is global in scope and directed against "the West" as a whole, seen as a cultural system pitted against Islam. He concluded that anyone who thinks clearly can easily work out which groups are truly fighting for Islam today.[54]

A decade earlier, al-Awlaki's ideology had been quite different. Beginning in 2000, he had begun to record a series of lectures on the lives of Muhammad, other prophets, and their companions. These

English-language recordings proved immensely popular and brought him a substantial following. Al-Awlaki was confident, eloquent, and witty, able to relate classical Islamic stories to life in the West today. Though he lacked credentials as a religious scholar, he was regarded as a charismatic popularizer with a talent for engaging commentary. When the 9/11 attacks occurred, he told journalists: "There is no way that the people who did this could be Muslim, and if they claim to be Muslim, then they have perverted their religion." He condemned attacks on civilians, irrespective of the oppression their governments were responsible for—on this basis, he opposed the US war on Afghanistan as much as the 9/11 attacks. He said that while America was responsible for propping up repressive governments in the Middle East, it was not a military enemy, and he hoped bin Laden's views would not win support. In speaking of the concept of jihad, he made the now commonplace distinction between its "greater" form of spiritual struggle and its "lesser" form of physical force in self-defense. Jihad was, he said, first a personal struggle to be a better person and the struggle of a community to rid itself of corruption. He also told journalists:

> And if there is an invading force from outside, then we would, too, struggle to defend ourselves, and that is where armed combat occurs. So actually, fighting is only a part of the jihad, and it's considered to be a defensive force in order to protect the religion.[55]

He drew a distinction between terrorism that targets civilians, which he opposed, and insurgencies within specific local contexts that aimed to defend Muslims against military occupations, which he might support. As a teenager at college in the late 1980s he had spent a summer visiting Afghanistan, including spending time with the anti-Soviet mujahideen, who were then supported by the US government. And in the 1990s he seems to have supported the Chechen insurgency against the Russian army. Certainly the US government, which investigated him thoroughly after 9/11, viewed al-Awlaki as a moderate. Indeed, as the imam at the largest mosque in the Washington, DC, metropolitan area, he was invited to a lunch event at the Pentagon, in an attempt by the US Army to reach out to mainstream American Muslims, and he gave a Friday sermon on Capitol Hill.[56]

The following year the FBI conducted a series of antiterrorist raids on Muslim educational, research, business, and charitable organizations in northern Virginia, where al-Awlaki was based. Angered at the raids, which seemed to target organizations just because they were Islamic, al-Awlaki told his congregation how agents had held women and children at gunpoint and handcuffed them for hours. "If you don't struggle for your rights," he said, "you will be stripped away from them, step by step, until you have nothing left." He called on American Muslims to unite and work with "Islamic organizations with a political orientation and a civil rights orientation" to challenge the war on terror, which had become, he said, a "war against Muslims."[57] The raids had led al-Awlaki to make radical criticisms of the war on terror and to view it as an attack on his religion. But his objections were framed in the language of civil rights and the need to organize politically to defend the community. His references to Malcolm X and H. Rap Brown suggested that the right strategy for American Muslims was to draw on the history of black political radicalism and community struggle. "Their rights were not handed to them," he said, but were won through political activism. However, al-Awlaki himself told friends he was becoming increasingly disillusioned with the US's criminalization of Muslims and aggressive foreign policy, and that he planned to leave the country. In March 2002, he moved to the UK, where he continued to call for Muslim political activism to defend civil rights and oppose the foreign policy of the war on terror. Two years later he settled in Yemen's southern province of Shabwa.[58]

The first indication that al-Awlaki's position had shifted came in December 2005, with the online publication of his "Constants on the Path of Jihad" lecture. In it he translated into English a text by Yusuf al-Uyayri—a Saudi veteran of the anti-Soviet jihad in the 1980s who went on to be an al-Qaeda activist in Saudi Arabia before being killed by the Saudi regime in 2003—and used the translation as an opportunity to give his own commentary. The lecture begins by noting that powerful nations are "mobilizing on various fronts (i.e. religious, political, social, economic, media, popular mass, etc.)" to fight against Islam, and many Muslims are deceived into thinking they are not obliged to fight back. Al-Awlaki no longer thinks of jihad as primarily an inner struggle; it is now an individual obligation for all able Muslims globally to fight for the sake of Allah. Jihad, says al-Awlaki, is not just about personal improvement, or even about the liberation of particular localities from foreign occupations; its real purpose is "to wipe out *kufr* [unbelief] from the world," a struggle that will continue until the day of judgment. This means: "Jihad is global. It is not a local phenomenon." The picture is one in which jihad has been redefined as a global war to defend Islam from the West, without limits in time or place. At this point in al-Awlaki's trajectory, the precise methods to be used in this war remain unclear; what is significant is that it encompasses various kinds of force (military, cultural, ideological), is global in reach, and requires all Muslims to engage in it.[59]

In the summer of 2006, al-Awlaki was arrested by the Yemeni authorities. According to *New York Times* journalist Scott Shane, he was originally imprisoned in relation to a "tribal dispute," but after his initial arrest, the Yemeni government was told by then US director of national intelligence John Negroponte to keep him in prison. After being held for a year and a half, and with mounting pressure in Yemen to end his imprisonment, the US government reversed its decision.[60] Al-Awlaki was released without charge in December 2007, and shortly afterward gave an interview to Moazzam Begg, a British Muslim who had himself been incarcerated at Guantánamo Bay and later became a campaigner for the rights of prisoners. In a part of the conversation not published at the time, al-Awlaki told Begg he had been "abused" while in prison but did not want to go into details or make public allegations. He also said FBI agents questioned him during his detention and were aware of his treatment.[61]

Before his incarceration in Yemen, al-Awlaki had begun to see the world as locked in a global struggle between the West and Islam. Now, having been imprisoned and apparently tortured with the complicity of the US government, any remaining reservations about targeting civilians in the country of his citizenship were abandoned. Within months of his release he had launched a new Web site and blog. Much of his published material continued to take the form of advice on personal questions such as divorce and fasting, but he also began to announce his clear support for violence against the US. By the summer of 2009, al-Awlaki's mass e-mails were calling any Muslim who is "fighting on behalf of America . . . a heartless beast, bent on evil, who sells his religion for a few dollars."[62] The following March, in an interview with Al Jazeera, he publicly endorsed Umar Farouk Abdulmutallab's attempted bombing of the US-bound plane. He added that it "would have been better if the plane was a military one, or if it was a US military target," but US civilians, having voted for prowar candidates, were also legitimate targets.[63] In a later statement, he commented: "Isn't it ironic that the two capitals of the war against Islam, Washington, DC, and London, have also become among the centers of western jihad? Jihad is becoming as American as apple pie and as British as afternoon tea."[64] If there had been a propensity to terrorist violence among American Muslims, this would have been the period when significant numbers of al-Awlaki's followers, those attracted to his earlier lectures on the lives of figures from Islamic history, would have taken up arms—taking advantage, for example, of the easy access to guns in the US—to carry out shooting sprees. What actually happened was that the widespread following he had built up dissipated as his new views became evident through documents such as "44 Ways of Supporting Jihad."

How can the transformation of al-Awlaki's views in the decade before his death be explained? Certainly there is no evidence to suggest that a religious awakening led to his adoption of a radically different theology. His theological understanding of jihad had always included a notion of military force as necessary to defend Islam under certain circumstances. Whereas before he had felt the necessity of military force only in specific local contexts, where Muslims were trying to liberate themselves from foreign occupations, by the end of 2005 he had begun to believe Muslims were involved in a global struggle rather than just a series of local wars, and that that struggle had both ideological and military dimensions. From a theological point of view, the key question in advocating such a position is whether it violates the belief, strongly grounded in Islamic jurisprudence, that being a citizen is a form of a contract to follow state laws, violation of which cannot be justified even when that state is at war with majority-Muslim nations or Muslim nonstate actors. But the change in al-Awlaki's position cannot be traced to a change in his theological position on the Islamic exhortation to honor contracts. In fact, nowhere in his published material does he attempt an answer to the well-known theological objection to his position.[65] He does, of course, present an Islamic discourse to legitimize his new idea of a multidimensional global war. But what is striking is how his global war concept mirrors the discourse of the war on terror itself, which also imagines no geographical limits and refers to a multidimensional conflict with physical and ideological spheres. Al-Awlaki was a keen student of this discourse, and familiar with the RAND Corporation's calls for a "battle of ideas" to create a "moderate" pro-Western Islam—what he called "RAND Islam."[66] What was essentially new in al-Awlaki's statements from late 2005 onward was not his theological position but a reinterpretation of the political circumstances that Muslims were in. The ultimate source of his idea of a global war to defend Islam was the militarized identity politics of the global war on terror itself.

"A Call to Jihad," a lecture he gave in 2010, gives his own account of how his new position emerged.

> We are not against Americans for just being Americans. We are against evil, and America as a whole has turned into a nation of evil. What we see from America is the invasion of [inaudible] countries; we see Abu Ghraib, Bagram, and Guantánamo Bay; we see cruise missiles and cluster bombs; and we have just seen in Yemen the death of twenty-three children and seventeen women. We cannot stand idly in the face of such aggression, and we will fight back and incite others to do the same. I for one was born in the US. I lived in the US for twenty-one years. America was my home. I was a preacher of Islam involved in nonviolent Islamic activism. However, with the American invasion of Iraq and continued US aggression against Muslims, I could not reconcile between living in the US and being a Muslim. And I eventually came to the conclusion that jihad against America is binding upon myself just as it is binding on every other able Muslim.[67]

If this account of what prompted al-Awlaki's support for terrorism against the US is correct, and there seems no reason to doubt it, then his radicalization is consistent with the historical pattern of political activists adopting a belief in terrorism when political action fails to bring about change—from the French anarchists who began bombing campaigns after the defeat of the Paris Commune, to the Algerian FLN struggling to end French colonialism, to the Weather Underground's "Declaration of a State of War" following state repression of student campaigns against the Vietnam war.

Mainstream radicalization analysts who have looked at al-Awlaki's evolution are confronted with a dilemma. According to their theories, it cannot have been the politics of the war on terror that drove him from political activism to supporting violence against the US; there must instead have been a significant psychological or theological process. Since no such process is evident from what is known of his life after 9/11, they try to shift the point in time at which he became radicalized to an earlier date and assume the process occurred then, during a period we have less information on. This would imply either that the definition of radicalization has been widened so far as to include any kind of political opposition to the status quo or that when he was officially considered a moderate, his public statements were just a cover, and he was secretly already an advocate of violence against the US. In support of the latter, radicalization analysts point to the allegation that in 2000 and 2001, three of the 9/11 hijackers attended mosques where al-Awlaki was an imam.[68] Yet despite repeated investigations, no evidence has ever emerged to prove that this was anything more than coincidence, which is what the FBI itself concluded.[69]

Official radicalization models failed to grasp how al-Awlaki had become a supporter of violence against the US. They also encouraged the idea that his online propaganda was an ideological virus that could infect young Muslims in the West and spawn an upsurge in terrorist attacks. The official reason given by the Obama administration for the extrajudicial killing of al-Awlaki is that he had an active operational role in al-Qaeda in the Arabian Peninsula. The Department of Justice's sixteen-page white paper outlining its claimed legal basis for targeted killings asserts that the government may lawfully kill a US citizen if "an informed, high-level official" decides that the target is a high-ranking figure in al-Qaeda or an affiliated group who poses "an imminent threat of violent attack against the United States" and that capturing him is not feasible.[70] The phrase "imminent threat" is used broadly enough to cover anyone who can be presented as active with al-Qaeda and affiliated organizations. A necessary condition for such killings to be considered permissible under international law is that they take place on a battlefield; but the war on terror is seen as involving, in principle, a global battlefield, and drone strikes have taken place in Pakistan, Yemen, and Somalia, all places where the US is not formally at war. Whatever the attempts to give a pseudolegal gloss to the kill list policy, it is likely the real reason Anwar al-Awlaki was killed is that he was seen as a radicalizer whose ideological activities were capable of driving Western Muslims to terrorist violence. But having this role is only plausible if models of radicalization in which a jihadist ideology mechanically causes people to be violent are accepted. There is only one case in which there is any apparent evidence that al-Awlaki's statements worked according to this model—that of Roshonara Choudhry, who attempted to stab the British parliamentarian Stephen Timms at his constituency office in May 2010. During interviews with police officers afterward she spoke about listening to hundreds of al-Awlaki's lectures and, as a result, coming to believe that she had an obligation to carry out acts of violence in defense of Islam. But she also talked about her anger at the Iraq war and said she targeted Timms because he had voted in support of it.[71] It is difficult to know from the available material exactly how religious ideology and political beliefs combined to cause her to attempt the stabbing. But it is precisely because the relationship between ideas and actions is ambiguous that, as a matter of principle, ideas should not be criminalized. If the real reason the Obama administration decided to kill al-Awlaki was to prevent his ideological virus from reaching Western audiences, then it not only based its decision on a flawed model of radicalization, it also violated this liberal principle in the most egregious way possible. Moreover, there were other options that could have been explored. Fawaz A. Gerges, a political scientist at the London School of Economics, notes that Yemen officially charged al-Awlaki with incitement to violence in October 2010. He suggests that if a fair trial had been promised, a deal could have been struck with local leaders in southern Yemen to hand al-Awlaki over to the Yemeni authorities to face prosecution; one key leader had already said in an interview at the time that he would consider such a proposal.[72]

In cases where American Muslims have carried out acts of violence, or attempted such acts, the same picture emerges. The perpetrators speak about political circumstances leading them to their actions rather than religious ideology. In February 2006, Faisal Shahzad, then a Pakistani immigrant living in New York, was wrestling with the question of how Muslims should respond to the wars in Iraq and Afghanistan, the plight of the Palestinians, and anti-Muslim racism in the West. He wrote in an e-mail message to a group of friends that Islam forbids the killing of innocent civilians. But equally he could not see how peaceful protest would bring about change: "Can you tell me a way to save the oppressed? And a way to fight back when rockets are fired at us and Muslim blood flows?" After millions-strong demonstrations failed to prevent the Iraq war, there were no easy answers to those questions. Three years later the questions had become more personal. In 2009, President Obama expanded the drone strikes campaign in Pakistan. While the US media dreamed of the new technology's possibilities for risk-free killing without geographical constraint, in Pakistan the death toll mounted, particularly in Shahzad's Pashtun homeland. US drones killed ninety-eight innocent civilians in Pakistan in 2009, according to the London-based Bureau of Investigative Journalism.[73] In April, Shahzad sent another e-mail to friends, attacking Pakistani politicians for failing to defend the country from such attacks.[74] By this time Shahzad seems to have resolved his earlier questions and come to believe that the killing of civilians could be justified as part of a supposed defensive war against the West. A couple of months later he traveled to Pakistan to seek out the Taliban, and the following May he tried to detonate a car bomb in Times Square. At his arraignment he told the court that his attempted attack was in response to the US's occupation of Iraq and Afghanistan and its drone strikes in Somalia, Yemen, and Pakistan. He said he considered himself "a mujahid, a Muslim soldier." The judge replied that his intended victims were not combatants invading other countries, but civilians.

"Well, the people select the government," replied Shahzad, grasping at whatever arguments he could muster. "Including the children?" the judge asked. There was a long pause before Shahzad finally said: "Well, the drone hits in Afghanistan and Iraq, they don't see children, they don't see anybody. They kill women, children, they kill everybody."[75] Again, it was the war on terror's own actions that a terrorist was mimicking.

In the case of Nidal Hasan, the army psychiatrist who carried out the Fort Hood attack, it appears that he had been struggling with his role in the US military since the launch of the 2003 Iraq war. On the one hand, his loyalty to the US military required that he might one day be asked to fight Muslims in other parts of the world in wars he considered unjust; on the other hand, did his loyalty to Muslims in other parts of the world require that he leave the US military—or even fight against it? The militarized identity politics of the war on terror were playing out on the deepest levels of his being. From 2003 to 2007, while he was a resident in the psychiatric program at the Walter Reed National Military Medical Center in Bethesda, Maryland, he openly questioned whether he could engage in combat against other Muslims, and asked whether he would qualify for conscientious objector status. He did not. In an academic presentation that he was required to give, he chose to discuss Islamic interpretations of the legitimacy of violence. He confided to a colleague that he applied for his next posting, at the nearby Uniformed Services University of the Health Sciences, to avoid being deployed to fight in a majority-Muslim country. In another presentation he asked whether the war on terror was actually a war on Islam, and he proposed a research study on whether Muslims in military service had conflicts between their loyalty to the US and their loyalty to fellow Muslims in other parts of the world.[76] At the end of December 2008 Hasan e-mailed Anwar al-Awlaki asking for "some general comments about Muslims in the US military." In total he sent eighteen e-mails and received two replies, neither of which answered his original question or suggested any course of action. Hasan was assigned to the Darnall Army Medical Center at Fort Hood, Texas, in July 2009, and he conducted psychiatric sessions with soldiers traumatized by their participation in the wars in Iraq and Afghanistan.

Based on his patients' accounts, he requested that his military superiors investigate possible war crimes. The request was declined.[77] In August Hasan's car was vandalized: after the perpetrator was arrested, it emerged that he had noticed Hasan's Muslim bumper sticker and was motivated by Islamophobia. Two months later the US Army told Hasan he would be deployed to Afghanistan shortly; his long-standing dilemma was now a matter of practical urgency rather than academic discussion. He could no longer contain within himself the split between his two antagonistic identities.[78] The following month he entered the Fort Hood deployment center and opened fire with a semi-automatic pistol fitted with laser sights, killing twelve US soldiers and one Department of Defense employee and injuring forty-two others.[79]

CHAPTER 5

Hearts and Minds

> But though I was initially disappointed at being categorized as an extremist, as I continued to think about the matter I gradually gained a measure of satisfaction from the label.
>
> —Martin Luther King, Jr., *Letter from Birmingham City Jail*

In April 2010, Talya Lador-Fresher, then Israel deputy ambassador to the UK was invited to speak at Manchester University in the north of England. The previous year Israel had mounted the devastating attack on Gaza known as Operation Cast Lead, which had been condemned by the prominent South African jurist Richard Goldstone in the months leading up to Lador-Fresher's lecture. He had been asked to lead a fact-finding mission for the UN Human Rights Council on the war in Gaza, and its report described the Israeli Defense Forces' war crimes and possible crimes against humanity. In Manchester, where students had been clashing bitterly over the issue of Israel and Palestine for years, Palestinian rights activists planned to challenge the deputy ambassador over the allegations in Goldstone's report as she delivered her lecture. However, strict security arrangements meant activists were prevented from entering the building. Hoping to confront Lador-Fresher as she left the university, they assembled at the exit to the university's car park. When her car emerged, they blocked it for a few seconds before the vehicle pushed through the crowd and sped away.[1] One of those who stood in front of the car was Jameel Scott, a seventeen-year-old student and member of the Socialist Workers Party. Jameel was hit by the vehicle as it pushed through the protesters, and was lifted onto its hood, leaving him with a minor limp.

The protest provoked a furious reaction from Ron Prosor, then Israeli ambassador to the UK:

> What is going on at British taxpayer-funded universities is shocking. Extremism is not just running through these places of education, it is galloping. My ears are ready and waiting to hear the strongest condemnation of this behaviour both from the heads of campus and the local authorities.[2]

Shortly afterward, officers of Greater Manchester Police turned up at Jameel's home and arrested him on suspicion of racially aggravated public disorder. Lador-Fresher alleged that he had thrown himself at the car's windscreen several times while chanting anti-Semitic slogans. This was soon contradicted by a security guard at the university who witnessed the incident, and no charges were pursued against Jameel. However, the matter did not end there. Since 2008, Greater Manchester Police had been one of the forces running an antiextremism project known as Channel—part of Britain's Preventing Violent Extremism program—that sought to profile young people who were not suspected of involvement in criminal activity but nevertheless were regarded as drifting toward extremism. Through an extensive system of surveillance involving, among others, police officers, teachers, and youth and health workers, would-be radicals were identified and given counseling, mentoring, and religious instruction in an attempt to reverse the radicalizing process. In some cases individuals were rehoused in new neighborhoods to disconnect them from local influences considered harmful. Across the UK, between 2007 and 2010, 1,120 individuals were identified by the Channel project as potentially traveling on a radicalization pathway. Of these, 290 were under sixteen years old and fifty-five were under twelve. Over 90 percent were Muslim (the rest were mainly identified for potential involvement in far Right extremism).[3] By the end of 2012 almost 2,500 people had been identified by the Channel project as possible risks.[4] The official guidance for the project—influenced by Sageman's and Wiktorowicz's focus on socialization and cognitive openings—listed indicators of potential radicalization such as abandoning current associates in favor of a new social network, experiencing a crisis of identity or family separation, and expressing "real or imagined grievances."[5]

Being a teenager, having a Muslim father (though not himself identifying as Muslim), joining a left-wing political party, and being involved in the incident at the university seem to have been the factors that led police to consider Jameel a radicalization risk and to decide to initiate a Channel "intervention." Officers of the North West Counter-Terrorism Unit (CTU) began by contacting Jameel's parents, his aunt, and his school. Then they approached Jameel himself and told him they were referring him to something called the Channel project because they considered him vulnerable to Islamist or far Left radicalization. He was told he would be on the project for two to three years, but if his behavior improved, he would be left alone after a year. A program of counseling with two officers from the CTU was initiated. The officers met with Jameel at his aunt's house to discuss concerns about his "political trajectory." They said they were worried that Jameel had been at a political demonstration at a young age. Conversations focused on the people he associated with: fellow members of the Socialist Workers Party and its various spin-off campaigns, such as Unite Against Fascism and the antiracist cultural group Love Music Hate Racism. They wondered whether he was being "groomed" by older people and asked him for names of activists and their political affiliations. Officers visited his school before left-wing demonstrations in Manchester and advised him not to attend and not to talk to other students about such events. "It was bullshit. It was completely and utterly exaggerated but scary at the time," says Jameel. When his political science teacher organized an educational trip to the Conservative Party conference in Manchester, officers contacted the school and ensured Jameel could not participate. This was for his own safety, they told him; they were concerned he was falling in with a bad crowd. Jameel said:

> I was bemused by the whole two-year process . . . It was quite clear that I wasn't in the terrorist category, but I was told that I'm being monitored and mentored by an antiterrorist project.

Jameel told the police he did not know anybody involved in terrorism or violence.

> People at most will put bike locks around their neck and chain themselves to a fence. They're activists.

But Jameel felt the officers, who he thought "very friendly," had been given

> very vague concepts from the top [that were] not an attempt to curb terrorism [but] an attempt at depoliticization, spreading fear, and making people actually feel unsafe around their neighbors.

His parents, his aunt, and his college were all contacted repeatedly by officers in an effort to put pressure on him to end his political activism. On one occasion officers telephoned Jameel's mother and told her it would be good to move the family to a different neighborhood, and that the CTU could have the local authority housing department find her a new home.

> I remember being quite offended by the fact that I'd made a political choice to actually engage with politics, and the people who I actually talk and discuss with are being accused of grooming me for future political extremist activity. [The officers] were always trying to be mentors and role models . . . Obviously, I didn't appreciate it, because I didn't need mentoring or role modeling, because I was just exercising my right to protest.[6]

"The Pool in Which Terrorists Will Swim"

In Britain, the new thinking on radicalization that emerged in national security circles beginning in 2004 became the basis for one of the most elaborate programs of surveillance and social control attempted in a Western state in recent decades. The Preventing Violent Extremism program, known as Prevent for short, was launched by Tony Blair's government in 2006. At its heart was a belief that, alongside the investigative work carried out domestically by police forces and the domestic intelligence agency MI5, which were focused on intercepting those whose activities were criminalized under the UK's wide-ranging antiterrorist legislation, it was necessary to develop a program directed at a wider population whose activities, behaviors, and beliefs were not criminal but, according to government officials, indicative of extremism. In the former category were hard interventions: criminal investigations, deportations of foreign nationals, and the imposition of control orders, which, without the need for a trial, allowed the government to subject suspects to a curfew, electronic tagging, and restrictions on visitors, travel, and Internet access.[7] But in the language of counterterrorism, "soft interventions" aimed at a broader group were also needed. Radicalization theories assumed would-be terrorists traveled through a series of stages toward extremism, only the last of which involved actual criminal activity. Intelligence officials argued that the government could not wait until extremism turned into terrorism; there had to be interventions earlier in the process. There were to be two kinds: one focused on individuals, and the other aimed at whole communities. At the individual level, policing needed to go upstream in the radicalization process, tackling extremists who had not crossed the threshold into behavior prosecutable as criminal activity but were seen as at risk of doing so. Partnerships between community organizations, police forces, and local authorities were meant to identify such individuals—guided by the government's radicalization model. At the community level, the same partnerships would enable an ideological challenge to radicalism. Moderate Muslim leaders were to be empowered with government funding to win over hearts and minds and secure allegiance to Western liberal democracy, in an effort to isolate extremists and prevent their ideas from spreading.[8] With a budget of hundreds of millions of pounds, Prevent became, in effect, the government's Islam policy.

Charles Farr, who was then the head of the counterterrorism department at Britain's foreign intelligence agency, MI6, and had worked on covert operations in Afghanistan and Jordan, was selected to run the new program.[9] He described its basic approach.

> There is a group of people that have been radicalized and are committed to violent extremism, and the only solution to that group of people in this country is criminal investigation and prosecution. There is a much larger group of people who feel a degree of negativity, if not hostility, towards the state, the country, the community, and who are,

> as it were, the pool in which terrorists will swim, and to a degree they will be complicit with and will certainly not report on activity which they detect on their doorstep. We have to reach that group, because unless we reach that group, they may themselves move into the very sharp end, but even if they do not, they will create an environment in which terrorists can operate with a degree of impunity that we do not want . . . That is to a degree what Prevent is all about.[10]

The primary way in which Prevent's success was being measured, said Farr, was in ascertaining whether government programs were "changing community attitudes."[11] MI5 had worked a year before with GCHQ, the national communications surveillance agency, and local police forces, running a coordinated intelligence-gathering operation called Project Rich Picture, which built up a list of eight thousand Muslims considered to be extremists.[12]

The Prevent program had a vast budget and operated across several government departments. Authorities responsible for schools, universities, prisons, probation services, youth crime prevention, and the arts were all drawn into the policy. Police forces recruited three hundred new staff across the country to work on Prevent in existing counterterrorism teams.[13] Half the Prevent budget went to the Foreign and Commonwealth Office, which launched propaganda campaigns in Pakistan and the Middle East to "counter extremists' false characterization of the UK as a place where Muslims are oppressed." Half a million pounds was used to produce a series of television commercials to be aired in Pakistan featuring prominent British Muslims.[14] "A dedicated team of key language specialists [worked] to explain British policies and the role of Muslims in British society, in print, visual and electronic media."[15] Across England and Wales, £20 million a year was made available to local authorities and community organizations to fund projects to combat extremist ideology. In theory, local authorities were meant to organize a consultation process with the community to decide whether a problem of extremism existed in the area and, if so, how best to tackle it. In practice, all of the ninety-four local authority areas with more than two thousand resident Muslims (according to the 2001 census, the first to ask a question about religion) became involved in Prevent, under pressure from the regional government offices that channeled central government policy. Funding was allocated in direct proportion to the number of Muslims present in each area. The government's assumption was that the best measure for the level of extremism was the size of the local Muslim population, which, as one government e-mail put it, was "a rough and ready proxy for risk of radicalization."[16] It was a formula that constituted a form of religious profiling and would have been vulnerable to legal challenge under antidiscrimination laws had it been made public at the time.

In the first couple of years of Prevent's implementation, the flow of money into local areas aimed at strengthening mainstream Muslim civil society. Muslim populations were drawn into a farrago of projects, ranging from the benign to the ridiculous. Community groups made DVDs about Islamophobia and put on plays about tolerance. Young Muslim boys were recruited to participate in basketball, football, and boxing sessions. Muslim women were given leadership training. Imams were taught English and taken on trips to the British Museum. Mosques got money for refurbishment and training in good governance. Government funding spawned a Muslim arts scene. Many Muslims welcomed the various initiatives but worried that such services were only available under the banner of a counterterrorism program singling out Muslims for attention. Often organizations providing such services were less than transparent about where the money came from, fearing they'd lose credibility if seen as linked to the police's counterterrorist units. In many areas, established community leaders, without much support in the communities they claimed to represent but with close relationships to the local authority, found they could obtain Prevent funding for pet projects without needing to go through the usual processes of accountability. In Bradford, the Council of Mosques—an umbrella organization formed over twenty-five years earlier and a long-standing gatekeeper to Bradford's Muslims—was seen as well suited to carry out Prevent work. "We're not looking for new organizations to spring up," a local authority manager said; bypassing established organizations would mean "a period of chaos."[17] In the absence of a genuine process of democratic decision making, sectarian conflicts occasionally sprung up between different parts of the Muslim population, as rival community leaders competed for money. A local authority worker in the Midlands described the allocation of Prevent funding as a "nod nod thing" involving "jobs for the boys."

> A lot of patriarchal politics is being played out, and there is a real issue of community leaders. Who has the right to be a community leader? Where does gender fit in? Some savvy and well-connected Muslim groups just take money and do what they want with it, because they are friends with the right people. This is where corruption and divisions set in.[18]

Meanwhile, the flow of resources into Muslim communities attracted the attention of other sections of the local population where deprivation was equally intense but no stream of government funding had been introduced on the basis of ethnic or relgions identity. Instead of uniting communities to work together on shared issues, Prevent tore at the already fragile social fabric, pitting Muslim against non-Muslim in competition for local favors from the state.

The main effect of Prevent in this initial period was to draw Muslim civil society organizations more closely into the orbit of government funding without civil servants worrying too much about how those organizations spent the money. Over time, as central government sharpened its agenda, the Prevent program became more ideological. A new version of the program was launched in 2009 with a greater emphasis on projects that directly combated what was referred to as "the ideology which sustains terrorism" and those who "undermine our shared values."[19] In a speech announcing the new program, government minister Hazel Blears defined this ideology as a

> belief in the supremacy of the Muslim people, in a divine duty to bring the world under the control of hegemonic Islam, in the establishment of a theocratic Caliphate, and in the undemocratic imposition of theocratic law on whole societies.

This "ideology" is rooted "in a twisted reading of Islam" and is the root cause of terrorism, she said, and fighting it required Britons be less tolerant.

> This country is proud of its tradition of fair play and good manners, welcoming of diversity, tolerant of others. This is a great strength. But the pendulum has swung too far.[20]

The Prevent program's head, Charles Farr, gave another definition of extremist ideology.

> [There are] views in some quarters here that Western culture is evil and that Muslims living in this country should not engage with Western cultural organizations, for want of a better term, with Western culture itself . . . There is nothing violent about that, and it is not necessarily going to lead to terrorism, but it does seem to me to be unreal for this or any other government not to say that they are going to challenge that.[21]

Risk and Ideology

The influence of counterinsurgency thinking on Prevent was clear. Government documents introducing the program spoke repeatedly of isolating extremists from mainstream Muslims, of winning over the hearts and minds of the majority in the targeted community, of establishing a coordinated strategy across a range of policing and nonpolicing agencies, of strategic communications, and of an intensive intelligence-gathering effort to build up detailed information on extremists and the wider Muslim population—all hallmarks of counterinsurgency strategy. But pursuing a counterinsurgency program within Britain itself in this way was unprecedented. To do so implied blurring conventional boundaries between the foreign and domestic spheres, between military and police operations, and between physical force and a battle of ideas. As the UK government's 2008 National Security Strategy put it:

> The distinction between "domestic" and "foreign" policy is unhelpful in a world where globalisation can exacerbate domestic security challenges . . . Similarly, the traditional contrast between "hard" and "soft" power obscures . . . More generally, the major security challenges require an integrated response that cuts across departmental lines and traditional policy boundaries.[22]

In this new era, all government departments needed to be plugged in to the machinery of counterterrorism. And the local authority chief executive in Lancashire was as significant to the government's integrated response as the army commander in Lashkar Gah. The Prevent program pressed staff of the former to see themselves as engaged on an ideological battlefield whose human terrain was Muslim citizens—a very different self-conception from that of a public servant accountable to the people. Counterinsurgency models, which had been crafted in overseas colonial settings, were now to be applied domestically to the enemy within.

This blurring of boundaries also meant the collision of two different modes of policing practice. The conventional view of the criminal justice system involves the notion of a ladder of escalating evidence thresholds that the state needs to cross before it is entitled to use increasing levels of coercion. To stop and search someone normally requires reasonable suspicion; to arrest someone requires more solid evidence of a crime; to charge someone requires a probability that such evidence will stand up in court; and to imprison someone requires evidence beyond the reasonable doubt of a jury of peers. On the other hand, counterinsurgency thinking starts from the need to gather intelligence on the contours of an ideological terrain. Knowledge of the ideological process by which a moderate becomes an extremist is necessary to develop a strategy to prevent and reverse such radicalization—quite a different kind of knowledge from evidence of criminal wrongdoing. Whereas criminal justice thinking asks whether someone is involved in terrorist activity, counterradicalization thinking asks whether someone's beliefs constitute a risk of extremism. With Prevent, domestic counterterrorism agencies dealt much more systematically in risk assessment. From one perspective, this transition seemed reasonable. Given the harm terrorism does, it might be argued, the state ought to widen its definition of the threat beyond those actively inciting, funding, or preparing terrorist activity. But there were a number of problems with such an approach. First, it assumed radicalization models can accurately describe a causal relationship between extremist ideas and terrorist actions, and that such models were capable of generating predictions statistically significant enough to base counterradicalization interventions on.

Yet such models did not stand up to scrutiny. Second, it led governments to consider the expression of certain ideas unacceptable. What this meant in practice was that you could be a target for counterterrorist initiatives even if you were fully law abiding. From both the pragmatic perspective of stopping terrorism and the point of view of civil liberties, there were deep problems.

A third danger was that British Muslims became, in the imaginations of counterterrorism officials, not citizens to whom the state was accountable but potential recruits to a global insurgency threatening the state's prospects of prevailing in Iraq, Afghanistan, and elsewhere. Because radicalization theory mistook attitudes of disaffection and opposition to foreign policy for signs of an extremist risk, state actors came to see a cross section of young Muslims as potential terrorist recruits rather than as dissenters who simply opposed the war on terror. They came to view young Muslims as a whole as on a knife edge, balanced between the ideology of al-Qaeda and allegiance to Western states. What was obscured by the imposition of this binary frame of moderate and extremist on the multitudinous tapestry of British Muslim life was precisely the new forms of identity young Muslims were creating beyond either of these poles. Instead they became the target for ideological campaigns aimed at changing their beliefs and attitudes through strategic communications programs. The narrow focus on stopping terrorism became confused with a wider project of reshaping the cultural identities of Muslims.[23]

That project was in part a matter of intervening on questions of theological interpretation. An organization called Radical Middle Way received £350,000 of Prevent money to organize a road show of "mainstream Islamic scholarship" to tour Britain to "counter extremist propaganda" and "denounce it as un-Islamic."[24] In Walsall, imams were given training "to identify individuals who show signs of misinterpreting the Quran."[25] In Bradford, the Council of Mosques was given £80,000 to develop a teaching resource for madrassas that seemed to gloss religious texts with Prevent-friendly messaging. Prevent officials occasionally spoke as if theological categories had inherent political meanings. For example, Salafis were classed as extremists and Sufis as moderates, or Deobandis as extremists and Barelvis as moderates. In effect, the government began to promote its own version of a good Islam to counterpose to al-Qaeda's bad Islam. Noticing these trends, Asma Jahangir, the United Nations' special rapporteur on freedom of religion or belief, pointed out in her 2008 report on the UK:

> It is not the Government's role to look for the "true voices of Islam" or of any other religion or belief. Since religions or communities of belief are not homogenous entities it seems advisable to acknowledge and take into account the diversity of voices . . . The contents of a religion or belief should be defined by the worshippers themselves.[26]

A specialists' unit was established at the Home Office in 2007 to develop an expertise in the ideological campaigning aspects of Prevent. The Research, Information and Communication Unit (RICU) had twenty-nine staff members by 2009 and a budget of over £4 million.[27] Each week they sent out a briefing to local Prevent officials across the country, providing a list of current issues thought to be of concern to Muslims and the key points of the government's narrative, so that the latter could be effectively communicated and the legitimacy of the war on terror shored up in public discourse. RICU also trained local authorities on techniques of strategic communication for countering radicalization, produced briefings on using appropriate terminology, conducted polling on Muslim attitudes, and commissioned academic research on the identity of young Muslims, how young Muslims used the Internet, and the impact of different counterextremism messages on domestic and foreign Muslim audiences.[28] In many ways, RICU was a revival of the Information Research Department (IRD) that was established at the Foreign Office in 1948 and continued to operate throughout the cold war. The IRD's aim was to fight a battle of ideas against communism and anticolonial nationalism by seeking to influence what journalists and intellectuals wrote. IRD officials fed confidential information on alleged communists within the UK labor movement during briefings of the media and various government agencies, and worked with the CIA to covertly fund cultural activities aimed at discrediting communism.[29] Dean Godson, a neoconservative who while research director at the Policy Exchange think tank had a strong influence on Prevent policy, wrote a 2006 article in *The Times* in which he called for a revival of such cold war techniques in the war on terror.

> During the cold war, organisations such as the Information Research Department of the Foreign Office would assert the superiority of the West over its totalitarian rivals. And magazines such as *Encounter* did hand-to-hand combat with Soviet fellow travellers. For any kind of truly moderate Islam to flourish, we need first to recapture our own self-confidence.[30]

As informed readers would have known, *Encounter* was covertly funded by the CIA. Today the battle of ideas—the state's attempt to set the terms of public discourse on extremism—takes place on blogs, Facebook, and YouTube and in chat rooms rather than in the pages of literary journals, and it is there, and in local communities, that Prevent focuses its attempts at influence warfare.

Dissent as Extremism

In March 2010, the far Right, Islamophobic English Defence League (EDL) planned to march through the town of Bolton in the north of England. The day before the demonstration, two local authority workers handed out leaflets across the mosques in Bolton after Friday prayers, telling congregants not to go to the demonstration and to stay away from the town center. Students were also given letters at schools, advising them not to go to the town center on the Saturday. In effect, Muslims were being asked to remain at home or in their own neighborhoods while the demonstration took place. It was "community lockdown time," as one local activist put it.[31] On the day itself, Muslim families stayed indoors, shops in Muslim areas closed for the day, and the police formed a ring around the town center to turn young Muslims away if they tried to head into town. The result was that the EDL managed to occupy the town center largely unchallenged by local Muslims. Like the EDL demonstration itself, the counterdemonstration by the Unite Against Fascism group was made up mainly of people from out of town. Its leaders were arrested early in the day and, from then on, antifascist protesters were easily contained by the police, while the EDL was able to marshal in front of the town hall. In the past the police had found it difficult to prevent local young people from confronting far Right groups when they marched through northern towns unless they deployed large numbers of officers in Asian areas and risked the kinds of violent confrontations that took place in Oldham, Burnley, and Bradford in 2001. In the Prevent era, a new approach was possible. Central to managing events on the day was the Bolton Council of Mosques, which had been generously supported with Prevent money and was embedded in a counterradicalization partnership with the local authority and the police. Police commanders could thus rely on the Council of Mosques and the local authorities to follow their lead. Representatives from the Council of Mosques agreed to the police's recommendation that Muslims be prevented from entering the town center, and they sat with police officers in the operational control center for the day, helping identify young people on closed-circuit television screens. From the point of view of the police, the EDL was not an extremist threat. The real danger was that the EDL's presence would foment radicalization among local young Muslims. The best way to prevent this, reasoned the police, was to keep young Muslims off the streets. But to the local Muslim population, this meant that their right to protest against the anti-Muslim EDL was dispensed with. Their frustration was directed as much at their own community "representatives" as at the police.

Community leaders who were more interested in building up their own ethnic fiefdoms than in advocating on behalf of the people they claimed to represent could be relied on to parrot the official line: terrorism was caused by the virus of extremism and best eradicated with an injection of British values. Prevent created a mini-industry of groups and organizations willing to give the government's message a Muslim face. Those who took a different view—for example, on questions of foreign policy—were put under pressure. On the eve of the publication of a new version of the Prevent strategy in March 2009, the government wrote a letter to the Muslim Council of Britain, the most prominent national Muslim organization, stating that unless its then deputy general secretary, Daud Abdullah, resigned, it would sever relations with the organization. Abdullah had recently signed the so-called Istanbul declaration, which called for Muslims to resist Israel's blockade of Gaza. Home Office civil servants said the key test of extremism for national Muslim organizations was whether they were willing to completely condemn Hamas. Of course, no other national organization was asked to criticize the human rights abuses of their coreligionists in other parts of the world.

At a local level, the test of extremism was more insidious. There was no objective definition, but in practice it included questions of foreign policy—young Muslims' views on the presence of British troops in Afghanistan, for example—and also revolved around nebulous questions of culture, identity, and British values. As a Muslim youth worker managing a Prevent-funded project in London told me: "The push for Britishness causes alienation. We become the 'other.' We need to be studied, managed, contained. Every conference we go to on Prevent frames things this way."[32] If Prevent's aim was to promote liberal values, it involved making judgments of people's attitudes in a most illiberal way. As Birmingham councilor Salma Yaqoob pointed out, this would end up being counterproductive.

> By denying the legitimacy of democratic opposition to government foreign policy from Muslims, and by promoting and recognising only those Muslims who toe the line, government policy is serving to strengthen the hands of the genuine extremists; those who say that our engagement in the democratic process is pointless or wrong. The danger of this approach is that it serves to squeeze the democratic space for dissent within the Muslim community. If Muslim organisations are reluctant to provide the space for sensitive discussions for fear of extremist's accusations, where are these young people to go? Where will their views and concerns get an airing? The answer is obvious. They will be expressed in private and secret, with the genuine extremists keen to provide listening ears and simplistic solutions.[33]

Beyond this pragmatic argument, there is a deeper political point: any minority population that reduces its identity to what is acceptable to others should fear for its rights. In the early years of the US civil rights movement, Martin Luther King Jr. was considered an extremist. Eventually he was presented in mainstream America as the moderate voice and counterposed to newer, more radical extremists. But King understood that without these extremists on the horizon, his own movement would have been much less successful. So, too, Britain's Muslims need their Malcolm Xs as much as their moderates.

Once the new Conservative and Liberal Democrat coalition government came to power in the summer of 2010, much of the Prevent funding for Muslim civil society organizations was cut back. At the same time, the policy was even more tightly focused on a definition of extremism that covered any rejection of British values, and ideology was placed firmly at the center of its analysis of radicalization. A more explicit catalog of opinions defined which beliefs would count as indicators of extremism, such as believing "the West is perpetually at war with Islam; there can be no legitimate interaction between Muslims and non-Muslims in this country or elsewhere; and that Muslims living here cannot legitimately and or effectively participate in our democratic society."[34] The coalition government's June 2011 review of the Prevent policy was clearer than ever that such nonviolent extremism is a conveyor belt to terrorism. A growing number of public service professionals were drawn into participating in the Channel project, and, facing criticism for its exclusive focus on Muslim populations, steps were taken to include a small number of right-wing and left-wing extremists in its processes of identification and intervention. Above all, there was a renewed push for counterextremism work at universities and colleges.[35] Teaching staff at universities faced mounting pressure to pass on to Prevent police officers information about Muslim students who seemed depressed, were estranged from their families, bore political grievances, or visited extremist Web sites.[36] On at least one occasion a student union passed the membership list of a student Islamic society to counterterrorist police. The nine hundred names and other personal details were then shared with the CIA.[37]

By 2011, it was becoming apparent that the mechanisms established through Prevent were proving adaptable to a range of different political tasks. An e-mail sent in January from Scotland Yard's Counter Terrorism Command to University College London (UCL) staff responsible for Prevent illustrated the new atmosphere:

> As the student population is returning to "work," we anticipate a renewed vigour in protests and demonstrations. The picture is currently building and we are monitoring the situation.

The e-mail added:

> I would be grateful if in your capacity at your various colleges that should you pick up any relevant information that would be helpful to all of us to anticipate possible demonstrations or occupations, please forward it onto me.

Large-scale student protests had erupted in London a couple of months earlier in opposition to rising tuition fees. The police had not anticipated such a level of anger and were now eager to shore up their intelligence gathering on students' political activities. In the same month, Dean Godson of the Policy Exchange think tank organized a seminar on the student protests, titled The Rise of Street Extremism. The term "extremism" was clearly being used to refer to any form of radical opposition. Peter Clarke, the former head of the Counter Terrorism Command at Scotland Yard, told the audience of security officials: "We need to—mentally at least—compare the ambitions of some of the current crop of protesters and the terrorists. The distinction to my mind is not so much about their intention as in our response to it."[38] The student population had become more working-class and ethnically diverse than ever before, and was increasingly active in protests against, for example, Israel's military offensives, tuition fees, and the withdrawal of maintenance grants to enable young people to attend college. In this context, campus activism was framed as the next form of extremism to be tackled through the Prevent apparatus. Because of the program's failure to distinguish between extremist ideas and terrorist violence, its structures were eminently suited to the task of countering the new protest movements against hemorrhaging public services and the racketeering of the 1 percent. Occupy London—the peaceful protest camp outside St. Paul's Cathedral modeled on Occupy Wall Street—was soon classified as an extremist threat, according to police documents made public under the Freedom of Information Act.[39]

In Britain, the special branches have historically formed the backbone of political policing. These units, based in each of the local forces, focused on threats of subversion, i.e., the radical Left, the peace movement, trade unionists, environmentalists, animal rights activists, and Irish nationalists. They acted as the local eyes and ears of the security state, having developed a close working relationship with MI5, which did not itself make arrests or launch prosecutions.[40] The end of the cold war made the political policing role of MI5 and the special branches much harder to justify, and although the old structures remained in place, they lacked a clear role. The terrorist attacks of 9/11 and 7/7 provided the pretexts for a substantial reorganization. The special branches were reconfigured as counterterrorism and counterterrorism intelligence units to work alongside MI5's eight newly opened regional offices across England. The number of police officers deployed on counterterrorism rose from seventeen hundred to three thousand between 2003 and 2008, and MI5's staff almost doubled in size, to around thirty-five hundred.[41] With Prevent, political policing had come back in a new form. Britain's security bureaucracy once again widened its reach to a stance that focused on political subversion (now billed as radicalization) rather than on threats of violence to the civilian population. Prevent was, in effect, an experiment in new forms of countersubversion for the twenty-first century, with young Muslims as a convenient testing ground. Because the old deference to the security apparatus had weakened, it was harder for MI5 and the police to operate without scrutiny, as they largely did during the cold war. But by drawing a range of nonpolice agencies into their intelligence-gathering web and wrapping their work in the language of antiextremism, they were able to introduce wide-ranging surveillance of people identified on the basis on their political beliefs and lawful activities.

Strategic Essentialism

Prevent's success rested on finding reliable Muslim partner organizations that could deliver the government's counterextremism message. With unprecedented intensity, the question of who was to speak for

Britain's Muslim population was raised. On the one hand, Muslims were pictured as a monolithic bloc appropriately represented by a single, unelected organization whose officials could sit in private meetings with government ministers and negotiate an agreement on the position of Muslims in British society. On the other hand, that such a form of leadership was even necessary betrayed the anxiety that Muslims were not really a monolith at all but divided about who they were and where their interests lay. It was not that community leaders were being asked to represent a preexisting community so much as to create and sustain the fiction that one existed. What was really being asked was who was to speak *to* Britain's Muslims, not *for* them.

In the early 1990s, the government had welcomed the formation of the Muslim Council of Britain (MCB), seeing it as a suitable candidate for this job: a body of moderate Muslims that, in return for official patronage, could channel political discontent within Muslim communities in a manageable form. That a number of MCB activists were linked to the Jamaat-i-Islami—the oldest organization representing political Islam in South Asia—was less important than its willingness to do the government's bidding. With the launch of wars on Afghanistan and Iraq after 9/11, the MCB's position became more fraught. Grassroots pressure forced it to refrain from any acquiescence in the Afghan occupation, and it argued forcefully that the war on Iraq would increase terrorism. The MCB was increasingly criticized as an extremist organization, and in the summer of 2006, ministers announced it would no longer be favored as the leading representative of Muslims in Britain.

Over the following years, two organizations stepped forward to attempt to fill the gap, both strongly guided by powerful outside networks, both seeking to become actively involved in the government's surveillance apparatus, and both declaring their support for the official analysis that ideology was driving radicalization and foreign policy was of little relevance. The first, the Sufi Muslim Council (SMC), received at least £203,000 of Prevent funding in 2008 and 2009 to establish itself as a community leadership organization.[42] Road shows and conferences were organized, a television channel launched, and a leading public relations consultancy, Blue Rubicon, hired to coordinate a marketing strategy. Prince Charles and government ministers publicly backed the group. A US-based neoconservative activist, Hedieh Mirahmadi, who was involved in setting up SMC along with a small network of British Muslims, said the organization was part of an attempt, supported by the government, to promote Sufism as a preferable form of Islam. "We deliberately saw Sufism as more moderate than Salafism," she says.[43] The RAND Corporation, the leading US think tank on military affairs, had argued the year before that Western governments should fight a "battle of ideas" against "Islamist extremism" in Europe by empowering traditionalists and Sufis, who it said were the "natural allies of the West."[44] In Washington, Mirahmadi has since been actively pushing for a more forceful US counterradicalization policy that would increase demands on American Muslims for ideological conformity: "The community needs to be pressured to challenge ideology—like Prevent did in Britain. We need to bug the community to get active on this.[45]

Among the projects linked to SMC was a youth center aimed at Muslims in the Longsight area of Manchester, for which a Prevent funding application of half a million pounds was submitted. The center was to provide sports facilities and offer career advice, as well as religious guidance aimed at providing a counterextremism narrative. "Some of the centre's activity will be diversionary," stated the funding application. "However the real focus will be on counter/de-radicalising people." For these people, "spiritual, theological and ideological training" would be used to challenge their views. The bid also recommended the inclusion of free IT facilities, as it was "good for monitoring which websites people were visiting," and "intelligence gathering" was stated as one of the rationales for the center. Asking people to register as members to use the center would help "to collect data and build a database." And "two-way sharing of information with local (policing) agencies" would take place, including in order to identify young people in the neighborhood who would be "targeted and then sought out to bring them into the programme."[46]

It became clear fairly quickly that the SMC lacked any credibility with young Muslims and would be unable to perform the leadership and surveillance roles expected of it by the government.

A second attempt at creating an astroturf Muslim organization was the Quilliam Foundation. It was established in April 2008 by Ed Husain (author of the best-selling *The Islamist* published a year earlier) and Maajid Nawaz, both of whom had been activists in Hizb ut-Tahrir before becoming disillusioned and embracing the government's Prevent agenda. The foundation was hugely effective in legitimizing the official narrative of radicalization. For a while Husain and Nawaz—young, articulate, and always sharply dressed—were ubiquitous in the media and on the conference circuit, arguing that political issues such as the Iraq war were not all that relevant in explaining terrorist attacks in Britain. Rather, they said, the root problem was the politicization of Islam, and the best way to prevent terrorism was for states to create a Western Islam that was reliably apolitical. The foundation launched an extensive program of radicalization awareness training sessions for thousands of police officers and officials working in local authorities around the country, promoting their good Muslim–bad Muslim message.[47] With backing from government ministers, it advised schools on the behaviors that "could indicate a young person is being influenced by extremists and developing a mindset that could lead them to accept and undertake violent acts." The indicators its training listed included expressions of political ideology, such as support for "the Islamic political system"; a focus on scripture as an exclusive moral source; a "conspiratorial mindset"; seeing the West as a source of evil in the world; and literalism in the reading of Muslim texts.[48]

The Quilliam Foundation received over £1 million of government Prevent funding in its first two years.[49] But things came unstuck in late 2009 after Ed Husain gave an interview to the *Guardian* in which he acknowledged Prevent was "gathering intelligence on people not committing terrorist offences" and said that to do so was "good" and "right."[50] This proved somewhat embarrassing at a time when ministers were trying to reassure the public that Prevent did not involve intelligence gathering but was a form of community engagement and assistance. The government was forced to distance itself from the foundation. The following year, Husain and Nawaz hoped they might return to favor with the new Conservative-led coalition government that came to power in May 2010. Their chances looked good, given that the neoconservative MP Michael Gove, who was education minister in the new government, was on the foundation's board. Gove's cranky 2006 book, *Celsius 7/7*, had called for a new cold war against "Islamism," recommended Britain carry out assassinations of terrorist suspects to send "a vital signal of resolution," and said a "temporary curtailment of liberties" would be needed to prevent "Islamism" from destroying Western civilization.[51] Among fellow Tories, Gove was seen as a veritable expert on Muslims in Britain. Were Gove's recommendations to be implemented, the Quilliam Foundation could certainly be of use to the new government. Husain and Nawaz decided to advertise their services by producing a blueprint for how Prevent policy might be taken in a more hardline direction. The document, meant only for private discussion by ministers and senior advisers, argued for tackling "a broader Islamist ideology," and included a list they had drawn up of groups to be banned from public funding and government engagement, including most of the major Muslim organizations in the UK. The idea of such a list had first been mooted by Charles Moore, the chairman of the Policy Exchange think tank, in a speech in March 2008 on a "possible conservative approach to the question of Islam in Britain." The government, he argued, should maintain a list of Muslim organizations that, while not actually inciting violence, "nevertheless advocate such antisocial attitudes that they should not receive public money or official recognition." In this category would fall any groups with links to the Muslim Brotherhood or the Jamaati-i-Islami, as well as individuals such as Tariq Ramadan.[52] But the Quilliam Foundation's blueprint was leaked, and the plan had to be dropped. By the end of 2010 the foundation's credibility with the government was in shreds, and it lacked any grassroots community base to fall back on. Funding had dwindled to a trickle, and most of its staff had to go. With the US government increasingly interested in importing British thinking on countering radicalization, Ed Husain left the UK to take up a fellowship at the Council on Foreign Relations (CFR) in Washington, while Maajid Nawaz began to work with Google's think tank, Google Ideas, on its counterradicalization program, also in partnership with the CFR.

Multiagency Surveillance

It is entirely appropriate for the police and MI5 to place Muslims under surveillance if there is a reasonable suspicion of their active involvement in terrorism. It is also right that channels are available for other professionals, such as youth workers and teachers, to provide information to the police if there are reasons to believe an individual is involved in criminality. But, as noted above, Prevent sought to draw professionals providing nonpolicing local services into routinely providing information to the counterterrorist police not just on individuals who might be about to commit a criminal offense, but also on the political and religious opinions and behaviors of young people. A major part of Prevent was the fostering of much closer relationships between the counterterrorist policing system and providers of nonpolicing local services to facilitate these kinds of flows of information on individuals considered at risk of extremism.

The attempt to integrate policing with agencies of local government can be traced back to the early 1980s, with the reorganization of policing under Metropolitan Police Commissioner Kenneth Newman (who had previously served as chief constable of the Royal Ulster Constabulary in Northern Ireland). New legislation sought to incorporate social and welfare agencies into the policing process. This was presented as a supportive form of "community policing," but its purpose was to embed police surveillance in schools and other agencies providing public services. This new approach, of coordinating police work with social agencies, was reflected in the 1982 Police and Criminal Evidence Bill, which in its original version, proposed a power to search confidential records held by professionals.[53] Civil rights lawyer Paul Boateng noted that the bill raised the prospect of civil liberties abuses as "the proper professional distinctions between the roles of social workers, probation officers, local government workers, teachers and policemen, become confused."[54] Grassroots campaigns for police accountability in the early 1980s led to some diminution of these dangers, and the power to search records was dropped by the time the bill became the Police and Criminal Evidence Act 1984. Nevertheless, the idea that social agencies should coordinate their work with the police took hold, and it led to these multiagency partnerships becoming common practice.

After 7/7, security officials in Britain studied how their Dutch counterparts had responded to the murder of filmmaker Theo van Gogh by a Dutch Muslim radical the year before. The Amsterdam municipal authority had been influenced by Wiktorowicz's model of radicalization and begun a comprehensive counterradicalization program that was subsequently replicated in other Dutch and Scandinavian cities. Its starting point was the idea of embedding surveillance in a range of formal and informal agencies, in the hope of creating an early warning system to detect radicalization.[55] Not just the police but social workers, teachers, and community activists were recruited into the web of counterterrorism intelligence gathering. In Amsterdam an agency named the Information House was the hub where nonpolicing professionals could be briefed on the indicators of extremism and the resulting flows of information were collated and, where necessary, shared with the security services. Since most of the would-be extremists identified were law-abiding, the interventions that followed could not normally involve criminal prosecution. Instead, mentoring, counseling, religious instruction, or various forms of disruption were applied. The Channel project, which is the part of Prevent aimed at individual interventions, was the same idea adapted for the British context. The structures of informal surveillance that already existed as multiagency partnerships to tackle gangs, antisocial behavior, and so on, were for the first time appropriated for counterterrorism purposes. In doing so, their potential as tools for monitoring and influencing the political opinions of young people in a suspect community was realized.

The Channel project is shrouded in secrecy. The official guidance documents are vague on how individuals are identified and referred to the project, and exactly what actions are taken thereafter. One states that "expressed opinions" are one of the potential indicators of radicalization and notes that among the kinds of opinion that might indicate a risk are the "rejection of the principle of the rule of law and of the authority of any elected Government in this country." Home Office officials say a key indicator of radicalization is the opinion that the West is at war with Islam. Prevent training sessions provide further guidance on how to spot an extremist; about fifteen thousand local authority staff have received Workshop to Raise Awareness of Prevent (WRAP) training on indicators of radicalization.[56]

Those working on the Channel project are bound by confidentiality agreements that prevent them from speaking openly. Nevertheless, based on interviews with five youth workers who have participated in providing Channel interventions across four English cities, and with four other youth workers who have been asked to participate in identifying young people at risk in various locations, it has been possible to sketch the kinds of behaviors that lead the Channel project to certain young people, and what kinds of actions follow. One youth worker, who says he has been asked to work with the most hard-core cases identified in his city, found no cases in which there was any chance of the young person heading toward terrorism. It was rather that they had strong political opinions about Muslims in Britain or other parts of the world. The youngest person he worked with was nine years old. He felt referrals were coming because teaching staff nowadays were less likely to handle racism and interethnic conflict in the classroom, and instead sent them to the Channel project for management; in the past teachers would have engaged students to resolve such issues. In one case a young person was referred because he had accused the teacher of racism in the treatment of Muslims in the classroom. None of the young people referred to this youth worker had adopted anything like a systematic ideology, nor was there any real interest in or knowledge of Islam—just conspiracy theories mixed with a Manichean identity politics.

Another youth worker spoke of a case in which a young person was referred to Channel for handing out a Hizb ut-Tahrir leaflet, which he had done in response to other students handing out far Right British National Party leaflets. In other cases young people were reportedly referred for expressing strong views on Palestine, against British forces in Afghanistan, or for visiting radical Web sites. One youth worker told me he

> had a host of requests from the police to collude with them; for example, asking us for names of people at meetings, and [calling us with requests] like, "Oh, can you just have a conversation with . . .". When

> we refuse, we have been told by the police that "you are standing in our way," and they have tried to undermine our organization. We have been threatened, but we have refused to share the beliefs, views, and opinions of people we work with.[57]

Another youth worker said:

> You're supposed to report back information to the Prevent Board, such as mapping movements of individuals. You have to provide information if an individual is at risk. But you also need to give information about the general picture, right down to which street corners young people from different backgrounds are hanging around on, what mosques they go to, and so on. There is probably a perception that these are benign procedures, and [that] it is an extension of a general attitude that already exists, for example, in the mapping of antisocial behavior.[58]

In 2008, the government published a tool kit to encourage schoolteachers to contribute to the Prevent program. It requested that they monitor pupils for the warning signs of extremism, offered guidance on detecting trigger points in vulnerable children, and recommended that schools "form good links with police and other partners to share information."[59] Police officers working on Prevent compiled lists of primary and secondary schools in their neighborhoods, sorted by the level of risk they were thought to present, and sought to recruit teachers as sources of intelligence. An e-mail sent by the West Midlands Police CTU in 2009 about the Channel project asked its recipients, who included schoolteachers and youth workers:

> I do hope that you will tell me about persons, of whatever age, you think may have been radicalised or be vulnerable to radicalisation . . . Evidence suggests that radicalisation can take place from the age of four.

Those on the Channel project would receive

> sessions with learned scholars of Islam who can refute the messages the radicalisers are giving out to people and show them the context of lines they may have been given from the Qur'an.[60]

I telephoned the officer who sent out the e-mail and asked him how a four-year-old might be identified as radicalizing. He told me that they might draw pictures of bombs on their exercise books or say things like, "All Christian people are bad," "We need an Islamic state," or "My daddy says all Western people should be killed." Visiting nursery schools to brief teachers on spotting these kinds of signs was useful, he said, because younger children would not be clever enough to know what to keep private.[61] The idea, it seemed, was to use young children as sources of intelligence on their parents. One youth worker I spoke to believed strong pressure from the police was leading to increasing numbers of young people being identified simply for articulating strong political opinions, for example, about British forces in Afghanistan.

The cases of young people who have been identified as at risk are discussed by a panel led by the police but including other professionals. It is based on these assessments that a program of mentoring or religious instruction might be recommended, in an effort to transform the person's ideology. Youth workers or other professionals are expected to report back to the panel after each session with details of the discussions that took place and whether the young person is still a potential threat. There are a variety of approaches. In some cases the emphasis is on addressing emotional issues or frustrations at being denied opportunities to progress in life. Counseling and perhaps help finding a job are provided. In other cases ideological and theological arguments are used to challenge the individual's worldview.

Often the young person does not know he is being targeted for intervention as part of a Preventing Violent Extremism initiative. Parents also may not know, especially if there is a suspicion that the family is the source of the extremist ideas. In one case a youth worker was asked to meet with a young person at school and befriend him without his being aware that he had been identified as at risk. Over time he was given mentoring in a bid to change his views about the war in Afghanistan. The youth worker involved pointed out to me that people who really advocated violence would never engage with such a mentoring process. But those who are referred to Channel, he said, have softer views that are more about identity than violence, and are usually driven by a sense that Western foreign policy is riddled with double standards and inconsistencies. Making the argument that Muslims living outside the house of Islam (*dar al-Islam*) are religiously obliged to follow the laws of the country of their residence is one part of how he responds. Another is to try to get young people to open up about their feelings about being Muslim in Britain, which usually includes descriptions of raw experiences that underlie their political views. Youth workers involved with Channel interventions are paid according to the number of cases they take on, and on the length of time each takes to resolve; there is therefore an incentive for them to talk up the problem of extremism in a local neighborhood, and to prolong the intervention itself.

In the official literature, Channel has two faces. On the one hand, it is presented as providing support for vulnerable individuals, in a way analogous to child protection measures designed to prevent young people from suffering abuse. On the other hand, it is also referred to as having an intelligence-gathering dimension. Norman Bettison, the former chief constable of West Yorkshire Police and one of the architects of Channel, put it as follows:

> [It] has the dual aims of linking community engagement with the generation of community intelligence with a view to intervening, with partners and the community themselves, where risk is identified.

Police officers implementing Channel therefore are

> a kind of hybrid of the two roles that have been identified as the central pillars for this approach—community engagement and developing community intelligence.[62]

Channel case files are held for a minimum of six years and can be kept indefinitely if it is thought necessary to do so. In one local authority, a document outlining the legal basis for the Channel project states that the data it collects are to be held until the subject is one hundred years old.[63] Given that these files contain detailed personal information about suspected young radicals' political and religious opinions, who they associate with, and other details about their private lives, the questions of who has access to this material, and under what circumstances, are crucial. Since individuals are not identified on the basis of criminal suspicion, it would be inappropriate for the information in the case files to be made available to MI5 or police counterterrorism investigators unless there were some separate basis to reasonably suspect the individuals of involvement in serious criminal activity. If they are shared, Channel would clearly be a significant adjunct to MI5's general intelligence-gathering work, providing a trove of data that would interlock with other forms of surveillance—but obtained with the collusion of public service providers and community organizations unaware that their data gathering was ending up as MI5 intelligence. Prevent head Charles Farr has refused to say under what circumstances MI5 would be able to access Channel data. In a carefully worded reply to this question he states that anyone who is the subject of an MI5 investigation should not simultaneously be subject to the Channel process. This was meant to reinforce the impression that there is a strong demarcation between the investigative work of MI5 and the community-based work of Prevent, and to reassure us that the Channel project would not be used by MI5 as another window into the lives of people already being investigated. There are two points to be made about this. First, MI5 already has wide-ranging surveillance powers to target subjects considered a national security threat, and so the extra window would in any case add little. Second, individuals referred by schools and universities are presumably on occasion already under MI5 investigation. Unless data is in fact shared between MI5 and the Channel project, how would the kinds of overlaps that Farr is ruling out be avoided in practice? But the real problem is that Farr's attempt at reassurance does not rule out the more likely scenario that the Channel project provides a way to obtain data on the lives of those on the periphery of social networks already being investigated by MI5. The Channel project is probably seen by MI5 as a cheap way of gaining detailed information about individuals not considered a national security threat themselves but who may associate with those who are. This would explain its apparent emphasis on gathering information on family members and others in a young person's social network. In any case, the police counterterrorism units that hold these case files include embedded MI5 officers, who would presumably be able to access this data straightforwardly.[64] Further clarification on these questions has been rebuffed by Farr with the boilerplate statement that "it has been the established policy of successive governments to neither confirm nor deny in response to questions concerning the intelligence and security agencies."[65]

Not only does the Channel project raise substantial issues of privacy; it is also discriminatory. Since it seems to function in part on the basis of treating religious behaviors as indicators of extremism, and because over 90 percent of its cases have involved Muslims, it appears to be a form of profiling based on religious identity. There are also a number of pragmatic difficulties which call the project into question. First, there is no reason to think that a nebulous Islamic identity politics, which seems to be what usually serves as an indicator of risk, is in any way a precursor to carrying out acts of violence against fellow citizens. When some young Muslims are alienated by their own society and see some of the wars the US and UK governments are fighting, they may come to believe the West is indeed at war with Islam. But there is no evidence to support the assumption that such opinions can be taken as indicators of a terrorist threat. Second, by recruiting nonpolicing professionals to engage in what is, in effect, a counterterrorism intelligence-gathering role, their own professional norms of trust and confidentiality are undermined. There is an obvious tension between the imperatives of policing, which is based on gathering information about people, and those of education, which is based on empowering students to think critically and learn how to express their views in effective ways. Young people should be able to fully express their opinions in schools and youth clubs without becoming entangled in the counterterrorism system. Indeed, enabling young people to do so is a surer way of reducing the attraction of political violence than a government-led program of ideological manipulation. But, for a state with a deeply unpopular foreign policy, a generation of young people able to critically analyze what is happening in the world and organize themselves to change it is perhaps a greater source of anxiety than terrorism itself.

CHAPTER 6

No Freedom for the Enemies of Freedom

> We shall provoke you to acts of terror and then crush you.
>
> —C. B. Zubatov, tsarist police director

In August 2010, twenty-one-year-old Antonio Martinez posted a message on his Facebook page.

> When are these crusaders gonna realize they cant win? How many more lives are they willing to sacrifice. ALLAHUAKBAR. [*sic*]

The following month, he commented:

> The sword is cummin the reign of oppression is about 2 cease inshallah . . . don't except the free world we are slaves of the Most High and never forget it! [*sic*]

A couple of days later, he added:

> Any 1 who opposes ALLAH and HIS Prophet PEACE.Be.upon.Him I hate u with all my heart.[1] [*sic*]

Martinez had grown up in a Nicaraguan family living in the Maryland outskirts of Washington, DC, and been involved with drugs and petty crime as a teenager. But he eventually had found work in construction and started looking to religion to provide meaning to his life. In his journal, he began to list quotations from the Bible, and wrote about his admiration for samurai warriors who gave their life in battle, adding:

> Oh, how I wish for the same fate, to be remembered forever as a fearless warrior.[2]

He was baptized, but Christianity did not seem to work for him. "He said he tried the Christian thing. He just really didn't understand it," remembered a former girlfriend.[3] Then he converted to Islam, which friends said helped him get his life under control.[4] He changed his name to Muhammad Hussain and on his Facebook page began to describe himself as "just a yung brotha [*sic*] from the wrong side of the tracks who embraced Islam."[5] But the version of Islam Martinez embraced was very different from that practiced by the rest of the local Muslim population. Martinez began to visit radical Web sites at a public library, such as the Revolution Muslim site run by Younes Abdullah Muhammad, whom we met in Chapter 3.[6] His postings on Facebook began to reflect his newfound view that the West was at war with Islam and oppressing Muslims around the world. Within a couple of months a member of the local Muslim community, who earlier had been recruited as an FBI informant, spotted the Facebook postings, and identified Martinez to federal agents.[7]

Martinez's online activity was entirely lawful. He was simply expressing religious and political opinions, protected activity under the First Amendment to the Constitution. Large numbers of people in the US believe, like Martinez, that the West is at war with Islam, not because they have been brainwashed by radical Web sites or preachers but because they read the news and concluded that the US government institutionally has a specific view of Islam that makes it more likely to use military violence against Muslim populations. Indeed, there are a significant number of people within the US's own national security apparatus who also believe the West is at war with Islam. In 2011, military officers undergoing training at the Joint Forces Staff College were told:

> Islam has already declared war on the West, and the United States specifically, as is demonstrable with over thirty years of violent history.

A presentation by Lieutenant Colonel Matthew A. Dooley, which was subsequently leaked to *Wired* magazine, argued for

> taking war to a civilian population wherever necessary (the historical precedents of Dresden, Hiroshima, Nagasaki, being applicable to the Mecca and Medina destruction . . .).

He added:

> Islam must change or we will facilitate its self-destruction.[8]

Although the opinions Martinez expressed were lawful and shared by significant numbers of others, one might still wonder whether young Muslims holding them are more likely to become involved in terrorist activity in the future. If so, one could ask, should law enforcement agencies concentrate resources on such individuals as part of a preventive strategy against terrorism? The FBI believes so and justifies its view through academically informed radicalization models that it says can be used to assess what individuals' lawful religious and political activities indicate about their progression toward terrorism. Like the NYPD's model of radicalization discussed in Chapter 4, the FBI's model has four stages an individual passes through, from converting to Islam to becoming a jihadist terrorist.[9] In the first stage, "frustration and dissatisfaction with the current religious faith leads the individual to change belief systems," and watching "inflammatory speeches and videos" on the Internet makes them vulnerable to further radicalization. In the second stage an individual identifies with "a particular extremist cause" without necessarily wanting to take action in support. Interacting with extremist materials on the Internet drives the individual further along the process "from conversion to jihad." Once the convert has "accepted the radical ideology" but not necessarily gotten involved in actual activities to advance the cause, he or she has reached the third stage, one step away from active terrorism.[10] It is not hard to see how applying the FBI's radicalization model to Martinez's case could create the impression that he posed a significant risk. He was certainly a world apart from the ruthlessly effective terrorists that television shows like *24* and *Homeland* routinely depict, and no one believed he was connected to any organized group. But it is such teenagers and young men whom the FBI regards as the greatest domestic security threat to the United States. To the FBI, al-Qaeda is no longer a structured organization able to recruit Western Muslims, train them, and conduct sophisticated, coordinated operations. It is instead an ideology that pushes some young Muslims along a four-stage path of radicalization until they become do-it-yourself terrorists who need no structured support from anyone else.

Moreover, FBI agents believe that just monitoring young people in these radicalization stages is insufficient. They claim surveillance alone is unreliable, because it risks missing crucial developments that, they say, can occur over as little as a few months. Equally, the FBI believes that in other cases it could be years before low-level radicalism moves to involvement in actual terrorist activity, by which time the case may have been dropped because a period of surveillance failed to indicate any criminal activity. Given these perceptions, as well as the demand that the FBI adopt counterterrorism as its top priority and the requirement that it take a preemptive stance on perceived threats, a more aggressive strategy has inevitably followed. That strategy is provocation: the use of agents provocateurs to test if individuals expressing radical views can, in circumstances carefully engineered by the government, be pushed into criminal activity, so that they can then be arrested and prosecuted. As a RAND Corporation study puts it, agents provocateurs need to be used to "lubricate" suspects' decision making.[11] The assumption is that if an FBI undercover agent or informant can, through elaborate sting operations lasting many months, create circumstances that manipulate radicalized young people into conspiring to commit acts of terror—with the FBI supplying fake weapons—then that is sufficient evidence to demonstrate that a person was already on a radicalization journey to becoming a terrorist. If the key difficulty of a preventive approach to counterterrorism is knowing whether someone who is not currently a terrorist is going to become one in the future, the FBI's solution is to ask a different question: can someone who is not currently a terrorist be made into one by the FBI?

This is what the FBI did in Martinez's case. The informant who had reported his Facebook postings was given the task of befriending him. After a little while the informant told Martinez he wanted him to meet an "Afghani brother" who shared their views—actually an FBI undercover agent. Search warrants were issued for the library computers Martinez had used, and Facebook agreed to release records of all of Martinez's postings and traffic.[12] The full details of the ensuing conversations between Martinez, the informant, and the undercover agent have not been made public. Some were recorded—but key moments were not—due to what the FBI called "recording machine malfunction," particularly in the early stages, when Martinez seemed to change from having vague thoughts about the oppression of Muslims to having a definite plan of action focused on attacking a local army recruiting center.[13] At some point in the developing relationships Martinez began to speak more specifically about wanting to join what he called "the ranks of the mujahideen." In one online exchange, he wrote:

> Jihad is all I think about when i sleep, when I wake up, sometimes i cry cuz im not there and kaffur [nonbelievers] killing all our brothers and sisters.[14][*sic*]

By now he was planning to travel to Pakistan or Afghanistan.

> Each and every Muslim in this country . . . knows that America is at war with Islam and they're not doing anything about it . . . No one is stepping up to do anything. We have to be the ones to pull that trigger.[15]

Soon the plan to travel abroad changed to carrying out an attack on a local army recruiting center in Catonsville, Maryland. Martinez asked the informant to purchase a rifle for the purpose. The FBI undercover agent suggested that instead he could arrange to provide a car bomb. At another meeting three weeks later the undercover agent showed Martinez an SUV and what he said were bomb components and a detonation device. The only problem was that Martinez could barely drive, so he had to practice driving around a parking lot. The attack was planned for the next morning. Martinez parked the SUV, laden with the fake bomb outside the target—the Armed Forces Career Center on Baltimore National Pike—before retreating with the informant to a vantage point and attempting to detonate the bomb, in what he thought would be his first strike against the Muslim-oppressing US military. But instead of the expected explosion, FBI agents rushed in and arrested him. Martinez was charged with the attempted use of a weapon of mass destruction and attempting to murder federal officials. He later pled guilty and was sentenced to twenty-five years in prison.

Martinez's story is far from unusual—it is in fact a textbook case of current FBI tactics in the domestic war on terror. Investigative journalist Trevor Aaronson has examined forty-nine terrorist prosecutions since 9/11 which involved an FBI agent provocateur. Among them were most of the high-profile terrorism cases over the last ten years. In all of them someone working for the FBI "provided not only the plan but also the means and opportunity for the terrorist plot."[16] Without the FBI's help in supplying money, weapons, and often a specific plan of attack, the accused would not have had the capability to carry out any plot. In many cases, there is evidence suggesting that FBI agents provocateurs manipulated vulnerable people with mental health or drug addiction problems into conspiring in acts of planned violence they would otherwise have had no intention of carrying out. The most significant conversations between the agents provocateurs and the defendants were not recorded on these occasions (which, as Aaronson notes, is implausibly explained by technical failures).

I Was an Islamist for the FBI

In December 2001, the FBI arrested Shahed Hussain for running a fake driver's license scam. He was a Pakistani immigrant granted political asylum in the 1990s, and now faced federal charges and deportation. Like many Muslim immigrants after 9/11 who were charged with criminal offenses, he was offered the chance to stay in the US without time in prison if he agreed to work as an informant for the FBI. And Hussain soon discovered that his abilities as a fraudster could be of use to the government. In 2003, based in Albany, New York, he manipulated two law-abiding men—Mohammed Hossain and Yassin Aref—into involvement in what they thought was a business loan deal. When prosecutors brought the case to court they presented the deal as a terrorist fund-raising operation, and the two men received fifteen-year sentences. When the prosecuting attorney was asked by journalists whether there was anything to connect Aref to terrorism, he said: "Well, we didn't have the evidence of that, but he had the ideology."[17] The FBI then used Hussain for other covert work, in Pakistan and London, before he returned to the US and settled in Newburgh, a dilapidated, poverty-stricken town sixty miles north of New York City, where he implanted himself in the local Muslim community, posing as a wealthy businessman. After a year searching for would-be targets, most of whom guessed he was an FBI agent, he met James Cromitie, a forty-five-year-old African American who was an occasional visitor to the local mosque. He worked night shifts at Walmart, and had served two years in prison in the 1980s for selling crack cocaine. When they first met in the mosque parking lot, Cromitie said: "Did you see what they did to my people over there? In Afghanistan. Those motherfuckers." Hussain had found his quarry.[18]

Hussain worked on Cromitie for four months, showering him with flattery, cash, and free meals. These conversations were not recorded by the FBI (and many later recordings had gaps—again, equipment malfunction was blamed), but by the end of it, it seems Cromitie was captivated by the lavish generosity of his new rich friend and happily joined in conversations laced with anti-Semitism about attacking synagogues. But he was less than enthusiastic about doing anything beyond talk. When Hussain gave him a camera to photograph potential targets, he immediately sold it for fifty dollars. For months, he did nothing. Then he disappeared for six weeks, telling Hussain that he was moving to North Carolina; in fact, he remained in Newburgh and just wanted Hussain to stop pursuing him. But Hussain kept up the pressure, telling Cromitie he had not done anything to advance the plan: "You've not started on the first step, brother. Come on." Only when Cromitie lost his job and became desperate for money did he get back in touch with Hussain, who offered to pay him $250,000, provide him with a two-week holiday in Puerto Rico, a barbershop business, and a BMW if he agreed to participate in a scheme to bomb two Bronx synagogues. "I told you, I can make you $250,000, but you don't want it, brother," Hussain said. Cromitie, who knew Hussain by the fake name Maqsood, gave in: "OK, fuck it. I don't care. Ah, man. Maqsood, you got me." Hussain later testified in court that "$250,000" was code for the plot, not an offer of payment, but this seems unlikely—he acknowledged that he had told neither his FBI handlers nor Cromitie about the sum's supposed secret meaning. Later Cromitie tried to withdraw from the scheme, telling Hussain he could not do it, to which Hussain replied that his terrorist "brothers" might cut off his head.[19]

Cromitie was given the task of recruiting others from Newburgh's Muslim community. Three other African-American men—Onta Williams, Laguerre Payen, and David Williams (not a relative of Onta)—were all roped in and also offered large sums of money. Onta Williams, whose mother had a crack cocaine addiction, had started selling drugs at the age of fourteen and had spent time in prison. Payen suffered from schizophrenia, had been in and out of mental health facilities, and kept bottles of urine in his bedroom.[20] David Williams had become a Muslim as a teenager after an uncle had introduced him to the religion. But other relatives had introduced him to selling drugs, and he served five years in prison. He settled in Queens, New York; when he was released at the age of twenty-four he found a job in a restaurant and enrolled in college. But when his younger brother Lord fell ill with liver cancer, he decided to return to Newburgh to help his mother, who had to leave her job to care for him. Realizing David feared for his brother's life and the family was unable to afford adequate health care, Hussain offered to pay for a liver transplant on the understanding that David would join his scheme.[21]

Payen said barely anything in the meetings between Hussain and the four other Newburgh men. But Cromitie and the two Williamses soon realized that the more extravagant their conversations about criminal activity became, the more money Hussain handed out. They began to put on a show for him, saying things they thought he would like to hear and expecting to be rewarded with cash. Cromitie claimed to have stolen guns, thrown bombs at police stations, been jailed for murder, and visited Afghanistan, none of which was true. Little did he realize that Hussain was manipulating him far more effectively than he was manipulating Hussain. When Hussain was not around to harangue the others into developing the plot, nothing happened. The supposed terrorists preferred to sit around getting stoned and playing video games. According to his aunt, David Williams was hallucinating on PCP throughout the entire period, barely aware of what was happening.[22] Indeed, he would have likely been in prison at this time were it not for FBI agents pulling strings to postpone a pending larceny case against him so he could be caught in their sting instead.[23] None of the four men had money, cars, contacts, weapons, or ideas of their own to contribute. Hussain supplied the plan, the vehicles, and the equipment. When Hussain gave Cromitie eighteen hundred dollars and asked him to buy a gun, the supposedly hardened criminal was unable to score a deal and had to return with the money unspent.

A few days before the attacks Hussain had planned, he drove the four men to Connecticut and showed them a fake missile system that he said could be used to shoot down military airplanes—they talked about using the weapon at Stewart Airport, near Newburgh. It is far from clear what the four Newburgh men were thinking at this point. They later claimed they were planning to scam Hussain for the money they had been promised (which they had been told was waiting for them in a UPS mailbox) and then disappear without actually doing anything. To a certain extent, this is consistent with their behavior. On the other hand, Hussain's promises of vast sums of money may have tempted them to be part of a plot; there is some evidence that they thought it would only involve property damage to empty buildings. What is certain is that without Hussain's money and manipulation, they would never have been involved in terrorism.

On May 20, 2009, Hussain drove the four men to the Bronx, where Cromitie had the job of placing what he thought were explosive devices in the trunks of parked cars outside two synagogues while the others acted as lookouts. An FBI SWAT team appeared as Cromitie returned to Hussain's car, smashed through the car's windows, and arrested the men, charging them with attempting to use weapons of mass destruction. The news coverage of the case presented the four as America-hating terrorists dedicated to mass violence and motivated by radical Islam.

In reality, there was nothing to suggest Cromitie and his crew were potential al-Qaeda recruits. What seemed to initially draw Cromitie into the FBI's plot was his anger at US foreign policy. For the other three, it was being Muslim, poor enough to be vulnerable to cash inducements, and gullible enough to believe they were really going to receive thousands of dollars for an operation they were completely incapable of carrying out. The three had not expressed radical views or outrage at the oppression of Muslims in other parts of the world prior to Hussain's appearance. The Newburgh four were simply struggling to survive in the face of poverty, addiction, and mental health issues. The money spent by the government on securing their convictions—Hussain received $100,000 in wages and expenses—could have given them the support they needed to turn their lives around, whether a living wage in a regular job or the health care services they needed. David Williams's aunt, Alicia McWilliams, characterizes the case as a television show put on by the government rather than a genuine criminal investigation.

> Instead of wasting all this money to make a TV production, you could open up a job training center in Newburgh. These are all ex-offenders. You know what Newburgh looks like. Newburgh is the most impoverished county.

She compares what happened to her nephew to earlier government programs directed at African-American activism.

> COINTELPRO. The Black Panthers. The use of informants in churches, back in the 1940s and 1950s. This is happening all over again. But now the profile is Muslims. It just has a different name, and they're using different terms.[24]

Although Judge Colleen McMahon gave each of the Newburgh four twenty-five-year prison sentences, she nevertheless criticized the FBI's approach.

> Only the government could have made a terrorist out of Mr Cromitie, a man whose buffoonery is positively Shakespearean in its scope . . . I believe beyond a shadow of a doubt that there would have been no crime here except [that] the government instigated it, planned it, and brought it to fruition.[25]

In theory, the FBI's provocation tactics should be held to account when cases come to trial, but this has not happened. In every case where defendants have attempted an entrapment defense in post-9/11 terrorist trials, it has been unsuccessful. Such a defense involves two parts: first, showing by a preponderance of the evidence that the government induced the defendant to commit the crime; second, if the defendant succeeds in proving inducement, the burden is on the government to prove beyond a reasonable doubt that the defendant had a predisposition to commit the crime. In the end, these cases come down to a subjective judgment of whether the defendants were predisposed to terrorism. So far juries have accepted the prosecutors' flawed argument that radical views—such as anger at foreign policy—are evidence of a predisposition to commit terrorist acts. Implicitly, juries in these cases have endorsed the central proposition in the official analysis of radicalization: ideology causes violence.[26] In effect, Muslims have been criminalized for behaviors associated with the early stages in a fallacious model of radicalization—though such behaviors are entirely lawful, according to the First Amendment.

Even putting aside such civil liberties issues, there are serious problems from a pragmatic point of view. At the very least, a significant statistical correlation between the ideological indicators of radicalization and terrorist violence would have to be demonstrated in order to give some support for the view that ideology causes terrorism. It would also be necessary to show that provocation is the most effective way for a counterterrorist system to respond to it. On both counts, there are serious objections. As we saw in Chapter 4, academic attempts to substantiate a link between radicalization indicators (such as expressions of religious ideology) and terrorist violence fall flat when properly scrutinized. Such studies always seek to trace the ways in which an individual's belief in a radical ideology emerges, on the assumption that radical ideologies cause violence—but this is precisely what needs to be demonstrated rather than assumed. In fact, expressing particular religious beliefs or anger at foreign policy are poor predictors of the likelihood of an individual becoming a terrorist. Moreover, a counterterrorism system that monitors radicalization indicators, assuming that they have predictive value, may well be worse at avoiding attacks than one focused more narrowly on individuals inciting, financing, or preparing to carry out acts of terror. Amassing vast quantities of information on large numbers of so-called radical persons makes it harder to spot the terrorism intelligence that is actually significant. More often than not, when the US government has failed to prevent terrorist acts, it is not because the intelligence was missing but because its significance was not identified amid the huge tracts of surveillance data the national security state collects.

Since 9/11, this problem has become far worse, as the FBI increasingly sees its counterterrorism role as collecting broad-based intelligence on radicalization that is unconnected to any specific criminal act. Key to this shift have been changes to the FBI's internal rules, known as the Attorney General's Guidelines. These were originally introduced in 1976, following the revelations of abuses in the FBI's Hoover-era countersubversion programs, such as COINTELPRO, which sought to discredit, harass, and criminalize legitimate political movements. The guidelines clarified that the FBI's role was not to conduct open-ended domestic intelligence operations. Intrusive investigative techniques could only be used when there were

> specific and articulable facts giving reason to believe that an individual or group is or may be engaged in activities which involve the use of force or violence and which involve or will involve the violation of federal law.[27]

The basis for starting such investigations had to be recorded, so that an audit trail was available if allegations of government abuse were later raised. However, over time, the guidelines were gradually adjusted so that the authority to collect information became less and less dependent on having evidence of completed or impending criminal acts.

After 9/11, the FBI adopted a preemptive stance on countering terrorism—what John Ashcroft, then attorney general, repeatedly promoted as a new "paradigm of prevention."[28] The belief was that the usual principles of the rule of law—investigating individuals when there was a reasonable suspicion of criminal intent—were insufficient for tackling terrorism. Surveillance had to be broadened to a wider group suspected of radicalization. In line with this, Ashcroft revised the FBI's guidelines so that the threshold for counterterrorism investigations was significantly lowered.[29] Whereas earlier, informants could be used only when there was strong evidence of criminal activity, after 9/11 they could be employed much more widely. Philip Mudd, who in 2006 became associate executive director of the National Security Branch of the FBI, explained the consequences of the new preventive approach: "By definition, if you are preventative, there will be people dragged into those investigations who did not do something wrong."[30] Mudd was recruited to lead the process of transforming the FBI into a spy agency on the model of Britain's MI5, of moving the bureau beyond investigating individual cases to a wide-ranging gathering of information on American Muslim communities in general. He had previously been deputy director of the CIA's Counterterrorism Center, during the period when it tortured terrorism suspects, and in the run-up to the Iraq war, when he liaised with then secretary of state Colin Powell prior to his notorious speech at the UN, which was based on fabricated intelligence. Mudd introduced a program at the FBI called "domain management" that involved producing electronic maps showing in detail where ethnic groups were clustered, cross-referencing such information with databases of financial transactions, charitable-giving activities, jobs held, and so on. This then became the basis for allocating resources and informant recruitment to specific neighborhoods—effectively, a form of ethnic profiling.[31] The FBI's Domestic Investigations and Operations Guide, which implements The Attorney General Guidelines, calls on agents to refrain from profiling "solely" on the basis of race, ethnicity, national origin, or religion. But they permit the collection of information regarding ethnic behaviors "reasonably believed to be associated with a particular criminal or terrorist element of an ethnic community"—which, given the FBI's model of radicalization, would allow for all kinds of Muslim religious practices to be subject to surveillance. Also permitted is the identification of "locations of concentrated ethnic communities [and] the locations of ethnic-oriented businesses and other facilities," which presumably includes mosques.[32]

In 2008, a new set of guidelines was introduced by Ashcroft's successor, Michael Mukasey, that explicitly defined the FBI as "an intelligence agency as well as a law enforcement agency" and authorized the mass collection and circulation of surveillance data regardless of its connection to any unlawful conduct as conventionally understood.[33] (More recently, Mukasey has appeared at a conservative conference spouting Islamophobic conspiracy theories.)[34] From March 2009 to March 2011, FBI agents conducted 42,888 national security assessments—preliminary investigations of people or groups—following the new guidelines, which relax the requirement that suspicions have a factual basis.[35] In carrying out "assessments" the FBI can use informants, informal interviews, and physical surveillance without any time limitation.[36] By 2011, the bureau had introduced Field Intelligence Groups to all of its fifty-six field offices and reportedly raised the number of intelligence analysts from 1,100 in October 2001 to nearly 3,000.[37] Of its $8.1 billion budget, $4.9 billion was allocated to intelligence and counterterrorism.[38] Mark F. Giuliano, assistant director of the FBI's Counterterrorism Division, boasted that they had successfully transformed it from an investigative agency into an intelligence agency—in other words, the bureau was now gathering vast amounts of information unconnected to specific criminal acts.[39] Models of radicalization gave the illusion that collecting information this way was somehow still tethered to preventing crime. But the truth was that the FBI's transformation had probably made it less effective at detecting actual terrorist plots, while the ones it was busily manufacturing with agents provocateurs gave the superficial appearance of an efficient counterterrorism program.

The use of agents provocateurs has a long history. In his account of the tsarist secret police, known as the Okhrana, Maurice Laporte described provocation tactics as "the foundation stone" of a police state.[40] The Okhrana's innovative filing system, in which cards were held on half a million Russians—with cross-referenced political friends, nonpolitical acquaintances, and persons in contact with friends of the suspect but not known to him personally—remains the basis of modern intelligence gathering—except today agencies use specialty software applications that are capable of far more efficient processing of much greater amounts of social network data than the paper-based techniques of a century ago.[41] The model of the tsarist police state found its way to the US colonial regime in the Philippines when the constabulary's Information Section was established there in 1901 by Henry Allen, who had earlier worked as an American military attaché in Russia in the 1890s.[42] The section cultivated hundreds of paid Filipino agents across the country, making it "scarcely possible for seditionary measures of importance to be hatched without our knowledge," as Allen wrote to President Theodore Roosevelt.[43] The techniques of compiling dossiers on dissidents' private lives, spreading disinformation in the media, and planting agents provocateurs among militants were applied to combating radical nationalist groups in Manila. Control over information proved as effective a tool of colonial power as physical force. During World War I, notes historian Alfred W. McCoy,

> police methods that had been tested and perfected in the colonial Philippines migrated homeward to provide both precedents and personnel for the establishment of a US internal security apparatus . . . After years of pacifying an overseas empire where race was the frame for perception and action, colonial veterans came home to turn the same lens on America, seeing its ethnic communities not as fellow citizens but as internal colonies requiring coercive controls.[44]

On this basis, a domestic national security apparatus emerged. By the late 1950s the FBI's COINTEL program had systematized these techniques, using provocateurs and informants to infiltrate the Left, Puerto Rican nationalists, the student movement, the civil rights movement, and some far Right groups. About 1,500 of the 8,500 American Communist Party members were likely FBI informants in the early 1960s. By the end of the decade, agents who had previously worked in US foreign intelligence were transferring to the burgeoning field of domestic intelligence to spy on radical movements· A key part of the strategy was the manipulation of political activists into committing criminal acts so that the FBI could arrest and prosecute them. Agents provocateurs initiated disruptions of meetings and demonstrations, fights between rival groups, attacks on police, and bombings.[45] At least one provocation ended in death. On May 15, 1970, Seattle police shot and killed Larry Eugene Ward as he fled the scene of an attempted bombing at a real estate office that had been accused of maintaining racial segregation in the city. It emerged that Ward had been recruited to place the bomb by an FBI informant as part of a plan to undermine the Black Panthers.[46]

As of 2008 the FBI had a roster of at least fifteen thousand informants—the number was disclosed in a budget authorization request that year for the $12.7 million needed to pay for software to track and manage them. The proportion who are assigned to infiltrate Muslim communities in the United States is unknown but likely to be substantial, given the FBI's prioritization of counterterrorism and its analysis of radicalization. There are also thought to be three times as many unofficial community sources of information, known as "hip pockets."[47] While many informants are motivated by financial reward, others do so under pressure to resolve immigration problems. In these cases, Muslims without permanent residence status in the US are threatened with deportation unless they work for the FBI. The Department of Homeland Security (DHS) even has a special route to permanent residence, known as an S green card, which can be issued to immigrants working as informants for the FBI—it has been dubbed the "Snitch" green card. And, under the secret "Controlled Application Review and Resolution Program," the DHS allows the FBI to delay or deny citizenship applications from persons who are Muslim or perceived to be so.[48] Others are pushed into becoming informants by threats of criminal prosecution or the release of embarrassing personal information. Journalist Trevor Aaronson reports that a former top FBI counterterrorism official told him: "We could go to a source and say, 'We know you're having an affair. If you work with us, we won't tell your wife.'"[49]

Another motivation for becoming an informant is to have oneself removed from the no-fly list. The case of Michael Migliore, a twenty-three-year-old convert to Islam, illustrates the kinds of pressure the FBI can bring to bear. He was placed on a no-fly list after he refused to meet with the FBI without a lawyer present. He believes federal agents wanted to question him because he had at one time been a casual acquaintance of Mohamed Osman Mohamud, who was charged with involvement in a bomb plot in Portland, Oregon, following an FBI agent provocateur operation. If the FBI wanted to recruit Migliore as an informant, it would explain why the presence of a lawyer would cause them consternation. When Migliore decided to relocate to Italy to live with his mother, he was forced to travel by ship to Europe, as he was barred from flying from the US. But as his liner approached Southampton, British police approached in a speedboat, boarded, and detained him for around nine hours of questioning, apparently at the behest of the FBI. British Special Branch officers confiscated his cell phone, a flash drive, and a book of Arabic grammar under Schedule 7 antiterrorist legislation, which allows for detentions and searches at ports of entry and makes it a criminal offense to refuse to answer questions.[50]

The use of a provocation strategy to secure terrorism convictions among American Muslims has had a number of far-reaching consequences beyond the impacts on the individuals prosecuted. Given the large numbers of informants operating in Muslim-American communities, mosque congregations and Muslim community organizations understand that there is the possibility of an informant jotting down names and conversations and passing the information to the government. With the prosecutors of the war on terror blurring the distinctions between First Amendment–protected speech and criminal activity, many feel it is safest to avoid discussing certain topics, such as Western foreign policy, except with one's closest friends and family. Relationships of trust within Muslim communities are thereby eroded, as people consider open discussions risky. Those who hold views critical of the government choose not to express themselves publicly. As fear takes hold, the traditional avenues of political activism, such as taking to the streets to protest, are less likely to occur. According to official theories of radicalization, an atmosphere in which political opposition to US imperialism cannot be freely expressed by Muslims helps prevent terrorism. But in reality, the more those angry at foreign policy see their community paralyzed by fear and reluctant to express itself openly, the more likely it becomes that some will end up supporting terrorism. A strong, active, and confident Muslim community enjoying its civil rights to the full and able to engage with young people on issues they feel strongly about is the best way of preventing violence.

A second consequence of the provocation strategy is the distorting effect on perceptions of the domestic terrorist threat. The FBI has generated a stream of terrorist convictions that are considered genuine by policy makers and analysts. That these cases would not have existed without FBI fabrication is ignored. This means that mainstream analysis of the scale and nature of the terrorist threat is in part a self-fulfilling prophecy, reflecting the FBI's choices of whom to target. If the numbers of people arrested in a particular year go up, it is as likely to be because of a step-up in the number of agent provocateur operations the FBI is carrying out as the result of an independent increase in terrorist plotting. If Muslims constitute the majority of those indicted for terrorism in the US, this is in large part a product of whom the FBI is deciding to target in provocation operations rather than an objective measure of where the threat of terrorism comes from. In the two decades leading up to 2010, 348 people were killed in acts of political violence committed by the American far Right in the United States. Of course, a much larger number of people died in the 9/11 attacks, carried out by Muslims present in the US as foreign visitors. But the number of people killed in acts of political violence carried out by Muslim-American citizens or long-term residents of the US is much smaller: twenty people between 1990 and 2010.[51] Yet because the FBI considers Muslim Americans a special risk, it targets them with agents provocateurs to a far greater degree than it does the far Right. The result is that every two months or so the FBI announces another high-profile arrest of a Muslim terrorist suspect, keeping the US on its war on terror footing and sustaining the multibillion-dollar homeland security industry, while the far Right threat is downplayed. In turn, the stereotype of Muslims as inherently prone to terrorism is perpetuated.

Consider, for example, the case of James Cummings, a neo-Nazi from Maine. After inheriting $2 million, he managed to acquire a supply of radiological materials, and may have been planning to build a dirty bomb—before his wife killed him in 2008 after she had suffered years of domestic abuse.[52] The case was barely reported in the media. Likewise, white supremacist William Krar, of Noonday, Texas, maintained a weapons cache containing automatic machine guns, remote-controlled explosive devices, sixty pipe bombs, and a hydrogen cyanide bomb capable of destroying a thirty-thousand-square-foot building. No press release was published by the Department of Justice when he was arrested in 2003, as is standard practice in terrorism-related cases involving Muslims, and no press conference was called to announce the discovery of chemical weapons. Indeed, Krar would not have been arrested had he not sent a package containing counterfeit documents to the wrong address by mistake.[53] When the US Department of Homeland Security produced an intelligence report on the far Right four months after President Obama took office in 2009, the reaction from conservatives was so vitriolic that the report was repudiated and the unit that produced it effectively blocked from doing any further monitoring work.[54] In the 1990s, the FBI used sting operations to target violent far Right activists, but most of the more recent arrests were not the result of undercover work—the discovery of Cummings's and Krar's weapons caches were both accidental. On the other hand, in recent years the FBI has infiltrated groups of peace campaigners, pro-Palestinian activists, environmental protesters, and nonviolent anarchists.[55]

As well as distorting the overall perception of threat, agent provocateur operations can also have serious disruptive effects in particular localities. In October 2010, Farooque Ahmed was arrested in northern Virginia after an operation involving an FBI agent provocateur. He appears to have been planning to travel to Afghanistan to fight against the US military presence there, but as part of a sting operation, the FBI hatched a plan for him to bomb subway stations on the DC Metro.[56] Though the idea to attack the Metro originated with the FBI, the arrest caused officials to become concerned that the DC subway network was indeed vulnerable to terrorism. Security was beefed up in response to the imagined plot, and physical and mechanical bag searches were introduced. Officials argued that even if the idea to bomb the Metro had come from the FBI, now that it was public, it had to be taken seriously as a plot that might be emulated by others.[57] Another hidden cost was the disbanding of a local women's group that called itself Hip Muslim Moms, of which Ahmed's wife happened to be a member. The group was tarred by association after the media coverage of his high-profile arrest and ended its activities, though his wife was not accused of any crime. It had been involved in such radical activities as coupon clipping, exchanging recipes, and watching *Sex and the City*.[58]

Centers of Influence

In May 2010, FBI agents in Houston, Texas, hurriedly organized a lunch meeting with about thirty leaders of the city's Muslim community. Faisal Shahzad, a Pakistani-born US citizen from Connecticut, had just attempted to set off a car bomb in Times Square. The agents informed the leaders who gathered at an Indian restaurant that, in the wake of the attempted attack in New York, the FBI would be visiting Muslims in the Houston area to gain more information on the potential radicalization of young people in the community. The meeting had been coordinated by Ghulam Bombaywala, a local Pakistani-American businessman and close associate of the FBI. Those present were shown FBI slides purporting to explain the process of radicalization and the warning signs to look out for. The meeting was typical of attempts by FBI field offices across the US to cultivate relationships with people they describe as centers of influence in Muslim communities. Such community partnerships are seen by the government as central to countering radicalization among American Muslims.

Bombaywala is a strong supporter of this approach and, over the last few years, has built up close friendships with local FBI agents working on counterterrorism. He was known for having run a successful chain of restaurants in the 1990s. After 9/11 he got involved in community activities, believing Muslim leaders and the FBI had a shared interest in preventing the radicalization of the young. Using his influence as a key source of private funding for mosques, he encourages imams to look out for unfamiliar young people who join the congregations, for those who stop attending and appear to drop out of their social network, and for those who change their appearance. He says:

> The FBI is really helping us to know what to look for . . . If you see someone changing overnight, growing a big beard and starting to wear different clothes, we need to find out what is happening. Maybe that kid needs some help . . . You never know if somebody is giving him bad advice.[59]

The idea that growing a beard or starting to wear traditional Islamic clothing are signs that someone is drifting into terrorism has been absorbed from the FBI's four-stage radicalization model. Bombaywala also gives occasional sermons in mosques on the responsibilities Muslims have in post-9/11 America.

> I tell people that, after 9/11, freedom of speech, freedom of press, freedom of religion, take an empty shoe box, put all of them in it, and put them in the closet. America is no longer the same as before 9/11. Just be a responsible citizen.

He says that Muslims should avoid "loose talk," which he defines as

> anti-American sentiment or anything to do with 9/11, or anything to do with Iraq or Afghanistan. Why make these kinds of statements when you really don't need to?

Every Thursday the thirty or so mosques in Bombaywala's network get an e-mail outlining the main bullet points that should be mentioned in that week's sermon.

> Whatever the message we want to give to the common man, through the imams, every Friday there is 500 to 1,000 people in front of these guys, and in their sermon, they can talk about all this stuff.[60]

In one case, says Bombaywala, his community network played a role in providing actionable intelligence to an FBI counterterrorist investigation. One of those convicted, Pakistani student Adnan Mirza, was sentenced to fifteen years in prison in part for conspiring to provide material support to the Taliban in the form of a $550 donation. He says he was sending the money to a government-approved hospital in Pakistan and that, in the end, the funds were used on local charity projects in Houston. A friend of Mirza's turned out to be an FBI informant; he had also been befriended by an undercover agent. After arriving in the US in August 2001, Mirza had enrolled at Houston Community College and become active in a project to help the homeless. He also started a local radio program designed to educate Americans about Islam. At the time of writing, he has filed a motion alleging he was provided with ineffective legal counsel.[61]

Steve Gentry, the executive manager of the FBI's counterterrorism program in Houston, estimates that a quarter of its investigations are initiated as a result of information from Muslim community partners. Agents in his office say that as well as providing intelligence, community relationships are also crucial as a way to convey a counterradicalization narrative to the Muslim community. One example occurred in 2011, when NATO forces began bombing operations in Libya, and the FBI drew up lists of Libyan residents in the US to be interviewed—eventually, more than eight hundred across the US.[62] In the past, such broad-based interviewing provoked allegations of ethnic profiling. Nowadays the FBI preempts potential opposition by informing its community partners in advance of what it is doing and they work together to manage any ensuing anger.[63]

The Libya example illustrates the extent to which the FBI's counterterrorism activities are intimately linked to military operations abroad. In the command-and-control center at the FBI's new office building in Houston, along with clocks for each of the time zones across the United States, there is also one for Iraq and one for Afghanistan. Before 9/11, the Houston field office had led the investigation into the financial crimes of Enron executives. But it no longer regards such work as a top concern; rather, its highest priority is ensuring Houston's strategic oil and gas infrastructure is secured from the threat of terrorism. According to one estimate, around a third of the office's agents working on counterterrorism have had military experience in the Middle East prior to joining the bureau. One such is Brad Deardorff, a supervisor of one of the city's five counterterrorism squads, who, like former FBI director Robert Mueller, used to be a marine. Deardorff believes the counterinsurgency principles he learned in Somalia have proved useful in his work on countering radicalization in the Muslim communities of Texas. In both places, he says, step one is to understand the culture of the community from which the threat emanates; step two is to identify the centers of influence in the community and build relationships with them that can result in both sources of intelligence on radicalization and the basis for an ideological campaign in the community against extremism.[64]

> We're looking at the social networks around people who are centers of influence. With more refinement, we've got youth groups who are either associated with subjects [of investigation] that we have, or we understand there's a vulnerability to recruitment there, or there's mobilization that we need to understand, political activism that we need to understand.

This kind of detailed knowledge of community social networks, says Deardorff, allows agents to contextualize intelligence that is coming in from other sources. But it also becomes the basis for a wider strategy of using soft power to fight an ideological battle, using centers of influence as more credible messengers than the US government would be itself.

Deardorff studied the UK's Prevent policy for his master's thesis, entitled "Countering Violent Extremism," that he wrote in 2010 when studying at the Naval Postgraduate School for a degree in homeland security. He was attracted to its "application of 'soft power' [to] combat terrorism at the ideological level."[65] The US, he wrote, was engaged in "an ideological war that will be fought on American soil, [a] war of ideas" that needed to draw on the lessons of counterinsurgency operations around the world.[66] Building relationships between federal agents and "centers of influence from both religious and cultural groups" was, he learned, essential for two reasons.[67] First, as sources of information on political and religious expressive activity that might count as an indicator of radicalization, they would bring "radicalizing individuals, as well as individuals who 'drop out' of the mainstream religious education, to the attention of law enforcement early in the radicalization process." Second, those relationships would enable centers of influence to promote messages on behalf of the government about the correct way to be a Muslim in America by promoting a greater affinity to "American-ness" and communicating "the moral and theological foundations of an alternative ideology to Islamist extremists."[68]

Whatever the legal definitions of free speech, in practice the right to free expression is also a matter of informal norms of acceptability—the unwritten rules that determine what kinds of opinions can be shared openly. The kinds of soft power arrangements

Deardorff advocated and put into practice worked by shifting these norms, making it difficult to express certain opinions. Bombaywala's instructions to Houston's Muslim population on the new limits of free speech after 9/11 were entirely consistent with this program. Muslim businessmen have played this center of influence role in several parts of the US, claiming to represent communities which their wealth had distanced them from. Often well-meaning but with little understanding of the importance of civil rights, they see their main task as reforming Muslim immigrants to make them more culturally American, while working with the government to combat a loosely defined extremism. Having absorbed the official narrative of radicalization, they end up, in effect, helping the government to manage dissent. The result is that strongly expressed criticisms of Western foreign policy become unacceptable and an atmosphere of self-censorship pervades. Bombaywala, for his part, feels he cannot be transparent with the community about his work with the FBI. "There is a lot of stuff the common man does not understand," he says. "You cannot talk openly about these kinds of things."[69]

In the imaginations of FBI agents, immigrant Muslim communities are made up of monolithic blocs headed by patriarchs—like the "tribes" many ex-military FBI agents thought they were confronting in Somalia, Iraq, and Afghanistan before they joined the bureau. What this ignores is that communities are complex tapestries, not only with different ethnic strands, but with multiple interwoven power relationships of class, gender, and age. Who represents Muslims is not something that can be decided by empirical indicators such as influence or the number of members in a congregation or an organization. Communities do not come ready-made with leaders—to identify one is to make a political choice. And potential leaders who take a civil rights stand are often vilified as conveyors of the extremist ideas that supposedly make people into terrorists. While the Obama administration has rhetorically embraced the idea of forging community partnerships with moderate Muslims in its domestic war on terror, in practice the role communities are allowed to play in preventing terrorism has been reduced to intelligence gathering and the self-policing of radical views.

Nor are community representatives always aware that their engagement with the bureau has an intelligence-gathering function. Documents released to the American Civil Liberties Union under the Freedom of Information Act in 2011 showed that the FBI in California used community outreach as an intelligence initiative to systematically collect and store information about Muslim Americans' religious and political opinions and affiliations, as part of the domain management program. Muslim participants in these outreach programs assumed their purpose was to provide a mechanism of FBI accountability, so that concerns about its practices could be addressed. Little did they realize the programs were yet another means of surveillance. Agents made records of social security numbers and other identifying information, and, on at least one occasion, data on political opinions. In another case an agent checked motor vehicle records on someone encountered at a Ramadan dinner at a San Francisco Islamic association. One attendee was described in the FBI's records as "very progressive" and another was described as "very Western in appearance and outlook."[70]

Many conservatives reject community partnerships outright, because they see Islam itself as the problem and view engagement with Muslim organizations as pandering to the West's enemies. In its place, they want every Muslim treated with suspicion. On the other hand, liberals generally find law enforcement partnerships with communities attractive, basing their views, in large part, on the turn to community policing in the 1990s, which seemed to many to have successfully reduced crime while minimizing violations of rights. William Bratton's time as chief of the Los Angeles Police Department (LAPD) is often cited as a model. The assumption is that when police departments build relationships with community leaders, a mutually beneficial exchange is enabled in which the police are educated on the needs of the community while the community grows to trust the police, and is more willing to share information. Conflict is reduced, and the apparent tension between fighting crime and respecting rights seems to fall away. The picture is one in which the police are neighborhood problem solvers, making sophisticated use of intelligence and building genuine relationships of trust with communities. In practice, community-oriented policing has never worked like this.

Usually it has been subsumed within a "broken windows" approach to law enforcement that emphasizes large numbers of arrests for "quality of life" and petty drug offenses to maintain order in working-class neighborhoods and to demonstrate that law enforcement is "invested" in the community. What is called community policing is, in most cases, anticommunity policing: it has resulted in huge increases in the numbers of African-American and Latino young people incarcerated for drug offenses that would not lead to indictments if they were committed by wealthier and whiter young people. True community policing would address itself to the underlying causes of America's social fractures rather than rely on a racialized criminal justice system to control disaffected populations.[71]

Whatever the merits of community-oriented policing to tackle drugs and gang-related crime, using it for counterterrorism is a different proposition. Community partnerships are unable to provide any means of accountability or shared decision making, because how the FBI investigates terrorism is decided in Washington, DC, and driven by political forces that Muslim-American organizations have been unable to challenge. Moreover, there is next to no information on terrorism that American Muslims can share with law enforcement agencies, no matter how much trust they have in them, because hardly any have come across terrorist recruitment. In practice, partnerships between the FBI and Muslim communities to tackle terrorism have been part of a top-down strategy to prevent radicalization that goes way beyond knowing about imminent crimes. The moderate Muslims who are recruited to such roles are rarely civil rights advocates with a commitment to government accountability; more often they are, in effect, advocates for the government, conveying its political message to community members rather than the other way around.

CHAPTER 7

Postboom

Woke up this morning
FB eye under my bed
Said I woke up this morning
FB eye under my bed
Told me all I dreamed last night, every word I said.
—Richard Wright, *The FB Eye Blues*

During the evening of November 4, 2008, as it was becoming clear that Barack Obama was headed for victory in the presidential election, Osman Ahmed received a phone call from his cousin to say her seventeen-year-old son, Burhan Hassan, was missing.

> We went to hospitals and police stations and couldn't find anything. Around midnight, we stopped, and slept, and thought, because of the election, he might have gone to a friend's home, to watch the results. [His] mum of course could not sleep. At seven in the morning, we reported to the police station that our child was missing.

Ahmed was told that two other Somali-American families in Minneapolis had reported their children missing that morning. He started to contact other families to try to find out whether anyone knew more. One family went to their son's apartment and found a flight itinerary listing all of the missing children bound for Somalia. They realized that their sons had gone to fight for al-Shabaab ("the youth" in Arabic), the Somali insurgent movement. Ahmed reflected:

> We never thought he would go back home, from where we fled civil war and chaos. That never came to our mind, that one day he would go back to Somalia and start fighting. It was a surprise.[1]

The family spent the following months working closely with the FBI to try to locate Burhan and facilitate his return to the US. Osman Ahmed appeared on national television to draw attention to the case and in March 2009 testified at a US Senate Homeland Security Committee hearing on al-Shabaab recruitment in America. Then, in May, Burhan called his mother. "If I come back to America," he asked, "will they arrest me and put me in Guantánamo?" She tried her best to reassure him and send him money to leave Somalia. It seemed as if he had decided to leave al-Shabaab.[2] But the family was told the following month that Burhan had been killed, most likely to prevent him from becoming an intelligence source for the US government.[3] Ahmed says:

> We used any effort, any money we had, any relatives back home to get him back. By the time we convinced him to come back, and sent him the money to buy a ticket and go across the border, they found out, and they killed him immediately, because he was an asset to the US government.[4]

Burhan was one of twenty-one young men thought to have traveled from Minnesota's Twin Cities between 2007 and 2009 to attend training camps in Somalia run by al-Shabaab, which was designated a foreign terrorist organization by the US State Department in February 2008. Recruits from Minneapolis were reported to have been involved in an ambush of Ethiopian troops in the summer of 2008. In October, Shirwa Ahmed, a twenty-six-year-old former college student in Minneapolis, carried out a suicide attack in northern Somalia, killing twenty-two people—which the FBI claimed was the first time a US citizen had carried out a terrorist suicide bombing. Mohamoud Hassan, who had studied engineering at the University of Minnesota and been vice president of the Minnesota Somali Student Union, was reported killed in September 2009, ten months after traveling to Somalia; he was the fifth from Minneapolis to die. He was twenty-three years old.[5] He was buried alongside his friend, Troy Kastigar, who had also been killed fighting for al-Shabaab. Kastigar was a young white man who grew up in suburban Hennepin County, became friendly with Somalis in Minneapolis, converted to Islam, and called himself Abdirahman.

In response to the disappearances, the FBI launched Operation Rhino, its largest terrorism investigation since 9/11. Bureau director Robert Mueller announced that Somalis were being radicalized in Minnesota. Senator Joseph Lieberman warned that the missing Somalis might "return to the US at any time—fully radicalized and trained in the tactics of terror—to launch attacks here—bringing to our cities the suicide bombings and car bombings we have so far escaped."[6] It was reasonable to ask whether al-Shabaab's American recruits presented a threat to the US, given the organization's acknowledged links to al-Qaeda. But the available evidence indicated al-Shabaab was exclusively focused on the regional war in East Africa, and its foreign recruits were useful for local propaganda purposes rather than as potential perpetrators of terrorist attacks in the West. Asked about the possibility of an al-Shabaab attack on the US, E. K. Wilson, who leads a team of FBI agents in the Minneapolis field office responsible for investigating terrorist threats from the Horn of Africa, told me: "There's no real information, no credible intelligence that it is in the works, or imminently in the plans, or it's going to take place."[7] Nevertheless, many attempted to talk up the threat. Tellingly, Congressman Peter King told a committee hearing on Muslim radicalization in July 2011 that to think of al-Shabaab as only engaging in attacks in East Africa was "a failure of imagination"; the ability to conjure fear scenarios was prized above evidence-based analysis.[8]

Counterterrorism officials refer to the period immediately following a terrorist attack, when investigators rush to identify the perpetrators and prevent any follow-up incidents, as the "postboom" moment. From late 2008 onward federal agents were in postboom mode regarding Somali Americans, even though there had been no incidents within the US. The Somali communities of Minneapolis and St. Paul were besieged.[9] Those who had volunteered to fight in Somalia may have been combatants only in a distant civil war, with no intention of attacking the US, but under American law they were guilty of terrorism, because al-Shabaab was a proscribed organization. By extension, anyone assisting others to travel to Somalia to volunteer for al-Shabaab by, for example, giving them money, could face charges of material support for terrorism. On this basis, federal agents claimed a wide-ranging pretext to place themselves everywhere that young Somalis gathered—on college campuses and in high schools, shopping malls, and libraries—to question them about those who had disappeared. Agents talked their way into homes without warrants, staked out mosques, and sought to recruit informants. Somali students reported being approached by FBI agents in campus libraries or receiving phone calls from agents instructing them to leave classes in order to answer questions.[10] To students at the University of Minnesota it appeared that FBI agents were compiling a list of Muslim students on campus and questioning them one by one about their identities, religious beliefs, and political opinions.[11] Somali Americans were stopped at airports and questioned for hours by officials of the Transportation Security Administration (TSA). In 2010, an off-duty TSA officer assaulted a Somali man in Minneapolis, saying that he hated Muslims and that Somalis should go back to Africa. He had threatened another Somali man with a loaded gun on a separate occasion.[12]

A few miles south of Minneapolis, at the Mall of America, where young Somalis often hung out, especially during Eid celebrations, security guards stopped and questioned an average of twelve hundred individuals a year as part of a counterterrorism initiative in which they shared information with law enforcement authorities. The mall staff collected personal information, including birth dates, ethnicity, and names of employers, along with surveillance images, all of which were then passed to the FBI via the local fusion center, a federally funded hub where surveillance data from various official and private sources is collated. Those questioned in nearly two-thirds of the cases were described as African American, people of Asian or Arabic descent, or other minorities.[13] Meanwhile, sending money to family members in Somalia became harder, as local banks came under government pressure to refuse to handle transactions with the country. In 2012, Somali Americans in Minneapolis protested outside branches of Wells Fargo after it refused to process wire transfers to

Somalia, leaving no financial institutions in Minnesota willing to handle such transactions—at a time when a devastating famine was hitting thousands of families dependent on remittances from the diaspora.[14]

Race, Rights, and Radicals

The Somali population in the Twin Cities is the largest in North America; thirty thousand people of Somali ancestry live in Minnesota, according to surveys carried out between 2008 and 2010.[15] The heart of the Somali community in Minneapolis is the Cedar-Riverside neighborhood east of the downtown area, which is known as Little Mogadishu. The tower blocks of Riverside Plaza, with their signature Mondrian-style colored panels, house more than three thousand Somalis in cramped conditions.[16] In St. Paul, two thousand people, the majority Somali, live at the Skyline Tower on St. Anthony Avenue; it is a similarly brutal concrete high-rise, appropriately nicknamed the Titanic. Somalis started arriving in Minnesota in the late 1980s, and the numbers increased in the following decade, as that country's civil war raged. Many families spent years in Kenya's Dadaab refugee camp before becoming among the select few given admittance to the US. Minnesota has a history of refugee settlement, and it became the principal location for Somalis settling in the US. But the public assistance available to refugees since the 1990s has declined, affecting access to adequate housing, food, and health care. There is a local stereotype that Somali refugees are lazily relying on welfare payments rather than searching for work, but it is inaccurate. Many families have a single parent struggling with mental health problems resulting from the civil war. Surveys carried out at the beginning of the twenty-first century found 37 percent of Somali women and 25 percent of Somali men in the Twin Cities had been tortured before arriving in the US and suffered ongoing physical and psychological problems as a result. More generally, their poverty is rooted in a lack of job opportunities coupled with discrimination. As researcher Ihotu Ali of Columbia University put it in a 2011 study, Somalis in Minnesota "are beginning to feel the wall and feel that they can't advance and move up . . . It's like they're learning what institutional racism is." That racism also takes violent forms. Shortly after 9/11, a sixty-six-year-old Somali man was assaulted while waiting at a bus stop, and later died in the hospital.[17]

As the federal investigation into the missing young men developed, dozens of friends and associates of those who had disappeared were subpoenaed to testify before a federal grand jury. The mass questioning by federal investigators gave rise to an atmosphere of fear, uncertainty, and confusion among Somalis in the Twin Cities. Nimco Ahmed, a Somali-American community organizer who now works for the Minneapolis City Council, remembers a group of young college students she knew who were subpoenaed.

> They just didn't know what to do. These kids were just in school. A lot of them knew that some of their friends ended up in Somalia, but they just didn't know how, when, why. People had a big phobia about what the FBI is. All of a sudden we became the target of the country. We were just the center of all investigation, and all types of people were told they had to talk to the FBI. So it was just a moment where everybody was just scared.[18]

Technically, most of the FBI interviews were voluntary, but those targeted were led to believe they were compulsory. The vague parameters of the legislation on material support of terrorism meant it was difficult to know whether speaking openly about contacts with the missing Somalis might be self-incriminating, and giving misleading information to the FBI could itself result in a conviction for the offense of making false statements to a federal agent. As part of the investigation, Abdow Munye Abdow, a twenty-six-year-old Somali American from Minnesota, was questioned at his place of work; he was later convicted of making false statements to FBI agents about who was in a car with him on a drive to San Diego. He received an eight-month sentence.[19] "There was just a broad sense of mistrust of the US government in general, and specifically of a national security agency like the FBI," notes special agent E. K. Wilson.

In early 2009, the local branch of the Council on American-Islamic Relations (CAIR), the national Muslim civil rights organization, began to assist Somalis who were looking for advice on how to handle the FBI's questioning. "It was especially important during that time for individuals to know and assert their constitutional rights," recalls Lori Saroya, executive director of CAIR's Minnesota office.

> We did training sessions across Minnesota, reaching over 30,000 Somalis. Our message was simple: "If you have information on any criminal activity taking place in your community, this is the time to speak out; you need to report it. But you need to protect and educate yourself too."

CAIR organized an attorney-referral network so that those being interviewed could have legal representation. "Having an attorney present was a safe way for community members to help with the investigation," says Saroya.[20] But CAIR's provision of legal representation in FBI interviews provoked condemnation from the organization's enemies in Washington. Congressman Peter King accused CAIR of fostering a policy of noncooperation with the FBI—evidence, he said, of a general lack of Muslim-American cooperation with law enforcement.[21] The question of whether attorneys could be present at interviews touched a raw nerve, because it threatened to set limits on what kinds of investigations the FBI could conduct. Applying the FBI's model of radicalization implied widening them beyond cases of suspected criminal activity and tracking individuals who displayed the indicators that they might be drifting toward becoming extremists. But a competent lawyer would resist the kind of informal questioning of young people's religious and political opinions that was aimed at detecting would-be radicals, on First Amendment grounds; broad-based questions about their social networks and everyday life would also likely be challenged. The presence of an attorney in interviews forced investigators to focus narrowly on terrorism rather than on the wide gamut of potential radicalization indicators.

The families affected by the disappearances faced a difficult dilemma. Should they work with the FBI to try to locate their sons, only for them to possibly receive lengthy jail sentences upon their return to America, or were there other ways to track down their children and help them leave al-Shabaab without involving the US government? After all, some of the young men who left in 2007 had grown disillusioned with the movement in Somalia and quietly returned to the US of their own accord. Stoked by the sense of fear, conflicts erupted in the community over this question, and over the wider one of whether the government could be trusted to treat Somalis fairly. Previous experience suggested not. After 9/11, police officers would drive around the Somali neighborhoods in Minneapolis, pick young kids up off the streets, take them to an alley across the city, beat them up, racially abuse them, and say things such as: "Fuck Islam." Somalis got used to police officers descending en masse onto the community over the smallest of altercations and using excessive force. Community activists had been trying to address these issues for years, using the conventional community liaison channels, and some progress had been made. But, unsurprisingly, suspicion of law enforcement agencies remained high.[22]

On the other hand, Osman Ahmed, and another of Burhan Hassan's uncles, Abdirizak Bihi, tried to convince the community that the best course of action was to not insist on the right to an attorney in FBI interviews, to identify any young person who seemed to have an Islamist ideology, and to accept that the Somali community had a deep problem of radicalization. They painted a wildly inaccurate picture of the Minnesota Somali community as inundated with al-Shabaab sympathizers, blurring the distinction between a vague belief in defending Somalia from foreign invaders and concrete activity in support of al-Shabaab. Ahmed warned a Senate committee hearing that al-Shabaab recruiters were

> well represented not only in certain mosques, but wherever Somali children and young adults are concentrated, such as community centers [and] charter schools operated by Somalis. They could sometimes pose as Somali community leaders and advise politicians and other agencies that are reaching out to the Somali community.[23]

And he informed FBI agents of his suspicions of other people's political opinions.

> We know individuals who are in favor of al-Shabaab, and any information or any suspicions we have, we share with law enforcement agencies.[24]

Assuming the young recruits must have been groomed by a hidden terrorist kingpin based in Minneapolis, Bihi and Ahmed accused the leaders of the largest of the city's mosques, the Abubakar As-Saddique Islamic Center, where many of the young recruits to al-Shabaab spent their spare time, of being the hidden brainwashers and financiers behind the disappearances. After placing the Salafi mosque under surveillance, and putting its officials on the no-fly list, the FBI eventually exonerated its leaders of these accusations. The mosque, in turn, charged Bihi and Ahmed with not having the community's interests at heart and of being stooges for the US government. Each side in the feud competed for federal favors and resources by claiming it was better placed to prevent the radicalization of young people. Bihi was one of the few American Muslims willing to support Peter King's congressional hearings on Muslim radicalization, at which he testified, and he was featured in the *Washington Post* as an exemplar of a new kind of Muslim community leader, one willing to take an active role in countering radicalization.[25] In a similar vein, Ahmed tried to convince Washington senators that they needed to fund Sufi theology within the American Muslim community which, he said, was inherently antiextremist.[26] Both Bihi and Ahmed hoped they could attract federal funding for counterradicalization work. Ironically, it was only by highlighting their supposed radicalization that the deeply impoverished Somali-American communities of the Twin Cities were likely to garner increased government resources. Ahmed did eventually become part of a federally funded project. He partnered with Stevan Weine, a psychiatrist at the University of Illinois at Chicago, to research the radicalization of Somali-American young men in Minnesota, with funding from the Department of Homeland Security's Science and Technology Human Factors and Behavioral Sciences Division.[27]

For their part, the Abubakar As-Saddique mosque leaders found that after an initial period of mutual suspicion, they could develop an even closer relationship with the FBI, leaving Ahmed and Bihi feeling betrayed by the federal government they had so publicly defended. Intelligence on the young Salafis who attended this mosque was the greatest prize for the FBI, and if mosque leaders could play a self-policing role in directing the congregation away from interest in Somali politics, then so much the better. In July 2011, a fight broke out at the mosque during a talk by the imam, in which he had tried to tell young people to focus less on what was happening in Somalia and more on their lives in Minneapolis. A young man stood up and accused mosque leaders of turning their back on Somalia and the struggle there, and then punched the mosque's executive director.[28]

For imams, community organizers, and other significant figures in the Somali community, this was a time of regular engagement with a range of federal agencies. The TSA, the Department of Homeland Security, the Department of Justice, and Customs and Border Protection began programs of community outreach to Somali Americans in the Twin Cities. The US military funded a young Somali-American woman from Minnesota to make a documentary video about radicalization. Community activists were funded by the State Department to visit Somali communities in Europe to talk about being American Muslims. The FBI's Minneapolis field office organized town hall events, meetings with elders, youth conferences, and community round tables to try to improve its credibility. Ostensibly these were opportunities for community members to raise their concerns about the way the investigations were being handled. But, as the FBI privately acknowledged, there was no possibility of the community influencing how the investigations were carried out. Rather, the FBI saw the meetings as a way to correct what its agents called "misperceptions" circulating in the community, such as that suspects in Somalia might be imprisoned without trial or targeted for drone killings (such community fears were consistent with official US policy, even in cases of suspects who were American citizens).[29] Another aim was to encourage community leaders to pass information to federal agents about young people. Special agent E. K. Wilson, for example, noted that "an absent father, without an older brother or uncle to step into that role" is a common denominator in a lot of cases of Somali radicalization. To this can be added other indicators of risk:

> An abrupt change in religious practices, a deviation from one group of friends, or one mosque, to another, for no apparent reason. Or maybe removing themselves from one peer group and becoming a loner and kind of deviating away from a particular religious group.

As a result of the bureau's outreach, said Wilson, Somali community leaders had been taught to treat these indicators as signs to watch out for and share with FBI agents. Thus, the bureau began to receive tips about young people exhibiting these behaviors, or about situations in which "this kid has all of a sudden been acting differently."[30]

In St. Paul, the local police department played a substantial role in counterterrorism intelligence-gathering, masking its activities with the language of community policing. The St. Paul Police Department (SPPD) developed a program called African Immigrant Muslim Community Outreach Program (AIMCOP), partly funded by a $670,000 grant from the Department of Justice (DOJ) in 2009. The idea of AIMCOP was to develop a community policing approach "to prevent radicalization, reduce violent crime, and increase crime prevention" in St. Paul's Somali-American community. Much of the program involved police officers conducting community outreach work, mentoring, and developing police-sponsored athletic leagues for young people. The thinking was that the more young Somalis could be given opportunities to interact with people outside their own community, the more they would likely integrate successfully into mainstream American society; moreover, it was hoped that such interactions would help them trust police officers.[31] The program also listed as one of its goals to "identify and intervene with individuals at risk of radicalization, gang involvement, and violent crime." "Radicalized youth" were to be identified, their details maintained in a database, and "up-to-date intelligence" shared with other law enforcement partners.[32] The SPPD presented itself to the DOJ as having a useful role to play in counterterrorism, being able to build relationships with the community more easily than federal agencies and thereby generate intelligence of use in preventing radicalization. And as the city's policing budget had been cut in an era of austerity, overtime opportunities for police officers were maintained through this program's federal funding.

The architect of AIMCOP was Assistant Chief Dennis Jensen, who based the program on a thesis he wrote while studying for a master's in homeland security at the Naval Postgraduate School's Center for Homeland Defense and Security, which had been created after 9/11 to cater to the demand for counterterrorism expertise in local and state law enforcement. Jensen's thesis stated:

> In the aftermath of September 11, 2001, it became abundantly clear that law enforcement agencies, both federal and local, lacked the ability to gather investigative data from the Muslim community. On a federal level, investigators not only lacked the contacts in the community, they actually harmed some relationships by their lack of cultural understanding when attempting to gather information . . . It is clear that building a strong relationship between the local police and the Muslim community is essential in defending America against acts of terrorism. Key to this relationship is trust between the groups and an understanding of cultural differences.[33]

Just as the counterinsurgency theorists emphasized the importance of cultural knowledge in fighting colonial wars, so ideas of culture had become important in domestic counterterrorism. The notion that there was a fixed, singular entity called Somali culture which could be an object of police knowledge took hold in law enforcement circles in the Twin Cities. Manipulation of this knowledge by government agencies would, it was believed, help integrate the community into the wider society and win its trust. Meetings with members of the community were the means by which this knowledge was to be both acquired and applied. "I don't know how old you are," Jensen asked me, "but do you remember in Vietnam they talked about winning the hearts and minds of people?"[34]

The starting point for Jensen was to approach those he called the "elders" in the community: "If the elders of the community come to trust the police officers, then most of the community will also cooperate wholeheartedly with the department."[35] Thereafter police officers were assigned to mentor young people at eight different public housing sites in St. Paul, for example, by helping with homework, and three hundred young Somalis were recruited to the Police Athletic League. Jensen hoped that getting involved in sports would mean "they're thinking about stuff like that instead of, you know, the ties to home."[36] Out of these relationships, Jensen claimed, the police department developed the cultural knowledge he hoped for (although the kinds of knowledge this process produced seemed bizarre: for example, he believed that, "with Somalis, particularly in their culture, it's okay to lie to people if it benefits the family").[37] The project also delivered significant intelligence in relation to radicalization. As an example, he said, information was obtained on mosques that were perceived as radicalized. That information was then passed on to FBI agents, with whom he met twice a week to share intelligence.[38] Jensen's pitch was that the local police department, less feared than the FBI, could be a richer source of community intelligence. He said:

> They really hate the FBI, for some reason. Sometimes the FBI did a little roughshod stuff after 9/11. But we get information from the community telling us who's bad, who's up to no good. Because we've had this five-, six-year relationship with them.[39]

I asked Sergeant Jennifer O'Donnell, who works on AIMCOP, how young people are identified as radicalized.

> Certainly, if we thought that there was a youth that was more isolated and withdrawn, we would certainly try to engage more. We have received some information about possible traveling back and forth to Africa. We pass all that information on to the FBI. I know that we've been told about problems in school, about problems with gangs, nothing specific on the big level of being recruited by al-Shabaab or anything like that.

Isn't being isolated or withdrawn fairly normal teenage behavior, I asked? "Right," she replied. "But if they're spending a lot of time on the Internet, and they change their attire, and they change their philosophy . . . They start talking about more radical things."[40] Again, the expression of radical opinions was being taken by a law enforcement agency as an indicator of potential terrorist risk without any awareness of the civil liberties issues raised. Indeed, the Department of Homeland Security now sees AIMCOP as a potential model for other city police departments.

A Nationalist Insurgency

At the heart of the FBI's investigation and the congressional hearings on Somali radicalization was the question of why a group of young Somali Americans, most born in Somalia but having spent the bulk of their young lives in the US, would have wanted to travel to an East African war zone and volunteer to fight on behalf of al-Shabaab. Members of the parents' generation within the Twin Cities Somali communities, who by and large considered themselves fortunate to have been able to flee Somalia and start new lives in the US, struggled to make sense of why their children would choose to go back. In July 2011, the House Committee on Homeland Security, chaired by Peter King, held a hearing that ostensibly aimed at answering the same question. Incredibly, during more than two hours of expert testimony, not a single mention was made of the political context of the 2006 Ethiopian invasion of Somalia, which was clearly an important part of why some Somali Americans volunteered to join the insurgency. Instead, witnesses giving evidence to the hearing indulged the fantasy of Muslim-American community leaders refusing to cooperate with law enforcement and argued that radicalization was fueled by the circulation of "anti-Western ideologies" and a lack of adherence to "American values." They even spent time considering the preposterous idea that al-Shabaab might be financed by Iran. In effect, the hearing became a discussion of the threat Somalis pose to America, seen largely as a problem of national loyalty rather than a matter of a few individuals volunteering to fight for al-Shabaab overseas.[41]

The US mainstream media has given Americans a hopelessly distorted image of Somalia. The 2001 film *Black Hawk Down*, a fairy tale of US military heroes fighting black Muslim terrorists, who die in great anonymous waves of bloodshed, was shot entirely from the point of view of American soldiers. The film is a heavily embroidered dramatization of the 1993 US mission to capture militia leader

Mohamed Farrah Aidid, in which over a thousand Somalis and eighteen Americans were killed, and it presents Somalis at best as charity cases, victims of a mess of their own creation; at worst, they are barbarous fanatics with a cultural propensity for tribal warfare. We learn nothing of Somalia's actual political history and the hand of the US in its collapse. Yet those events owe more to US cold war policy than to any cultural traits of the Somali people.

In the 1980s, the government of General Mohamed Siad Barre was a key US ally in Africa, and the US supplied it with hundreds of millions of dollars' worth of arms despite its well-known record of abuses. This level of outside military assistance was at the time unmatched in Africa's history, and it was intended to overwhelm the Soviet-backed communist government in neighboring Ethiopia.[42] Barre had taken power in Somalia in 1969, nine years after the country's independence from British and Italian colonialism. He was compelled in the 1980s to implement damaging structural adjustment programs in order to be allowed access to International Monetary Fund (IMF) loans, and this in turn led to the collapse of the pastoralist economy, a growing dependence on imported food, and increasingly high levels of urban unemployment.[43] By the middle of the decade, facing mounting opposition, Barre's regime was no more than a clan-based autocracy, imprisoning and executing opposition leaders. The withdrawal of IMF credit in 1988 caused the economy to collapse. The vast military arsenal Barre had amassed from US patronage was now deployed against his own population. The military officers who had been trained by the US in techniques of political repression were given free rein, particularly in the north, where a secessionist movement had risen up. Tens of thousands were killed and half a million became refugees in 1988 and 1989, leaving Somalia mostly for neighboring countries.[44] By 1991 the north had succeeded in breaking away, and Barre was expelled from power by an armed insurgency, leaving behind a bankrupt, starving, war-torn country. The politics of clan identity had hollowed out the state itself, fragmenting the nation into various armed factions that fought for control of Mogadishu over the subsequent decade, in the absence of a functioning central state.[45]

In late 2002, the US took over the former French colonial base at Camp Lemonnier in neighboring Djibouti and deployed nine hundred military and intelligence personnel to what was named the Combined Joint Task Force for the Horn of Africa. Somalia was identified as a breeding ground for terrorist attacks on America, though there were likely only a dozen al-Qaeda militants in the country. Nevertheless, various Somali militia groups were recruited by the CIA as part of the war on terror. Soon the militias were capturing and killing individuals they suspected of being Islamist radicals, usually imams and local prayer leaders who had nothing to do with terrorism. In some cases, they rendered their captives to the US forces at Djibouti. The CIA's hope was that a group of exiled warlords in Kenya, who had formed a government-in-waiting known as the Transitional Federal Government (TFG), would rule Somalia, once the agency-backed militia had control of the capital. But the effect of the CIA campaign was the opposite of what was intended. Resentment at the militia violence led to growing support for a grassroots network known as the Islamic Courts Union (ICU), which in 2006 succeeded in expelling the CIA-funded militias from Mogadishu.[46] The ICU was made up mainly of traditional mullahs, who taught the Qur'an in villages, and of local clerics, who dispensed justice according to their interpretation of shari'a law, in an effort to introduce some kind of order to the chaotic city. There was no talk of international terrorism, and the more militant youth wing, al-Shabaab, was a marginal element.[47] The courts proved popular largely because of the security they brought to much of the country after more than a decade of internecine violence, but they had no clear plan for governing. Members of the diaspora in Europe and North America felt they could travel back to Somalia more safely than before and, after returning from their visits, regaled others in Somali communities with stories of how, under the rule of the courts, crime and violence were nonexistent.

In Washington, there was consternation. The ICU was interpreted as part of the global Islamist threat, and the Bush administration began searching for new ways to take them on. They turned to Somalia's long-standing regional rival, Ethiopia, whose army was given funding and logistical support to carry out a unilateral invasion in December 2006.[48] Assisted by US air support and Special Operations forces on the ground, tens of thousands of Ethiopian troops were able to quickly overpower the ICU and install the TFG in power the following year. The Ethiopian invasion fostered tremendous resentment. Investigative journalist Jeremy Scahill writes:

> The [Ethiopian] occupation was marked by indiscriminate brutality against Somali civilians. Ethiopian and US-backed Somali [TFG] government soldiers secured Mogadishu's neighborhoods by force, raiding houses in search of ICU loyalists, looting civilian property, and beating or shooting anyone suspected of collaboration with antigovernment forces. They positioned snipers on the roofs of buildings and would reportedly respond to any attack with disproportionate fire, shelling densely populated areas and several hospitals, according to Human Rights Watch. Extrajudicial killings by Ethiopian soldiers were widely reported, particularly during the final months of 2007. Accounts of Ethiopian soldiers "slaughtering" men, women and children "like goats"—slitting throats—were widespread, Amnesty International noted. Both Somali Transitional Government forces, led by exiles and backed by the United States, and Ethiopian forces were accused of horrific sexual violence.[49]

The foreign invasion established a corrupt and dysfunctional government protected by African Union troops. It also gave rise to a nationalist insurgency, with al-Shabaab at the forefront of the forces combating the Ethiopian army and the TFG.

It is not difficult to see why—in this context—a trickle of young men in the diaspora would be attracted to the idea of answering al-Shabaab's call for volunteers to defend Somalia from US-backed invaders. The only English-language journalist who has interviewed young Somali-American recruits themselves about why they volunteered for al-Shabaab is Fatuma Noor of Kenya's *Nairobi Star*. In her interviews with recruits from the US in 2011, carried out as they prepared to enter Somalia from Kenya, we get the clearest sense of what lay behind their choices to leave their lives in the West. Nuno Ahmed, age eighteen, said:

> Young people like me are needed there [in Somalia] to protect our country. I can do something important over there compared to what

> I was doing back in the US . . . This is my choice and no-one has made me come here as my mother would like to believe. They have lived in Minnesota for too long and now they want to forget about home. But not me.

Another, twenty-three-year-old Abikar Mohamed, says: "We are all here to defend what we believe in. We are all here to protect Islam and we are going to do that at all cost." He adds that, once his family was granted US citizenship, he thought he "would enjoy the same treatment and rights as any other US citizen, but that was never to happen." Though finishing among the top five students in his Minnesota high school, he was unable to get a job or a college scholarship. A third recruit, Abdirahman Gullet, aged nineteen, talks about the mood in Minneapolis in 2008 after the FBI began its investigation into the disappearances. "We have all been seen as terror suspects. Police regularly storm our houses and conduct searches without permission," he says, and he recalls being taken off the street by the FBI for several hours of interrogation. Before these incidents, he says, joining al-Shabaab did not cross his mind. "I thought it was a stupid thing . . . Now I understand why. I have had firsthand experience."

As Noor puts it, the Ethiopian invasion prompted a "political awakening" among young Somalis in the diaspora, as word spread about the brutality of the occupation.[50] But that awakening would not have taken the form it did were it not for the barriers these young men faced in America. They perceived their lives in the US as marked by stigma, blocked opportunities, and the suspicious gaze of the national-security state. Ironically, the perception that Muslims were terrorists itself became one of the factors leading to some joining a group designated a terrorist organization. Once an initial few had made the journey and started to tell their peers back home tales of military heroism in defense of nation and religion, a recruitment chain started that rested mainly on international cell-phone calls and social media communication, with a small number of individuals in the Twin Cities each raising a couple of thousand dollars or so to cover travel costs.[51]

By 2009, al-Shabaab controlled most of southern Somalia and Mogadishu. The US government's invasion plan, which aimed at removing the threat of international terrorism from Somalia, had, as so often in the war on terror, made the problem worse. Thus, for the first time, a group with loose ties to al-Qaeda gained control of territory and began imposing its brand of Taliban-style rule, with beheadings, floggings, and amputations meted out on the spot to those who violated its edicts—including, on one occasion, the fatal stoning of a child victim of rape. At one point, musical ringtones on cell phones were banned for being un-Islamic. Even so, al-Shabaab's rhetoric remained focused on regaining control of the country rather than striking at the West. And the group could count on a modicum of support, due to the perception that it was the only force defending the nation. As even Peter King's star witness, Abdirazak Bihi, acknowledged:

> I know a lot of people in al-Shabaab in Somalia from neighbors I grew up with. Whether you like it or not, they are there because of nationalism but they don't agree with them a bit. Because Shabaab are the only people fighting to keep Somali borders, Somali pride, and Somali nationality and government, and bringing them together. Because every other group is not nationalistic, is corruptible, works for Ethiopia, or the UN, for the illiterate warlords, destroying the whole country.[52]

For young Somalis in Minnesota angry at US foreign policy in the war on terror, and who want to give expression to their opposition, al-Shabaab seems to be the only show in town. As several Minneapolis community organizers pointed out, conversations among young Somali Americans about Muslims being oppressed and Somalia being victimized, with the American government to blame, are fairly normal. They also noted that apart from al-Shabaab, there were no political groups attempting to pick up on those opinions and give them an organized expression, offering alternative forms of political activism to al-Shabaab's violent fundamentalism. And attempts by young Somali Americans to express themselves politically tend to become the object of government suspicion. Two days after he became a US citizen, Abdiwali Warsame, a thirty-year-old Minnesota bus driver, created a Web site, Somalimidnimo.com, or United Somalia, which quickly became popular in the diaspora. It expressed a variety of political opinions on Somalia but was strongly opposed to US intervention. In June 2012, Warsame received a Google Alert e-mail notifying him that his site had been mentioned in a document posted on the Internet. On opensource.gov, a federal Web site, he discovered that a government military contractor, the Virginia-based Navanti Group, had been commissioned by US Special Operations Forces to "counter nefarious influences" in Africa, and, as a result, had begun to monitor his site and compiled a confidential research dossier about its founder and its content. The dossier identified "opportunities" to conduct "Military Information Support Operations," more commonly known as psychological operations, that would target Somali audiences worldwide. The US military ought to consider a "messaging campaign," argued the dossier, by repeating comments posted on the site by readers opposed to al-Shabaab. This dossier was also passed to the local field office of the FBI, whose agents interviewed Warsame. At first the agents told him he was under criminal investigation, but after his attorneys intervened and he refused to meet bureau agents without a lawyer, the bureau stopped calling.[53]

Living in Fear

Officially the federal investigation into the disappearances from the Twin Cities was considered a success. By the end of 2009 the number of young Somali Americans trying to leave the US and volunteer for al-Shabaab seemed to have declined. A handful of people were convicted of donating four-figure sums to it. Its credibility was gradually undermined as people learned of its brutal violence against any Somalis who had a different view of the country's political future. To some extent, the heroic image of fighting a foreign occupation had waned. One of al-Shabaab's most famous members was Omar Hammami, known as Abu Mansour al-Amriki, or "the American," an Alabama-born convert who performed raps in propaganda videos. In April 2012, it was reported that al-Shabaab had fallen out with Hammami, apparently over ideological differences, and attempted to kill him.

Whether the federal investigation had also contributed to preventing further recruitment in Minnesota was unclear. On the one hand, the systematic surveillance of the community would have made it harder for new volunteers to reach Somalia; on the other hand, the tensions it generated could easily have further fueled the feeling that young Somalis faced a dismal future in the US. What was more certain was that the concept of radicalization that guided federal efforts to respond to the problem was an inadequate way of understanding the experiences of young Somalis in Minnesota, and that it had led to unwarranted surveillance of the everyday lives of young people in an entire community in the hope of finding the magical indicators of a drift to extremism. As community organizer Nimco Ahmed points out, the idea that members of the community could spot radicalization through a set of indicators is flawed.

> In fact, I could be a friend of a radicalized individual and never have to know. Which I actually did. I never knew they were radicalized until they left and did what they did.

The signs usually listed, such as changing to an Islamic dress style, apply to millions of people, she notes.

> And people are smart—they're not going to come saying I'm supporting al-Shabaab, or I'm doing this, or al-Qaeda this. Nobody's going to do that.[54]

A generation of young Somali Americans had seen their whole community treated as suspect. Local law enforcement had been drawn into surveillance of young people's political opinions. Community leaders of the targeted population had competed to establish themselves as useful to the government rather than as advocates for the people on whose behalf they claimed to speak. Opposition to the foreign and domestic policies of the war on terror had no outlet.

None of this went unnoticed by young Somali Americans themselves, who bore the brunt of official suspicion. At the University of Minnesota I met with a group of Somali-American students. After just a short while talking about their lives, their anger started to flow. "I think this is an image that the media has portrayed," begins one of the group. “The stereotype: oh, you’re Muslim, you’re a terrorist. Minnesota is a nice place, they don’t say nothing. But it’s an image war.” Another relates how she is questioned for three or four hours every time she leaves the country. “Even if you went nowhere near Somalia, they want to give you a hard time, they just wanted me to sweat. Even if we haven’t done anything wrong, they still give us a hard time.” Others agree, and began talking about being discriminated against for having a Muslim name or wearing head scarves. They speak of being prevented from traveling to visit family in Somalia because their names come up on the wide-ranging terrorist watch lists. “Every Muslim in America lives in fear to be blunt,” one of the young men comments.

> We developed that fear of when will they come knocking on our door. When will they come and interrogate you or harass you. They can start at any time. You don’t know if there’s a pending case against you, even though you know you didn’t do anything.

Another adds:

> There was the McCarthy era against communism. There was Vietnam, and the Viet Cong. There is now Islamophobia. And as Muslim Somali youth, we have so many things stacked up against us. For instance, we are black, we are immigrants, we’re Muslim.

The conversation soon turns to foreign policy.

> If you look at the foreign policy of America, the East African region, and especially Somalia since the 1980s, 1990s, even before that, in the cold war time, you see that America does not really show that it cares for us by its policies. It shows it wants to take resources, take what we have. That’s somehow what is going on throughout the world to the Muslim people. There is a sense of discrimination in this policy.[55]

One of the consequences of treating radicalization as the central problem, and thereby broadening the focus of counterterrorism from individuals engaged in political violence to a wider set of attitudes or beliefs, is that the political opinions of many young Somali Americans, as expressed above, came to be seen as indicators of risk and could not be given legitimate public outlets. The prominent community leaders these young people see supposedly speaking on their behalf say nothing of foreign policy, discrimination, or civil liberties. One of the group said:

> It's actually pitiful to say, but the Somali community has a lot of sellouts who portray themselves as Somali advocates or community leaders. They get the most air time because pretty much what they preach is what the government wants them to preach. I feel as if anybody that does try to step up gets intimidated and they recant from their earlier statements. You see all these people that are locked up without just cause, without due process. And then you start getting worried. It could be you, just because you spoke out. And to be honest, most of us feel that we don't have that so-called freedom of speech.[56]

This is where the counterradicalization paradigm ultimately led: to young people feeling their political views could not be freely expressed. As a consequence, the possibility of generating a radical politics that could provide a genuine alternative to al-Shabaab's fundamentalist violence was closed off.

CHAPTER 8

Twenty-First-Century Crusaders

> Historian T. R. Fehrenbach once observed that my home state of Texas and Israel share the experience of "civilized men and women thrown into new and harsh conditions, beset by enemies."
>
> —Texas governor Rick Perry, 2011

Katy is a neighborhood in the western suburbs of Houston, Texas. It takes its name from the old K-T railroad linking Kansas and Texas, which first made it possible to establish a settlement around what had until then been a mosquito-ridden creek. Today it is one of the wealthiest parts of the city and the center of Houston's energy corridor, where oil and gas corporations are headquartered. Their demands for technically skilled employees have brought a number of Muslim immigrants to the neighborhood, and in 2006, three brothers purchased an eleven-acre plot of land where they planned to build a mosque. Four years later a temporary structure, to be used as a prayer hall, and a playground were opened. Most mosques are built in multiracial, inner-city areas, where land is cheap. But in Katy, the site was located amid some of the most expensive residential real estate in the city.

Meanwhile, in the summer of 2010, a national debate raged on about whether the Cordoba Initiative, a New York–based Muslim organization, should be allowed to build a community center, known as Park51, in lower Manhattan. Though it was neither a stand-alone mosque nor located at ground zero, Islamophobic blogger Pamela Geller dubbed Park51 the "ground zero mosque" and cast it as an insult to the victims of 9/11, as if Muslims were collectively responsible for the terrorist attacks and could not therefore be welcome anywhere near the 9/11 site. Rupert Murdoch's *New York Post* and Fox News picked up the story and, with Newt Gingrich and Sarah Palin weighing in, the issue hit the mainstream media.

In Houston, Michael Berry, a talk show host on KTRH radio, said that if the center was built in New York, "I hope somebody blows it up . . . I hope the mosque isn't built, and if it is, I hope it's blown up, and I mean that."[1] Some residents of Katy had already begun to worry about the new mosque building springing up in their neighborhood and made attempts to pressure city officials to deny the necessary permits. But now the mood of animosity intensified. A businessman who lived next to the mosque and owned land surrounding it constructed posts around its perimeter, onto which he placed Christian crosses and stars of David, presumably to defend Judeo-Christian civilization from the newcomers. Then he began organizing pig-racing competitions on the land adjacent to the mosque, in a deliberate attempt at provocation. Hesham Ebaid, the president of the Muslim American Society of Katy, which runs the mosque, pointed out: "The pigs are not offensive. We just can't eat pigs. We are not offended by the animal. It's just an animal."[2]

Other incidents were more serious. Incendiary devices and beer bottles were thrown onto the mosque's driveway, and the words "Islam is evil" were painted onto a wall around the corner, where they remained two years later.[3] At the nearby Beckendorff Junior High School, an Arab-American eighth-grader needed surgery to repair his jaw after he was the victim of an attack, during which he was taunted with the words "terrorist," "Muslim, go home," and "you blow up buildings."[4] Located a short distance from the mosque is a barbeque restaurant famous locally for having a poster of a lynching. The man being hanged from a tree has had a Middle Eastern face superimposed on it. The caption says: "Let's play cowboys and Iranians." Hesham Ebaid acknowledges, "It's a challenging environment," but his efforts at courteous engagement—knocking on doors in the neighborhood to reassure locals, sending out dinner invitations on religious occasions, and organizing open days—seem to have calmed most of the neighbors.[5]

What was happening in Katy was a microcosm of a widespread pattern that unfolded across the US beginning during the summer of 2010. The American Civil Liberties Union reported at the end of 2010 that forty mosques were facing organized opposition. From Los Angeles to Brooklyn and from Seattle to Miami, existing and newly planned mosques were facing vandalism, harassment, angry protests, and attempts to deny building permits on spurious pretexts.[6] In Orange County, California, as congregants, including children, arrived at a mosque event in early 2011 to raise money for women's shelters and homeless people, hundreds of anti-Muslim protesters jeered, "Go back home"; "Terrorists"; and "U-S-A." A local councilwoman speaking at the protest said: "I know quite a few Marines who would be very happy to help these terrorists to an early meeting in paradise." Another protester said: "You're messing with Americans now. We're not England. We're not British. We're Americans." This referenced the canard that Britain's excessive multicultural tolerance had already enabled the country's submission to shari'a law.[7] In Portland, Oregon, a man who fire-bombed the Salman Alfarisi Islamic Center told police officers: "Jihad goes both ways. Christians can jihad too."[8]

Some perpetrators of Islamophobic violence had the courtesy to check the religious identity of their victims first. In August 2010, Ahmed H. Sharif, a Bangladeshi cabdriver, was stabbed in Manhattan after a passenger asked him: "Are you a Muslim?" When Sharif replied that he was, the passenger said, "Consider this a checkpoint," before pulling out a knife and slashing the driver's throat, face, and forearms. Had the cut to Sharif's throat been any deeper or longer, the driver would have died, said doctors.[9] In a bar in St. Petersburg, Florida, Bradley Strott struck up a conversation with Samad Ebadi, who happened to tell him he was Muslim. Strott responded by grabbing him by his shirt and stabbing him in the neck with his pocket knife.[10] In November 2012, seventy-two-year-old Ali Akmal was walking in Queens, New York, in the early hours, when two men approached him and asked, "Are you Muslim or Hindu?" When he responded, "I'm Muslim," they beat him viciously, leaving him in a critical condition, unable to walk or talk.[11] Earlier in the same month, fifty-seven-year-old Bashir Ahmad was walking up the steps to open the front door to al-Saaliheen mosque in Queens when he was approached from behind, stabbed several times, and bitten on the nose by an assailant yelling anti-Muslim slurs.[12]

In other cases, simply looking South Asian was sufficient. In December 2012, forty-six-year-old Sunando Sen was killed by an oncoming train after being pushed onto the rails at a Queens subway station by a woman who told officers she "pushed a Muslim off the train tracks because I hate Hindus and Muslims. Ever since 2001 when they put down the twin towers I've been beating them up." The attacker was wrong to think Sen a Muslim; he had a Hindu background.[13] Sikh men—whose turbans fit the stereotyped image that many Americans have of Muslim terrorists—are often the most visible of targets for Islamophobic attacks. In April 2011, two elderly Sikhs out walking in the Sacramento suburb of Elk Grove, California, were shot at. Surinder Singh was killed and his neighbor Gurmej Atwal seriously wounded. Six months earlier, in the same neighborhood, a Sikh cabdriver had been beaten by two men who yelled anti-Muslim slurs.[14] The following year a neo-Nazi, who had spent time in the white supremacist music scene, went on a shooting rampage at a Sikh temple in Oak Creek, Wisconsin, killing six people.[15] Although the story made national headlines, there was little reflection on the wider pattern of racist violence that the shootings were an example of. The next day, in Joplin, Missouri, a mosque was burned to the ground—the second arson attack on the building in two months.[16] Later in the same month a homemade bomb exploded outside an Islamic school in Chicago while fifty worshippers, including children, were attending a prayer service. The perpetrator had attempted to throw the bomb through a window.[17]

According to FBI statistics on hate crimes, after a dramatic increase following 9/11, the number of incidents of anti-Muslim violence declined steadily—until 2010, when it soared by 50 percent, and rose again the following year.[18] As Farhana Khera, director of the civil rights group Muslim Advocates, notes, "The FBI's hate crimes tracking system, which relies on voluntary reporting by local police departments, is deeply flawed," and likely to record much less than half the number of actual incidents.[19] But whatever the absolute numbers, the statistical trend of an upsurge from 2010 was consistent with a worsening Islamophobic mood in America's political culture—from antimosque campaigns, to mobilizations to ban shari'a law, to the stigmatization of President Obama as a secret Muslim, to high-profile congressional hearings on the radicalization of American Muslims.

"The English Lion Has Awoken"

In September 2009, the English Defence League (EDL) released a video on YouTube to help publicize a major demonstration in Manchester the following month. Filmed in a disused warehouse in Luton, the video shows around twenty men dressed in black lined against one wall of a large empty room, their faces concealed behind balaclavas. One of the men reads a prepared statement while another sets fire to a Nazi flag that has been hoisted in front of the men. The EDL spokesman says burning this flag will prove his organization is not a far Right group motivated by racism but simply opposes those he calls Islamic extremists. Addressing himself to these extremists, he announces: "We, the English Defence League, will contest your kind, as our forefathers did, relentlessly pursuing you in our quest to see all shari'a banished from our great democratic country. Long live the free." Anyone can join the EDL if they share this stance, he says, even antiextremist Muslims. Behind the men hang placards with the slogans "Black and white, unite and fight" and "We support Israel's right to exist." After the spectacle of the flag burning, the camera zooms in on one section of the EDL members to demonstrate from the skin color of their forearms that this gathering includes black men as well as white. In the description that accompanies the video on YouTube, a supporter has written: "How anyone can call this group far right fascist Nazis is beyond belief. Since when were Nazi groups multi-race? It's not racist to oppose Islamic Extremism!"

When this video was released the EDL had been in existence for just a few months. It had been formed following events in Luton earlier that year. In March 2009, Anjem Choudary, the leader of a small group that had taken various names since its original incarnation, al-Muhajiroun, was disbanded in 2004, organized a protest against a parade through Luton's town center of British troops recently returned from Afghanistan. His protest prompted a furious reaction from bystanders; a coalition of angry locals, members of violent football fan groups, and seasoned far Right activists came together to form the organization that would soon call itself the English Defence League. Making good use of the online and offline networks that already linked violent football fans and the far Right across the country, and picking up a significant number of young people via Facebook and YouTube who seemed to relate to its style of politics, the EDL was soon organizing demonstrations in several towns and cities across England, attracting up to two thousand people. The slogans at these early demonstrations included "Muslim bombers off our streets"; "Extremist Muslims go to hell"; "British voters say no to shari'a law"; "LBC [Luton Borough Council] sell out cowards"; "Our troops are heroes"; "We demand a St. George's Day parade"; "Ban preachers of hate"; and, more prosaically, "We are sick of this shit." Their demands included a ban on the building of mosques, a ban on wearing burkas, a ban on renaming Christmas, and the creation of a new criminal offense: calling for the introduction of shari'a law.

The EDL's September 2009 video is striking for a number of reasons. First, its format and style places the YouTube clip within a genre of video communiqués issued by various terrorist organizations since the 1970s. In its style of presentation, the EDL video imitates the very extremism it ostensibly opposes. And there is more unintended mimicry when one of the reporters who was invited to the warehouse suggests that the EDL's appearance in balaclavas might seem intimidating. The EDL leader replies by saying: "It's exactly the same as a burka." Second, in its graphic imagery of anti-Nazism, its reference to "forefathers" who also fought against extremism (presumably in World War II), and, most strikingly, in its appropriation of the socialist slogan "Black and white, unite and fight" (no longer against the bourgeoisie but against Muslim radicals), the video plunders antifascist imagery in an attempt to construct a popular front against Islamic extremism. Similarly, the reference to Israel's right to exist aims at announcing a rejection of the anti-Semitism that was central to far Right politics in the twentieth century and at establishing a new alignment of forces to confront the Islamic extremist enemy. Hence the formation within the EDL of a Jewish division, a gay division, and the prominence of a Sikh activist, Guramit Singh, at EDL demonstrations. The EDL thus went to great lengths to present itself as an organization that was not racist and as able to include within its ranks groups who are normally the targets of far Right violence. The concept of extremism was central to this positioning. By claiming to attack Muslim extremism rather than Muslims per se, the EDL hoped to dispel the suspicion that it was just another fringe, racist, far Right group.

In another EDL video, released shortly before its October 2009 demonstration in Manchester, another set of symbols is mobilized. To a pounding soundtrack, the video opens with pictures of sword-wielding crusaders, the red crosses on their shields and breasts mirroring the St. George cross that forms the EDL logo. "The English lion has awoken," announces the video. "The time has come to defend our land from 1,400 years of jihad that has finally washed up upon our shores." This is followed by a series of images of newspaper headlines which are arranged to suggest that Britain is on its way to "Islamification" within thirty years.

> Do you want your children and grandchildren to grow up under Islamic rule in this your Christian homeland? Second-class citizens in the place your forefathers fought and died for for you to live free.

The viewer is told that "Islam religiously teaches Moslems to convert Nations into Islamic rule" and that the government has been too politically correct to face up to this danger. Only a movement of English patriots taking to the streets can save the nation from shari'a. The Manchester demonstration will be a "day of reckoning." Apart from its crusader imagery (which, given the anti-Semitic violence of the crusades, tends to undermine the EDL's claim to be inclusive of Jews, let alone nonextremist Muslims), the power of this video lies in its sampling of newspaper headlines. There is little in the way of commentary or interpretation added to the headlines. Indeed, none is needed. The *Express*, *Mail*, and *Star* newspapers articulate a narrative wholly consistent with the EDL's own, with their daily diet of cartoon Muslim fanatics, secret shari'a courts, forced Islamic conversions, and no-go areas for non-Muslims—all tolerated by a politically correct, liberal, multicultural elite that has even abolished Christmas so as not to offend the enemy within.

There is ample evidence that the EDL's activities are accompanied by overt racism. EDL demonstrations have been marked by Nazi salutes, racist chanting, and racist violence. EDL activism overlaps significantly with that of the membership of the racist British National Party (BNP). Indeed, both of the EDL's senior leaders, Stephen Yaxley-Lennon (aka Tommy Robinson) and his cousin Kevin Carroll, were previously members of the BNP and have been convicted of criminal violence. Members of the West Midlands Division of the EDL have taken photographs of themselves standing in front of Ulster Volunteer Force flags, carrying imitation firearms.[20] At a demonstration on September 3, 2011, through the largely Muslim area of Tower Hamlets, East London (a favorite location for far Right mobilization since the Battle of Cable Street in 1936), Yaxley-Lennon told the crowd:

> We are here today to tell you, quite loud, quite clear, every single Muslim watching this video on YouTube: on 7/7, you got away with killing and maiming British citizens. You got away with it. You better understand that we have built a network from one end of this country to the other end. We will not tolerate it. And the Islamic community will feel the full force of the English Defence League if we see any of our citizens killed, maimed, or hurt on British soil ever again.

Again, the logic of Yaxley-Lennon's statement was identical to that of the terrorists he claimed to be contesting: both justify violence against a whole population deemed responsible for the violence of some of its members. After the murder in Woolwich in May 2013 of British soldier Lee Rigby, Yaxley-Lennon's threat was realized. As the EDL stepped up its street activity around England to capitalize on the incident, the number of racist attacks against Muslims escalated, including arson and bomb attacks on mosques in Grimsby, Muswell Hill, Walsall, and Tipton.[21]

Whatever overlaps exist, it would be wrong to see the EDL's rhetoric of antiextremism as simply a mask for more familiar forms of far Right politics. In fact, its ideology stems as much from the official antiextremist narrative of the war on terror as from the far Right tradition. According to conventional wisdom, the mobilization of far Right groups in Europe has pressured centrist politicians into adopting more xenophobic positions, leading to far Right ideas entering the mainstream. But the example of the EDL suggests the flow of ideology is more in the opposite direction. The EDL is a movement that appropriated the culturalist and reformist discourses of the official war on terror and gave them organizational form on the streets. It took literally the government's proposition that there is a war on Islamic extremism. It absorbed the notion from the government's Preventing Violent Extremism program that the enemy in this war is not a few individuals engaged in violence but an ideology embedded in Muslim communities. Likewise, the notion that Muslims can be categorized as extremist or moderate according to their allegiance to Western values was taken from statements of government policy. The repeated ministerial speeches attacking an imagined multiculturalist orthodoxy (most recently Prime Minister David Cameron's February 2011 speech in Munich) gave the EDL its belief that state multiculturalism is holding back the fight against Muslim extremism. All it adds of its own is the thought that the politicians running the war are too soft and cowardly, still too caught up in multicultural platitudes, to fight it properly, particularly on the home front—the streets of England—where the EDL fills the gap with its own form of militancy.[22] In its criticism of the state, the EDL uses the state's own discourse against it.

This suggests that appropriate analogies for the EDL can be found not only in traditions of European racist organizing but also in groups such as the anticommunist John Birch Society and Minutemen militia of the 1950s and 1960s, which forged often violent, far Right movements by appropriating official US cold war ideology. They turned it against the government with the accusation that communist infiltration had weakened its willingness to take on the enemy. Just as the activists of the John Birch Society were convinced that the fluoridation of public water was a communist plot (a theory wonderfully mocked in Stanley Kubrick's *Dr. Strangelove*), so the EDL bloggers warn of the "creeping shari'a" of halal food being offered on England's high streets. Conspiracy theory is essential to EDL's ideology, because only if the government can be presented as secretly in league or complicit with the enemy is there any need for the EDL to fight its own version of the war on terror.

From Anti-Semitism to Islamophobia

Postwar British fascism was never just a matter of hating minorities. It was also an ideology that sought to explain and give order to the social dislocation and depredations felt by the working class through a rival narrative to that of the Left. To achieve this, it presented immigration from the Caribbean and Asia as an alien corruption of the purity of the nation, but it paid equal attention to the ruling class that had allowed this to happen, a betrayal which far Right ideology explained with Jewish conspiracy theory. What appeared to be a British ruling class was, in fact, a mirage. Real power lay with the secret Jewish cabal that pulled the strings of international finance, the media, and the revolutionary Left, as supposedly revealed in *The Protocols of the Learned Elders of Zion*, the document forged by the tsarist secret police that purports to show how Jews manipulated world events to their advantage. While far Right street activism involved racist violence against African Caribbeans and Asians, far Right ideology saw the real problem as lying elsewhere: the Jews and their hidden agenda of destroying national identity by fostering the immigration and mixing of other races. As David Edgar put it in his 1977 analysis of the politics of the National Front (NF), the far Right "blames the Jews for the blacks."[23] Even as popular racism against Asians and African Caribbeans was the means by which young recruits were drawn into the far Right, anti-Semitism remained a necessary ideological component, because only Jews could play the role of the secret source of economic and political power that had weakened and corrupted the nation. To this extent, British fascist parties such as the NF and the BNP were correctly described as Nazi in their ideology.

Beginning in 1999, the BNP's new leader, Nick Griffin, embarked on a strategy of downplaying this neo-Nazi legacy. No doubt he still believed Jews secretly controlled the media—as his 1997 pamphlet "Who Are the Mindbenders?" argued—but publicly he tried to remodel the party along the lines of more successful European counterparts, such as the Front National in France, using the language of defending British cultural identity (rather than white racial identity) against a ruling elite that wanted to destroy it through immigration, multiculturalism, and appeasement of the Muslim enemy within. Instead of talk of a Jewish conspiracy, it was about those in power being too "cosmopolitan" to have the real interests of the British people at heart; and Islamic militancy was invoked to illustrate the dangers of immigration, capitalizing on the Islamophobia of post-9/11 Britain. This message, of course, resonated with many voters—it was, after all, little different from what had been shouted from a thousand newspaper columns since 9/11 and echoed in a more genteel form by both Labour and Conservative ministers. After 2001, the narrowing gap between the party's rhetoric and mainstream discourse meant the BNP was able to dramatically increase its electoral support, winning two seats in the European parliament in 2009 even while its active membership remained dominated by long-standing neo-Nazis and violent racists.

The significance of this can best be grasped by recalling the BNP's first election success, in 1993, when Derek Beackon won a seat on the Tower Hamlets council in East London with the slogan "rights for whites." At the time, his election was considered shocking enough to prompt a mass campaign that united mainstream politics against him, removing him from office the following year. A key part of that campaign was the argument that voting for the Labour Party rather than the BNP was a better way to address the issues people felt angry about, such as the lack of adequate public housing. Beginning in 2003, the BNP had at least ten councilors in office at any one time, with the real possibility of winning control of a borough or city council, such as that of Burnley. But the response of the political mainstream in that decade was rather different from the early 1990s. The Labour Party, having "modernized" from 1994, had lost its credibility as a vehicle for addressing working-class political concerns;

activists on doorsteps who wanted to dissuade would-be BNP voters were thus unable to offer a positive alternative. Moreover, the message from mainstream politics and popular newspapers was not that the BNP was fundamentally wrong but that it was exploiting legitimate grievances better addressed by responsible politicians from the major parties. If the best mainstream argument against the BNP was that it was irresponsible, then it was hardly surprising that it attracted substantial support among the large numbers of people who increasingly saw mainstream politics itself as devoid of any moral responsibility.

The weakness of this strategy was illustrated when Labour minister Jack Straw debated Nick Griffin on a specially staged edition of the BBC's *Question Time* program in 2009. While Griffin himself was discredited by his weird demeanor and incompetence as a rhetorician, Straw was unable to attack the BNP's actual policies on multiculturalism and immigration. To say precisely what was wrong in principle with the BNP's racist identity politics would have called into question the way Labour ministers themselves approached these issues. As Gary Younge noted in the *Guardian*, "Since New Labour's politics enabled the BNP, it is in no position to disable it."[24] In the last few years, the BNP's organizing capacity has been severely reduced, firstly by the leaking of its membership list and secondly by the financial burden of defending itself against a legal challenge to its racist membership policy. But these tactics targeted the messenger, not the message, allowing others to pick up where the BNP had left off. As it turned out, the EDL was well placed to do so. It had not organized as a conventional political party and had no formal members, so it was less vulnerable to the tactics that had been partially effective against the BNP. More significantly, the EDL was better able to tailor its ideology to current circumstances, as it owed its outlook to the war on terror. The BNP's opportunistic exploitation of Islamophobia after 9/11 carried it to a level of electoral support unimaginable in the 1990s. But, by virtue of its core membership, the party remained tethered to the neo-Nazi tradition and so, unlike the EDL, could not fully realize the potential of the post-9/11 context.

Given anti-Semitism's centrality to the European far Right of the twentieth century, the EDL's new relationship to right-wing Zionism is the most striking indicator of its break with conventional fascist ideology. Along with counterparts in other parts of Europe, the EDL not only eschews anti-Semitism but actively embraces militant Zionists in the defense of the West against its Islamist enemy. Historically, the far Right in Europe tended to oppose Israel, for purely anti-Semitic reasons. But the culturalist politics of the war on terror has reversed this position, with Israel seen as a Western bridgehead within enemy territory. In Belgium, the Flemish nationalist Vlaams Belang (VB) party—formed by members of the neo-fascist Vlaams Blok after it was banned in 2004 for promoting racism—has built links with the Israeli right and succeeded in gaining the support of a minority of Antwerp's Jewish voters. The VB is historically rooted in anti-Semitism and neo-Nazism, but nowadays Islamophobia has substituted for anti-Semitism, and its leader, Filip Dewinter, visits Israel to meet right-wing members of the Knesset. In 2005, he told the Israeli newspaper *Haaretz*:

> Islam is now the No. 1 enemy not only of Europe, but of the entire free world. After communism, the greatest threat to the West is radical fundamentalist Islam. There are already 25–30 million Muslims on Europe's soil and this becomes a threat. It's a real Trojan horse. Thus, I think that an alliance is needed between Western Europe and the State of Israel.[25]

In the Netherlands, Pim Fortuyn pioneered a similar new form of far Right politics founded on defending liberal values against Islamification, his own open homosexuality indicating the distinctiveness of this politics from the traditional far Right (an innovation the EDL's LGBT division later drew on). Fortuyn's party became the largest on Rotterdam's council before he was murdered by an animal rights activist in 2002. Geert Wilders, the leader of the third-largest political party in Holland, continued this new form of politics with the Islamophobic video *Fitna* and his call for a ban on the Qur'an. On his regular visits to Israel, Wilders has called for annexing the entire West Bank and pushing any would-be Palestinian state to the eastern bank of the Jordan River. According to Dutch newspaper reports, he receives substantial funding from the David Horowitz

Freedom Center, a major artery of the Islamophobia movement in the US.[26]

Like Wilders and Dewinter, the EDL highlights its sliver of Jewish support as a badge of postracialism. Its Jewish division made links to far Right Jewish groups in the US, such as the Jewish Task Force, led by Victor Vancier (national chairman in the 1970s of the terrorist Jewish Defense League), and gave it the credibility to forge links with Pamela Geller, the New York–based Islamophobic blogger, and her Stop the Islamization of America group. In September 2010, EDL leaders attended protests in lower Manhattan against the Park51 community center. A month after this visit, Rabbi Nachum Shifren, a Tea Party activist who believes that "the Muslim onslaught is at the gates," came to London to speak at an EDL rally, where he announced: "We will never surrender to the sword of Islam."[27] Around the same time, the EDL was noticed by US neoconservatives. The Hudson Institute, part of the Israel lobby in Washington, DC, published an article praising

> members of the EDL holding their flags with pride, putting their arms around men and women of every age and ethnicity . . . It seemed that the nationalism of the EDL was a cousin of American nationalism, in which everyone can be proud of his nation, and of being a citizen, under the flag of the nation.[28]

Earlier in 2007, US-based Islamophobic activists had begun to take an interest in forming a trans-Atlantic movement, involving various far Right groupings across Europe. Activists such as Pamela Geller and Robert Spencer had attended a 2007 conference called Counter Jihad in Brussels, along with Vlaams Belang leaders and Bat Ye'or, author of the Eurabia conspiracy theory (discussed below). To US Islamophobes the protests of the EDL seemed a welcome revolt against Islam by the native English. Britain had long appeared the most Islamized nation in an Islamizing continent, and London had become Londonistan, a city given over to Islamic domination and a warning sign of what would happen in the US if creeping shari'a was not halted.

Just as the older far Right narrative had had a structural need for a Jewish conspiracy theory to explain the purported complicity of national governments with their enemies, so too the EDL's rhetoric cannot dispense with conspiracy theory. After all, one might ask, why the need for popular mobilization for the antiextremist cause when the UK government already takes a tough stance on fighting radical Islam? The answer is that government rhetoric about fighting Islamism is mere appearance; behind the scenes ruling elites are secretly in league with the Islamic enemy. One account of how this is happening, popular with the EDL, is the Eurabia conspiracy theory, outlined in Bat Ye'or's 2005 book *Eurabia: The Euro-Arab Axis*. Her claim is that the Euro-Arab Dialogue—a program initiated by the European Community's political establishment, following the 1973 oil crisis, to forge closer links with Arab nations—was actually a secret plot by European politicians and civil servants to facilitate Muslim immigration, subjugate Europe, and transform the continent into an Arab colony, Eurabia. Like the Jewish conspiracy theory of the *Protocols*, no evidence is offered. Nevertheless, through the mainstream conservative writing of Oriana Fallaci, Niall Ferguson, and Melanie Phillips, the term "Eurabia" has come to be associated with an image of Europe as cowardly and weak in the face of Islamic intimidation, allowing itself to be colonized by an increasing Muslim presence.[29] But as well as making use of the Eurabia conspiracy theory, the EDL also borrowed heavily from the new shari'a conspiracy theories that Islamophobic networks in the US had been promoting.

The Shari'a Conspiracy Theory

There is no American equivalent to the EDL. Rather than building a street-based movement, the US Islamophobic far Right operates through networks of bloggers, pundits, activists, and propagandists who shape public opinion through the media. They rely on large amounts of funding and publicity from different parts of the conservative movement—from Tea Party activists to ultra-Zionists—and a number of mainstream media outlets and politicians willing to amplify their message. Most important, as with the EDL in Britain, their message resonates because it aligns with significant elements of the war on terror's official discourse. Although its influence was felt most strongly after the election of President Obama, the far Right's campaign began in the early years of the terror war, with attacks on pro-Palestinian campus activism.[30] In 2002, with growing support, particularly among students, for the rights of Palestinians, neoconservative activists such as Daniel Pipes and David Horowitz began to launch campaigns aimed at discrediting pro-Palestinian academics. Pipes set up Campus Watch, which posted dossiers on university professors who supported Palestinian rights and encouraged students to report remarks or behavior considered critical of Israel. Targeted professors were inundated with hostile e-mails, including death threats. A similar tactic had been used earlier by another Israel lobby organization, the Anti-Defamation League, which in the 1980s distributed a booklet containing "background information on pro-Arab sympathizers active on college campuses" to its student supporters.[31] In 2003, David Horowitz started DiscoverTheNetworks.org, a database that was intended to identify left-wing groups and individuals accused of enabling Islamism and undermining American values. Islamo-Fascism Awareness Week, organized by Horowitz in 2007, was another attempt to mobilize the same agenda on campuses. The emerging far Right Islamophobia network scored its first success that same year, with an attack on the Khalil Gibran International Academy, a secular Arabic-English elementary school planned to open in Brooklyn, New York. Without evidence, the school's principal, Debbie Almontaser, was accused of being a jihadist. Mayor Michael Bloomberg caved in and threatened to shut down the school, prompting her to resign.

By 2008, a group of well-funded Islamophobic activists had coalesced. Pamela Geller's blog Atlas Shrugs (named after Ayn Rand's novel) had come to prominence with the Khalil Gibran International Academy campaign. She worked closely with Robert Spencer, whose Jihad Watch Web site was run as a subsidiary of the David Horowitz Freedom Center. The Los Angeles–based millionaire couple Aubrey and Joyce Chernick used their foundation to fund Robert Spencer with close to a million dollars between 2004 and 2009. (They also donated significant funds to pro-Israel lobby groups in Washington, such as the Washington Institute for Near East Policy, of which Aubrey Chernick was a trustee.) ACT! for America, an Islamophobic citizen action network led by Brigitte Gabriel, formed in 2007 and modeled itself on the National Rifle Association; by 2009, it had 573 chapters, 170,000 members worldwide, and a $1 million annual budget. According to an investigation by the Center for American Progress, seven conservative foundations donated over $40 million to Islamophobic groups between 2001 and 2009.[32] A 2013 report by the Council on American-Islamic Relations identified thirty-seven US-based Islamophobic groups and estimated their combined revenue between 2008 and 2011 at $119 million.[33]

These groups and individuals work together to popularize a single, shared message, a shari'a conspiracy theory to play the same role for today's far Right that Jewish conspiracy theories had within traditional far Right ideology. For these new conspiracy theorists, Islamist terrorism is just the visible tip of a hidden jihad iceberg. Alongside the use of violence is the strategy of stealth jihad, which aims at the infiltration of national institutions and the assertion of Muslim demands through the legal system. Muslims advocating for their civil rights or seeking to win political office are therefore to be regarded not as fellow citizens but as agents of a secret plan to impose a totalitarian government on the world. Non-Muslims who stand with Muslims in challenging discrimination are *dhimmis*, the twenty-first-century equivalent of the cold war's fellow travelers, who have already internalized the status of second-class citizenship within an Islamo-fascist state. The provision of halal food, shari'a-compliant finance, or prayer breaks in workplaces is creeping shari'a, the first steps toward a society ruled by Islam. (Pamela Geller called for a boycott of Campbell's soup because halal versions are available.) Since the Islamic doctrine of *taqiyya* supposedly sanctions systematic lying to non-Muslims to help advance shari'a government, Muslims who say they interpret Islam as a religion of peace and tolerance are not to be trusted. Just as the early cold war produced the reds-under-the-bed phantasm of a vast network of communist agents operating in the US, the new conspiracy theorists hold almost every American and European mosque to be exploiting religious freedom to promote Islamic sedition. Underlying the whole fantasy is the culturalist belief that Islam is not a religion like Christianity and Judaism but a fanatical, totalitarian ideology aiming at political domination of the West. Shari'a—which is regarded by most practicing Muslims as a personal moral code open to multiple interpretations by different religious scholars—was taken to have only one possible meaning: a set of oppressive laws to be implemented by an Islamic state, supplanting the US Constitution.

With Barack Obama's selection as the Democratic Party's presidential candidate in 2008, the propagandists who wanted to convince America there was a secret Islamic conspiracy to take over the US, enabled by a liberal, cosmopolitan elite, found the perfect image for their campaign: Obama as a crypto-Muslim. To object to Obama's presidential bid because he is an African American would have been transparently racist. But to object to him because he is secretly in league with America's enemies—that was just responsible citizenship. The latter strategy was effective, because its racial meanings were sufficiently submerged to deflect straightforward accusations of racism yet still close enough to the surface to connect with America's racial imaginary.

During the election contest, an organization called the Clarion Fund received $17 million from Donors Capital, a conservative funding organization that is able to keep donations anonymous, to distribute twenty-eight million copies of a propaganda film, *Obsession: Radical Islam's War Against the West*, predominantly in swing states.[34] The film reproduced all the themes of the shari'a conspiracy theory and featured most of the activists in the Islamophobia network. On her Web site, Pamela Geller described Obama simply as "the jihad candidate." Fearful of his being associated with Islam, Obama's campaign responded to such propaganda by ensuring he was never seen with Muslims or defending their rights. At a rally in Detroit, aides removed women wearing hijabs from the crowd behind Obama so that they were not in photos of the candidate.[35] Well-known Muslim and Arab Americans, such as Keith Ellison and James Zogby, who volunteered to campaign for Obama in key states were told to stay away. A Muslim-American staffer on the campaign team resigned after a reporter for the *Wall Street Journal* asked about his religious background. The claim that Obama was a Muslim was described as a "smear" on the campaign's Web site rather than simply false. At no point did Obama respond to the accusation that he was a Muslim by pointing out that Muslims had as much right to be president as anyone else.[36]

After the election the far Right's propaganda became even more outlandish. Six months into his first term, Pamela Geller wrote that President Obama was

> using all branches of government to enforce the Shariah. [His is the] first Muslim presidency, just eight years after 9/11 . . . Everything this president has done so far has helped foster America's submission to Islam.

The US government, she said, was secretly controlled by Muslim extremists

> The enemy has infiltrated every department, every division of the federal government and the Obama administration, including the White House. The State Department [is] essentially being run by Islamic supremacists.[37]

Robert Spencer devised an ingenious theory to justify dismissing Obama's self-identification as Christian.

> Barack Obama was a Muslim as a child. He has never explained when or whether he left Islam at all. He identifies himself as a Christian now but it is, I think, perhaps salient to note that a Muslim can identify himself as Christian because Jesus Christ is a Muslim prophet in the *Qur'an* . . . And so it's not out of the realm of possibility that some individual, or possibly Barack Obama, could be a Muslim and identify himself as Christian without even meaning to say that he is a member of the classic Christian tradition at all . . . But certainly his public policies and his behavior are consistent with his being a committed and convinced Muslim.[38]

For the first time, the shariʿa conspiracy theory began to connect with significant strands of mainstream opinion. By August 2010, around a quarter of Americans thought Obama was a Muslim, according to a survey for *Time* magazine. When President Obama visited India in November 2010, a scheduled visit to the Sikh Golden Temple in Amritsar was canceled, because he would have been expected to cover his head, giving rise to the possibility of photographs of him "looking Muslim." Obama's aides reportedly came up with the idea of a modified baseball cap, in the hope that it would meet the requirement that visitors to Sikh temples cover their head while also looking suitably all-American. But the Golden Temple did not permit a baseball cap instead of a head scarf.[39] By 2011, a Public Religion Research Institute survey found only 38 percent of Americans correctly identified Obama as a Christian, 18 percent believed him to be a Muslim, and the rest said they did not know.[40]

At the same time, the shari'a conspiracy theory started to receive a favorable hearing in government and national security circles. Robert Spencer was invited to brief the US military, the FBI, and other intelligence agencies on jihad and Islam.[41] Another advocate of the shari'a conspiracy theory—Frank Gaffney, president of the Center for Security Policy (CSP)—began to be taken seriously by elements of the national security establishment. In January 2011, senior intelligence officials attended the launch of a CSP publication, *Shariah: The Threat to America*. The report modeled itself on the famous neoconservative "Team B" report of 1976, which is credited with providing the groundwork for Reagan's abandonment of détente policy in the cold war and shift of the US toward a more aggressive anticommunist position. The authors of the CSP report hoped to achieve an equally significant policy transformation in America's domestic war on terror, and they echoed all the usual shari'a conspiracy themes in their attempt to do so. The report made the culturalist argument that jihadist violence is "rooted in the Islamic texts, teachings, and interpretations that constitute shariah." Beyond terrorism itself, the report claimed Islamists were engaged in "stealthy jihad tactics [to] impose a totalitarian regime [through] multi-layered cultural subversion, the co-opting of senior leaders, influence operations, and propaganda." Many of the most prominent Muslim organizations in America were "front groups for the Muslim Brotherhood" and were succeeding "in insinuating shariah into the very heartland of America."[42] These "forces of shariah have been at war with non-Muslims for

1,400 years and with the United States of America for 200 years," and Europe was expected to be "an Islamic continent by the end of this century, if not before." Political correctness among academics and political and military leaders was fostering a "dhimmi" attitude in the face of this threat and hampering recognition of the ideological nature of the enemy.[43] America is doubly endangered, because in the 1960s the government lost the legal powers that should have been in place to defeat communism, and even these would not have been "adequate to shield us from a totalitarian ideology cloaked in religious garb." In response, the government needed to introduce bans on "those who espouse or support sharia [from] holding positions of trust in federal, state, or local governments or the armed forces," and imams and mosques that "advocate shariah in America" should face prosecution for sedition.[44] Since espousing shari'a, not in its caricatured form of mandating the stoning of women but as a moral code, is central to what most practicing Muslims believe, implementing these recommendations would, in effect, make believing in Islam a crime.

Later in the year the Florida-based Citizens for National Security (CNS) organization published a similar report, entitled "Homegrown Jihad in the USA: Muslim Brotherhood's Deliberate, Premeditated Plan Now Reaching Maturity." A meeting on Capitol Hill to promote the report was hosted by Congressman Allen West, an Iraq war veteran who was disciplined and relieved of his post as commander of an artillery unit after beating and threatening to kill an Iraqi prisoner in 2003.[45] A series of charts in the CNS presentation drew elaborate links from al-Qaeda and Hezbollah to mainstream Muslim America in an attempt to demonstrate a giant conspiracy to destroy the United States through stealth jihad. Fortunately for the survival of the free world, the Citizens for National Security had acquired the names of the six thousand active members of the Muslim Brotherhood in the US who were the agents of this conspiracy. The group had previously announced that they would release the names to the public at the meeting, but, on the day, they elected instead to share them only with select "responsible parties."

Allen West had repeatedly endorsed the shari'a conspiracy theory. He told a campaign meeting in 2010:

> We already have a Fifth Column that is already infiltrating into our colleges, into our universities, into our high schools, into our religious aspect, our cultural aspect, our financial, our political systems in this country. And that enemy represents something called Islam. And Islam is a totalitarian theocratic political ideology; it is not a religion.[46]

He later claimed, "There is an infiltration of the Sharia practice into all of our operating systems in our country, as well as across Western civilization."[47] Peter King, chair of the House Homeland Security Committee, also dipped into the shari'a conspiracy basket in the lead-up to his 2011 hearings on the radicalization of American Muslims. On *The Laura Ingraham Show*, King claimed "80 percent of the mosques in this country are controlled by radical imams." The source for this statistic was a single, unsubstantiated statement made by a Californian Muslim cleric in 1999. The cleric later admitted that his definition of an extremist mosque was one that was "focus[ed] on the Palestinian struggle."[48]

Since 2010, when Oklahoma voters passed a constitutional amendment prohibiting judges from considering foreign laws (code for shari'a) in their decisions, over two dozen states have proposed or passed similar legislation on the presumption that there is a secret plan to impose shari'a law on the US. Most of the legislation has been drafted according to templates developed by New York–based lawyer David Yerushalmi, whom we met in Chapter 2. The Oklahoma statute was later struck down by federal court judges, who pointed out that its advocates had not been able to find any actual examples of a shari'a problem to be addressed. Those claiming shari'a law was infiltrating courts across the US only ever cited one example: a 2009 New Jersey case in which a judge denied a woman a restraining order against her husband, who was accused of repeatedly beating and sexually assaulting her. The basis for the judge's decision was that there was no criminal intent because the Muslim defendant genuinely believed his religion entitled him to sexual relations on demand (which many Muslims would deny). The decision was clearly wrong under state law, because there is no "cultural" defense for breaking the law, and the New Jersey Appellate Court reversed it.[49] But this single decision became the basis for the fantasy that shari'a was covertly sweeping the American legal system, propelled by a hidden conspiracy of Islamists. An August 2011 survey found 30 percent of Americans believed Muslims in the US were seeking to replace the Constitution with shari'a law. The number is double among those who consider Fox News a trustworthy source of news.[50]

By the time of the 2012 Republican primaries, candidates were hoping to pick up on the undercurrents of shari'a paranoia in the electorate. Newt Gingrich was ahead of the game; he had already said in a speech to the neoconservative American Enterprise Institute in July 2010 that shari'a "is a mortal threat to the survival of freedom in the United States and in the world as we know it."[51] Other Republican candidates tried to catch up by endorsing the conspiracy theory in more forceful ways. Herman Cain condemned what he called the "attempt to gradually ease Sharia law and the Muslim faith into our government," said he would introduce a special loyalty test for Muslims wanting to serve in his administration, and claimed the majority of American Muslims have extremist views.[52] Michele Bachmann declared that shari'a "must be resisted across the United States" and demanded that national security officials investigate Muslim Brotherhood infiltration into the highest levels of the federal government.[53] In a McCarthyite letter to the State Department inspector general, she accused Huma Abedin, a top aide to Secretary of State Hillary Clinton, of being a Muslim Brotherhood "operative." Her only evidence was that other people in Abedin's family were "connected" to the Muslim Brotherhood.[54] The irony is that figures on the Christian Right who believe religious texts should be the basis on which laws are formed have more in common with the Muslim Brotherhood's ideology than American liberals like Abedin.

All this adds up to what we might call, with Senator Joseph McCarthy, "a conspiracy on a scale so immense as to dwarf any previous such venture in the history of man." And, in a sense, this is a return to what Richard Hofstadter diagnosed in 1963 as the "paranoid style" in American politics, now with an equal audience among the European far Right.[55] The conspiratorial conception of power of the early cold war, or the anti-Semitic conspiracy theories that had such an influence in the twentieth century, saw their enemies as hugely powerful and able to direct world history through secret control of the media and the economy, or even through techniques of brainwashing. Anti-Semites viewed Jews as both an outcast subclass threatening the purity of the social body, and also as a secret class above society able to manipulate events to maintain its power. All racisms have some kind of double aspect. Racialized immigrants, for example, are always both lazy and stealing our jobs; they both refuse to integrate into our society while also secretly infiltrating it. But anti-Semitism was historically unique in positioning Jews as constituting both a cosmopolitan superpower and a species of subhumans. For the first time, the far Right has now begun to think of Muslims in the same way. The new conspiracy theorists ascribe to Islam magical powers to secretly control Western governments while at the same time see in it a backward, seventh-century ideology whose followers constitute a dangerous underclass. The political logic of this shari'a conspiracy theory is clear: its supporters hope to pressure American liberals to abandon any remaining support for the civil rights of American Muslims on the grounds that Islam is not a religion but a totalitarian political ideology and therefore not entitled to protection under the First Amendment. Uniting behind this campaign are Christian Right groups, such as the American Family Association, right-wing Zionists, conservative foundations, and elements of the national security apparatus.

The rising influence of far Right Islamophobia at the end of the first decade of the twenty-first century was largely responsible for creating the political atmosphere in which an upsurge in anti-Muslim violence in the US became likely. Islamophobic violence was not a spontaneous reaction to terrorist attacks. It emerged nine years after 9/11 and, while the Fort Hood shooting in late 2009 and the attempted car-bomb attack on Times Square in May the following year had given Islamophobes hooks around which to mobilize, by themselves these attacks could not have generated the worsening climate that followed. The government had for years been telling Americans to expect more terrorism, even suggesting attacks would likely involve weapons of mass destruction. When actual incidents did occur, they were, if anything, less disturbing than what had been predicted.

But Islamophobic campaigning only has the effect it does because its message resonates with the culturalist and reformist Muslim problem narratives that infuse the discourse of US government agencies. The view that there is a deep, internal struggle taking place within Muslim communities, between our values and Islamist extremism, that the wars the US is fighting are a necessary response to a violence-prone Islamist ideology, and that American Muslim political leadership needs to be pressed to demonstrate its loyalty to American values—all this is not confined to a far Right fringe but is official analysis as well, and is supported by liberals in the Obama administration as much as by conservatives. Domestically liberals tend to maintain a rhetorical defense of First Amendment rights and pursue a cultural policy of assimilating moderate Islam into the mainstream of America. Obama's Department of Justice makes some limited efforts to prosecute hate crimes and defend the rights of Muslims to build mosques. But such efforts are ultimately undermined by the deeper structures of official thinking on extremism. Government counterterrorism officials hold there to be a domestic ideological threat of Muslim extremism that is serious enough to warrant the extrajudicial killing of US citizens who advocate extremist ideologies. That threat is, under Obama, usually understood in terms of a reformist narrative that distinguishes between good Muslims and bad Muslims—the former defined by their embrace of American values, the latter by their support for an extremist ideology that causes terrorism. But that still leaves in place the misguided assumptions of a Muslim problem and the militarized identity politics of a war between the West and radical Islam. It is no surprise, then, that a survey of likely voters in May 2012 found that 63 percent believed there was a conflict in the world today between Western civilization and Islamic nations.[56] The basic assumptions of the war on terror have remained largely in place throughout the Obama years.

Terrorism in Oslo

On July 22, 2011, as news emerged of a major terrorist attack taking place in Norway, the *Wall Street Journal* went to press while the identity of the perpetrator was still unknown. On the presumption that only a Muslim could be responsible, the newspaper's editorial claimed Norway had been targeted because it is "a liberal nation committed to freedom of speech and conscience, equality between the sexes, representative democracy and every other freedom that still defines the West."[57] The reflexes entrenched by nearly ten years of war on terror thinking had led the editorial writer to feel confident that the attacker's motivation could already be known. As it turned out, the car bomb in Oslo, followed by a shooting spree on the island of Utøya that left seventy-seven dead—the worst terrorist attack in Europe since the Madrid bombings of 2004—had been carried out in the name of a "counterjihadist" rather than a jihadist ideology. Anders Behring Breivik, whose fifteen-hundred-page manifesto, *2083—A European Declaration of Independence*, was published online on the day of the attacks, believed that European elites were pandering to multiculturalism and enabling an "Islamic colonisation of Europe." Like the *Wall Street Journal* editorial writer, he believed Norway's values were under threat from radical Islam.[58]

Breivik wrote his manifesto in English, presumably to attract British and American readers. Much of the document consists of advice to fellow far Right terrorists on weapons, bomb making, body armor, physical training, rituals to maintain ideological commitment, music to listen to, political marketing, and the potential use of chemical, biological, and nuclear weapons. He claims to be a member of a secret group of new crusaders founded in London in 2002 by representatives from eight European countries "for the purpose of serving the interests of the free indigenous peoples of Europe and to fight against the ongoing European Jihad." One section of *2083* describes the ranks, organizational structure, initiation rites, uniforms, awards, and medals being used by this secret Knights Templar group. These parts of the manifesto—and a section in which he interviews himself, narcissistically listing his favorite music, clothes, and drinks—appear to be its only original content. The bulk of the document is a compilation of texts copied from Breivik's favorite Web sites. Its opening chapters, a long section on "cultural Marxism" and political correctness, are plagiarized from *Political Correctness: A Short History of an Ideology*, a book published online in 2004 by the Free Congress

Foundation, a Washington-based lobby group founded by Paul Weyrich, one of the most influential activists of the US Christian Right and architect of the evangelical movement's entry into US politics during the 1980s. In this section, Breivik has replaced references to "America" in the original text with "Western Europe." The writers Breivik cites most often are Robert Spencer, Ba'et Yor, and "Fjordman," a Norwegian who has written for the US-based *Gates of Vienna* and *Jihad Watch* Web sites.

The key argument of the manifesto is that Europe has been taken over by a pro-multiculturalist elite, which is imposing its ideology of cultural Marxism in order to undermine native European culture. Endorsing the Eurabia thesis, Breivik sees multiculturalism as facilitating the "Islamic colonisation of Europe [through] demographic warfare." And the clock is ticking: "We have only a few decades to consolidate a sufficient level of resistance before our major cities are completely demographically overwhelmed by Muslims." Through its control of the media, universities, and mainstream political parties, the multiculturalist elite has prevented the possibility of democratic opposition, claims Breivik. While individual Muslims do not necessarily follow its precepts, Islam is "a political ideology that exists in a fundamental and permanent state of war with non-Islamic civilisations, cultures, and individuals," which means that the more Muslims there are in Europe, the more Islam's inherent violence manifests itself. If this trend is not reversed, he predicts, a European civil war will break out between nationalists and Muslims allied with multiculturalists. Finally, Breivik justifies his violence by arguing for "a pre-emptive war, waged in order to repel, defeat or weaken an ongoing Islamic invasion/colonisation, to gain a strategic advantage in an unavoidable war before that threat materialises."

The formal structure of the manifesto's argument corresponds to the conventional neo-Nazi doctrine of race war, in which, before it is too late, whites rise up against governments that have tried to dilute their racial purity. The standard strategy of neo-Nazism has been to actively encourage such a war by launching attacks on minorities—to provoke a violent reaction that would awaken the white majorities to the necessity of racial struggle, sending thousands of recruits into the ranks of the nationalist movement. This was what David

Copeland was hoping for when, in 1999, he planted nail bombs in London's black and Asian neighborhoods and in a gay bar, killing three people and injuring over a hundred. There are elements of this provocation strategy in Breivik's manifesto too. He argues for attacks on Muslim cultural events to incite "violent riots and various forms of Jihadi activities"; these, he hopes, will in turn "radicalise more Europeans" and spiral, until more Europeans "come to learn the 'true face of Islam' and multiculturalism." But he singles out the multiculturalist elites as the primary targets for violence, hoping that terrorism will "penetrate the strict censorship regime" and damage the multicultural ideology. "In order to wake up the masses, the only rational approach will be to make sure the current system implodes." Hence the mass murder at Utøya of the next generation of Labor Party leaders.

While Breivik's narrative formally resembles the race war of neo-Nazism, he reframes this doctrine by substituting culture for race, Muslims for blacks, and multiculturalists for Jews. He explicitly rejects the race war concept and calls instead for a cultural war in which "absolutely everyone will have the opportunity to show their loyalty to our cause, including nationalist European Jews, non-European Christians or Hindu/Buddhist Asians." Like the EDL, he uses a culturalist framework to forge new alliances. Yet he also speaks of his "opposition to race-mixing" and wants "to prevent the extinction of the Nordic genotypes." Of Jews, he writes:

> So, are the current Jews in Europe and US disloyal? The multiculturalist (nation-wrecking) Jews ARE while the conservative Jews ARE NOT. Approx. 75% of European/US Jews support multiculturalism while approx. 50% of Israeli Jews does the same. This shows very clearly that we must embrace the remaining loyal Jews as brothers . . . There is no Jewish problem in Western Europe (with the exception of the UK and France) as we only have 1 million in Western Europe, whereas 800 000 out of these 1 million live in France and the UK. The US on the other hand, with more than 6 million Jews (600% more than Europe) actually has a considerable Jewish problem.

Casting Jews as both potential allies (if they join in fighting Islam) and a demographic threat (if there are too many), Breivik is simultaneously anti-Semitic and pro-Zionist. The picture that emerges is far from consistent, with old far Right ideas of race war being reworked with newer culturalist notions.

The overwhelming majority of Breivik's source material comes from Web sites of the US far Right Islamophobia network. Europe has repeatedly been presented on these sites as on the verge of cultural extinction as a result of Muslim immigration. A 2007 blog post by Fjordman gives Breivik the title of his manifesto and his core argument:

> We are being subject to a foreign invasion, and aiding and abetting a foreign invasion in any way constitutes treason. If non-Europeans have the right to resist colonisation and desire self-determination then Europeans have that right, too. And we intend to exercise it.[59]

In a section discussing the EDL, Breivik praises the organization for being the first youth movement to transcend the old-fashioned race hate and authoritarianism of the far Right. He urges "conservative intellectuals" to help ensure the EDL continues to reject "criminal, racist and totalitarian doctrines." But he also considers them "dangerously naïve" in thinking their objectives can be achieved by means of street protests.

Certainly, Breivik's manifesto shares much of the culturalist politics of the EDL and the US Islamophobia network and strongly reflects their far Right themes: the view of Islam as an extremist political ideology; the emphasis on multiculturalism as enabling Islamification; conspiracy theories about Islamic infiltration; the rejection of old-style racism; and support for right-wing Zionism. For bloggers such as Pamela Geller and Robert Spencer, the references to their writings in his manifesto must have been unnerving. Even so, Geller responded to the Oslo massacre with characteristic gusto. Less than two weeks afterward, she wrote:

> Breivik was targeting the future leaders of the party responsible for flooding Norway with Muslims who refuse to assimilate, who commit major violence against Norwegian natives, including violent gang rapes, with impunity, and who live on the dole . . . all done without the consent of the Norwegians.

The left-wing youth camp on the island of Utøya was, she added, an "antisemitic indoctrination training center." She did not think Breivik's actions were justified, but, she added, there was "also no justification for Norway's antisemitism and demonization of Israel."[60]

We should be wary of drawing straight lines of causality between far Right ideology and individual acts of violence—such claims are as weak with regard to far Right terrorism as with so-called jihadist terrorism. It is nevertheless possible to say what kinds of political circumstances make terrorist attacks such as Breivik's more likely. The key factor is ten years of war on terror rhetoric that has entrenched a militarized identity politics as the default way of understanding our place in the world. The major theme of Breivik's manifesto was the argument that political correctness and multiculturalism had weakened national identity and encouraged Islamic extremism, bringing European nations to a crisis point. As Breivik himself correctly noted in the first week of his trial, this view was held by "the three most powerful politicians in Europe"—Nicolas Sarkozy, Angela Merkel, and David Cameron.[61] The uncomfortable truth is that a central plank of a terrorist's narrative was shared by heads of Western governments.

CHAPTER 9

Dream Not of Other Worlds

> The less the orthodox political sphere seems responsive to the demands of those it excludes, the more those demands can assume a pathological form, blowing apart the very public arena in which they had previously sought a hearing. Terrorism is among other things a reaction to a politics which has grown vacuously managerial.
>
> —Terry Eagleton, *Holy Terror*

Mainstream popular culture in the period since 9/11 has remained slavishly faithful to the official narratives of the war on terror. While at the margins—for example, in underground hip-hop—a radical critique can be found, a narrow and limited consensus has suffused the cultural center ground of the US and the UK. Spaces for questioning have been made available only on entirely pragmatic matters—for example, on whether torture and war actually work as means for preventing terrorism or whether they end up making the problem worse. Films such as *Zero Dark Thirty* (2012) and Britain's Channel 4 production *Complicit* (2013) consider the use of torture an acceptable topic of discussion—an indication that the terror war has permanently broken the earlier consensus that torture is an absolute wrong. The limits of acceptable discourse are illustrated even more starkly by considering what passes for a "liberal" take in popular cultural depictions. If *24* was the quintessential television drama of the war's early phase—with its ticking-time-bomb scenarios glorifying torture, its mass killings of US civilians by weapons of mass destruction, and its constant stream of one-dimensional terrorist enemies—*Homeland* is hailed as a liberal alternative, more appropriate to the Obama era, and its focus on the psychology of radicalization. Indeed, the show—broadcast on Showtime in the US and on Channel 4 in the UK—is said to be the president's favorite program.

Homeland's key plot themes are the infiltration of the US administration by Muslim extremists (a nod to Islamophobic conspiracy theories), suspicion of ordinary Muslim Americans, especially converts, and the psychological turmoil of the leading Muslim character, who is caught between his all-American family and the pull of extremist indoctrination. Nick Brody, a white American marine, is captured and held prisoner by al-Qaeda in Iraq (later this becomes the Taliban in Afghanistan—the two are apparently interchangeable) until he is freed eight years later. Returning to the US as a war hero, Brody tries to maintain a normal family life while hiding the fact that he has converted to Islam. The CIA's Carrie Mathison, whose character is reportedly based on an actual CIA analyst (who also inspired the lead in *Zero Dark Thirty*), suspects Brody has been won over to the terrorist cause and begins a rogue surveillance operation to prove her theory; she also has an affair with her subject. His suicide mission to kill the vice president and a host of other government officials is abandoned after a last-minute conversation with his daughter. He then plots to get elected to Congress and take a senior role in the administration in order to subvert US foreign policy. Mathison induces Brody to confess during an interrogation, and he agrees to work as a double agent. Meanwhile, Abu Nazir, the al-Qaeda leader who recruited him, enters into an implausible alliance with Hezbollah to avenge an Israeli strike on an Iranian nuclear facility by attacking the US. Nazir somehow manages to enter the US with teams of heavily armed commandoes, which engage in various confrontations before kidnapping Mathison and forcing Brody to kill the vice president. Season two ends with a car bombing at the CIA's headquarters.

Brody's character has more emotional depth than any other terrorist on US television. And there is a strand to the plot that tries to acknowledge the ways foreign policy decisions made in Washington can end up being counterproductive. Brody's indoctrination is presented as bound up with his anger at a US drone strike on a school that resulted in the death of Issa, Nazir's son, whom Brody had taken under his wing. These aspects of the show—which point to terrorism as not a pure evil but rooted in psychological processes—are the basis for its liberal credentials. They are also consistent with the discourse of radicalization that shapes the current phase of the war on terror. Like official accounts, *Homeland* presents radicalization as closely tied to Islamic culture and identity. All of the major Muslim characters are terrorists: from convert Brody to Roya Hammad, a Palestinian television journalist based in Washington who has easy access to the corridors of power and secretly plots on behalf of al-Qaeda, to Professor Raqim Faisel and his blond American wife, Aileen, who converted to Islam while living in Saudi Arabia as a teenager. The series' lack of concern for the differences between Hezbollah and al-Qaeda, or between Iraq and Afghanistan, coupled with its ridiculous portrayal of Beirut as a terrorist enclave give an impression of terrorism as a general cultural problem in the Middle East disconnected from specific political contexts. On multiple occasions in *Homeland*, terrorists struggle between an attraction to Western culture and their commitment to terrorism. A source of intelligence on Hezbollah shares information because of her love of American films. A Saudi diplomat working for al-Qaeda agrees to share intelligence so that his daughter can receive the benefits of Western culture. Brody's inner conflict between his love for his children and the pull of his indoctrination is depicted as an identity crisis, a battle between American values (symbolized by his family life) and Islamic values (presented as implying terrorism). Implicitly, *Homeland* is suggesting that the more culturally Muslim you are, the more likely you are to be a terrorist.

Brody is the only significant Muslim character on any US television drama program. He also happens to be a terrorist. Aspects of Muslim life, such as praying and reading the Qur'an, receive one of their only portrayals in US television drama in a storyline that is all about whether a convert to Islam should be suspected of terrorism. Brody's wife, Jessica, for a while embodies traditional American family values in the series: upon Brody's unexpected return from captivity, she abandons her relationship with his friend Mike for the sake of her marriage vows and thereafter struggles against the odds to hold the family together. She reacts angrily when she discovers

Brody is a Muslim, not because of the deception but because "these are the people who tortured you" and who would "stone" his daughter "to death in a soccer stadium."[1]

The true hero of *Homeland* is Saul Berenson, Mathison's thoughtful CIA mentor whose cultural knowledge and fluency in Arabic are presented as enabling him to pursue terrorist enemies by cultivating reliable informants rather than launching gung-ho missions. Yet he also believes in racial profiling when necessary, on one occasion giving his team instructions on how to conduct an investigation: "We prioritize. First the dark-skinned ones." At this point we have already been reassured that he has no problem with dark-skinned people. Following the usual cliché, his career with the agency has wrecked his relationship with his wife, Mira, who is Indian. In other words, profiling is seen as necessary for operational reasons and not the reflection of an individual agent's racial prejudice. Galvez, a Muslim member of the CIA team, has a negligible role until he is suspected by Mathison of working with al-Qaeda, largely because of his religion. Thus both of the series' CIA heroes find it necessary to profile on the basis of race or religion, at least on occasion. Racial discrimination is presented as a regrettable but understandable tactic that even America's best agents are likely to succumb to when investigating terrorist threats. Torture is not the universal solution it was on *24*, but it can still be an essential item in *Homeland*'s counterterrorism tool kit, so long as it is used in conjunction with Mathison's soft skills. Brody is stabbed through the hand by an interrogator, but only so that Mathison can step in afterward and present herself as the good cop, using empathy rather than force to win his cooperation.

US policies in *Homeland* are essentially benign but occasionally undermined by rogue cliques, who lead the government astray into counterproductive excesses. The show gives Mathison and Berenson multiple opportunities to voice their concerns about such excesses from within the national security system. But the only Muslim voices raising political issues do so as terrorists. The show's depictions of Muslim opposition to US foreign policy involve characters trying to justify terrorism, from Brody's martyrdom video to Mathison's interrogation of Hammad to Nazir's angry exchange with Mathison during her kidnapping. In line with the official radicalization narrative, political dissent and terrorism are collapsed into each other: the only Muslim voice is the terrorist voice. Indeed, Brody's prominence as the kind of Muslim who can make it to mainstream television is telling. The reality television series *All-American Muslim*, which tried to portray the everyday lives of Arab-American families in Dearborn, was taken off the air after conservatives pressured advertisers to pull their support. And for a number of years until the launch of Al Jazeera America in August 2013, deep opposition prevented Al Jazeera's English-language news channel from being allowed access to US cable networks.[2]

Welcome then to the latest stage of the war on terror. Muslim Americans are not automatically to be considered terrorists, but their culture remains a source of suspicion for its radicalizing effects. Their vulnerability to radicalization is understood as tied to identity conflicts and inner psychological processes that need to be tracked with widely deployed surveillance and an intelligent understanding of cultural context. The hard power of overwhelming force is complemented with soft power techniques and cultural knowledge to secure cooperation. With a liberal gloss of nuance, the war on terror continues to sustain Islamophobia, but in ways that are less susceptible to political challenge. Occasional pragmatic criticism of individual US actions as counterproductive insulates the wider structures of policy from substantial opposition. Above all, Muslim criticism of US policies is seen as no more than a precursor to terrorism, rendering absent any notion of Muslim political dissent.

The Right to Solidarity

Drive north from downtown Dallas, past the anti-Obama billboards that ask "Where's the birth certificate?" and others with a Jerusalem skyline and the caption "Israel will protect the holy land for all," and after thirteen miles you reach the suburb of Richardson, where a small Muslim population has made its home. On one block, amid the usual bars and burger joints, you can find a Pakistani grocery store and a Middle Eastern café where young Arab Americans sit in the courtyard smoking hookahs. This small pocket of Muslim

America in the northern suburbs of Dallas, surrounded by the city's prevailing conservative Christian culture, was home to the Holy Land Foundation, the largest Muslim charity in the United States until it was shut down by the Bush administration in the months after 9/11. The trial of the leaders of the Holy Land Foundation, the "Holy Land Five," highlights the limits placed on American Muslim political organization from the early years of the war on terror.

The Holy Land Foundation's purpose was to raise funds from Muslim-American communities to provide humanitarian aid to, among other groups, Palestinian charities called *zakat* committees—voluntary groups charged with administering the charitable donations that Islamic tradition considers mandatory. The Red Cross, the United States Agency for International Development, and the United Nations have all used Palestinian *zakat* committees as a way to distribute aid with low overhead. Historically, such committees have been well respected, politically neutral, and trustworthy local providers of food, clothing, and other relief to Palestinians living in the Occupied Territories. However, throughout the 1990s, Israeli officials pressured the US government to prosecute the Holy Land Foundation for its use of *zakat* committees. An investigation was begun in 1993 and coordinated with Israeli security agencies. Meetings of the foundation were secretly recorded by the FBI. Then, in the months after 9/11, the Treasury Department designated the foundation a terrorist organization, seized its assets, and put the charity out of business. In 2004, its leaders were indicted and accused of providing material support to Hamas. The government charged that from 1995 to 2001, the Holy Land Foundation sent approximately $12.4 million outside of the United States with the intent to willfully contribute funds, goods, and services to Hamas.[3] After an initial partial acquittal, the trial was reassigned to a new judge, and the Holy Land Five were eventually convicted in 2008, receiving sentences ranging from fifteen to sixty-five years.

The charge against the five was not that they sent money directly to Hamas, or that the money they sent to help Palestinians was intended for terrorist uses. Rather, the claim was that the *zakat* committees were run by Hamas and that, by providing charitable support to *zakat* committees, the foundation helped Hamas win the hearts and minds of the Palestinian people.[4] From a legal perspective, the prosecution strategy was striking for two reasons. First, to support the claim that the *zakat* committees were controlled by Hamas it relied on two witnesses, an agent of the Israel Security Agency and an officer of the Israel Defense Forces, who were able to testify anonymously, making it impossible for the defense to properly question them. Matthew Levitt, of the pro-Israel lobby group the Washington Institute for Near East Policy, also testified as an "expert" on Hamas. Second, the prosecution admitted dozens of documents seized from other Muslim-American activists and used these to name three hundred Muslim organizations as "unindicted co-conspirators" in the case, including some of the most prominent national Muslim organizations, such as the civil rights–focused Council on American-Islamic Relations, the mainstream Islamic Society of North America, and the North American Islamic Trust, which holds the deeds of many American mosques. The usual restrictions on hearsay evidence were put to one side, which meant that the groups on the list had allegations made against them that could not be challenged in court.

At no point were the *zakat* committees themselves designated as terrorist entities by the US government. And despite the hundreds of wiretapped phone calls and a mass of seized documents, prosecutors could find no firm evidence of a connection between the Holy Land Foundation and Hamas after 1995, when Hamas was designated a terrorist organization in the US and funding it became illegal. It was true that the Holy Land Foundation had been established by exiled activists who had a worldview shaped by political Islamic movements in the Middle East, such as the Muslim Brotherhood, and that Hamas was itself founded by the Palestinian branch of the Muslim Brotherhood. In the early 1990s, US-based activists in this milieu generally agreed with Hamas's rejection of the Oslo accords; so, too, did many secular Palestinians on the grounds that the Oslo process was unlikely to lead to the creation of a viable Palestinian state. They might also have agreed with Hamas's use of violence to resist Israel's occupation, just as today many agree with the violent rebellion in Syria against the Assad regime, which the US government also supports. But once Hamas was designated a terrorist entity in the US in 1995, the Holy Land leaders took steps to ensure compliance with US law. Indeed, representatives of the foundation met with Treasury Department officials in the 1990s seeking guidance on the implications for charitable work in Palestine, and were given the impression that donating to *zakat* committees would be lawful. But prosecutors in the Holy Land trial deliberately conflated general ideological support for the Muslim Brotherhood worldview with material support for Hamas. What the trial indicated was that after 9/11 even the minimal level of solidarity with their fellow Muslims in other parts of the world that the Holy Land Foundation had attempted would, in effect, be criminalized as a form of terrorism.[5] It was an eminently political prosecution that demonstrated how the widening of material support legislation could be used to convict major Muslim organizations in the US of being terrorists. It sent a message to Muslim America that after 9/11 Islamic political activism in solidarity with Palestinians had been criminalized.

In October 2012, the US Supreme Court declined to hear an appeal of the Holy Land Foundation case, marking the end of any judicial process. Four of the Holy Land Five were transferred to Communications Management units, special terrorist-holding prisons in Terre Haute, Indiana, and Marion, Illinois, where those accused of mainly al-Qaeda–related crimes face severe restrictions on communicating with the outside world. Counterterrorism officials in Washington, DC, strictly monitor telephone conversations, which are limited to two fifteen-minute calls each week, and a screen prevents physical contact with family members during the two four-hour visits allowed each month.[6]

As much as it set a legal precedent for criminalizing Muslim solidarity, the Holy Land trial also had the effect of inaugurating a conspiratorial view of Muslim politics in the US. The trial enabled the release of a transcript of an FBI covert recording of a meeting of Islamic activists held in Philadelphia in 1993, and of documents seized during an FBI raid of an Islamic activist in Annandale, Virginia, in 2004. These texts are held to constitute evidence of a wide-ranging Muslim Brotherhood conspiracy to take over the US and impose shari'a law, using seemingly benign national advocacy organizations as the vehicles to achieve this goal. Yet an objective reading of the material easily dispels such fantasies. The transcript of the Philadelphia meeting reveals nothing more than a conversation by a group of activists sympathetic to political Islam, frustrated by the recent Oslo accords, worried about the shifting atmosphere in the US political debate, and trying to explore how they might lawfully continue to support Palestinian charities without being demonized. Among the seized documents, the most often referred to in shari'a conspiracy theories is the so-called Explanatory Memorandum, apparently drafted by an activist called Mohammed Akram Adlouni in 1991. The document is a summary of its author's opinions, which he requested be added to the agenda of the next meeting of a group of pro–Muslim Brotherhood activists. The group itself did not commission the document. In one paragraph the author writes:

> The process of settlement is a "Civilization-Jihadist Process" with all the word means. The Ikhwan [Brothers] must understand that their work in America is a kind of grand Jihad in eliminating and destroying Western civilization from within.[7]

The document concludes with a list of Muslim organizations; this has been interpreted as a list of Muslim Brotherhood front groups, but the document itself does not describe them as such, instead lamenting the fact that they do not "all march according to one plan."[8] In the hands of conspiracy theorists, this document has been read as revealing a hidden extremist agenda behind a mask of Muslim moderation, demonstrating that leading American Muslim organizations are engaged in a secret plot to destroy Western civilization by infiltrating the government and manipulating the media. As such, the Explanatory Memorandum has become the *Protocols of the Learned Elders of Zion* of the shari'a conspiracy theory, its credibility enhanced by its being submitted as evidence in a terrorism prosecution. But even putting to one side the question of whether the views expressed in the document are shared by any actual organizations, it is clear that what is actually being proposed is the building of an organizational structure in the US that can act in political solidarity with other Muslim Brotherhood organizations around the world, while also proselytizing to Americans that Islam represents a better model of civilization than Western liberalism. All of this is lawful activity. The Muslim Brotherhood is not a terrorist organization and has never been designated one by the US government.

Convinced that a secret Muslim Brotherhood plot exists, and that the Obama administration has prevented the FBI from properly investigating it, shari'a conspiracy theorists have conducted their own freelance investigations of Muslim organizations. For example, in preparing his book *Muslim Mafia: Inside the Secret Underworld That's Conspiring to Islamize America*, coauthored with Paul Sperry, P. David Gaubatz, a former special agent in the US Air Force Office of Special Investigations, had his son Chris grow a beard, pretend to be Muslim, and spend six months "undercover" as an intern at the head office of the Council on American-Islamic Relations (CAIR), one of the few national organizations that campaigns for the civil rights of Muslims in the US. Chris managed to remove a quarter of a ton of documents from the office and record three hundred hours of video footage.[9] Among the shocking revelations produced by this daring investigation: CAIR engages with federal agencies to influence government policy; it advises Muslims of their rights when questioned by law enforcement officials; it provides legal assistance to individuals accused of terrorism; it organizes protests against firms accused of discriminating against Muslims; it has a public relations strategy; it owns real estate; and individuals working at CAIR have occasionally lived in the same neighborhood as a person charged with terrorism. Ironically, CAIR's efforts to organize for Muslims to take internships on Capitol Hill is described as "spying" and "infiltration." In conclusion, Gaubatz and Sperry recommend that "investigators and the public" should understand certain "red flags signaling extremism," including wearing a beard that is "a fistful in length" but with a trimmed mustache, wearing a silver ring on the right hand, and wearing robes that "cut above the ankle and contain black stitching."[10] This feverishly imaginative book was endorsed by Republican congresswoman Sue Myrick, and led to a group of lawmakers demanding that the government investigate CAIR, which thereafter struggled to free itself from the stigma of suspicion. It was again accused of extremism during the congressional hearings on Muslim radicalization initiated by House Homeland Security Committee chair Peter King in 2011.

In fact, as an organization, CAIR has followed the typically American, twentieth-century tradition of using identity politics to establish a Washington interest group. It seeks to defend the constitutional rights of individual Muslims, protest against media stereotypes, and defend the reputation of Islam as a religion. Prior to the intimidating climate of the war on terror, activists in CAIR had ambitions to shift US policy on the Middle East. But since then the main emphasis has been on an antidefamation and antidiscrimination agenda that roots itself in the US Constitution, similar to that deployed by other Washington lobby groups asserting minority interests. Like many Muslim organizations, CAIR has judged that lobbying on foreign policy issues is likely to be ineffectual in the current period, and it does not even mention foreign affairs on its Web site. And it has shied away from a wider, popular mobilization in defense of Muslim political freedoms in the US.

The shariʿa conspiracy theory has chimed with flawed radicalization models to generate a mood in which Muslim political organization and expression are inherently suspect. Good Muslims are implicitly expected to abandon Islamic political activism and the global solidarity it implies. Distancing oneself from political opposition to American foreign policy becomes the only way Muslims can be accepted in American culture. American national identity is usually seen as more open than Britishness, and certainly, in the US, there is nothing that directly compares to the explicit demands in the UK that immigrants and communities of color integrate into British values. But American culture has its assimilatory thrusts, too, that work in less obvious but equally powerful ways. Those tendencies have been bound up in the late war on terror with the securitization of Muslim culture and a current of official thinking on radicalization that embraces an acceptable way to be an American Muslim, one that abandons a politics of solidarity with Muslims in other parts of the world. On occasion this position has been fostered by the hard power of state criminalization, at times by the soft power of government counterradicalization initiatives. But it also results from the general Islamophobia of American political culture. The consequence is that Muslims lose the freedom to shape their identity on their own terms, and their only acceptable integration with America involves giving up affiliations with Muslims in other parts of the world.

The extent to which pro-Israel lobby groups have cultivated such an atmosphere has reflected their anxiety that the Muslim-American population is growing, and that the political influence of Muslims in the US might one day reflect their numbers, making less viable the defense of a Western foreign policy that shields Israel from sanctions for its occupation policy. The talk of Muslim infiltration betrays this anxiety that American Muslims could begin to deploy their weight in American society as equal citizens, and be able to speak as effectively in defense of Palestine as some Jews do in defense of Israel. The pro-Israel propagandist Daniel Pipes, a central figure in the American Islamophobia movement, relayed his fear of a growing Muslim-American population at an American Jewish Committee convention in 2001:

> I worry very much, from the Jewish point of view, [at] the presence, and increased stature, and affluence, and enfranchisement of American Muslims, because they are so much led by an Islamist leadership that this will present true dangers to American Jews.[11]

Pipes's understanding of this Islamist leadership is conveyed in a later comment:

> If Ayatollah Khomeini and Osama bin Laden represent Islamism 1.0, the prime minister of Turkey, Recep Tayyip Erdogan and the French intellectual Tariq Ramadan represent Islamism 2.0. The former are more deadly, but the latter will likely do greater long-term damage.[12]

The "damage" of an "Islamism 2.0" represented by figures like Ramadan is presumably that the US foreign policy of one-sided support of Israel will be increasingly challenged. No one knows the exact number of American Muslims in the US, but it is likely to approach the size of the American Jewish population—around six million—over the next decade, and the number of young, American-born Muslims is set to increase significantly in the coming years.[13]

For all its rhetoric, the real fear that lies behind US Islamophobia is not the Muslim fanatic but the possibility that this new generation of American Muslims might express itself politically.

Tahrir Square

If conservatives after 9/11 viewed political Islamic organizations as united in a worldwide conspiracy to overthrow Western civilization, liberals have tended to distinguish between moderate and extremist organizations on the basis of whether such organizations accommodate themselves to perceived Western interests and values. The debate between conservatives and liberals thus revolved around the question of whether political Islam can be incorporated into the liberal capitalist order or whether the former is necessarily an extremist threat to the latter. The stale public debate that has recurred through the war on terror, on whether Islam is culturally compatible with democracy, has usually been a proxy for consideration of this essentially political question. What both sides in the debate neglected to properly consider were the social and political injustices that create the fertile ground in which extremism grows.

The US response to Arab peoples themselves rising up in mass movements for dignity and equality is illustrative of these limitations. Conflict in the Middle East has been seen by conservatives as rooted in a cultural failure of Islam to adapt itself to modernity rather than as a political aspiration to freedom from Western-backed regimes. The assumption has been that Muslims could not generate their own democracy. The eruption of a transformative movement in Egypt in 2011 finally demonstrated in practice that this culturalist assumption does not hold. Popular sovereignty, not God's sovereignty, was the basis of the Tahrir Square protests; Muslims and Christians marched together. The slogans were demands for rights, dignity, and social justice. All of this confounds the clash of civilizations thesis, which holds that "Islam has bloody borders."[14] Equally, it undermined Obama's dialogue of civilizations approach, which sought to address the people of the Middle East as a culturally distinct Muslim world rather than as populations whose demands are political. It is no surprise that Obama's response to the fall of his erstwhile ally Hosni Mubarak was muddled. The events of 2011 drastically undermined the administration's strategy of restabilizing US Middle East policy through strengthened multilateral alliances with governments in Muslim-majority countries and using soft power public diplomacy to recognize moderate Islam as a legitimate cultural and religious identity. It turned out that US recognition of Islam was not the shortcut to winning hearts and minds that planners had anticipated. The people of the Middle East were more concerned with the US foreign policy of supporting oppressive regimes than its views on cultural questions about Islam and the West. And the strategic alliance with the Egyptian security services, which the Obama administration relied on in its war on terror, placed it on the wrong side of the barricades in 2011. Administration officials thus worried that the Egyptian revolution was "very chaotic" and would struggle to "find an equilibrium." What was needed was an "orderly transition" in which limited reforms could be made while maintaining US interests.[15] The administration's hope was for a managed process that would leave Egypt's strategic alliance with the US unaltered. The State Department stepped up talks with the Muslim Brotherhood, the leading organized political force among the opposition to Mubarak, in an attempt to achieve this. To the shari'a conspiracy theorists this was further evidence of the infiltration by Muslim Brotherhood supporters of the Obama administration. But the reality was that the Egyptian revolution had made the Brotherhood a potential power broker that the US government chose to engage with to secure its interests.

By the beginning of 2012, Obama liberals such as the journalist Fareed Zakaria—always a reliable bellwether of administration thinking—were no longer treating the Brotherhood as an extremist threat but seeing it as a potential stabilizing force that could, on the model of Prime Minister Erdogan in Turkey, partner with the military, continue neoliberal economic policies, avoid excessive anti-Western populism, and leave in place Mubarak's security arrangements with Israel and the US.[16] After Brotherhood leader Mohamed Morsi was elected president of Egypt, *Time* magazine featured him on its cover and described his seven years at universities in California, where he became a fan of the Trojans, the University of Southern California's football team, and acquired the nickname "Mo."[17] This assimilation of Morsi into American culture signaled that US establishment media were now able to conceive of the possibility of a Muslim Brotherhood government acting as a shock absorber for the Egyptian revolution's more radical impulses and bringing stability to the most populous Arab nation. The formula was an implicit pact between the Brotherhood leadership and the military, in which the generals would be able to maintain their hold on the deep state and continue profiting from their business interests while the Brotherhood pursued its cultural agenda. This, of course, left unaddressed the processes of social and economic marginalization that had driven Egypt's revolutionary protests in the first place. Liberal media in the US were correct to belatedly adopt a measure of nuance in their accounts of political Islam. But they were unable to grasp that the real problem was the Brotherhood's inability to offer an alternative economic model to the neoliberalism that produced Egypt's vast inequalities. The predominantly cultural formulae of Islamic movements are a poor basis upon which to resolve the political and economic challenges faced by postcolonial societies. Political Islam has historically reconciled itself to Western capitalism, despite its rhetorical opposition. Political scientist Fawaz Gerges has described the Muslim Brotherhood as "new capitalists," supportive of the interests of the business class and eager to reassure Western powers of its commitment to free-market principles: "The architect of the Brotherhood's economic policy, the millionaire businessman Khairat al-Shater, has silenced voices within the organisation that call for a more egalitarian, socialist approach."[18] Indeed, political Islam is usually content to play a role shoring up capitalist social relations, offering itself as an efficient cultural glue to resolve the antagonisms such relations generate, a process in which women and minorities are likely to pay the heaviest price. Despite continuing mass mobilizations on the streets, the more radical desire for economic, political, and social transformation that Tahrir Square represented was ignored by the Morsi government. Such a transformation, in which the people of the Middle East might begin to free themselves from the vested interests of pro-Western business and military classes, was the US's real fear of radicalization and the basis for its improvised response to the events of 2011. Indeed, once it became clear in 2013 that the Brotherhood would be unable to prevent such a radicalization in Egypt, despite its attempts to present itself as aligned with Western interests, the Egyptian military returned to power by appearing as the embodiment of the people's unmet demands; and the US government gave its blessing to what amounted to a military coup, with Secretary of State John Kerry describing the military intervention as "restoring democracy."[19] As Egyptian-American journalist Sharif Abdel Kouddous put it:

> In securing the military's fiefdom, the Brotherhood was left to its own devices to manage civilian politics. Yet the generals needed political stability in order to enjoy their economic empire, and the June 30, [2013], uprising threatened a complete state collapse, prompting them to intercede to protect their core interests.[20]

When the military began its brutal crackdown on dissent—killing hundreds of unarmed protesters—it knew it did so with the support of the US government. A token and temporary reduction in US aid to the Egyptian military did not alter their underlying strategic partnership. And with the generals once again monopolizing power, the US media's brief flirtation with Morsi ended. In the *New York Times*, David Brooks defended the military's power grab on the culturalist grounds that Egypt lacks "the basic mental ingredients" for democracy, while conservative magazines such as *Commentary* and *National Review* cheered on the violent suppression of opposition.[21]

Defending Dissent

This book has argued that the radicalization discourse of the current phase of the war on terror conceives of Western Muslims as locked in an ideological battle between, on the one hand, a moderate Islam that is seemingly apolitical but implicitly supportive of Western governments, and, on the other, an inherently violent extremist Islam. How is "extremism" defined in this discourse? At times the term has a theological meaning, referring, for example, to Salafi or conservative religious beliefs; it is also sometimes given an identitarian meaning, referring to the idea of a global Islamic identity that emphasizes one's affiliations with other Muslims around the world over one's national citizenship; on occasion it assumes a more explicitly political meaning, referring to radical opposition to Western governments. As a proportion of young Muslims in the West seem to fall under these various definitions of extremism, and extremist ideology is assumed to be a precursor to terrorist violence, the perception has grown that large numbers of young Muslims are on the verge of becoming al-Qaeda terrorists. Political and cultural disaffection is then misread as terrorist radicalization. With these assumptions in place, policies have been devised that would not make sense if the actual, negligible extent of al-Qaeda activism among Western Muslims was properly acknowledged.

Having conceived of radicalization in this way, tackling it implies the mass surveillance of the religious and political lives of Muslim populations. In the US, thousands of informants in Muslim communities have been recruited to this end. In the UK, nonpolice public service providers are drawn into the process of gathering intelligence on those suspected of radicalism. In both countries the state has criminalized expressions of Islamist ideology. Sting operations in the US have been deployed against those thought to be traveling on a radicalization journey. The grim legacies of COINTELPRO-style countersubversion policing have been revived. The UK state's Channel project uses a different approach, one in which young people are subjected to soft interventions designed to shift them away from extremist ideology while every aspect of their lives is scrutinized by police counterterrorist units. These have a less harmful impact on the lives of those targeted compared to US-style sting operations. But the Channel project nevertheless raises the question of whether it is appropriate to target young people on the basis of ideological expressions the government believes to be problematic, and then trying to manipulate them into adopting more acceptable opinions, all the while gathering detailed information about their private lives.

Some in the US have tried to import Britain's Channel project, seeing it as a liberal alternative to the FBI's sting operations. For example, Mohamed Elibiary, a Muslim activist from the northern suburbs of Dallas, has conducted his own Channel-style soft interventions in partnership with the FBI since 2008. Elibiary personally engages in counseling and mentoring young people to divert them from their extremist opinions while briefing the FBI on his progress. Such initiatives are rare, because in order to share information on the young person involved, high levels of trust are needed between the FBI and the activist carrying out the intervention.[22] And yet, the closer the relationship, the more the activist is, in practice, a state agent whose efforts to shift a young person's political or religious opinions begin to resemble state intrusion into personal ideology. The UK, meanwhile, is beginning to import the FBI's sting techniques and apply them to countering radicalization. In an unprecedented case that came to trial in Manchester in 2011, Munir Farooqi was convicted of preparing for acts of terrorism, inciting murder, and disseminating terrorist publications. Two undercover police officers had befriended Farooqi, pretended to convert to Islam, and spent a year repeatedly raising questions of jihad and the war in Afghanistan.[23] At the time of writing, Farooqi is appealing his conviction.

The close coordination between US and UK counterterrorism officials is illustrated by another development. The British government now has a policy of revoking the citizenship of suspected Islamist extremists while they are outside the UK in order to pave the way for US actions against them. Two British nationals who were stripped of their UK citizenship were subsequently killed in US drone strikes in Somalia.[24] Another British national, Somali-born Mahdi Hashi, is currently imprisoned in New York. Before 2012, he was a youth worker in Camden, London, where he had been pressured by MI5 officers to become an informant. He refused but was threatened with harassment. His citizenship was withdrawn while he was visiting Somalia in 2012, making it impossible for him to return to the UK. He was then imprisoned at a secret site in neighboring Djibouti, where he was threatened with torture and questioned by CIA and FBI officers. Because his British citizenship had been revoked by the Home Office, he was not entitled to consular assistance, and UK ministers could wash their hands of him. Only months later did his family track him down in a New York detention center, where he had been rendered to face charges of providing material support to al-Shabaab.[25]

Everyday life for communities under state surveillance programs increasingly resembles the patterns described in classic accounts of totalitarianism. There is the same sense of not knowing whom to trust, of choosing one's words with special care when discussing politics, and of the arbitrariness and unpredictability of state power. The thousands of American Muslims on the US government's no-fly list, for example, have no idea why their names are on it. Is it because they share a name with a suspected terrorist? Is it because someone with a grudge has phoned the government with false information? There is no way of knowing. No one can be sure whether the telephone call to relatives in Iran is wiretapped, whether Facebook posts are read by officials, or whether the new face in the mosque congregation is an informant. They have heard the stories, so they are careful—just in case.

Totalitarian rule thrives on its subjects' ignorance of the extent to which the surveillance system is monitoring their lives. The possibility, rather than the fact, of surveillance is enough to generate fear, anxiety, and informal pressures to conform, to downplay dissenting opinions, to declare one's absolute loyalty. Thus an enforced culture of self-censorship emerges in communities that used to express their political opinions freely. Linda Sarsour, an Arab-American community activist from Brooklyn, New York, notes:

> We're Arabs, we talk about politics all the time. Politics is all we do! Every coffee shop, it's either al-Jazeera or a soccer game on TV. This new idea that we must be suspicious of those who speak about politics—something's wrong.[26]

Humor is often the way people cope with this subtle psychological terror. The jokes American Muslims tell about state surveillance will be eerily familiar to those who lived under the East German Stasi; they are a way of acknowledging the same anxiety. Occasions on which political issues might be tentatively discussed by Muslim Americans usually begin with a humorous reference to the wiretapped phone or the presence of an informant.[27] Such humor is also an acknowledgment that the surveillance regime has been normalized in their everyday lives. Sunaina Marr Maira, a New England community activist, has written of how she and her colleagues began to develop

> strategies to manage the unspoken anxiety about the intrusion of state powers into everyday life, by self-consciously drawing attention to this constant possibility of surveillance. We made jokes about FBI videotaping and wiretapping, dressing for the camera, and possible informants in our midst . . . Our humor, I think, was a way to grapple with the unknown and ever-present reach of state powers.[28]

After repeated FBI interrogations over a six-month period in 2002, in which he was asked about every aspect of his life, Hasan M. Elahi, an artist and scholar at the University of Maryland, began to produce a Web site that automatically documented every flight he took, every place he visited, every financial transaction, and every meal he ate—a darkly humorous parody of the national-security state's obsession with quotidian detail. "There are 46,000 images on my site," he writes. "I trust that the FBI has seen all of them."[29]

The East German Stasi is estimated to have had one intelligence analyst for every 166 citizens. Adding regular informants brings the number to one spy for every 66 citizens.[30] The FBI reportedly has at present 10,000 intelligence analysts and agents working on counterterrorism and 15,000 paid informants.[31] Exactly how many of them are focused on Muslims in the United States is unknown; there is little transparency in this area. But given the emphasis the FBI has placed on preventing Muslim terrorism, it is reasonable to estimate that at least two-thirds are assigned to spy on Muslims. Taking the usual estimate of the Muslim population in the United States of 2.35 million, this would mean that the FBI has a spy for every ninety-four Muslims in the United States—before the resources of the National Security Agency, regional intelligence fusion centers, and the counterterrorism resources of local police departments, such as the NYPD, are added. This suggests that Muslims in the United States are likely to be exposed to levels of state surveillance similar to that which the East German population faced.

The collapse of East Germany's communist system and the opening of the Stasi's files gave regular citizens the uncanny experience of discovering their names in state intelligence documents and finding out who among their circles of friends was an informant. The 2011 leaking of some NYPD intelligence files has already begun giving individual Muslims the same disturbing experience. Numerous businesses, cafés, restaurants, and mosques in New York became aware that the NYPD considers them hot spots and deploys informants to monitor them. And the recent outing of a small number of NYPD informants has meant that some have found out that relationships they thought of as genuine friendships were actually covert attempts to gather intelligence. Asad Dandia, a nineteen-year-old student at City University of New York, has spoken of becoming aware that a friend was an informant.

> I met him through the Muslim Student Association's Facebook connections. He had told me he wanted to become a better person and to strengthen his faith. So I took him in, introduced him to all of my friends, got him involved in our extracurricular activities. I would wake him up for prayer every morning. He even slept over at my house . . . When I was texted the news [that he was an informant], the shock caused me to drop my phone. It took me twenty-four hours to get myself together.[32]

Another student at City University, Jawad Rasul, saw his name listed when a file on Muslim students became public in 2012, and that was when he discovered a friend of his was an informant. "You always hear about the NYPD spying on this group or that group, but having your name come up, it just brings everything home."[33]

Our current models of totalitarianism, largely derived from the cold war, are poorly equipped to make sense of these practices. Whether derived from fiction or historical studies, they usually picture a narrow, ideologically driven elite controlling the mass of the population. Such a state of affairs is normally assumed to be incompatible with a formal democratic process and a liberal economy. But the experience of the war on terror suggests that, if the same tools of totalitarian rule are applied only to racialized groups rather than the population as a whole, the trappings of democracy can be maintained for the majority. (Numerous other examples—such as China—have long demonstrated the compatibility of a liberalized economy with state authoritarianism.) The key to such a seemingly inconsistent "democratic totalitarianism" is a racialized discourse of fear that constructs Muslims as a cultural threat to the liberal order. It is the race principle that enables the separation of Muslims from the usual liberal norms of rights and citizenship. And it is on the basis of race thinking that Muslim dissent is read only as the intrusion of alien, illiberal cultural values into the public sphere and rarely as an attempt to use the political process to hold states accountable to their own liberal standards. From this perspective, the totalitarianism of the war on terror intersects with other racialized regimes, such as the war on drugs and the militarized policing of immigration, in which similar patterns of discriminatory surveillance, brutality, and incarceration are central.[34]

So long as the unspoken assumption that these measures will only be directed at racialized subjects—Muslims, African Americans, undesired immigrants, asylum seekers—remains valid, then the consent of the majority can be secured. And if this racialized totalitarianism begins to overreach and step on the freedoms of others—through, for example, overbearing screening at airports or by trying to introduce universal identity cards—such excesses can be quickly corrected while preserving the essential structure of the system. Moreover, since a transformative politics is more likely to emerge from racialized sections of society, the special measures the state reserves for these populations prove useful tools for maintaining the status quo. The analysis of totalitarianism today therefore requires a critical understanding of the centrality of race—but in a more radical way than managed by Hannah Arendt, who ultimately saw it as merely one of various possible precursors.

But as even the Stasi eventually discovered, no system of surveillance can ever produce total knowledge. Indeed, the greater the amount of information collected, the harder it is to interpret its meaning. The relevant information in the majority of recent US terrorist attacks was somewhere in the government's systems, but its significance was lost amid a morass of useless data. More significantly, what is obscured by the demands for ever greater surveillance and information processing is that security is best established through relationships of trust and political empowerment. A society that has blocked a section of its population from shaping a process of political transformation is one that has hollowed out its democracy until what's left is an empty, technocratic consensus in which real politics is disavowed. When radical political contestation is suffocated, the processes by which societies reinvent themselves and resolve their social tensions are neutered, and in the absence of a genuinely emancipatory alternative, the only possible outlet for the impulses generated by social and economic marginalization is the fake radicalism of armored identity politics, conspiracy theories, and apocalyptic fantasies.

Ending the War on Terror

Among the youth workers participating in the British government's program to tackle extremism, the more independently minded have realized that the real problem is the absence of any alternative to the managerial politics of mainstream liberalism. The young people they work with have not been radicalized by Anwar al-Awlaki or Nick Griffin. Their accounts of the world are more likely to involve conspiracy theories about Tupac or the Illuminati. Among those from Muslim backgrounds, there is no knowledge or interest in the content of Islamic ideology, only a pulp millenarianism and what one youth worker refers to as a "pseudo-Islamism" that reduces Islam to "a set of clichés." He adds that they share with young people supportive of the far Right a "totally uncritical way of looking at the world" that is apolitical, conspiratorial, and narrowly identitarian. The underlying principle of this worldview, reflecting the wider culturalist prejudices of our age, is that all societal problems are to be blamed on the fixed culture of the "other." Such attitudes are common and can, of course, connect with racist violence of various kinds, though youth workers say the risk of it leading to terrorism is negligible. To tackle it requires understanding its roots in the current context of depoliticization. Javaad Alipoor, a youth worker in Bradford who deals with issues of extremism among young people from a variety of backgrounds, points out:

> It is not a political way of thinking. When daily political discourse is completely shorn of any emotion and it's just a tedious administrative question of Ed Miliband versus David Cameron, then, of course, this

> repressed emotional core politics is going to come out in these crazy ways. I think there's a wider problem, which is, there's no politics. As radical as young people's worldviews are supposed to seem, in their racism, or their crazy religious millenarianism, in reality they are all built on the understanding that nothing about the fundamental socio-economic constellation can actually change, that no one ever talks about class, no one ever talks about capitalism, no one ever talks about working-class access to the world and the good things in life. The problem is that we don't have any politics. And so people's revulsion at the existing state of things manifests itself in all these crazy ways.[35]

In contrast to this political analysis, official thinking on extremism assumes that flawed structures of identity are the problem. A void is imagined to exist among white, working-class young people where a positive sense of national identity ought to be; a lack of identification with Britishness is supposed to be equally destructive of the proper integration of young Muslims. The absence of an appropriate sense of identity creates an opening for an extremist mind-set to fill the void. Part of the blame lies in excessive multiculturalism, which supposedly encourages the value of different cultures while not endorsing the majority identity. The answer, accordingly, is to revive national belonging by defining it in terms of the shared liberal values from which both Muslims and the white, working class are currently seen as alienated. On this view, the liberal state positions itself as a neutral mediator between the various forms of extremism that confront it, and sees its role as developing forms of identity politics that can draw marginal populations into accepting its values. In the latest iteration of this thinking, far Right extremism and Islamist extremism are seen as mutually reinforcing threats to the liberal order; extremism in one community provokes support for extremism in an opposing group, in a spiral of demonization—a process of "cumulative radicalization."[36] The response, liberals argue, should be a generic antiextremism that treats all forms of it as rooted in the same psychology of blocked identity formation that creates an opening for ideological mind-sets (a view that renders irrelevant the twentieth-century tradition of Left antifascism, which treated extremism as a political problem of class societies). Among the groups adopting this depoliticized model of extremism is the think tank Google Ideas, which has developed counterradicalization programs in which former radicals speak of their struggles to construct a positive sense of identity.

The limitation of this approach is that the liberal state is absolved of its role in creating an environment in which identitarian political violence occurs. Liberalism's promise (latterly in the form of multiculturalism) is that it provides the best means of enabling the coexistence of different ways of life within a single polity. But liberalism always had a different meaning too: not just a way of "reconciling many ways of life" but a way of life itself into which lesser peoples needed to be civilized.[37] The more the war on terror has emphasized this view of liberalism, in which it becomes a transcendent identity politics of its own rather than a space where various identities come together, the less liberalism has been able to play the role of neutral mediator. Instead it appears to its interlocutors as a one-sided demand that they simply substitute one form of identity politics for another, giving up their current ethnic, racial, or religious affiliations in favor of a "progressive nationalism."[38] This is unlikely to be very appealing to would-be extremists, who are characterized by their rejection of the liberal political game and a belief in the complete bankruptcy of the mainstream. But while the extremist is positioned as an outsider, as a force alien and disruptive of liberal democratic capitalism, he is in fact a symptom of the very system he despises. The al-Qaeda wannabe is no more than the mirror image of the official discourse of the war on terror, simply inverting the terms in the culturalist clash of civilizations rhetoric. Equally, the far Right activist gets the idea that he is at war with Islamic extremism from the very governments he rejects as hopelessly co-opted by an empty cosmopolitanism. This suggests that, in the end, liberals will be unable to solve their problems with extremism unless they can construct forms of political identification that reach beyond questions of cultural identity and speak to the wider context of neocolonialism, social and economic inequality, and the collapse of working-class representation.

For these reasons, programs that emphasize intense scrutiny of, and limitations on, radical opinion and religious behavior in the name of tackling radicalization are counterproductive. In the case of the Boston bombings, for example, the real missed opportunity to intervene before the attack was not some piece of intelligence that might have been picked up had the government been given greater surveillance powers. Rather, it came three months earlier, when bombing suspect Tamerlan Tsarnaev stood up during a Friday prayer service at his mosque—the Islamic Society of Boston, in Cambridge—to angrily protest the imam's sermon. The imam had been celebrating the life of Martin Luther King Jr., which Tsarnaev thought was selling out. According to one report, Tsarnaev was then kicked out of the prayer service for his outburst.[39] Since 9/11, mosque leaders have been under pressure to eject anyone expressing radical views rather than to engage with them and seek to challenge their religious interpretations, address their political frustrations, or meet their emotional needs. That policy has been forced on mosques by the wider climate of excessive surveillance. It has made mosque leaders wary of even having conversations with those perceived to be radicals for fear of attracting official attention. They fear that every mosque has a government informant listening for radical talk. Unsurprisingly, this means most people are reluctant to engage with young people expressing radical views.

The Tsarnaev brothers were said to be angry about US foreign policy in Afghanistan and Iraq, possibly drawing parallels with their own experiences as refugees from Russia's brutal wars of counterinsurgency in the Caucasus. But because discussions of foreign policy have been off-limits in mosques since 9/11, they were unlikely to have had their anger acknowledged, engaged, challenged, or channeled into nonviolent political activism. The heavy surveillance of Muslims has meant there is no room for mosques to engage with someone like Tamerlan Tsarnaev, listen to him, challenge those of his ideas that might be violent, or offer him emotional support. Instead, Muslims have felt pressured to demonstrate their loyalty to America by steering clear of dissident conversations on foreign policy. Flawed models of the radicalization process have assumed that the best way to stop terrorist violence is to prevent radical ideas from circulating. Attempting to reconstruct the motivation for the bombings is fraught with difficulty; there can be little certainty in such matters. But pathological outcomes are more likely when space for the free exchange of feelings and opinions is squeezed.

No one could have predicted from Tsarnaev's outburst that a few months later he would be suspected of carrying out an act of mass murder on the streets of Boston. And we do not know what would have made a difference in the end. But a community able to express itself openly, without fear, whether in the mosque or elsewhere, should be a key element in efforts to prevent terrorism. What is needed is less state surveillance and enforced conformity and more critical thinking and political empowerment. The role of communities in countering terrorism is not to institute self-censorship but to confidently construct political spaces where young people can politicize their disaffection into visions of how the world might be better organized, so that radical alternatives to terrorist vanguardism can emerge. Radicalization—in the true political sense of the word—is the solution, not the problem. Genuine emancipatory movements eschew the tactic of terrorism, because they locate themselves among the people; violence has only a defensive role in such movements.[40] Terrorism is not the product of radical politics but a symptom of political impotence. "The very fact of individual acts of terror," wrote Leon Trotsky, "is an infallible token of the political backwardness of a country and the feebleness of the progressive forces there."[41]

Anyone who seeks to extinguish the lives of civilians in acts of terrorism deserves universal contempt. But to condemn terrorism without hypocrisy today requires also a questioning of the normalized violence of the war on terror. The question of terrorist violence carried out by extremist or ideological nonstate actors is inseparable from the wider background of state violence that is defined as normal, necessary, and rational. They feed each other in a savage cycle of war and murder. Martin Luther King Jr. well understood how individual violence at home is intricately linked to state violence abroad—although this part of his message is downplayed in official celebrations of his life. Speaking in 1967, he told an audience at Riverside Church in New York:

> As I have walked among the desperate, rejected, and angry young men, I have told them that Molotov cocktails and rifles would not

> solve their problems. I have tried to offer them my deepest compassion while maintaining my conviction that social change comes most meaningfully through nonviolent action. But they asked, and rightly so, "What about Vietnam?" They asked if our own nation wasn't using massive doses of violence to solve its problems, to bring about the changes it wanted. Their questions hit home, and I knew that I could never again raise my voice against the violence of the oppressed in the ghettos without having first spoken clearly to the greatest purveyor of violence in the world today: my own government.

His efforts at what might now be called "preventing violent extremism" among young Americans depended on first opposing the violence of US foreign policy, a point that remains as valid today in the era of the terror war's global battlefield. Equally relevant today is King's understanding that "the giant triplets of racism, extreme materialism, and militarism" are interwoven in societies that place "profit motives and property rights" above human beings.[42] It is time once again to heed King's message of peace by ending the war on terror, and unraveling the racisms and totalitarianisms it fostered.

Afterword

In the year since I completed writing *The Muslims Are Coming!*, its analysis has, unfortunately, been repeatedly confirmed. The US and UK are in the midst of yet another round of counterterrorism initiatives, supported as ever by a compliant corporate media and so-called experts on terrorism who are paid to endorse official fear-mongering. The threat this time comes in the form of the Islamic State (ISIS), described by security officials on both sides of the Atlantic as the "greatest terror threat ever"—a preposterous claim that, of course, goes unchallenged.[1] The pattern is the familiar one repeated over the last decade: the group's spectacular violence is not seen as the product of a political context in part created by US and UK foreign policy; instead, it is assumed to be the result of "extremism," that bad version of Islamic belief which somehow takes hold of Muslim minds.

Ignored is the legacy of the 2003 Iraq War and the subsequent spurring on of sectarian divisions there to shore up a failing military occupation. ISIS, says British premier David Cameron, cannot be "defined by a war ten years ago" and nor, he claims, is it in any way connected to sectarianism.[2] The group's origins in Abu Musab al-Zarqawi's al-Qaeda in Iraq and, by extension, the insurgency against the US-UK occupation are thus forgotten. Also not addressed is an Anglo-American Syria policy that has amounted to fostering a balance of forces between the Bashar al-Assad regime and the various opposition factions—a win-win situation for Western security officials who fear that the Syrian government and its Islamist opposition are both equally dangerous to Israel, the Gulf allies, and the West. Having made that grim calculation, these same officials now panic at the consequences of their policy: the seizure of significant territory by ISIS and the danger, real but exaggerated, that young men participating in the conflict will commit acts of violence in European and American cities.

In response, our governments, once again, bomb *them* over there in the hope that this will prevent their bombing *us* over here.

While television news programs assist ISIS's propaganda efforts by hyping its video releases, a veil of silence is drawn over the obvious symbolism of the orange jumpsuits its Western victims are forced to wear. It would not be appropriate for commentators to point out that ISIS is, to some degree, mimicking the mediated violence of the Guantánamo prison camp. At the same time, the US and UK governments support the Gulf elites—surely the greatest force of religious reaction in the region—with multimillion-dollar arms deals; the early private financing of ISIS by those elites is now politely ignored by London and Washington.[3] To cap it all, the US media and political class cheer Israel's mass slaughter of children in Gaza. Netanyahu's line "Today they are against Israel, tomorrow they will be against you" was pitched perfectly for an American public long encouraged to think of Palestinians as inherently fanatical.[4] Again, the cry of "Muslim extremist!" serves to camouflage the politics of empire.

In Britain, Cameron's government proposes that a "generational struggle against a poisonous and extremist ideology" is to be fought domestically by prosecuting en masse those who travel to Syria and Iraq.[5] British passport-holders may be barred from re-entry, and the use of new powers to strip British nationals of their citizenship is being stepped up. Legislation passed in 2014 enables the British government to remove the citizenship of naturalized citizens, even if to do so would render them stateless. The policy is advertised with the slogan that "citizenship is a privilege, not a right." But citizenship is the right that enables all other rights; removing it is the gateway to all manner of abuses, including torture and extra-judicial killing by drone strike. Alongside this, the Justice and Security Act (2013) makes it possible for court proceedings to be held in secret so that the activities of the UK and US intelligence services, particularly any involvement in torture, can be shielded from public scrutiny. Meanwhile, the Channel "de-radicalization" program described in Chapter 5 is to be placed on a statutory basis, meaning a likely increase in the numbers placed on the scheme. By the end of 2013, 153 children under the age of eleven had already been identified as potential terrorists under the program, testimony to the embedding of security surveillance even in the lives of Muslim preteens.[6]

In the US, conservative pundits continue to normalize fear of Muslims. In June 2014, Fox News anchor Bill O'Reilly railed that Robert Bergdahl, the father of freed Taliban prisoner Bowe Bergdahl, "looks like a Muslim," because he has a beard and spoke some words of Pashto. By August, with the ISIS panic in full flow, Fox News reported that the group was planning to send terrorists to enter Texas over the Mexican border. Neoconservatives have for years fantasized that Latin America might become an "operational base to wage asymmetric warfare against the United States," in the words of an American Enterprise Institute report.[7] For the US Right, the phantasm of Muslim terrorists crossing the Mexico border is the ideal scare scenario, uniting the threats of terrorism and immigration in a single image of evil. It did not matter that there was no actual evidence of a terrorist plot to cross the Mexican border. The Obama administration joined the fray, with inflated accounts of the threat ISIS presents to the US, and a focus on immigration suggested by Chairman of the Joint Chiefs of Staff General Martin Dempsey: "Because of open borders and immigration issues, it's an immediate threat, that is to say, the fighters who may leave the current fight and migrate home."[8]

Viewers who switched away from the news might have caught the latest season of Fox's *24*, which was broadcast in 2014. Its storyline revolved around Muslim terrorists launching drone strikes on London with the help of a Julian Assange–type figure who naively supplies the necessary technology. Naturally, a show that depicts WikiLeaks and Muslims in collaboration is far more likely to appear on US television than a drama about the thousands of actual civilian victims of drone strikes in Yemen, Somalia, and Pakistan, whose stories are systematically hidden from view.

One result of the unrelenting demonization is racist and political violence on British and American streets. Two cases stand out for the way the victims were deliberately targeted for their political activism. Member of Parliament George Galloway was repeatedly punched in a west London street in August 2014 by a man who objected to his criticism of Israel. A week later, Linda Sarsour, a prominent Palestinian-American campaigner, whom I interviewed for *The Muslims Are Coming!*, was chased and threatened with beheading while walking near her Brooklyn office.[9]

If there is one area where the official consensus on national security is on the defensive, it is in relation to the National Security Agency (NSA) and its mass surveillance of our digital lives, which Edward Snowden's whistle-blowing made public in 2013. Concerned technologists and privacy activists ensured a continuous focus on the NSA's collection policies. Less attention was paid to the experiences of the individuals and communities specifically monitored by the NSA. In July 2014, Glenn Greenwald and Murtaza Hussain published an article that named NSA targets and showed how individuals were placed under surveillance despite there being no reasonable suspicion of their involvement in criminal activity.[10] All of those named were prominent Muslim Americans. One NSA document instructed staff on how to draw up a target list for surveillance; in place of the target's real name, the memo used "Mohammed Raghead" as a fake name. Yet the story attracted scant attention.

The following month, Jeremy Scahill and Ryan Devereaux published another report for *The Intercept*, which revealed that, under the Obama administration, the number of people on the National Counterterrorism Center's no-fly list had increased tenfold to 47,000. Leaked classified documents showed that the Center maintains a database of terrorism suspects worldwide—the Terrorist Identities Datamart Environment—which contained a million names by 2013, double the number of four years earlier. This database included 20,800 persons within the US, who were disproportionately concentrated in Dearborn, Michigan, with its significant Arab-American population.[11] Again, the story was largely ignored: there was little interest in reports of Arab Americans as targets of government surveillance.

Few realize that effectively challenging the NSA's surveillance programs means also rejecting the idea that certain communities can justly be surveilled on the basis of their ethnicity or religion. The resulting failure to engage with the American Muslim experience—or indeed the black experience—of being monitored by the government has given rise to a "national conversation" on state surveillance that is almost entirely focused on the privacy rights of the white middle class.

Yet it is precisely communities racialized by state surveillance that have been most effective in opposing it. In New York, the campaign against the Police Department's surveillance of Muslims has drawn its strength from building alliances with other groups affected by racial profiling: Latinos and African Americans who suffer from hugely disproportionate rates of stop and frisk. In California's Bay Area, a grassroots campaign successfully halted plans to open a Domain Awareness Center that had received funding from the Department of Homeland Security and would have intensified such surveillance. Various constituencies were able to unite on the issue, including homeless people, the poor, Muslims, and African Americans, all of whom would have been among the Center's targets had it opened. Similarly, a "demographics unit" planned by the Los Angeles Police Department, which would have profiled communities on the basis of race and religion, was shut down after a campaign that united various groups.

While these grassroots campaigns pointed to one possible avenue of change, from Connecticut came news of a legal victory that suggested an alternative approach to federal terrorism prosecutions. Talha Ahsan and Babar Ahmad had been extradited to the US from Britain in 2012, accused of providing "material support" for terrorism, and held for two years in solitary confinement. Under these conditions of psychological pressure, and no doubt calculating that, whatever the merits of their cases, the odds of acquittal in a US terrorism prosecution were stacked against them, each agreed to a plea bargain, meaning Ahmad faced a maximum sentence of twenty-five years and Ahsan fifteen.

The charges against them related to a website, Azzam.com, which was hosted in Connecticut from 1999 to 2001. This was the loose tie to the US that enabled the case to be prosecuted in the US's normally more punitive judicial system, rather than in Britain. But it also meant the case could not be pursued in the usual sites for federal terrorism prosecutions and took place instead in New Haven, where, it turned out, the chief judge, Janet C. Hall, had not internalized the flawed logic that usually underpins such cases.

At the sentencing hearing in July 2014, the government alleged that Azzam.com was an al-Qaeda support operation, and that someone who supported the Chechen insurgents and the Taliban must have had the "mindset" of an al-Qaeda supporter. But Judge Hall was skeptical. When prosecutors noted Azzam.com had republished Osama bin Laden's 1996 declaration of war against the US, she said the *New York Times* had done so as well. The court was shown a gruesome video, available on Azzam.com, of a Chechen militant executing a Russian soldier. This was evidence, said the government, that those involved in the site knew they were supporting perpetrators of war crimes. Judge Hall's reply was striking: the US government also commits war crimes, so its supporters would likewise be guilty of terrorism charges if that were a sufficient basis for prosecution. When prosecutors bandied around words like "jihad," Hall demanded precise definitions that distinguished between violence against civilians and self-defense against combatants. A key piece of the government's case—a document sent unsolicited to Azzam.com containing classified information on the movements of a US navy battle group—was interpreted by the judge as further evidence that Ahsan and Ahmad were not intent on harming the US: they had typed up the information but never used it or passed it on. Her concluding statement rejected the usual vocabulary of "extremism" and "radicalization." Ahmad, she said, was mistaken in being supportive of the Taliban but there was no evidence of support for al-Qaeda. Ahsan had similarly erred in supporting the Taliban before 9/11 but had never endorsed violence. She described them as motivated not by fanaticism but a desire to end oppression.

Judge Hall issued minimal sentences: Ahmad's time already served in prison in Britain was deducted and his release estimated for about thirteen months' time; Ahsan was sentenced to time served and released into the custody of immigration officers to be returned to the UK as a free man. For the first time in a post-9/11 terrorism case, a US judge decided to break with the usual deference to the government and assess the merits of the prosecution freed from official models of "radicalization" and the associated mythology of "extremist mindsets."

There is, of course, no immediate prospect that this approach will spread to other terrorism prosecutions. Instead, the machinery of mass surveillance, racialized criminalization, and extra-judicial killing presses on.

September 2014

Acknowledgments

The writing of this book was supported by a grant from the Open Society Fellowship. Parts of Chapters 4 and 8 first appeared as articles in *Race and Class* (54: 2, October 2012) and in *Critical Muslim* (no. 3, 2011). I am grateful to the editors of both journals for permission to reproduce sections of the articles here. The people who helped in the writing of this book are too numerous to mention by name, but I would particularly like to thank all those who agreed to meet with me or be interviewed. Especially helpful was the assistance I received from Fahd Ahmed, Hishaam Aidi, Amna Akbar, Harmit Athwal, Jenny Bourne, Nancy Chang, Lisena DeSantis, Mohamed Dirie, Liz Fekete, Mike German, Stephen Hubbell, Deepa Kumar, Kate Martin, Nancy Murray, Fattum Mutahr, Faiża Patel, Wendy Patten, Bipasha Ray, Rizwaan Sabir, A. Sivanandan, and Hazel Waters. None of them, of course, is responsible for the opinions I have expressed here. Andy Hsiao at Verso did a careful and thoughtful job of editing the original manuscript. Finally, I am grateful to Tanuka Loha for the warm support, insightful comments, and careful analysis she provided during the writing of this book.

Notes

INTRODUCTION

1 Phone interview with Omar Regan, July 18, 2012.

2 *Criminal Complaint, USA v. Luqman Ameen Abdullah et al.*, United States District Court for the Eastern District of Michigan, October 27, 2009, 2.

3 Ibid., 3.

4 Interview with Imam Abdullah Bey el-Amin, Detroit, March 31, 2011.

5 Phone interview with Andrew Arena, April 7, 2011.

6 "Report Re: Death of Imam Luqman Ameen Abdullah," Civil Rights Division, United States Department of Justice, October 13, 2010.

7 Malcolm X Grassroots Movement, "Black People Executed without Trial by Police, Security Guards, and Self-Appointed Law Enforcers, January 1–June 30, 2012," July 16, 2012.

8 The Obama administration has not completely ended extraordinary rendition but seeks to legitimize the practice by using antitorture diplomatic assurances from recipient countries and posttransfer monitoring of detainee treatment. Amrit Singh, *Globalizing Torture: CIA Secret Detention and Extraordinary Rendition*, Open Society Foundations, New York, 2013, 7.

9 "Establishing a New Normal: National Security, Civil Liberties, and Human Rights under the Obama Administration—An 18-Month Review," American Civil Liberties Union, July 2010.

10 Hillary Clinton, "Remarks on the Killing of Usama bin Ladin," Treaty Room, Washington, DC, May 2, 2011.

11 "Lawfulness of a Lethal Operation Directed against a US Citizen Who Is a Senior Operational Leader of al-Qa'ida or an Associated Force," Department of Justice (undated).

12 "Empowering Local Partners to Prevent Violent Extremism in the United States," White House, August 2011.

13 Mark Mazzetti, Charlie Savage, and Scott Shane, "How a US Citizen Came to Be in America's Cross Hairs," *New York Times*, March 9, 2013.

14 Nasser al-Awlaki, "The Drone that Killed My Grandson," *New York Times*, July 18, 2013, A23.

15 "Obama's Top Adviser Robert Gibbs Justifies Murder of 16-year-old American Citizen", wearechange.org (October 23, 2012), available at http://www.youtube.com/watch?v=7MwB2znBZ1g, accessed April 7, 2013.

16 Erik Nisbet, Michelle Ortiz, Yasamin Miller, and Andrew Smith, "The 'Bin Laden' Effect: How American Public Opinion about Muslim Americans Shifted in the Wake of Osama bin Laden's Death," School of Communication, Ohio State University, July 20, 2011.

17 Christopher Hitchens, "Londonistan Calling," *Vanity Fair*, June 2007.

18 Samuel P. Huntington, *Who Are We? The Challenges to America's Identity*, New York: Simon & Schuster, 2004, 262.

19 Mahmood Mamdani, *Good Muslim, Bad Muslim: America, the Cold War, and the Roots of Terror*, New York: Doubleday, 2004.

20 Alana Lentin and Gavan Titley, *The Crises of Multiculturalism: Racism in a Neoliberal Age*, London: Zed Books, 2011, 69.

21 "Fighting Anti-Muslim Racism: An Interview with A. Sivanandan," *IRR News*, March 15, 2010, irr.org.uk, accessed July 25, 2013.

22 FBI Counterterrorism Division, "The Radicalization Process: From Conversion to Jihad," May 10, 2006, 10.

23 Mitchell D. Silber and Arvin Bhatt, "Radicalization in the West: The Homegrown Threat," New York Police Department Intelligence Division, 2007, 85.

24 Charlie Rose, *This Morning*, CBS News, January 11, 2013.

25 See, for example, Glenn Greenwald and Spencer Ackerman, "How the NSA Is Still Harvesting Your Online Data," *Guardian*, June 27, 2013.

26 Gianfranco Sanguinetti, *On Terrorism and the State: The Theory and Practice of Terrorism Divulged for the First Time*, London: B. M. Chronos, 1982.

27 United States Senate, "Final Report of the Select Committee to Study Governmental Operations with Respect to Intelligence Activities," April 26 1976, 11.

28 United States Senate, "Final Report of the Select Committee to Study Governmental Operations with Respect to Intelligence Activities: Cointelpro—The FBI's Covert Action Programs Against American Citizens," April 23, 1976.

29 Ward Churchill and Jim Vander Wall, *The COINTELPRO Papers: Documents from the FBI's Secret Wars Against Dissent in the United States*, Cambridge, MA: South End Press, 2002.

30 Tony Shaw, "*The Russians Are Coming! The Russians Are Coming!* (1966): Reconsidering Hollywood's Cold War 'Turn' of the 1960s," *Film History*, 22: 2, 2010, 244.

31 Ibid., 244.

32 Ibid., 245–46.

33 The phrase "The Muslims Are Coming!" was the title of a 1990 *National Review* article by Daniel Pipes, which claimed "Western European societies are unprepared for the massive immigration of brown-skinned peoples cooking strange foods and maintaining different standards of hygiene . . . All immigrants bring exotic customs and attitudes, but Muslim customs are more troublesome than most." *National Review*, November 19, 1990, 28–31.

34 Katrina Trinko, "GOP Congressman: 'Increase Surveillance' of Muslim Community," *National Review*, April 19, 2013.

35 Alison Sullivan, "Gohmert: US Should Deport Chechen Immigrants with Violent Proclivities," *Houston Chronicle*, April 19, 2013.

36 *Indictment, United States of America v. Dzhokhar A. Tsarnaev, aka "Jahar Tsarni,"* United States District Court for the District of Massachusetts, June 27, 2013, 5.

37 "House of Commons," *Hansard*, June 3, 2013, col. 1235.

38 Ibid., col. 1245.

39 Vikram Dodd and Andrew Sparrow, "Theresa May's Plans to Tackle Extremism Face Backlash," *Guardian*, May 27, 2013.

40 Boris Johnson, "By Standing United, We Can Isolate the Virus of Islamism," *Telegraph*, May 26, 2013.

41 *Indictment, United States of America v. Dzhokhar A. Tsarnaev*, 4.

42 Janet Reitman, "Jahar's World," *Rolling Stone*, July 17, 2013.

43 Leo Hickman, "Woolwich Attack Witness Ingrid Loyau-Kennett: 'I Feel Like a Fraud,'" *Guardian*, May 27, 2013.

44 Rachel Shabi, "British Tolerance Is Never a Given: Post-Woolwich, It Must Be Defended," *Guardian*, July 2, 2013.

45 Eqbal Ahmad, "Terrorism: Theirs and Ours," in Carollee Bengelsdorf, Margaret Cerullo, and Yogesh Chandrani, eds, *The Selected Writings of Eqbal Ahmad*, New York: Columbia University Press, 2006.

46 Ed Moloney, "Rep. King and the IRA: The End of an Extraordinary Affair?" *New York Sun*, June 22, 2005.

47 Randy Blazak, "Isn't Every Crime a Hate Crime?: The Case for Hate Crime Laws," *Sociology Compass*, 5: 4, 2011, 248.

48 Arun Kundnani, "Blind Spot? Security Narratives and Far-Right Violence in Europe," International Centre for Counter-Terrorism, The Hague, May 2012, 3.

49 National Consortium for the Study of Terrorism and Responses to Terrorism, "Far-Right Violence in the United States: 1990–2010," University of Maryland, August 2012.

50 Thirteen people were killed in the Fort Hood shooting in November 2009 that was carried out by Nidal Malik Hasan, an American citizen. In June 2009, Abdulhakim Mujahid Muhammad, an African American who changed his name from Carlos Bledsoe after he converted to Islam, shot at a military recruiting office in Little Rock, Arkansas, killing Private William Long and wounding Private Quinton Ezeagwula. One person was killed in the July 2006 shooting at the Jewish Federation of Seattle, which was carried out by Naveed Afzal Haq, who grew up in Washington State. Three passengers were killed in the 2002 Los Angeles airport shooting; the perpetrator, Hesham Mohamed Hadayet, was a permanent resident of the US. One person was killed in the 1997 Empire State Building shooting, carried out by Ali Hassan Abu Kamal, who had been living in the US on a nonimmigrant visa. The murder of Rashad Khalifa in Tucson in 1990 by two members of the Jamaat ul-Fuqra group appears to have been politically motivated and carried out by US citizens. The term "jihadist" is, of course, inadequate to describe the various motivations involved in these murders.

51 Jorge Rivas, "CNN's John King Fails to Explain His 'Dark Skinned' Comment on Twitter," colorlines.com, April 19, 2013, colorlines.com, accessed July 24, 2013.

52 "Hardball with Chris Matthews," MSNBC, April 18, 2013.

53 Josh Halliday, "Woolwich Attack: BBC's Nick Robinson Apologises after 'Muslim' Description," *Guardian*, May 23, 2013.

54 "UK Mosque Bombing Suspect Also Accused of Muslim Man's Murder," Reuters, July 20, 2013.

55 Garrett M. Graff, "Homegrown Terror," *5280*, November 2011.

56 Brian Michael Jenkins, "Stray Dogs and Virtual Armies: Radicalization and Recruitment to Jihadist Terrorism in the United States Since 9/11," RAND Corporation, 2011, 6.

57 Kim Murphy, "Is Homeland Security Spending Paying Off?" *Los Angeles Times*, August 28, 2011.

58 Charles Kurzman, "Where Are All the Islamic Terrorists?" *Chronicle of Higher Education*, July 31, 2011.

59 John Mueller, "Six Rather Unusual Propositions about Terrorism," *Terrorism and Political Violence*, 17: 4, 2005, 488.

60 "Draft List of Deaths Related to the Conflict from 2002 to the Present", http://cain.ulst.ac.uk/issues/violence/deathsfrom2002draft.htm, accessed April 15, 2012.

61 "Human Costs of War: direct War Death in Afghanistan, Iraq, and Pakistan, October 2001–February 2013," Costs of War Project, Watson Institute for International Studies, Brown University, http://costsofwar.org/sites/default/files/HMCHART_2.pdf, accessed September 12, 2013.

62 Gilbert Burnham, Riyadh Lafta, Shannon Doocy, and Les Roberts, "Mortality after the 2003 Invasion of Iraq: A Cross-Sectional Cluster Sample Survey," *Lancet*, 368, October 21, 2006, 1421.

1. AN IDEAL ENEMY

1 Interview with Farasat Latif, Luton, June 3, 2011.

2 Phone interview with Farasat Latif, May 7, 2002.

3 Ibid.

4 Keith Poole, "Attack on Afghanistan: We'll Drive Extremists Out, Say Moderate Muslims: Luton," *Evening Standard*, October 31, 2001, 7.

5 Humayun Ansari, *"The Infidel Within": Muslims in Britain Since 1800,* London: Hurst & Company, 2004, 235.

6 David Docherty, David E Morrison, and Michael Tracey, *Keeping Faith? Channel Four and Its Audience*, London: J. Libbey, 1988, 11.

7 Figures supplied by the Institute of Race Relations, http://www.irr.org.uk/news/deaths-with-a-known-or-suspected-racial-element-1991-1999, accessed October 19, 2012.

8 Virinder Kalra, *From Textile Mills to Taxi Ranks: Experiences of Migration, Labour and Social Change*, Aldershot: Ashgate, 2000, 210.

9 Peter Ratcliffe, *Breaking Down the Barriers: Improving Asian Access to Social Rented Housing*, Coventry, Chartered Institute of Housing, 2001; "Racism in Oldham Housing," *Campaign Against Racism and Fascism*, no. 18, January/February 1994, 15.

10 Arun Kundnani, "From Oldham to Bradford: The Violence of the Violated," *Race and Class*, 43: 2, October 2001.

11 Herman Ouseley, *Community Pride, Not Prejudice: Making Diversity Work in Bradford*, Bradford: Bradford Vision, 2001.

12 Interview with Muhammad Najeib, Hull, UK, April 2, 2001.

13 Frantz Fanon, *The Wretched of the Earth*, London: Penguin, 1990, 190.

14 Ibid., 198.

15 Ibid., 255.

16 Suha Taji-Farouki, *A Fundamental Quest: Hizb al-Tahrir and the Search for the Islamic Caliphate*, London: Grey Seal, 1996, 187.

17 Olivier Roy, *Globalised Islam: The Search for a New Ummah*, London: Hurst, 2004.

18 Tariq Ramadan, *Western Muslims and the Future of Islam*, Oxford: Oxford University Press, 2004, 22, 35.

19 Shiv Malik, "My Brother the Bomber," *Prospect*, no. 135, June 2007.

20 David Cameron, *Speech to Munich Security Conference*, February 5, 2011.

21 Anne-Marie Bradley, "Bomber Was Huddersfield Drug Dealer," *Huddersfield Daily Examiner*, August 8, 2005.

22 Marc Lacey, "'Haboobs' Stir Critics in Arizona," *New York Times*, July 21, 2011.

23 *Muslim Americans: Middle Class and Mostly Mainstream*, Washington, DC: Pew Research Center, May 2007, 1; Karen Leonard, "American Muslims: Race, Religion, And Nation," *ISIM Newsletter*, Leiden, Netherlands: International Institute for the Study of Islam in the Modern World, April 2004.

24 Hishaam D. Aidi and Manning Marable, "Introduction: The Early Muslim Presence and Its Significance," in Manning Marable and Hishaam D Aidi, eds., *Black Routes to Islam*, New York: Palgrave Macmillan, 2009, 1.

25 Moustafa Bayoumi, "East of the Sun (West of the Moon): Islam, the Ahmadis, and African America," in ibid., 73.

26 Sherman A. Jackson, "Black Orientalism: Its Genesis, Aims, and Significance for American Islam," in ibid., 35.

27 Manning Marable, *Malcolm X: A Life of Reinvention*, New York: Viking Penguin, 2011, 103, 154.

28 Yvonne Yazbeck Haddad, *Not Quite American? The Shaping of Arab and Muslim Identity in the United States*, Waco, TX: Baylor University Press, 2004, 2–3; Pew Research Center, *Muslim Americans: Middle Class and Mostly Mainstream*, 1.

29 Dan Georgakas, "Arab Workers in Detroit," *MERIP Reports*, no. 34, January 1975.

30 Mary Bisharat, "Yemeni Farmworkers in California," *MERIP Reports*, no. 34, January 1975.

31 Interview with Rachid Elabed, Dearborn, Michigan, April 1, 2011.

32 Pew Research Center, *Muslim Americans: Middle Class and Mostly Mainstream*, 18.

33 Vijay Prashad, *Uncle Swami*, New York: New Press, 2012.

34 John Tehranian, "Selective Racialization: Middle-Eastern American Identity and the Faustian Pact with Whiteness," *Connecticut Law Review*, 40: 4, May 2008.

35 "Revisions to the Standards for the Classification of Federal Data on Race and Ethnicity," White House, Office of Management and Budget, October 30, 1997, http://www.whitehouse.gov/omb/fedreg_1997standards, accessed October 31, 2012.

36 Haddad, *Not Quite American?*, 20.

37 Elaine Hagopian, "Minority Rights in a Nation-State: The Nixon Administration's Campaign against Arab-Americans," *Journal of Palestine Studies*, 5: 1/2, Autumn 1975–Winter 1976.

38 Erik Skindrud, "Twenty Years Later, Still No Charges in Alex Odeh Assassination," *Electronic Intifada*, December 6, 2006, http://electronicintifada.net/content/twenty-years-later-still-no-charges-alex-odeh-assassination/6582, accessed October 31, 2012.

39 David Cole, *Enemy Aliens: Double Standards and Constitutional Freedoms in the War on Terrorism*, New York: New Press, 2005, 165.

40 Judith Gabriel, "Palestinians Arrested in Los Angeles Witch-Hunt," *MERIP Middle East Report*, no. 145, March–April 1987, 41.

41 Benjamin Netanyahu, ed., *Terrorism: How the West Can Win*, New York: Farrar, Straus, Giroux, 1986, 80–81.

42 Joseba Zulaika, "The Self-Fulfilling Prophecies of Counterterrorism," *Radical History Review*, no. 85, Winter 2003, 195.

43 Claire Sterling, *The Terror Network : The Secret War of International Terrorism*, New York: Holt, Rinehart, and Winston, 1981.

44 Lisa Stampnitzky, *Disciplining Terror: How Experts Invented "Terrorism,"* Cambridge: Cambridge University Press, 2013, 117–22.

45 Edward Said, "Identity, Negation and Violence," *New Left Review*, no. 171, September–October 1988, 47.

46 Reader List, A List on Media and The City, Information Politics and Contemporary Culture http://mail.sarai.net/pipermail/reader-list_mail.sarai.net/2001-September/thread.html, accessed October 25, 2012.

47 Suhail A. Khan, "America's First Muslim President," *Foreign Policy*, August 23, 2010.

48 Interview with Linda Sarsour, Brooklyn, New York, October 22, 2010.

49 Haddad, *Not Quite American?*, 33, 44.

50 Jean-Paul Sartre, *Anti-Semite and Jew*, New York, Schocken Books, 1948, 69.

51 *Muslim Americans: No Signs of Growth in Alienation or Support for Extremism*, Washington, DC: Pew Research Center, August 2011, 41.

52 Interview with Ghulam Bombaywala, Houston, Texas, April 16, 2011; phone interview with Ghulam Bombaywala, August 16, 2011.

53 Interview with Mahdi Bray, Washington, DC, October 21, 2010.

54 Interview with Dawud Walid, Detroit, March 29, 2011.

55 Interview with Rachid Elabed, Dearborn, Michigan.

56 Sikh Coalition Bay Area, *Civil Rights Report 2010*, 3.

57 Interview with Imam Johari Abdul-Malik, Falls Church, Virginia, January 24, 2011.

58 Haddad, *Not Quite American?*, 51.

59 Mucahit Bilici, "Homeland Insecurity: How Immigrant Muslims Naturalize America in Islam," *Comparative Studies in Society and History*, vol. 53, no. 3, 2011, 616.

60 https://www.soros.org/voices/911-10-religious-diversity-common-commitment, accessed November 1, 2012.

2. THE POLITICS OF ANTI-EXTREMISM

1 Bernard Lewis, "The Roots of Muslim Rage," *Atlantic Monthly*, September 1990.

2 Ibid., 60.

3 Samuel P. Huntington, "The Clash of Civilizations?" *Foreign Affairs*, Summer 1993, 22, 31–32, 35.

4 Mahmood Mamdani uses the term "culture talk" and Verena Stolcke uses the term "cultural fundamentalism" to refer to the same kind of thinking. See *Good Muslim, Bad Muslim: America, the Cold War, and the Roots of Terror*, New York: Doubleday, 2005; Verena Stolcke, "Talking Culture: New Boundaries, New Rhetorics of Exclusion in Europe," *Current Anthropology* 36: 1, 1995.

5 Philip Rucker and Joel Greenberg, "Romney Faces Palestinian Criticism for Jerusalem Remarks as He Heads to Poland," *Washington Post*, July 30, 2011.

6 Mehdi Semati, "Islamophobia, Culture and Race in the Age of Empire," *Cultural Studies* 24: 2, March 2010.

7 W. E. B. Du Bois, *The Conservation of Races*, Washington, DC: American Negro Academy, 1897; Alana Lentin and Gavan Titley, *The Crises of Multiculturalism: Racism in a Neoliberal Age*, London: Zed Books, 2011, 69.

8 Étienne Balibar, "Is There a 'Neo-Racism'?" in Tania Das Gupta, Carl E. James, Roger C. A. Maaka, Grace-Edward Galabuzi, and Chris Andersen, eds., *Race and Racialization: Essential Readings*, Toronto: Canadian Scholars' Press, 2007, 85.

9 Samuel P. Huntington, *Who Are We? The Challenges to America's Identity*, New York: Simon & Schuster, 2004, 262.

10 Edward Said, *Orientalism*, New York: Vintage Books, 1978.

11 Edward Said, *Covering Islam*, New York,: Fodor's Travel Guides, 1996.

12 Eqbal Ahmad, "Islam and Politics," in *The Selected Writings of Eqbal Ahmad*, New York: Columbia University Press, 2006.

13 Deepa Kumar, *Islamophobia and the Politics of Empire*, Chicago: Haymarket Books, 2012, 81–94.

14 George W. Bush, *Speech to Joint Session of Congress*, September 20, 2001.

15 Todd S. Purdum, "Bush Warns of a Wrathful, Shadowy and Inventive War", *New York Times*, September 17, 2001, A2.

16 Richard T. Cooper, "General Casts War in Religious Terms," *Los Angeles Times*, October 16, 2003.

17 Michael Hirsh, "Bernard Lewis Revisited," *Washington Monthly*, November 2004.

18 Tony Blair, *Speech to World Affairs Council*, Los Angeles, August 1, 2006.

19 Liz Fekete, *A Suitable Enemy: Racism, Migration and Islamophobia in Europe*, London: Pluto Press, 2009.

20 Christopher Caldwell, *Reflections on the Revolution in Europe: Immigration, Islam, and the West*, New York: Anchor Books, 2010, 116.

21 Stephen Steinberg, "The Role of Race in the Devolution of the Left," *Logos*, 10: 2, 2011.

22 John Casey, "One Nation: The Politics of Race," *Salisbury Review* 1, Autumn 1982.

23 Quoted in Stolcke, "Talking Culture," 3.

24 Anthony Browne, "Britain Is Losing Britain," *The Times* (London), August 7, 2002, 2.

25 Office for National Statistics, *Population Estimates by Ethnic Group 2002–2009*, 2011, 6.

26 Anthony Browne, "How the Government Endangers British Lives," *Spectator*, January 25, 2003, 12.

27 Anthony Browne, "Fundamentally, We're Useful Idiots," *The Times*, August 1, 2005. In 2008, Browne was appointed policy director of the London mayor, Boris Johnson.

28 "Little-Known Lawyer Extends Anti-Islam Voice to Mainstream," *The Forward*, July 22, 2011.

29 David Yerushalmi, "On Race: A Tentative Discussion," *The McAdam Report*, no. 585, May 12, 2006, 7, 8, 10.

30 Hishaam D. Aidi, "Slavery, Genocide and the Politics of Outrage: Understanding the New Racial Olympics," *Middle East Report*, no. 234, Spring 2005.

31 Paddy Hillyard, *Suspect Community: People's Experience of the Prevention of Terrorism Acts in Britain*, London: Pluto Press, 1993.

32 Douglas Murray, *What Are We to Do About Islam?*, Pim Fortuyn Memorial Conference on Europe and Islam, The Hague, February 2006.

33 Shubh Mathur, "Surviving the Dragnet: 'Special Interest' Detainees in the US after 9/11," *Race and Class*, 47: 3, 2006.

34 David Cole, *Enemy Aliens: Double Standards and Constitutional Freedoms in the War on Terrorism*, New York: New Press, 2003, 26; Nancy Murray, "Profiled: Arabs, Muslims, and the Post-9/11 Hunt for the 'Enemy Within,'" in Elaine C. Hagopian, ed., *Civil Rights in Peril: The Targeting of Arabs and Muslims*, Chicago: Haymarket Books, 2004, 31.

35 Somini Sengupta, "Ill-Fated Path to America, Jail and Death," *New York Times*, November 5, 2001, 1.

36 Louise Cainkar, "The Impact of the September 11 Attacks on Arab and Muslim Communities in the United States," in John Tirman, ed., *The Maze of Fear: Security and Migration after 9/*11, New York: New Press, 2004, 216–18.

37 Ibid., 215.

38 Moustafa Bayoumi, "Racing Religion," *New Centennial Review*, 6: 2, Fall 2006, 275.

39 Sahar Aziz, *The Muslim "Veil" Post-9/11: Rethinking Women's Rights and Leadership*, Institute for Social Policy and Understanding and the British Council, 2012, 3.

40 Ibid., 14–16.

41 Cainkar, "The Impact of the September 11 Attacks," 227–28.

42 Ayaan Hirsi Ali, "Muslim Rage and the Last Gasp of Islamic Hate," *Newsweek*, September 17, 2012.

43 David Cohen, "Violence Is Inherent in Islam—It Is a Cult of Death," *Evening Standard*, February 7, 2007.

44 Ayaan Hirsi Ali, "The Problem of Muslim Leadership," *Wall Street Journal*, May 27, 2013.

45 Tony Karon, "Condi in Diplomatic Disneyland," *Time*, July 26, 2006.

46 Bernard Lewis, "Communism and Islam," *International Affairs*, 30: 1, January 1954, 9.

47 George W. Bush, *Speech to the National Endowment for Democracy*, October 6, 2005.

48 Paul Berman, *Terror and Liberalism*, New York: Norton, 2004, 49–51.

49 Ibid., 60.

50 Peter Beinart, *The Good Fight: Why Liberals—and Only Liberals—Can Win the War on Terror and Make America Great Again*, New York: Harper Collins, 2006, xii.

51 Ibid., 94.

52 Nick Cohen, *What's Left? How Liberals Lost Their Way*, London: Fourth Estate, 2007; Ed Husain, *The Islamist: Why I Joined Radical Islam in Britain, What I Saw Inside and Why I Left*, London: Penguin Books, 2007.

53 Berman, *Terror and Liberalism*, 99.

54 Ibid., 184, 191.

55 Uwe Backes, *Political Extremes: A Conceptual History from Antiquity to the Present*, Abingdon: Routledge, 2010, 85–86.

56 Ibid., 97–98.

57 Arthur M. Schlesinger Jr., *The Vital Center: The Politics of Freedom*, Boston: Houghton Mifflin, 1962, 40.

58 Ibid., 104.

59 Francis Fukuyama, "After Neoconservatism," *New York Times*, February 19, 2006.

60 Angel Rabasa, Cheryl Benard, Lowell H. Schwartz, and Peter Sickle, *Building Moderate Muslim Networks*, Santa Monica, CA: RAND Corporation, 2007, iii.

61 Marc Sageman, *Leaderless Jihad: Terror Networks in the Twenty-First Century*, Philadelphia: University of Pennsylvania Press, 2008, 94, 160.

62 George Jones, "Terrorism Fight Is Our Cold War, Says Brown," *Telegraph*, July 3, 2007; interview with Andrew Marr, *Sunday AM*, BBC1, July 1, 2007.

63 Frances Stonor Saunders, *The Cultural Cold War: The CIA and the World of Arts and Letters*, New York: New Press, 2000.

64 Interview with Home Office civil servant, London, May 24, 2011.

65 Paul Dixon, "'Hearts and Minds'? British Counter-Insurgency from Malaya to Iraq," *Journal of Strategic Studies*, 32: 3, June 2009.

66 John Mackinlay, "Counter-Insurgency in Global Perspective—An Introduction," *RUSI Journal*, 152: 6, December 2007, 6.

67 David J. Kilcullen, "Countering Global Insurgency," *Journal of Strategic Studies*, 28: 4, August 2005, 610.

68 *Field Manual 3-24—Counterinsurgency*, Washington, DC: US Army and Marine Corps, 2006, 1-1.

69 David H. Petraeus, "Beyond the Cloister," *American Interest*, July/August 2007.

70 Ibid.

71 Joe Klein: "David Petraeus' Brilliant Career," *Time*, August 22, 2011, 15; "The Return of the Good Soldier," *Time*, July 5, 2010, 20–23; "Can Obama and Petraeus Work Together?" *Time*, June 24, 2010.

72 Barton Gellman, "Spyfall," *Time*, November 26, 2012, 26.

73 Mahmood Mamdani, *Define and Rule: Native as Political Identity*, Cambridge, MA: Harvard University Press, 2012; Laleh Khalili, "The New (and Old) Classics of Counterinsurgency," *Middle East Report*, no. 255, Summer 2010.

74 George Packer, "Knowing the Enemy," *New Yorker*, December 18, 2006.

75 David H. Price, *Weaponizing Anthropology: Social Science in Service of the Militarized State*, Oakland, CA: AK Press, 2011, 105.

76 Thomas Friedman: "Mideast Rules to Live By," *New York Times*, December 20, 2006, A29; "Tribes with Flags," *New York Times*, March 23, 2011, A27.

77 Ryan Lizza, "The Consequentialist," *New Yorker*, May 2, 2011.

78 Walter Pincus, "Don't Ignore Western Europe, Terrorism Expert Warns US," *Washington Post*, September 8, 2005, A9.

79 Francis Fukuyama, "Identity and Migration," *Prospect*, no. 131, February 25, 2007.

80 Robert S. Leiken, "Europe's Angry Muslims," *Foreign Affairs*, July/August 2005, 120, 122.

81 Marc Sageman, "The Next Generation of Terror," *Foreign Policy*, February 19, 2008.

82 Timothy Garton Ash, "We Are Making a Fatal Mistake by Ignoring the Dissidents within Islam," *Guardian*, March 14, 2007.

83 Timothy Garton Ash, "Wake Up, the Invisible Front Line Runs Right through Your Back Yard," *Guardian*, September 13, 2007, 37.

84 Garton Ash, "We Are Making a Fatal Mistake."

85 Launch of Quilliam Foundation, London: British Museum, April 22, 2008.

86 Saba Mahmood, "Secularism, Hermeneutics, and Empire: The Politics of Islamic Reformation," *Public Culture*, 18: 2, 2006, 326–27.

87 "Security Council Meeting of World Leaders Calls for Legal Prohibition of Terrorist Incitement, Enhanced Steps to Prevent Armed Conflict," United Nations Security Council, September 14, 2005, http://www.un.org/News/Press/docs/2005/sc8496.doc.htm, accessed October 1, 2006.

88 Ben Hayes, "'White Man's Burden': Criminalising Free Speech," *Statewatch*, 18: 1, January–March 2008, 18–20.

89 Home Office, Press Release on Tackling Terrorism—Behaviours Unacceptable in the UK, August 24, 2005.

90 Gareth Peirce, "Was It Like This for the Irish?" *London Review of Books*, April 10, 2008, 6, 8.

91 "Teen Charged Over Facebook Post on UK Soldiers Killed in Afghanistan," *Metro*, March 12, 2012; "Facebook Rant Man Spared Jail," *Independent*, October 10, 2012.

92 Nick Cohen, "We Have to Deport Terrorist Suspects—Whatever Their Fate," *Observer*, November 5, 2006.

93 Husain, *The Islamist*.

94 Michael Ignatieff, *The Lesser Evil: Political Ethics in an Age of Terror*, Princeton: Princeton University Press, 2004.

95 Gwyn Prins and Robert Salusbury, "Risk, Threat, and Security: The Case of the United Kingdom," *RUSI Journal*, 153: 1, February 2008, 23.

96 Timothy Garton Ash, "Divided Loyalties: Why Young British Muslims Are Angry," *Globe and Mail*, August 10, 2006.

97 Sageman, *Leaderless Jihad*, 160.

98 Ibid., 102.

99 US Department of Homeland Security, *National Strategy for Homeland Security*, October 2007, 22.

100 Between September 2001 and March 2011, 421 persons were charged for terrorism-related offenses in the UK, mainly Muslims but also some others. There are no published figures on the proportion who were accused of what the government calls

"al-Qaeda inspired" terrorism. However, since April 2005, 87 percent of those charged were classified as being involved in "international" terrorism, which is the term the intelligence services use to designate terrorism related to the Middle East and al-Qaeda. Assuming this proportion holds for the entire period, we can estimate that 366 people have been charged with offenses related to international terrorism over the ten years. The total Muslim population in Britain is approximately 2.4 million. The Center on Law and Security at the New York University School of Law counts 310 persons charged with jihadist terrorism-related offenses in the US over the ten-year period following 9/11. Other sources have different numbers, some higher and some lower. There is uncertainty over the size of the Muslim population in the US, with estimates varying from approximately 2.35 million to 6 million. Depending on the population estimate, it may be concluded that the number charged with international/jihadist terrorism as a proportion of the total Muslim population is approximately the same in the US and the UK. *Operation of Police Powers under the Terrorism Act 2000 and Subsequent Legislation: Arrests, Outcomes, and Stops and Searches, Great Britain 2010/11*, Home Office, October 13, 2011, 10, 23; Richard Kerbaj, "Muslim Population 'Rising 10 Times Faster than Rest of Society,'" *The Times* (London), January 30, 2009); *Terrorist Trial Report Card: September 11, 2001–September 11, 2011*, New York: Center on Law and Security, New York University School of Law, 2011, 7; *Muslim Americans: Middle Class and Mostly Mainstream*, Pew Research Center, May 22, 2007.

101 Garrett M. Graff, "Homegrown Terror," *5280*, November 2011.

102 Maryclaire Dale, "'Jihad Jane' Admits to Conspiracy to Support Terrorists, Murder," *Christian Science Monitor*, February 1, 2011.

103 Alexandra Frean, "Unexploded Car Bomb in Times Square 'Amateurish One-Off' Terrorism Attempt," *The Times* (London), May 2, 2010.

104 Andrea Elliot, "Bombing Suspect's Long Path to Times Square," *New York Times*, May 16, 2010, A1.

105 Peter Bergen and Bruce Hoffman, *Assessing the Terrorist Threat: A Report of the Bipartisan Policy Center's National Security Preparedness Group*, Bipartisan Policy Center, September 2010, 4, 16, 29.

106 Barak Ravid, "Dennis Ross' 'Red Line' to the White House," *Ha'aretz*, January 30, 2012.

107 J. Scott Carpenter, Matthew Levitt, Steven Simon, and Juan Zarate, *Fighting the Ideological Battle: The Missing Link in US Strategy to Counter Violent Extremism*, Washington Institute for Near East Policy, 2010, 10–11.

108 *Transcript of Secretary Napolitano's Remarks to the America-Israel Friendship League*,

Washington, DC: US Department of Homeland Security, December 3, 2009, http://www.dhs.gov/ynews/releases/pr_1259860196559.shtm, accessed March 6, 2010.

109 Caroline Preston, "Homeland-Security Officials to Meet with Foundation Leaders," *Chronicle of Philanthropy*, February 11, 2011.

110 President Obama, *Empowering Local Partners to Prevent Violent Extremism in the United States*, August 2011, Washington, DC: White House.

111 "McDonough Discusses White House's Counterterrorism Plan," NPR Radio, August 3, 2011, http://www.npr.org/2011/08/03/138962413/mcdonough- discusses-white-houses-counterterrorism-plan, accessed August 10, 2011.

112 "Obama Envoy Claims Islam Is Answer to Violence," *World Net Daily*, April 3, 2011, http://www.wnd.com/2011/04/282741/, accessed November 26, 2012.

113 Rashad Hussain and al-Husein N. Madhany, *Reformulating the Battle of Ideas: Understanding the Role of Islam in Counterterrorism Policy*, Washington, DC: Saban Center for Middle East Policy, Brookings Institution, 2008, 2.

114 John Brennan, Speech at New York University Law School, February 13, 2010.

115 Anne Barrowclough, "'Fedex Delivered'—How Secrets of Bin Laden Funeral Were Kept from Sailors," *The Times* (London), November 23, 2012, 23.

116 *Terrorist Trial Report Card: September 11, 2001–September 11, 2011*, New York: Center on Law and Security, New York University School of Law, 2011, 19.

117 David Cole, "39 Ways to Limit Free Speech," *New York Review of Books* blog, April 20, 2012, http://www.nybooks.com/blogs/nyrblog/2012/apr/19/39-ways-limit-free-speech, accessed April 20, 2012.

118 Samuel J. Rascoff, "Establishing Official Islam? The Law and Strategy of Counter-Radicalization," *Stanford Law Review*, 64, February 2012.

119 Lentin and Titley, *The Crises of Multiculturalism*, 192.

120 Timothy Garton Ash, "Freedom and Diversity: A Liberal Pentagram for Living Together," *New York Review of Books*, November 22, 2012.

3. THE ROOTS OF LIBERAL RAGE

1 Phone interview with Younes Abdullah Muhammad, March 30, 2011.

2 *Statement of Facts, USA vs. Jesse Curtis Morton*, United States District Court for the Eastern District of Virginia, February 2, 2012.

3 Phone interview with Younes Abdullah Muhammad, March 30, 2011.

4 Younus Abdullah Muhammad, *By All Means Necessary: In Pursuit of the Objectives Amidst Improving Odds—Assessing the Role and Responsibilities of Those Left Behind in the War on Islam* (New York, December 2008), 27.

5 *Real Time with Bill Maher*, HBO, April 30, 2010.

6 "Clarifying the South Park Response and Calling on Others to Join in the Defense of the Prophet Muhammad," revolutionmuslimdaily.blogspot.com, accessed April 22, 2010.

7 *Zachary Chesser: A Case Study in Online Islamist Radicalization and Its Meaning for the Threat of Homegrown Terrorism*, US Senate Committee on Homeland Security and Governmental Affairs, February 2012.

8 Phone interview with Younes Abdullah Muhammad, March 30, 2011.

9 "We Are All Osama bin Laden," Islam Policy, islampolicy.com, May 8, 2011.

10 Army of God, armyofgod.com, accessed December 19, 2012.

11 *Sentencing Factors, USA vs. Jesse Curtis Morton*, United States District Court for the Eastern District of Virginia, June 14, 2012.

12 Mark Steyn, *America Alone: The End of the World as We Know It*, Washington, DC: Regnery Publishing, 2006, 123.

13 Arthur M. Schlesinger Jr., *The Vital Center: The Politics of Freedom*, Boston: Houghton Mifflin, 1962, xxiii–xxiv.

14 Terry Eagleton, *Ideology: An Introduction*, London: Verso, 1991, 4.

15 Domenico Losurdo, "Towards a Critique of the Category of Totalitarianism," *Historical Materialism*, 12: 2, 2004, 50–51.

16 Corey Robin, "Dragon-slayers," *London Review of Books*, 29: 1, January 4, 2007.

17 Hannah Arendt, *The Origins of Totalitarianism*, New York: Meridian Books, 1958, 311.

18 William Pietz, "The 'Post-Colonialism' of Cold War Discourse," *Social Text*, no. 19/20, Autumn 1988, 69.

19 Arendt, *The Origins of Totalitarianism*, 185–91.

20 Samantha Power, "The Lesson of Hannah Arendt," *New York Review of Books*, April 29, 2004.

21 Losurdo, "Towards a Critique of the Category of Totalitarianism."

22 Karl Popper, *The Open Society and Its Enemies, Vol. I: The Spell of Plato*, Princeton: Princeton University Press, 1966, 9.

23 Ibid., 393.

24 Ibid., 268–69.

25 Ibid., 265.

26 Giorgio Agamben, *State of Exception*, Chicago: University of Chicago Press, 2005.

27 Manfred Berg, "Black Civil Rights and Liberal Anticommunism: The NAACP in the Early Cold War," *Journal of American History*, 94: 1, June 2007.

28 Tarak Barkawi and Mark Laffey, "The Postcolonial Moment in Security Studies," *Review of International Studies*, no. 32, 2006, 332.

29 Gianfranco Sanguinetti, *On Terrorism and the State: The Theory and Practice of Terrorism Divulged for the First Time*, London: B. M. Chronos, 1982, 3.

30 Donatella della Porta, *Social Movement Studies and Political Violence*, Centre for Studies in Islamism and Radicalisation, Department of Political Science, Aarhus University, Denmark, September 2009, 9.

31 According to Home Office figures, the number of people convicted of terrorism-related crimes in Britain more than doubled between 2003, when the Iraq war began, and 2006, before halving again by 2009. *Operation of Police Powers under the Terrorism Act 2000 and Subsequent Legislation: Arrests, Outcomes, and Stops and Searches Great Britain, 2010/11*, UK Home Office, October 13, 2011, 29–30.

32 Jeroen Gunning and Richard Jackson, "What's So 'Religious' about 'Religious Terrorism'?" *Critical Studies on Terrorism*, 4: 3, December 2011, 381.

33 Melanie Phillips, "To Defeat Islamic Terror, We Must First Acknowledge What It Is," *Daily Mail*, May 27, 2013.

34 Talal Asad, *The Idea of an Anthropology of Islam*, Occasional Paper, Center for Contemporary Arab Studies, Georgetown University, 1986, 13.

35 Leonard Binder, *Islamic Liberalism: A Critique of Development Ideologies*, Chicago: University of Chicago Press, 1988, 177.

36 Sayyid Qutb, *Milestones*, New Delhi: Islamic Book Service, 2001, 49.

37 Binder, *Islamic Liberalism*, 177.

38 Qutb, *Milestones*, 61.

39 Binder, *Islamic Liberalism*, 188.

40 National Commission on Terrorist Attacks upon the United States, *The 9/11 Commission Report: Final Report of the National Commission on Terrorist Attacks upon the United States*, New York: Norton, 2004, 51.

41 Adnan A. Musallam, *From Secularism to Jihad: Sayyid Qutb and the Foundations of Radical Islamism*, Westport, CT: Praeger, 2005, 169.

42 "Bookseller Ahmed Faraz Jailed Over Terror Offences," BBC News, December 13, 2011, bbc.co.uk/news.

43 Victoria Brittain and Asim Qureshi, "Banning Books in Britain, Fifty Years after Lady Chatterley," *Our Kingdom* openDemocracy.net, December 17, 2011, accessed December 10, 2012.

44 Ed Husain, *The Islamist: Why I Joined Radical Islam in Britain, What I Saw Inside and Why I Left*, London: Penguin Books, 2007; Yahya Birt, "The Islamist: A Review," *Fug's Blog*, fugstar.blogspot.com, accessed June 19, 2008.

45 Tariq Ramadan, *Western Muslims and the Future of Islam*, Oxford: Oxford University Press, 2004, 26.

46 Paul Berman, "Who's Afraid of Tariq Ramadan?" *New Republic*, June 4, 2007.

47 Tariq Ramadan, "Blair Can No Longer Deny a Link Exists Between Terrorism and Foreign Policy," *Guardian*, June 4, 2007.

48 David Goodhart, "An Open Letter to Tariq Ramadan," *Prospect*, no. 135, June 2007.

49 Nick Cohen speaking at the Hay Festival, May 27, 2007.

50 Nick Cohen, *What's Left? How Liberals Lost Their Way*, London: Fourth Estate, 2007, 260.

51 Andrew Anthony, *The Fallout: How a Guilty Liberal Lost His Innocence*, London: Jonathan Cape, 2007.

52 Ibid., 234.

53 Ibid., 123–24.

54 Martin Amis, *The Second Plane: September 11: 2001–2007*, London: Jonathan Cape, 2008, 50.

55 Johann Hari, "The Two Faces of Amis," *Independent*, January 29, 2008.

56 Amis, *The Second Plane*, x.

57 Ginny Dougary, "The Voice of Experience," *The Times* (London), September 9, 2006.

58 Alberto Toscano, *Fanaticism: On the Uses of an Idea*, London: Verso, 2010, 99–101.

59 Adam James Tebble, "Exclusion for Democracy," *Political Theory*, 34: 4, August 2006.

60 Alexis de Tocqueville, *Democracy in America*, Ware, UK: Wordsworth Editions, 1998, 358.

61 Losurdo, "Towards a Critique of the Category of Totalitarianism," 53.

62 Agamben, *State of Exception*.

63 Samuel P. Huntington, *Who Are We? The Challenges to America's Identity*, New York: Simon & Schuster, 2004, 262.

4. THE MYTH OF RADICALIZATION

1 Caroline Elkins, *Britain's Gulag: The Brutal End of Empire in Kenya*, London: Jonathan Cape, 2005, 106–7.

2 Walter Laqueur, "Terror's New Face," *Harvard International Review*, 20: 4, 1998.

3 Peter Neumann, "Perspectives on Radicalisation and Political Violence: Papers from the First International Conference on Radicalisation and Political Violence,"

London, January 17–18, 2008, London: International Centre for the Study of Radicalisation and Political Violence, 2008, 4.

4 Immanuel Kant, "An Answer to the Question: 'What Is Enlightenment?'" 1784. In Immanuel Kant, *Practical Philosophy*, New York: Cambridge University Press, 1996.

5 Mark Sedgwick, "The Concept of Radicalization as a Source of Confusion," *Terrorism and Political Violence*, 22: 4, 2010, 480–81.

6 Frances Stonor Saunders, *Who Paid the Piper?: The CIA and the Cultural Cold War*, London: Granta Books, 1999, 214.

7 Walter Laqueur, "The Terrorism to Come," *Policy Review*, August/September 2004, 51, 53, 55–6.

8 Daveed Gartenstein-Ross and Laura Grossman, "Homegrown Terrorists in the US and UK: An Empirical Examination of the Radicalization Process," Washington, DC: Foundation for the Defense of Democracy, 2009, 11, 14, 26–27, 29, 35, 52–54.

9 Wajahat Ali, Eli Clifton, Matthew Duss, Lee Fang, Scott Keyes, and Faiz Shakir, "Fear, Inc.: The Roots of the Islamophobia Network in America," Washington, DC: Center for American Progress, 2011, 18–19.

10 Gartenstein-Ross and Grossman, "Homegrown Terrorists in the US and UK," 8.

11 Daveed Gartenstein-Ross, "Home", http://www.daveedgr.com, accessed March 25, 2012.

12 Marc Sageman, *Understanding Terror Networks*, Philadelphia: University of Pennsylvania Press, 2004; Marc Sageman, *Leaderless Jihad: Terror Networks in the Twenty-First Century*, Philadelphia: University of Pennsylvania Press, 2008.

13 "Marc Sageman", Philadelphia: Foreign Policy Research Institute, http://www.fpri.org/about/people/sageman.html, accessed April 15, 2012.

14 Elaine Sciolino and Eric Schmitt, "A Not Very Private Feud over Terrorism," *New York Times*, June 8, 2008.

15 Sageman, *Leaderless Jihad*, 23, 66, 70, 75–81, 83–84, 88, 94, 102, 155, 160.

16 Sageman, *Understanding Terror Networks*, 1.

17 Ibid., 120.

18 Ibid., 135.

19 Quintan Wiktorowicz, *Radical Islam Rising: Muslim Extremism in the West*, Oxford: Rowman & Littlefield, 2005.

20 See cables for October 25, 2007, "EUR Senior Advisor Pandith and S/P Advisor Cohen's visit to the UK," and April 18, 2008, "Proposals for ambassador's CT fund."

21 Dina Temple-Raston, "New Terrorism Adviser Takes a 'Broad Tent' Approach," *Morning Edition*, NPR, January 24, 2011, npr.org.

22 Wiktorowicz, *Radical Islam Rising*, 3, 6, 17, 20.

23 Ron Suskind, *The Way of the World: A Story of Truth and Hope in an Age of Extremism*, New York: HarperCollins, 2008, 200–202.

24 Sean O'Neill and Yaakov Lappin, "I Don't Want You to Join Me, I Want You to Join bin Laden," *The Times* (London), January 17, 2005, 5.

25 Wiktorowicz, *Radical Islam Rising*, 210.

26 Ibid., 12.

27 Leon Trotsky, "The History of the Russian Revolution, Volume Two: The Attempted Counter-Revolution", 1932, Marxists Internet Archive http://www.marxists.org/archive/trotsky/1930/hrr/intro23.htm>, accessed March 27, 2012.

28 Mitchell D. Silber and Arvin Bhatt, "Radicalization in the West: The Homegrown Threat," New York Police Department Intelligence Division, 2007, 2, 6–7, 10, 31, 85. The NYPD stated in a subsequent "clarification" that the report did not mean to imply that behaviors such as growing a beard could be indicators for the purposes of surveillance.

29 Ibid., 20.

30 Deposition by Thomas Galati in *Handschu v. Special Services Division*, United States District Court, Southern District of New York, June 28, 2012, 31.

31 Associated Press, "Highlights of AP's Pulitzer Prize-winning Probe into NYPD Intelligence Operations" http://www.ap.org/media-center/nypd/investigation, accessed April 21, 2012.

32 Adam Goldman and Matt Apuzzo, "NYPD Shadows Muslims Who Change Names," Associated Press, October 26, 2011.

33 Matt Apuzzo and Adam Goldman, *Enemies Within: Inside the NYPD's Secret Spying Unit and Bin Laden's Final Plot Against America*, New York: Touchstone, 2013, 66–68, 73, 283.

34 Galati, *Handschu v. Special Services Division*, 124.

35 Alan Feuer, "The Terror Translators," *New York Times*, September 17, 2010.

36 Faiza Patel and Andrew Sullivan, "A Proposal for an NYPD Inspector General," New York: Brennan Center for Justice at New York University School of Law, 2012, 1.

37 Adam Goldman and Matt Apuzzo, "Informant: NYPD Paid Me to 'Bait' Muslims," Associated Press, October 23, 2012.

38 Chris Hawley and Matt Apuzzo, "NYPD Infiltration of Colleges Raises Privacy Fears," Associated Press, October 11, 2011.

39 Leonard Levitt, "Lone Wolves or Sheep?," NYPD Confidential, nypdconfidential.com, March 19, 2012.

40 Russ Buettner, "Man Sentenced in Plan to Bomb Manhattan Synagogue," *New York Times*, April 27, 2013, A19.

41 Adam Goldman and Matt Apuzzo, "Documents: NY Police Infiltrated Liberal Groups," Associated Press, March 23, 2012.

42 Michael Greenberg, "New York: The Police and the Protesters," *New York Review of Books*, October 11, 2012.

43 Ramzi Kassem, "The Long Roots of the NYPD Spying Program," *Nation*, June 13, 2012.

44 Jason Leopold and Matthew Harwood, "Hacked Intel E-Mail: NYPD Involved in 'Damn Right Felonious Activity,'" Truthout, truthout.org, September 4, 2012, accessed January 21, 2013.

45 John Miller, "Violent Islamist Extremism: Government Efforts to Defeat It," testimony before the United States Senate Committee on Homeland Security and Governmental Affairs, May 10, 2007.

46 Olivier Roy, "Al Qaeda in the West as a Youth Movement: The Power of a Narrative," MICROCON: A Micro Level Analysis of Violent Conflict, Policy Working Paper 2, Brighton, UK: Institute of Development Studies, University of Sussex, November 2008, 2.

47 Ibid., 3, 15.

48 Jonathan Githens-Mazer and Robert Lambert, "Why Conventional Wisdom on Radicalization Fails: The Persistence of a Failed Discourse." *International Affairs*, 86: 4, 2010.

49 Donatella della Porta, "Social Movement Studies and Political Violence," Denmark: Aarhus University Centre for Studies in Islamism and Radicalisation Process, School of Business and Social Science, September 2009, 9.

50 *Final Report of the William H. Webster Commission on the Federal Bureau of Investigation, Counterterrorism Intelligence, and the Events at Fort Hood, Texas, on November 5, 2009*, 36.

51 There is an indication that al-Awlaki may already have been placed on a "kill or capture" list in late 2009. Dana Priest, "US Playing a Key Role in Yemen Attacks," *Washington Post* January 27, 2010, A1.

52 US Department of Homeland Security Secretary Janet Napolitano, "Nine Years after 9/11: Confronting the Terrorist Threat to the Homeland," statement before the United States Senate Committee on Homeland Security and Governmental Affairs, September 22, 2010.

53 Alexander Meleagrou-Hitchens, "As American as Apple Pie: How Anwar Al-Awlaki Became the Face of Western Jihad," London: International Centre for the Study of Radicalisation and Political Violence, 2011, 30–31, 84.

54 Anwar al-Awlaki, "44 Ways to Support Jihad," January 2009.

55 Brian Handwerk and Zain Habboo, "Attack on America: An Islamic Scholar's Perspective—Part 1," *National Geographic*, September 28, 2001, news.nationalgeographic.com, accessed March 28, 2013.

56 Scott Shane and Souad Mekhennet, "Imam's Path from Condemning Terror to Preaching Jihad," *New York Times*, May 8, 2010.

57 Anwar al-Awlaki speech, northern Virginia, March 2002. Exact date unknown.

58 Shane and Mekhennet, "Imam's Path."

59 Anwar al-Awlaki, "Constants on the Path of Jihad," December 2005.

60 Transcript of "The Rise of Anwar al-Awlaki" event, Carnegie Endowment for International Peace, Washington, DC, June 1, 2010.

61 Phone interview with Asim Qureshi, August 24, 2011.

62 *Final Report of the William H. Webster Commission*, 67–68.

63 "Interview: Anwar al-Awlaki," Al Jazeera, February 7, 2010, aljazeera.com, accessed March 29, 2013.

64 Anwar al-Awlaki, "Western Jihad Is Here to Stay," March 2010.

65 Andrew March, "Anwar al-'Awlaqi against the Islamic Legal Tradition," New Haven: Yale Law School, September 2010.

66 Anwar al-Awlaki, "Battle for the Hearts and Minds," May 2008.

67 Anwar al-Awlaki, "A Call to Jihad," March 2010.

68 Meleagrou-Hitchens, "As American as Apple Pie;" J. M. Berger, "The Myth of Anwar al-Awlaki," *Foreign Policy*, August 10, 2011.

69 Shane and Mekhennet, "Imam's Path."

70 US Department of Justice, Memo, "Lawfulness of a Lethal Operation Directed Against a US Citizen Who Is a Senior Operational Leader of al-Qa'ida or an Associated Force," White Paper.

71 Vikram Dodd, "Roshonara Choudhry: Police Interview Extracts," *Guardian*, November 3, 2010.

72 Fawaz A. Gerges, "Al-Qa'eda in the Arabian Peninsula: Does It Pose a Threat to Yemen and the West?" Washington, DC: Institute for Social Policy and Understanding, 2011, 19.

73 "Pakistan Drone Statistics Visualized," Bureau of Investigative Journalism, July 2, 2012, thebureauinvestigates.com, accessed March 24, 2013.

74 Andrea Elliott, Sabrina Tavernise, and Anne Barnard, "Bombing Suspect's Long Path to Times Square," *New York Times*, May 16, 2010, A1.

75 Lorraine Adams with Ayesha Nasir, "Inside the Mind of the Times Square Bomber," *Observer*, September 19, 2010.

76 US Senate Committee on Homeland Security and Governmental Affairs, *A Ticking Time Bomb: Counterterrorism Lessons from the US Government's Failure to Prevent the Fort Hood Attack*, February 2011, 27–30.

77 Brooks Egerton, "Fort Hood Captain: Hasan Wanted Patients to Face War Crimes Charges," *Dallas Morning News*, November 17, 2009.

78 Joseba Zulaika, "The Terror/Counterterror Edge: When Non-Terror Becomes a Terrorism Problem and Real Terror Cannot Be Detected by Counterterrorism," *Critical Studies on Terrorism*, 3: 2, 2010, 252.

79 *Final Report of the William H. Webster Commission.*

5. HEARTS AND MINDS

1 Marco Schneebalg, "The Press Has Exaggerated Anti-Israel Protests in Manchester," *Haaretz*, May 6, 2010.

2 Marcus Dysch, "Israel Deputy Ambassador 'Shocked' by Manchester Attack," *Jewish Chronicle*, April 29, 2010.

3 Home Office, "Channel Data 2007–2010," document released under the Freedom of Information Act, May 2011.

4 Secretary of State for the Home Department, "CONTEST: The United Kingdom's Strategy for Countering Terrorism—Annual Report," London, March 2013, 22.

5 HM Government, "Channel: Supporting Individuals Vulnerable to Recruitment by Violent Extremists: A Guide for Local Partnerships," March 2010, 9–10.

6 Interview with Jameel Scott [pseudonym], conducted by Rizwaan Sabir, Manchester, October 22, 2011.

7 In 2012, control orders were replaced with Terrorism Prevention and Investigation Measures, effectively a rebranding of the same powers.

8 Department for Communities and Local Government, "Preventing Violent Extremism Pathfinder Fund: Guidance Note for Government Offices and Local Authorities in England," London, February 2007, 5.

9 David Leppard, "Terror Chief Tipped to Head MI6," *The Times* (London), September 21, 2008; Anne McElvoy, "On Her Majesty's Not-So-Secret Service," *The Times* (London), October 4, 2009.

10 House of Commons Home Affairs Committee, "Project CONTEST: The Government's Counter-Terrorism Strategy: Ninth Report of Session 2008–09," July 7, 2009, Ev 29.

11 Ibid., Ev 74.

12 Jason Bennetto, "MI5 Conducts Secret Inquiry into 8,000 Al-Qa'ida 'Sympathisers,'" *Independent*, July 3, 2006.

13 Secretary of State for the Home Department, "Pursue, Prevent, Protect, Prepare: The United Kingdom's Strategy for Countering International Terrorism," March 2009, 13.

14 "Pro-West Ads to Target Extremism," BBC News, February 23, 2009, news.bbc.co.uk, accessed September 8, 2009.

15 MI5 Security Service, "Countering International Terrorism: The Battle of Ideas," mi5.gov.uk, accessed October 1, 2009.

16 Private e-mail from a government department to an arm's-length official body, 2007.

17 Interview with local authority manager, Bradford, April 28, 2009.

18 Interview with local authority worker, August 18, 2009.

19 "Pursue, Prevent, Protect, Prepare," 10, 13.

20 Hazel Blears, "Many Voices: Understanding the Debate About Preventing Violent Extremism," lecture at the London School of Economics, February 25, 2009, communities.gov.uk, accessed February 26, 2009.

21 Home Affairs Committee "Project CONTEST," Ev 26.

22 Cabinet Office, "The National Security Strategy of the United Kingdom: Security in an Interdependent World," March 2008, 8.

23 UK Home Office, "The Prevent Strategy: A Guide for Local Partners in England: Stopping People Becoming or Supporting Terrorists and Violent Extremists," London, 2008, 16.

24 Gordon Brown, Statement on National Security, London, October 28, 2007; "Countering International Terrorism: The Battle of Ideas," MI5 Security Service.

25 Walsall Council, "Building Resilience—Priorities For Action: Delivering the Prevent Strategy in Walsall 2008/09–2010/11," August 2009.

26 Asma Jahangir, Report of the Special Rapporteur on Freedom of Religion or Belief: Mission to the United Kingdom, United Nations, February 7, 2008, 21.

27 House of Commons, "Hansard Written Answers," London, January 12, 2009.

28 Home Affairs Committee, "Project CONTEST," 21, 26; Home Office Research, Information and Communications Unit, "Counter Terrorism Communications Guidance: Communicating Effectively with Community Audiences," London, 2007); spinprofiles.org, accessed August 29, 2009.

29 Robin Ramsay, "The Influence of Intelligence Services on the British Left", *Lobster*, 1996, http://www.lobster-magazine.co.uk/articles/rrtalk.htm, accessed October 9, 2013.

30 Dean Godson, "The Feeble Helping the Unspeakable," *The Times* (London), April 5, 2006, timesonline.co.uk.

31 Interview with community activist, Bolton, June 14, 2011.

32 Interview with youth worker, London, April 30, 2009.

33 Salma Yaqoob, "Government's PVE Agenda Is Failing to Tackle Extremism," *Muslim News*, November 28, 2008.

34 Secretary of State for the Home Department, *Prevent Strategy*, London: HM Government: June 2011, 20.

35 Ibid.

36 Ryan Gallagher and Rajeev Syal, "University Staff Asked to Inform on 'Vulnerable' Muslim Students," *Guardian*, August 29, 2011.

37 Syma Mohammed and Robert Verkaik, "CIA Given Details of British Muslim Students," *Independent*, April 1, 2010.

38 Peter Clarke speech, The Rise of Street Extremism conference, Policy Exchange, London, January 10, 2011.

39 Kevin Rawlinson, "Police Face New Questions Over Approach to Protest Groups," *Independent*, January 6, 2012.

40 Tony Bunyan, *The History and Practice of the Political Police in Britain*, London: Quartet Books, 1983.

41 Jenny Percival, "New Strategy Will Train Shop and Hotel Managers to Tackle Terrorist Threats," *Guardian*, March 24, 2009.

42 Hansard, London: House of Commons, April 23, 2009, Columns 872W, 878W; Department for Communities and Local Government press release, "Empowering Community Leaders," March 17, 2009.

43 Interview with Hedieh Mirahmadi, Washington, DC, July 27, 2011.

44 Angel Rabasa, Cheryl Benard, Lowell H. Schwartz, and Peter Sickle, *Building Moderate Muslim Networks*, RAND Corporation, 2007, 74.

45 Interview with Hedieh Mirahmadi.

46 Haras Rafiq, "Funding Application to the Home Office's 'Counter and De-Radicalisation Fund for Community Organisations,'" Manchester: Crescent Network Ltd, 2009.

47 Quilliam Foundation, "Progress Report 2008–09," London, April 2009, 14.

48 Teachernet teachernet.gov.uk, accessed May 6, 2009.

49 Richard Kerbaj, "Government Gives £1m to Anti-Extremist Think-Tank Quilliam Foundation," *The Times* (London), January 20, 2009.

50 Vikram Dodd, "Spying Morally Right, Says Thinktank," *Guardian*, October 16, 2009.

51 Michael Gove, *Celsius 7/7*, London: Weidenfeld & Nicolson, 2006, 45, 103, 136.

52 Charles Moore, Keith Joseph Memorial Lecture, Centre for Policy Studies, London, March 10, 2008), cps.org.uk, accessed September 1, 2008.

53 Lee Bridges, "Policing the Urban Wasteland," *Race and Class*, 25: 2, Autumn 1983, 39.

54 Paul Boateng, "The Police, The Community and Accountability," in *Scarman and After: Essays Reflecting on Lord Scarman's Report, the Riots and Their Aftermath*, Oxford: Pergamon Press, 1984, 158.

55 Colin Mellis, Amsterdam and Radicalization: The Municipal Approach, PowerPoint presentation, City of Amsterdam, 2007.

56 "Prevent Strategy," 58.

57 Interview with youth project manager in the north of England, April 3, 2009.

58 Interview with youth project manager in London, May 5, 2009.

59 Department for Children, Schools, and Families, *Learning Together to Be Safe: A Toolkit to Help Schools Contribute to the Prevention of Violent Extremism*, London, October 2008, 8, 13.

60 E-mail correspondence from Steve Pursglove, West Midlands Police Counter Terrorism Unit, October 26, 2009.

61 Telephone interview, Steve Pursglove, November 19, 2009.

62 Norman Bettison, "Preventing Violent Extremism—A Police Approach," *Policing*, 3: 2, May 2009, 135.

63 Metropolitan Police, Information Sharing Agreement for the Purposes of the Channel Project in Waltham Forest, London, 2009.

64 Association of Chief Police Officers, Memorandum Submitted to Parliament, 2008.

65 Private correspondence, June 22, 2011.

6. NO FREEDOM FOR THE ENEMIES OF FREEDOM

1 *Criminal Complaint: USA v. Antonio Martinez aka Muhammad Hussain*, US District Court for the District of Maryland, December 8, 2010.

2 Tricia Bishop, "Terror Suspect Ordered Held Until Trial," *Baltimore Sun*, December 14, 2010.

3 Don Markus and Andrea F. Siegel, "Man Accused in Bomb Plot Had Prior Criminal Charges," *Baltimore Sun*, December 10, 2010.

4 Tricia Bishop, "Would-be Catonsville Bomber Sentenced to 25 Years in Prison," *Baltimore Sun*, April 6, 2012.

5 Tricia Bishop, "Maryland Man Pleads Guilty in Terrorist Bomb Plot," *Baltimore Sun*, January 26, 2012.

6 Nick Madigan, "Man Accused in Catonsville Bomb Plot Urged Holy War, Feds Say," *Baltimore Sun*, February 10, 2011.

7 Tricia Bishop, "New Details Revealed in Catonsville Terrorism Investigation," *Baltimore Sun*, September 27, 2011.

8 Noah Shachtman and Spencer Ackerman, "US Military Taught Officers: Use 'Hiroshima' Tactics for 'Total War' on Islam," *Wired*, May 10, 2012 wired.com.

9 FBI Counterterrorism Division, "The Radicalization Process: From Conversion to Jihad," May 10, 2006.

10 Ibid., 5, 7, 8.

11 Brian Michael Jenkins, *Stray Dogs and Virtual Armies: Radicalization and Recruitment to Jihadist Terrorism in the United States Since 9/11*, Santa Monica, CA: RAND Corporation, 2011, 18.

12 Madigan, "Man Accused in Catonsville."

13 Tricia Bishop, "Retired Agent Faults FBI's Handling of Terrorism Investigation," *Baltimore Sun*, November 4, 2011; *Criminal Complaint: USA v. Antonio Martinez aka Muhammad Hussain*, 13.

14 Bishop, "Retired Agent Faults."

15 Justin Fenton and Tricia Bishop, "Arrest Made in Plot to Blow Up Baltimore-Area Military Recruiting Center," *Baltimore Sun*, December 8, 2010.

16 Trevor Aaronson, *The Terror Factory: Inside the FBI's Manufactured War on Terrorism* (Brooklyn, NY: Ig Publishing, 2013), 197.

17 Petra Bartosiewicz, "To Catch a Terrorist," *Harper's*, August 2011, 38.

18 Transcript of recorded conversations in *United States v. James Cromitie et al.*, Suffern, NY, October 12, 2008, 16.

19 Graham Rayman, "Small-Time Terrorists," *Village Voice*, March 2–8, 2011, 11.

20 Paul Harris, "Newburgh Four: Poor, Black, and Jailed Under FBI 'Entrapment' Tactics," *Guardian*, December 12, 2011.

21 Interview with Alicia McWilliams, New York, March 21, 2011.

22 Ibid.

23 Ibid.

24 Ibid.

25 Harris, "Newburgh Four."

26 Center for Human Rights and Global Justice, New York University School of Law, "Targeted and Entrapped: Manufacturing the 'Homegrown Threat' in the United States," 2011.

27 Emily Berman, "Domestic Intelligence: New Powers, New Risks," Brennan Center for Justice at New York University School of Law, 2011, 11.

28 David Cole, "Are We Safer?" *New York Review of Books*, March 9, 2006.

29 Berman, "Domestic Intelligence," 14.

30 Philip Mudd, "Intelligence Collection and Law Enforcement: New Roles, New Challenges," speech at symposium at the Brennan Center for Justice at NYU School of Law, March 18, 2011.

31 Scott Shane and Lowell Bergman, "FBI Struggling to Reinvent Itself to Fight Terror," *New York Times*, October 10, 2006.

32 Berman, "Domestic Intelligence," 24.

33 Ibid., 21.

34 Alex Seitz-Wald, "Bush AG Tells CPAC: 'The Vast Majority' of Muslims Want to Impose Sharia Law," *Salon*, salon.com, March 16, 2013, accessed March 19, 2013.

35 Charlie Savage, "FBI Focusing on Security Over Ordinary Crime," *New York Times*, August 24, 2011.

36 Berman, "Domestic Intelligence," 22.

37 Jerome P. Bjelopera and Mark A. Randol, *The Federal Bureau of Investigation and Terrorism Investigations*, Washington, DC: Congressional Research Service, April 27, 2011, 2.

38 Petra Bartosiewicz, "Deploying Informants, the FBI Stings Muslims," *Nation*, July 2–9, 2012.

39 Mark F. Giuliano, "The Post 9/11 FBI: The Bureau's Response to Evolving Threats," Washington Institute for Near East Policy, April 14, 2011.

40 Quoted in Hannah Arendt, *The Origins of Totalitarianism,* Cleveland, OH: Meridian Books, 1958, 422.

41 Zeev Ivianski "Provocation at the Center: A Study in the History of Counter-Terror," *Terrorism: An International Journal*, 4, 1980, 59.

42 Alfred W. McCoy, *Policing America's Empire: The United States, the Philippines, and the Rise of the Surveillance State* (Madison: University of Wisconsin Press, 2009), 104.

43 Ibid., 105.

44 Ibid., 294.

45 Noam Chomsky, "Domestic Terrorism: Notes on the State System of Oppression," *New Political Science*, 21: 3, September 1999.

46 Jon R. Waltz, "Staked Out for Slaughter," *Nation*, July 5, 1971.

47 Aaronson, *The Terror Factory*, 44.

48 *Muslims Need Not Apply: How USCIS Secretly Mandates the Discriminatory Delay and Denial of Citizenship and Immigration Benefits to Aspiring Americans*, American Civil Liberties Union, August 2013.

49 Aaronson, *The Terror Factory*, 102.

50 Nick Baumann, "Michael Migliore, the FBI, and Shadowy Interrogations Abroad," *Mother Jones*, September 22, 2011.

51 National Consortium for the Study of Terrorism and Responses to Terrorism, *Far-Right Violence in the United States: 1990–2010*, University of Maryland, August 2012. See also n. 50, Introduction.

52 Eric Russell, "Officials Verify Dirty Bomb Probe Results," *Bangor Daily News*, February 11, 2009.

53 Paul Krugman, "Noonday in the Shade," *New York Times*, June 22, 2004.

54 Department of Homeland Security Office of Intelligence and Analysis, "Rightwing Extremism: Current Economic and Political Climate Fueling Resurgence in Radicalization and Recruitment," April 7, 2009.

55 Matthew Rothschild, "FBI Infiltrates Twin Cities Anti-War Group," *Progressive*, January 14, 2011; Colin Moynihan and Scott Shane, "For Anarchist, Details of Life as FBI Target," *New York Times*, May 28, 2011.

56 Spencer S. Hsu, "Suspect in DC Metro Bomb Plot Sought to Fight US Troops Overseas, Records Say," *Washington Post*, October 29, 2010.

57 Phone interview with Michael German, October 29, 2010.

58 Tara Bahrampour, "Hip Muslim Moms Group Undone by D.C. Metro Bomb Plot," *Washington Post*, October 29, 2010.

59 Interview with Ghulam Bombaywala, Houston, April 16, 2011; phone interview with Ghulam Bombaywala, August 16, 2011.

60 Phone interview with Ghulam Bombaywala, August 16, 2011.

61 Affidavit of Adnan Mirza, *United States v. Adnan Mirza*, United States District Court, Southern District of Texas, Houston Division, March 15, 2013.

62 Richard Esposito and Jason Ryan, "FBI Has Interviewed 800 Libyans about Terror Threat," ABC Newsabcnews.com, April 7, 2011, accessed March 9, 2013.

63 Phone interview with Steve Gentry, August 16, 2011.

64 Interview with Brad Deardorff, Houston, April 15, 2011.

65 Robert B. Deardorff, "Countering Violent Extremism: The Challenge and the Opportunity," Master's thesis, Naval Postgraduate School, December 2010, i.

66 Ibid., 9, 10, 87.

67 Ibid., 11.

68 Ibid., 98–99, 110.

69 Interview with Ghulam Bombaywala. Houston, April 15, 2011.

70 Jerry Markon, "FBI Illegally Using Community Outreach to Gather Intelligence, ACLU Alleges," *Washington Post*, December 1, 2011.

71 Michelle Alexander, *The New Jim Crow: Mass Incarceration in the Age of Colorblindness*, New York: New Press, 2010.

7. POSTBOOM

1 Interview with Osman Ahmed, Minneapolis, September 23, 2011.

2 Richard Meryhew, "Tormented Mother Grieves Son Who Heeded A Fatal Call," *Minneapolis Star Tribune*, July 13, 2009.

3 Richard Meryhew, "5th Twin Cities Somali Man Is Killed in War-Torn Homeland," *Minneapolis Star Tribune*, September 5, 2009.

4 Interview with Osman Ahmed.

5 Meryhew, "5th Twin Cities Somali Man Is Killed."

6 Senator Joseph Lieberman, Opening Statement on "Violent Islamist Extremism: al-Shabaab Recruitment in America," hearing before Senate Committee on Homeland Security and Governmental Affairs, March 11, 2009.

7 Interview with E. K. Wilson, Minneapolis, September 21, 2011.

8 Representative Peter King, Opening Statement on Al-Shabaab's Muslim American Radicalization, hearing before House Committee on Homeland Security, July 29, 2011.

9 Andrea Elliott, "A Call to Jihad, Answered in America," *New York Times*, July 12, 2009, A1.

10 Interview with Lori Saroya, Minneapolis, September 22, 2011.

11 Focus group with Somali-American students, Minneapolis, September 21, 2011.

12 Randy Furst, "Minneapolis Man Pleads Guilty to Civil Rights Crime," *Minneapolis Star Tribune*, August 10, 2011.

13 G. W. Schulz, Andrew Becker, and Daniel Zwerdling, "Mall of America Visitors Unknowingly End Up in Counterterrorism Reports," Center for Investigative Reporting and NPR, *All Things Considered*, September 7, 2011.

14 Allie Shah, "Protesters Seek Bank's Money-Wiring Help," *Minneapolis Star Tribune*, May 11, 2012.

15 Chris Williams, "New Census Data: Minnesota Somali Population Grows," Associated Press, October 27, 2011.

16 Stevan Weine, John Horgan, Cheryl Robertson, Sana Loue, Amin Mohamed, and Sahra Noor, "Community and Family Approaches to Combating the Radicalization and Recruitment of Somali-American Youth and Young Adults: A Psychosocial Perspective," *Dynamics of Asymmetric Conflict*, 2: 3, November 2009.

17 Ihotu Ali, "Staying Off the Bottom of the Melting Pot: Somali Refugees Respond to a Changing US Immigration Climate," *Bildhaan: An International Journal of Somali Studies*, 9, 2011, 96–97, 100, 106.

18 Interview with Nimco Ahmed, Minneapolis, September 19, 2011.

19 *Chanhassen Man Sentenced for Obstructing Investigation of Missing Somali Men*, press release from U.S. Attorney's Office, District of Minnesota, July 16, 2010.

20 Interview with Lori Saroya.

21 United States House of Representatives Committee on Homeland Security, hearing on the American Muslim Response to Hearings on Radicalization within Their Community, June 20, 2012.

22 Interview with Abdirazak Bihi, Minneapolis, September 21, 2011.

23 Osman Ahmed, testimony on "Violent Islamist Extremism: Al-Shabaab Recruitment in America," hearing before Senate Committee on Homeland Security and Governmental Affairs, March 11, 2009.

24 Interview with Osman Ahmed, Minneapolis, September 23, 2011.

25 Eli Saslow, "Muslim Activist in Minnesota Struggles as One-Man Counter against Lure of Terrorism," *Washington Post*, July 8, 2011.

26 Interview with Osman Ahmed.

27 Stevan Weine and Osman Ahmed, "Building Resilience to Violent Extremism Among Somali-Americans in Minneapolis-St. Paul: Final Report," National Consortium for the Study of Terrorism and Responses to Terrorism, a Department of Homeland Security Science and Technology Center of Excellence Based at the University of Maryland, August 2012.

28 Interview with Hassan Jama and Sheikh Abdirahman Sheikh Omar, Minneapolis, September 24, 2011.

29 Interview with E. K. Wilson.

30 Ibid.

31 Interview with Dennis Jensen, St. Paul, September 23, 2011.

32 City of Saint Paul Police Department, African Immigrant Muslim Community Outreach Program: Project Summary, 2009.

33 Dennis L. Jensen, "Enhancing Homeland Security Efforts by Building Strong Relationships Between the Muslim Community and Local Law Enforcement," master's thesis, Naval Postgraduate School, Monterey, California, 2006, 91.

34 Interview with Dennis Jensen.

35 Jensen, "Enhancing Homeland Security Efforts," 60.

36 Interview with Dennis Jensen.

37 Ibid.

38 "Alumnus Combats Somali Radicalization in St. Paul," *Education Report*, Naval Postgraduate School Center for Homeland Defense and Security, 2011, 12.

39 Interview with Dennis Jensen.

40 Interview with Jennifer O'Donnell, St. Paul, September 23, 2011.

41 Al-Shabaab's Muslim American Radicalization, hearing before House Committee on Homeland Security, July 29, 2011.

42 Mohamed Diriye Abdullahi, "In the Name of the Cold War: How the West Aided and Abetted the Barre Dictatorship of Somalia," in Adam Jones, ed., *Genocide, War Crimes, and the West: History and Complicity*, London: Zed Books, 2004, 247.

43 Michel Chossudovsky, *The Globalisation of Poverty: Impacts of IMF and World Bank Reforms*, London: Zed Books/Third World Network, 1997, 102.

44 Chris Searle, "Agony and Struggle in Northern Somalia," *Race and Class*, 34: 2, October–December 1992.

45 Ken Menkhaus, "State Collapse in Somalia: Second Thoughts," *Review of African Political Economy*, 30, 97, September 2003.

46 Jeremy Scahill, *Dirty Wars: The World is a Battlefield*, New York, Nation Books, 2013, 66, 191–201.

47 Ghaith Abdul-Ahad, "Diary," *London Review of Books*, November 3, 2011.

48 Andrew England, "Ethiopia 'Holding Suspects' after US Strike in Somalia," *Financial Times*, January 11, 2007, 7; Barbara Slavin, "US Support Key to Ethiopia's Invasion," *USA Today*, January 8, 2007; David Axe, "WikiLeaked Cable Confirms US' Secret Somalia Op," *Wired*, December 2, 2010, wired.com, accessed December 20, 2012.

49 Scahill, *Dirty Wars*, 224.

50 Fatuma Noor, "My Encounter with American-Somali Jihadist in Nairobi," *Nairobi Star*, June 27, 2011.

51 Elliott, "A Call to Jihad, Answered in America"; Patrick Condon, "Charges against 8 in Missing Somali Case Unsealed," Associated Press, November 23, 2009.

52 Interview with Abdirazak Bihi.

53 Craig Whitlock, "Somali American Caught Up in a Shadowy Pentagon Counterpropaganda Campaign," *Washington Post*, July 8, 2013.

54 Interview with Nimco Ahmed.

55 Focus group with Somali-American students, Minneapolis, September 21, 2011.

56 Ibid.

8. TWENTY-FIRST-CENTURY CRUSADERS

1 "CAIR: Texas Radio Host Urges Bombing of NY Mosque," PR Newswire, May 27, 2010.

2 Interview with Hesham Ebaid, Katy, Texas, April 14, 2011.

3 "Mosque in Katy, Texas, Divides Town," UPI, September 8, 2010.

4 "CAIR: Texas Muslim Student Targeted by Slurs Has Jaw Broken," PR Newswire, February 4, 2010.

5 Interview with Hesham Ebaid.

6 American Civil Liberties Union, "Map—Nationwide Anti-Mosque Activity," aclu.org, accessed November 20, 2010.

7 Richard Adams, "The Ugly Face of Islamophobia in Orange County, California," *Guardian*, March 3, 2011.

8 Nigel Duara, "Man Arrested for Hate Crime in Fire at Ore. Mosque," Associated Press, August 25, 2011.

9 Karen Zraick and Andy Newman, "Student Arraigned in Anti-Muslim Stabbing of Cabdriver," *New York Times*, August 25, 2010.

10 Chad Cookler, "Deputies: St. Pete Man Stabbed Victim Because He's Muslim," *ABC Action News*, February 5, 2011, abcactionnews.com, accessed, January 26, 2013.

11 "NYPD: Suspects Savagely Attacked Elderly Man in Queens After Asking If He Was Muslim," WCBS, November 30, 2012, newyork.cbslocal.com, accessed January 26, 2013.

12 "Stabbing at Queens Mosque May Be Bias Attack," Fox New York, November 18, 2012.

13 Marc Santora, "Woman Is Charged with Murder as a Hate Crime in a Fatal Subway Push," *New York Times*, December 29, 2012.

14 Lee Romney, "Attack on Sikh Men Triggers Outcry in Elk Grove, Calif., and Beyond," *Los Angeles Times*, April 11, 2011.

15 Joe Heim, "Wade Michael Page Was Steeped in Neo-Nazi 'Hate Music' Movement," *Washington Post*, August 7, 2012.

16 "US Mosque Burned to Ground," *Daily Telegraph*, August 6, 2012.

17 Josh Stockinger, "Homemade Bomb Goes Off outside Muslim School," *Chicago Daily Herald*, August 14, 2012.

18 Paul Fanlund, "In Wake of Wisconsin Temple Murders, Muslims Remain 'Enemy du Jour,'" *Capital Times*, December 17, 2012,

19 United States Senate Judiciary Subcommittee on Constitution, Civil Rights, Human Rights, and the Law, testimony by Farhana Khera at hearing on protecting the civil rights of American Muslims, March 29, 2011.

20 Paul Jackson, "The EDL: Britain's "New Far Right" Social Movement," Northampton, UK, Radicalism and New Media Research Group, University of Northampton, 2011.

21 Cahal Milmo and Nigel Morris, "Ten Attacks on Mosques since Woolwich Murder," *Independent*, May 27, 2013; James Meikle, Matthew Taylor, and Vikram Dodd, "Police Investigate Fire at Islamic Community Centre in Muswell Hill," *Guardian*, June 5, 2013; "Ben Quinn, "Device outside Mosque Was Bomb," *Guardian*, June 23, 2013; Vikram Dodd, "Police Investigate Nail Bomb Explosion Near West Midlands Mosque," *Guardian*, July 12, 2013.

22 Mission Statement, English Defence League, englishdefenceleague.org, accessed January 26, 2013.

23 David Edgar, "Racism, Fascism and the Politics of the National Front," *Race and Class*, 19: 2, 1977.

24 Gary Younge, "When You Watch the BNP on TV, Just Remember: Jack Straw Started All This," *Guardian*, October 21, 2009.

25 Adi Schwartz, "Between Haider and a Hard Place," *Haaretz*, August 28, 2005.

26 Tom-Jan Meeus, "Grote Geld Voor Wilders Ligt in VS," *NRC Handelsblad*, January 25, 2012.

27 "Rabbi Shifren's Speech at the EDL Demonstration," *Jewish Chronicle*, October 25, 2010.

28 A. Millar, "The English Defense League: The New Face of Anti-Islamist Protest in Europe?" Hudson Institute, September 22, 2010, hudson-ny.org , accessed June 30, 2011.

29 Matt Carr, "You Are Now Entering Eurabia," *Race and Class*, 48: 1, 2006.

30 Max Blumenthal, "The Great Islamophobic Crusade," December 20, 2010, maxblumenthal.com, accessed January 26, 2013.

31 Kristine McNeil, "The War on Academic Freedom," *Nation*, November 11, 2002.

32 Wajahat Ali, Eli Clifton, Matthew Duss, Lee Fang, Scott Keyes, and Faiz Shakir, "Fear, Inc.: The Roots of the Islamophobia Network in America," Center for American Progress, August 2011, 15, 22, 65–69.

33 *Legislating Fear: Islamophobia and its Impact on the United States*, Washington, DC: Council on American-Islamic Relations, 2013, 1.

34 Ibid., 17.

35 "Muslims Decry Banning of Hijab-Wearing Women at Obama Event," Agence France-Presse, June 19, 2008.

36 Suhail A. Khan, "America's First Muslim President," *Foreign Policy*, August 23, 2010.

37 "Pamela Geller Op-Ed in World Net Daily: Obama's Islam," *Atlas Shrugs*, June 10, 2009, atlasshrugs2000.typepad.com, accessed January 27, 2013.

38 "Spencer Interview: Is Obama a Muslim?" *Jihad Watch*, April 29, 2010, jihadwatch.org, accessed January 27, 2013.

39 Pranab Dhal Samanta, "No Headscarf, Obama May Skip Golden Temple Visit," *Indian Express*, October 19, 2010.

40 "Only Four-in-Ten Correctly Identify Romney as Mormon," Public Religion Research Institute/Religion News Service, July 25, 2011.

41 Ali et al., "Fear, Inc.," 44–45.

42 Center for Security Policy, "Shariah: The Threat to America (an Exercise in Competitive Analysis)—Report of Team 'B' II," Washington, DC, 2010, 6, 10, 13, 14, 17.

43 Ibid., 13–14, 16, 19, 128.

44 Ibid., 9, 21.

45 Thomas E. Ricks, "Commander Punished as Army Probes Detainee Treatment," *Washington Post*, April 5, 2004, A13.

46 Tim Murphy, "Rep. Allen West's (Very, Very) Stealth Jihad," *Mother Jones*, July 26, 2011.

47 Ali et al., "Fear, Inc.," 29.

48 "Zombie Lie: Right Still Clinging to Decade-old fabrication about Radicalized Mosques," *Media Matters for America*, February 2, 2011, http://mediamatters.org/print/research/201102020008, accessed March 6, 2011.

49 Abed Awad, "The True Story of Sharia in American Courts," *Nation*, June 13, 2012.

50 Robert P. Jones, Daniel Cox, William A. Galston, and E. J. Dionne, Jr., "What it Means to Be American: Attitudes in an Increasingly Diverse America Ten Years After 9/11," Brookings Institution and Public Religion Research Institute, Washington, DC, 2011, 2.

51 Scott Shane, "In Islamic Law, Gingrich Sees a Mortal Threat to US," *New York Times*, December 21, 2011.

52 Justin Sink, "Cain: Majority of US Muslims Share Extremist Views," *The Hill*, November 14, 2011.

53 Awad, "The True Story of Sharia in American Courts."

54 Alex Seitz-Wald, "Her Muslim Witch Hunt," *Salon*, July 13, 2012, salon.com, accessed July 17, 2012.

55 Richard Hofstadter, *The Paranoid Style in American Politics*, New York: Vintage, 2008.

56 Rasmussen Reports, "63% See Conflict between Islam and the West," May 14, 2012.

57 "Terror in Oslo," *Wall Street Journal*, July 23, 2011.

58 Anders Behring Breivik, "2083—European Declaration of Independence," 2011.

59 "Native Revolt: A European Declaration of Independence," *Brussels Journal*, March 16, 2007, brusselsjournal.com, accessed January 27, 2013.

60 Pamela Geller, "Summer Camp? Anti-Semitic Indoctrination Training Center," *Atlas Shrugs*, July 31, 2011, atlasshrugs2000.typepad.com, accessed January 27, 2013.

61 Helen Pidd, "Anders Behring Breivik Spent Years Training and Plotting for Massacre," *Guardian*, August 24, 2012.

9. DREAM NOT OF OTHER WORLDS

1 Laila al-Arian, "TV's Most Islamophobic Show," *Salon*, December 15, 2012, salon.com. In this section I have drawn on Anna Erickson's "*Homeland* as Almost Progressive," New York University, 2012.

2 Jorge Rivas, "Group Says Lowe's Is One of 64 Companies to Pull Ads From 'All-American Muslim,'" *Colorlines*, December 13, 2011, accessed December 13, 2011; Lorraine Ali and Marisa Guthrie, "Why American Cable Systems Won't Carry the al Jazeera Network," *Hollywood Reporter*, March 18, 2011.

3 *United States of America v. Mohammad el-Mezain, Ghassan Elashi, Shukri Abu Baker, Mufid Abdulqader, Abdulrahman Odeh, Holy Land Foundation for Relief and Development*, United States Court of Appeals for the Fifth Circuit, December 7, 2011, 10.

4 Ibid., 8.

5 *Ghassan Elashi, Shukri Abu Baker, Mufid Abdulqader, and Abdulrahman Odeh v. United States of America, Petition for a Writ of Certiorari*, United States Court of Appeals for the Fifth Circuit, 2012.

6 Alia Malek, "Gitmo in the Heartland," *Nation*, March 10, 2011.

7 "An Explanatory Memorandum on the General Strategic Goal for the Group in North America," May 22, 1991.

8 Ibid., 32.

9 P. David Gaubatz and Paul Sperry, *Muslim Mafia: Inside the Secret Underworld That's Conspiring to Islamize America*, Washington, DC: WND Books, 2009, iii–iv.

10 Ibid., 301–2.

11 Daniel Pipes, "CAIR's Dirty Tricks against Me," *FrontPageMagazine.com*, September 7, 2007, frontpagemag.com, accessed September 20, 2013.

12 Daniel Pipes, "Islamists Impose Sharia by Stealth," *Australian*, November 6, 2009.

13 Pew Research Center, "The Future of the Global Muslim Population Projections for 2010–2030," Washington, DC, January 2011, 137.

14 Samuel P. Huntington, "The Clash of Civilizations?" *Foreign Affairs*, Summer 1993, 35.

15 Ryan Lizza, "The Consequentialist," *New Yorker*, May 2, 2011.

16 Fareed Zakaria, "The Real Threat in the Middle East," *Time*, January 23, 2012, 20.

17 Bobby Ghosh, "Morsi's Moment," *Time*, November 28, 2012.

18 Fawaz Gerges, "The New Capitalists: Islamists' Political Economy," *openDemocracy*, May 10, 2012, opendemocracy.net, accessed April 13, 2013.

19 John Kerry interview with Hamid Mir of Geo TV, Pakistan, August 1, 2013, state.gov, accessed August 3, 2013.

20 Sharif Abdel Kouddous, "What Led to Morsi's Fall—And What Comes Next?," *Nation*, July 5, 2013.

21 David Brooks, "Defending the Coup," *New York Times*, July 15, 2013, A19; Michael Rubin, "The Perils of Proportionality," *Commentary*, August 16, 2013; David Pryce-Jones, "Laboratory of Islamism—Egypt's Long Erosion by an Imperial Ideology," *National Review*, August 19, 2013.

22 Michael Jacobson, Terrorist Dropouts: Learning from Those Who Have Left, Washington, DC, Washington Institute for Near East Policy, Policy Focus, 101, 2010, 17; Arsalan Iftikhar, "Challenges of a Muslim 'Deradicalizer,'" *Providence Journal*, February 13, 2010.

23 Helen Carter, "Jihad Recruiters Jailed after Anti-Terror Trial," *Guardian*, September 9, 2011.

24 Chris Woods, Alice K Ross, Oliver Wright, "Exclusive: Secret War on Enemy Within," *Independent*, February 27, 2013.

25 Robert Verkaik, "British Man Who 'Vanished' after Being Stripped of Citizenship Says He Was Tortured and Forced to Sign a Confession by the CIA," *Mail on Sunday*, January 19, 2013.

26 Diala Shamas and Nermeen Arastu, *Mapping Muslims: NYPD Spying and Its Impact on American Muslims*, Muslim American Civil Liberties Coalition, Creating Law Enforcement Accountability & Responsibility, and Asian American Legal Defense and Education Fund, 2013, 20.

27 Ibid., 23–24.

28 Sunaina Marr Maira, *Missing: Youth, Citizenship, and Empire after 9/11* (Durham, NC: Duke University Press, 2009), 254.

29 Hasan M. Elahi, "You Want to Track Me? Here You Go, FBI," *New York Times*, October 29, 2011.

30 John O. Koehler, *Stasi: The Untold Story of the East German Secret Police*, Boulder, CO: Westview Press, 1999.

31 According to Senator Dianne Feinstein of the Senate Intelligence Committee, "The FBI now has 10,000 people doing intelligence on counterterrorism." Transcript of a news conference with Senators Dianne Feinstein (D-CA) and Saxby Chambliss (R-GA), June 6, 2013, washingtonpost.com, accessed July 26, 2013; Trevor Aaronson, *The Terror Factory: Inside the FBI's Manufactured War on Terrorism*, Brooklyn, NY: Ig Publishing, 2013, 44.

32 Shamas and Arastu, *Mapping Muslims*, 40.

33 Ryan Devereaux, "Muslim Student Monitored by the NYPD: 'It Just Brings Everything Home,'" *Guardian*, February 22, 2012.

34 Michelle Alexander, *The New Jim Crow: Mass Incarceration in the Age of Colorblindness*, New York: New Press, 2011.

35 Interview with Javaad Alipoor, Bradford, June 13, 2011.

36 Roger Eatwell and Matthew J. Goodwin, eds, *The New Extremism in 21st-Century Britain*, London: Routledge, 2010, 243.

37 John Gray, *Two Faces of Liberalism*, New York: New Press, 2002.

38 David Goodhart, *Progressive Nationalism: Citizenship and the Left*, London: Demos, 2006.

39 Andrew Tangel and Ashley Powers, "FBI: Boston Suspect Tamerlan Tsarnaev Followed 'Radical Islam,'" *Los Angeles Times*, April 20, 2013.

40 E. P. Thompson, "The Secret State," *Race and Class*, 20: 3, 1979, 235.

41 *The Case of Leon Trotsky: Report of Hearings on the Charges Made Against Him in the Moscow Trials, Thirteenth Session—Part 1*, New York: Merit Publishers, 1969, Marxists Internet Archive marxists.org, accessed April 18, 2013.

42 Martin Luther King, "Beyond Vietnam—A Time to Break Silence," speech, New York, NY: April 4, 1967.

AFTERWORD

1 Paul Cruickshank and Tim Lister, "Europe Faces 'Greatest Terror Threat Ever' from Jihadists in Iraq and Syria," cnn.com, June 19, 2014, accessed September 4, 2014, http://edition.cnn.com/2014/06/19/world/europe/lister-european-jihadists/index.html.

2 David Cameron, “Isil Poses a Direct and Deadly Threat to Britain,” *Sunday Telegraph*, August 16, 2014.

3 Vijay Prashad, “The Geopolitics of the Islamic State,” *The Hindu*, July 3, 2014, 8.

4 Richard Osley, “Israel-Gaza Conflict: Benjamin Netanyahu Warns of No Let Up in Raids Until Hamas Tunnels are Destroyed,” *Independent*, August 3, 2014.

5 Cameron, “Isil Poses a Direct and Deadly Threat to Britain”; Martin Bentham, “Brits Who Fight in Syria Face Life in Jail,” *Evening Standard*, February 3, 2014.

6 Simon Hooper, “Sharp Increase in Under-18s ‘at Risk’ of Being Radicalised into Jihadists,” *Independent*, March 23, 2014.

7 Roger F. Noriega and José R. Cárdenas, “The Mounting Hezbollah Threat in Latin America,” *American Enterprise Institute for Public Policy Research*, no. 3, October 2011, 1.

8 Department of Defense Press Briefing by Secretary of Defense Chuck Hagel and Chairman of the Joint Chiefs of Staff General Martin E. Dempsey, Pentagon Briefing Room, August 21, 2014, accessed September 4, 2014, http://www.defense.gov/transcripts/transcript.aspx?transcriptid=5491.

9 Thomas Tracy and Joseph Stepansky, “Arab Civil Rights Activists Attacked, Threatened with Beheading in Brooklyn,” *New York Daily News*, September 4, 2014.

10 Glenn Greenwald and Murtaza Hussain, “Meet the Muslim-American Leaders the FBI and NSA Have Been Spying On,” *The Intercept*, July 9, 2014, accessed August 1, 2014, https://firstlook.org/theintercept/article/2014/07/09/under-surveillance.

11 Jeremy Scahill and Ryan Devereaux, “Barack Obama’s Secret Terrorist-Tracking System, by the Numbers,” *The Intercept*, August 5, 2014, accessed August 7, 2014, https://firstlook.org/theintercept/article/2014/08/05/watch-commander.

Born and bred in London, **ARUN KUNDNANI** moved to New York in 2010 on a fellowship with the Open Society Foundations and now lives in Harlem. He is the author of *The End of Tolerance: Racism in 21st Century Britain*, which was selected as a *New Statesman* Book of the Year in 2007. A former editor of the journal *Race and Class*, he was educated at Cambridge and London Metropolitan University, and teaches at New York University.

On the Typeface

This book is set in Minion, a typeface designed by Robert Slimbach for Adobe Systems in 1990, which has become one of the few contemporary book faces to rival the classic types of Caslon, Bembo, and Garamond. Though it has no obvious precursor, it retains a calligraphic sentiment that Robert Bringhurst dubs "neohumanist" in his *Elements of Typographic Style.*

Telltale features of Minion include the subtle cant in the bar of the "e," the angular bowl of the "a," and the tapered bulbs that terminate the head of the "a" and the tails of the "y" and "j."

Minion's restrained personality and even color have made it a popular workhorse type, the narrow set width of which provides economy yet does not detract from its suitability for book settings.